A CONSTRUCTIVE SURVEY OF UPANISHADIC PHILOSOPHY

A CONSTRUCTIVE SURVEY OF UPANISHADIC PHILOSOPHY

BEING A SYSTEMATIC INTRODUCTION TO INDIAN METAPHYSICS

R. D. RANADE

Published by

FacsiMile Publisher
12 Pragati Market
Ashok Vihar, Ph-2
Delhi - 110052, India
Phone: 011-47034999
Email: www.facsimilepublishers.com
info@facsimilepublishers.com

Distribution Network
gyanbooks.com
India, USA, Canada, UK, Australia

ISBN: 978-93-7106-576-4 (PB)
First Published, 1920

2nd Impression 2025

Printed at: Gyan Press, Delhi.

A CONSTRUCTIVE SURVEY OF UPANISHADIC PHILOSOPHY
Author: R. D. RANADE

A CONSTRUCTIVE SURVEY OF UPANISHADIC PHILOSOPHY

BEING

A SYSTEMATIC INTRODUCTION TO INDIAN METAPHYSICS

BY

R. D. RANADE M. A.,

Director, Academy of Philosophy and Religion,

Formerly, Professor of Philosophy, Fergusson College, Poona.

PUBLISHED UNDER THE PATRONAGE OF THE LATE

CAPTAIN SIR PARASHURAMRAO BHAUSAHEB, K.C.I.E.,

Chief of Jamkhandi.

ORIENTAL BOOK AGENCY, POONA.

PREFACE

1. *The Occasion of the Work.*—Ever since the nucleus of the following Survey of Upanishadic Philosophy was presented for the first time to the public of Bangalore and Mysore in a series of lectures inaugurated under the Presidentship of His Highness the Maharaja Gaekwar of Baroda at the time of the foundation of the Sanskrit Academy in Bangalore in July 1915, the author has been bestowing continual attention on the substance of these lectures, and making them suitable for a thorough-going philosophical survey of the Upanishads, in the firm hope that what may thus be presented by way of exposition of Upanishadic philosophy will satisfy every seeker after Upanishadic truth by giving him in a brief, though in a very solid, compass all the chief points of Upanishadic thought in their full philosophical sequence. I must thank Pandit Mahabhagvat of Kurtkoti, now Shankaracharya of Karvir, and Mr. V. Subrahmanya Iyer, B. A., Registrar of the University of Mysore, for having given me an opportunity at that time of placing my thoughts on the Upanishads for the first time before the *élite* public of Bangalore and Mysore. It seems that the lectures were much appreciated in Bangalore at the time of their delivery, and His Highness the Maharaja Gaekwar advised that "the lectures be printed in English and the Vernaculars and distributed broad-cast, so that the knowledge imparted might be made widely available". But what through stress of other work and what through unforeseen difficulties that beset the progress of any important

undertaking, this volume could see the light of day only after the lapse of such a long period after the idea first sprang into my mind that the Upanishadic Philosophy was worth while presenting, and would serve as an incentive both to students of European and Indian thought alike.

2. *The Combination of Philosophy and Philology.*—Though I had begun my study of the Upanishads much earlier than 1915, it was in that year that I first conceived the idea of a presentation of Upanishadic Philosophy in terms of modern thought, while a literary inspiration in that direction came to me first from a lecture of the late Sir Ramkrishna Gopal Bhandarkar in February 1915. It was not long before I could discover that the Upanishads contained not one system of philosophy, but systems of philosophy rising one over another like Alps over Alps, and culminating in a view of Absolute Reality which was worthy of the fullest consideration of our contemporary Philosophers of the West. With that end in view and in order that the Upanishadic philosophy might be made intelligible to the Western mind, I boldly struck out the plan of presenting it according to the methods of Western thought, so as to make it understandable and appreciable by those who were trained to think according to those methods. It might easily be seen by casting a glance at the contents of this volume that the manner of presentation is strictly one which is amenable to the methods of Western philosophy. Another difficulty, however, stood in my way. In trying to present the spirit of Upanishadic philosophy in the garb of European thought, it was incumbent on me not to do injustice to the letter of Upanishadic philosophy. It was thus that philological considerations weighed with me equally with philosophical considerations. I had seen in my study of Greek Philosophy how much Dr. Burnet's method of interpreting the Early Greek Philosophers by reference to the Original Sources had revolutionised the study of Greek Thinkers, and I thought a similar presentation of Upanishadic Philosophy according to that method was certainly one which was worth while attempting. It was hence that I culled out Sources from Upanishadic literature, classified them into groups according to the various departments of Upanishadic thought, arranged them in philosophical sequence, and interpreted them with due regard to considerations of philology, taking care all the while that the philological interpretation of these Texts would not become so crude and unintelligible as not to appeal to students of philosophical thought. It was this problem of the combination of philology with philosophy that has made the task of an intelligent interpretation of the Upanishads in philosophic sequence so taxing and formidable. I leave it to the student of Upanishadic philosophy and philology to see how far I have succeeded in my attempt.

3. *The Place of the Upanishads in Indian Philosophy.*—The Upanishads indeed occupy a unique place in the development of Indian thought. All the later Systems of Indian Philosophy, as we believe has been shown in detail for the first time in the history of Upanishadic literature in the fourth Chapter of this work, have been rooted in the Upanishads. The indebtedness of particular systems of Philosophy to the Upanishads has been partially worked out by a Garbe or an Oldenberg ; but the entire problem of the relation of all the later Systems of Philosophy to the Upanishads has been hither-

to an unattempted task. Oldenberg has indeed fairly worked out both in his earlier volume on "Buddha" as well as in his later "Die Lehre der Upanishaden and die Anfänge des Buddhismus" how the Upanishads prepared the way for Buddhistic thought, and deserves praise for having attempted a hitherto unattempted task. Garbe in his "Samkhya-Philosophie" has discussed how far we could legitimately trace the origin of Sāṁkhya Philosophy to the Upanishads, and has come to the conclusion that the roots of the Sāṁkhya Philosophy cannot be traced to the oldest Upanishads (p. 27), but that the Sāṁkhya ideas came into existence only during the interval elapsing between the older period of the Bṛihadāraṇyaka and the Chhāndogya on the one hand, and the later period of the Kaṭha, the Śvetāśvatara, the Praśna, and the Maitri on the other. Garbe points out truly that the Ahaṁkāra of Chhāndogya VII. 25 is to be understood not as the egoism of Sāṁkhya philosophy, but as the mystical ego, and there is much truth in what Garbe says. He similarly makes a discussion about such conceptions as those of Sambhūti and Liṅga occurring in the earlier Upanishads, and comes to the conclusion that even they have no Sāṁkhyan connotation. So far so good. It is, however, when Garbe refuses altogether to find any traces of Sāṁkhya doctrine in the older Upanishads that it becomes impossible for us to go with him. Indeed, in our fourth Chapter we have pointed out how the conception of the three colours in the Chhāndogya must have led to the conception of the tri-coloured Prakṛiti in Sāṁkhya Philosophy (pp. 182-183), and as the Chhāndogya is recognised to be an old Upanishad all round, a general statement such as the one which Garbe makes that no traces whatever of Sāṁkhya doctrine are to be found in the older Upanishads becomes hardly convincing. As regards the Vedānta, also, we have tried to work out systematically in what respects all the later Vedāntic systems, the monistic, the qualified-monistic, and the dualistic, could be traced to the Upanishads as to a parent. Indeed, when we recognise that all the great commentators, Śaṅkara, Rāmānuja, and Madhva have made the Brahma-sūtras the pivot for their philosophical speculations, and when we remember also that the Brahma-sūtras were an aphoristic summary of the doctrines of the Upanishads, it would seem a little strange why we have not discussed the arguments of these philosophers at even greater length than we have done. There are however two reasons why we have not done so. In the first place, we wanted to take recourse to the objective method of presentation, going to the Texts of the Upanishads themselves, unbiassed by any theological interpretations of the Commentators whether on the Upanishads or the Brahma-sūtras. And, in the second place, it was thought desirable that a full discussion of all the theologico-philosophical points would best be reserved for a later volume on Vedānta philosophy proper. Indeed the Vedānta Philosophy stands to the Upanishads almost in the same relation in which the Philosophy of the Schoolmen stood to Aristotle. We might say about the theological disquisitions of these Commentators what Bacon said about the arguments of the Schoolmen, borrowing the idea from Ariston, that they "resemble more or less a spider's web, admirable for the ingenuity of their structure, but of little substance and profit": τοῖς μὲν ἀραχνίων ὑφάσμασιν εἴκαζεν, οὐδὲν μεν χρησίμους, λίαν δὲ τεχνικούς. This might be a little harsh judgment; but it shows how there is a fundamental difference in the methodologies of the Upanishads and the Vedānta.

In the one case, we have the intuitional method, in the other only the logical. We have no desire to exalt the intuitional at the expense of the logical. The intuitional, we believe, is not contradictory of the logical, but subsumptive of it. It must be remembered that we are not speaking here about the sub-relational intuitional method, but rather of the super-relational. Hence, even though we agree with Oltramare in his judgment that the Upanishads "regard the normal operations of Intellect as powerless to grasp Ultimate Reality" (p. 134), we differ from him when he says that "fearlessly and imperiously doth the Intuition of the Upanishadic Philosophers say fie to experience and give discharge to all demonstrations, while it does not even try to eliminate contradictions" (pp. 131-132). The relation of Intuition to Intellect raises a large philosophical problem, and, as we have said at a later place in this volume (pp. 339-341), we cannot enter into a philosophical discussion about their comparative competence to solve the problem of reality in a work professedly dealing with Orientalia.

4. *Examination of the Opinions of a few Orientalists.*—The work which has been accomplished by Western Scholars upon Upanishadic literature has not been by any means scanty. Though the volume of work turned out by them on Upanishadic literature is neither so large nor so profound as that turned out on Vedic literature, it is neither on the other hand either meagre or small. Towards the end of the present volume may be found a succint account of all the work that has been done on Upanishadic literature by scholars like Weber, Röer, Max Müller, Böhtlingk, Whitney, Deussen, Oldenberg, Oltramare, Hertel, and Hillebrandt. Deussen 's work on the Upanishads is a monument to his great scholar-

ship, industry, and insight, and so is the work of Oldenberg and Oltramare. We do not wish to enter here into a detailed examination of the various opinions held on the subject of Upanishadic literature by early scholars, which have become the common property of all Upanishadic students; we only wish to examine here a few of the latest utterances on the subject. When Hertel, for example, says in his brilliant, though somewhat one-sided, introduction to the Kenopanishad in his "Die Weisheit der Upanishaden," that Brahman in that Upanishad is not to be understood as "the World-Soul in which all the individual Souls ultimately merge", he forgets to notice the point that the aim of that Upanishad is simply to describe Brahman, in Wordsworthian fashion, as a power or a presence,

> "Whose dwelling is the light of setting suns,
> And the round ocean, and the living air,
> And the blue sky, and in the mind of man."

This must verily be the upshot of that Upanishad wherein we are asked to meditate on Brahman as the Reality in the world of Nature and in the world of Mind: *tasyaisha ādeśo yadetad vidyuto vyadyutadā itīti nyamīmishadā ityadhidaivatam; athādhyātmam yadetad gachchhatīva cha mano anena chaitad upasmaratyabhīkshṇam saṁkalpaḥ* (Kena IV. 29, 30). With all due deference to Hertel's favourite theme of the identification of Brahman with Fire, we must say that we cannot accuse the Upanishad of not having considered a point which is not the point at issue. The point at issue being the spiritual description of Brahman as a presence or power, it would be an *ignoratio elenchi* on the part of that Upanishad to go into the description of the Brahman as a "World-Soul in which all the other souls ultimately merge." Then, secondly, when Hertel points out that the Kenopanishad dispenses with the necessity of a Spiritual Teacher for the purpose of spiritual realization, that the Self must according to that Upanishad be regarded as capable of being realised simply by internal illumination, and that Umā in that Upanishad does in no way help Indra in realising the Absolute, he forgets entirely to notice the fact that the true *rôle* of a Spiritual Teacher consists just in the office which Umā has been performing, namely, like a lamp-post on the Pathway to God, of simply directing the benighted wanderer on the path of spiritual progress without herself going it. Dogmatic statements such as this about the teachings of Upanishads come merely out of taking partial views about a subject. This is also illustrated in Oltramare's accusation against the Upanishads in his "L 'Histoire des Idées théosophiques dans l'Inde" that "in affirming the identity of the Universal and the Individual Soul, from which follows necessarily the identity of all souls, the Upanishads have not drawn the conclusion—Thou shalt love thy neighbour as thyself" (p. 137). True that the Biblical expression "Thou shalt love thy neighbour as thyself" is not to be found in the Upanishads ; but it would be bold on the part of any writer on Upanishadic Philosophy to affirm that the sentiment is not present in the Upanishads. What else is the meaning of that Upanishadic dictum *yasmin sarvāṇi bhūtāni ātmaivābhūd vijānataḥ* (Īśa 7), except that a Sage, who has realised the Ātman, must see the Ātman in all human beings, must, in fact, regard all human beings as living in a Kingdom of Ends ? Finally, when Oldenberg in his brilliant work on the Upanishads "Die Lehre der Upanishaden" tells us that the true parallel for Upanishadic Philosophy is to be found rather in the teachings of Plotinus, the Sufis, and the Christian mystics like Eckhart than in the Philosophy of Kant, and when he therefore a little superciliously disposes of the teaching of the Upanishads by saying " Der eine der Weg der Mystik, der andre der Kants", we are tempted to say about Kant with a little variation upon what Aristotle said about Plato, "Let Kant be our friend, but let Truth be our divinity". When Oldenberg commends Kant by saying that the central principle of Kant's philosophy is the "Formbegriff," while that of Upanishadic Philosophy is the "Formlosigkeit," he is blinding himself to the fact that his Critique of Pure Reason was only the first premiss of a grand philosophical syllogism whose minor premiss and conclusion were respectively the Critiques of Practical Reason and Judgment, wherein conceptions of Goodness and Value supplemented the considerations of Pure Reason, for, on the grounds of Pure Reason, what philosophy could there be about the ultimate realities of human life, the Self, the World, and God, except a philosophy of paralogisms that paralyse, antinomies that make one flounder, and ideals which can never be realised at all ? The " Cognoscendo ignorari " of Augustine, the " Neti Neti " of Yājñavalkya, the " Weder dies noch das " of Eckhart, would be far more sure indexes of spiritual humility, and consequent possession of reality, than the self-satisfied and half-halting dictates of an Agnosticism on the grounds of Pure Reason, which must destroy knowledge in order to make room for faith.

5. *The Upanishads and Contemporary Thought.*—The comparison of Upanishadic Philosophy with Kant suggests the parallelism, in a number of points, of the philosophical thought of the Upanishads with the tendencies of Contemporary Thought. Time was when Upanishadic Philosophy was compared with the doctrine of Plato and Parmenides ; time was yet again when it was compared with the philosophies of Kant and Schopenhauer ; we, however, who live in the world of Contemporary Thought can scarcely afford to neglect its parallelisms with the tendencies of the thinking world of to-day. Anybody who will take the trouble to read the argument of the present work will see how very provocative of thought it would be for one who is interested in the tendencies of contemporary philosophy. Here, in the Upanishads, we have doctrines of Absolute Monism, of Personalistic Idealism, of Pluralism, of Solipsism, of Self-realisation, of the relation of Intellect to Intuition, and so forth,—doctrines which have divided the philosophic world of to-day. Had it not been for the fact that Comparative Philosophy, like a virgin consecrated to God, bears no fruit, the parallelism of Upanishadic Philosophy with the tendencies of Contemporary Thought would have even invited a volume on Comparative Philosophy. What we, however, would much rather like to have is a constructive than a comparative philosophy. With the advance of knowedge and with the innumerable means for communication and interchange of thought, the whole world is being made one, and the body of Western philosophers could ill afford to neglect the systems of Indian philosophy, and more particularly the Upanishads. The same problems which at the present day divide a Bradley from a Bosanquet, a Ward from a Royce, a Pringle-Pattison from a McTaggart, also divided the Upanishadic philosophers of ancient times. Here we have the same conflict of views about the relation between the Absolute and the Individual, the nature of Immortality, the problem of Appearance, and the Norm of human conduct. The *élan vital*, which, in Bergson, wears not much more than a physiological aspect, appears in Āruṇi (Chh. VI. 11) as a great organic force, only much more psychologised and spiritualised. The pyramidal depiction of Reality as on the basis of Space and Time with the qualitative emergence of Life and Mind and Deity in the course of evolution, which we meet with in Alexander and Lloyd Morgan, is present in those old Upanishads only with a stress on the inverted process of Deity as the primary existent, from which came forth Mind and Life and Space and Time in the course of devolution. The very acute analysis of the epistemology of Self-consciousness, which we meet with in the Upanishads, can easily hold its own against any similar doctrine even of the most advanced thinker of to-day, thus nullifying once for all the influence of that ill-conceived and half-thought-out bluster of an early European writer on the Upanishads that "they are the work of a rude age, a deteriorated race, and a barbarous and unprogressive community." Our presentation of the problems of Upanishadic philosophy would also lay to rest all the charges that are made against it on the supposition that it is a block-philosophy and does not allow of any differentiation inside it. For is it not a familiar charge that we hear made against Indian philosophy, that it is all Pantheism, Determinism, Karmism, A-moralism, and Pessimism? It would be out of place here to answer each and all of the charges that have been thus made against Indian Philosophy in general, and Upanishadic Philosophy in particular. If our present work brings to the notice of these critics the variety and wealth of Upanishadic ideas on every conceivable subject in the domain of philosophy, it should have fulfilled its *raison d'etre*. Thus, to say that the Upanishads teach only "an unreal morality, or a mere

Antinomianism ", would entirely miss the mark, because it would be a flank-attack and not directed against the main body of Upanishadic doctrine. Finally, to say that the Upanishads teach only a Pessimism is to entirely miss the tenor of Upanishadic Philosophy. For the simple reason that there is a phase of Pessimism in a certain portion of Upanishadic teaching, it does not follow that all Upanishadic teaching is pessimistic. It has been customary with European writers on Indian subjects to suppose that all was pessimism and sorrow before the days of Tagore in India, and that Tagore brought the evangel of joy and bliss from the West. It is nothing of the kind. Tagore 's philosophy of joy and bliss is only the crest-wave of that great huge ocean of blissful existence depicted in Upanishadic philosophy. If the present book points to any moral, it is the moral of the life of beatific vision enjoyed at all times by the Mystic. When Lord Ronaldshay, therefore, fixing himself, among other things, on a passage of the Upanishads, says in his book on " India, a Bird's eye-view" that pessimism infects the whole physical and intellectual life of India, and that the Indian Philosophers have never been able to paint any positive picture of bliss (p. 313), with all due deference to him we must ask him to see if the final upshot of Upanishadic Philosophy, as we have depicted it, would not enable him to revise his judgment. To the charge, finally, that even supposing that the Upanishads teach a doctrine of bliss, the bliss of the Indian is one thing and that of the Christian another, that the one is negative while the other is positive, ("Upanishads and Life" pp. 69, 70), we may say, as against Mr. Urquhart, in the first place, that we cannot conceive of any bliss being negative, for it would be a contradiction in terms, and in the second place, that this bliss is the same for all human beings whether they live in India or in Europe, for where the same intellect and feeling and will have been ordained to mankind by God, He has also made provision for a like consummation in each case. Oldenberg indeed has the candidness to admit, which these critics have not, that the opposite view is at least equally tenable that it should be inconceivable how the world which is "pierced by Brahman through and through" should ever wear a pessimistic aspect (pp. 115-116). Let those, however, who wish to find sorrow in the Upanishads, find sorrow, and those who wish to find bliss, find bliss! πάντων χρημάτων μέτρον ἄνθρωπος.

6. *The three-fold purpose of the Work.*—As may have been noticed from our previous discussion, the two chief purposes of the Work with which we have been hitherto concerned are to put into the hands of the Orientalists a new method for treating the problems of Indian Philosophy, and into the hands of European Philosophers a new material for exercising their intellects on. But these are not the only purposes with which the Work has been written. The ultimate purpose of the Work is the spiritual purpose. To that end, everything else is subservient. Time and oft have the Upanishads compelled a spiritual admiration from all Oriental Scholars, both European and Indian. Dr. Goldstücker said that the Upanishads formed the basis of the enlightened faith of India. R. C. Dutt, when he read the Upanishads, felt a new emotion in his heart, and saw a new light before his eyes. Ram Mohan Roy felt his whole life transformed when he happened to read a page of the Īśa Upanishad flying past him. Pratt regards the Upanishads as essentially

a religious rather than a philosophical work. Geden acknowledges how all the attempts at religious reform in India have taken their rise from the study of the Upanishads. Mead has gone to the length of calling the Upanishads a World-Scripture. From these utterances it may be seen in what high spiritual esteem the Upanishads have been held by Thinkers, both of the East and the West. If we may say so without exaggeration, there is no piece of literature in the whole realm of Indian Philosophy, except possibly the Bhagavadgītā, which is so truly religious as the Upanishads, and demands from young India an intellectual justification of her faith in the light of modern thought. Those who have observed the course of the development of European thought during the last half century know how very much it owes its existence, its inspiration, and its fulfilment to the establishment of the Gifford Lectures. It is a good sign of the times that the University of Calcutta should have risen to the occasion, and been a pioneer in establishing Lectureships by means of which a similar ambition might be fulfilled in India. The Upanishads well deserve to constitute a very important chapter in the World 's Philosophy of Religion. It will not be possible hurriedly to estimate the contribution which the Upanishads are likely to make to the formation of tendencies in Contemporary Thought. The trend of the present volume is to show how all the teachings of Upanishadic Philosophy converge towards the realisation of the mystical goal. We do not wish to enter here into any philosophical disquisition about the nature and meaning of Mysticism ; nor have we any desire to discuss how the Mystic criterion of reality compares with those of the Idealist, the Pragmatist, and the Realist. The veracity and the virility of any metataphysical theory is to be gauged by its power of making life more divine, and therefore more worth while living. Readers of the last Chapter of this volume may feel that, after all, the consummation that the Upanishadic philosophy affords is the realisation of the divine in the Individual Soul, and that it is not seen there working itself out in the social and political affairs of humanity. The practical application of the spiritual philosophy was, however, to come later on from the Bhagvadgītā, which taught a life of a disinterested activism on a spiritual basis, so that the divine purpose may come to be realised in the affairs of men. It cannot be denied that the Upanishads supply the philosophic foundation upon which the Bhagavadgītā later on erects its theory of spiritual activism. In either case, however, the mystical motive has been most predominant. It would be a problem for the Philosophy of the Immediate Future to place Mysticism on a truly philosophical basis. Rational Mysticism, which has been hitherto regarded as a contradiction in terms, must now be a truism. The author shall feel his labours amply rewarded if he finds that his exposition of the Upanishadic Philosophy makes a contribution, however small, to the realisation of this Ideal.

7. *The Academy of Philosophy and Religion and its Aims.*—The present work is the first publication of the Academy of Philosophy and Religion, an institution which has been recently founded in India with the purpose of bringing together all those who are interested in a philosophical investigation of the problem of God. This aim of the Academy is to be achieved primarily by Publications, embodying continued and sustained research in all the Philosophies and Religions of the world. There will also

be a number of Lectures from time to time on behalf of the Academy at great educational centres in India, which might also help the propagation of the cause of the Academy. The present centres of the Academy will be Poona, Bombay, and Nagpur, and so on, while the work of the Academy will be extended to other centres also in course of time. The Academy is intended to be an All-India Body, the Personnel of whose Council is drawn from representatives of all the Universities of India. For all those who are interested in the work of the Academy of Philosophy and Religion, there will be an Ashram at Nimbal, a Railway Station on the M. S. M. Railway in the District of Bijapur, which might be used as an intellectual and spiritual resort. If Bacon's maxim may be requisitioned for our present purposes, we may say that the Academy must take all philosophical and religious knowledge for its province, irrespective of differences of creed, caste, nation, or race. The universal vision which must inspire the work of the Academy may be made apparent from the following quotation from the preamble of its Prospectus : " The problem of finding the universal in the midst of particulars, the unchanging in the midst of change, has attracted the attention of every man of vision, whether he be Philosopher or Prince. Plato and Śaṅkarāchārya among Philosophers, Aśoka and Akbar among Princes are illustrations of the way in which this universal vision has been sought. Plato is known for nothing so much as for his synoptic vision of the universal among the particulars. Śaṅkarāchārya spent a lifetime in seeking to know that by knowing which everything else comes to be known. Aśoka, in one of his Rock-Edicts, forbade the decrying of other people's faiths,—for in that way he said one was doing disservice to one's own faith,—

and he taught the virtue of Concourse (Samavāya). Akbar sought after the universal vision by summoning a Council of Religion, for perchance, in that way, he thought that 'that lock whose key had been lost might be opened'. There is a far cry from the days of Plato and Śaṅkarāchārya, or of Akbar and Aśoka, to the present day. Knowledge has taken immense strides with the growth of time. Scientific inventions have enormously enriched the patrimony of man. The old order has changed, and a new one has taken its place. Nevertheless, the goal of human life as well as the means for its attainment have remained the same. Unquestionably, the search after God remains the highest problem even to-day, and a philosophical justification of our spiritual life is as necessary to-day as it was hundreds of years ago." More information about the Academy could be had from the Director of the Academy of Philosophy and Religion, Poona Branch, Poona, *or*, Nimbal, M. S. M. Railway, District Bijapur, India.

8. *Patronage for this Volume.*—I must express my heartfelt gratefulness to the late Shrimant Capt. Sir Parashuramrao Bhausaheb Patwardhan, K. C. I. E., Chief of Jamkhandi, to whose kind patronage the preparation of this volume has been entirely due. It is impossible for me to express adequately how much I owe to him and to his State, in which I was born and educated, and from which I was sent out into the literary world. At a time when the idea of free Primary Education was not even mooted in British India, Shrimant Appasaheb, the father of the late Chief, boldly conceived the idea of making even Secondary Education free in his Native State. It was only becoming in the generous successor of Shrimant Appasaheb to have been so kind in his pa-

tronage of letters as to even voluntarily offer to patronise this among a number of other projected publications. It pains me all the more that Shrimant Bhausaheb did not live to see the publication of this volume which was brought out under his generous patronage. He met a hero's death in trying to educate a wild tusker, and it is all the more to be mourned that he did not live to see the fulfilment of the projected series of works of which this is only the first. It is not too much to say that it was the promise of patronage which I received from the late Chiefsaheb of Jamkhandi that impelled me and my friend Dr. S. K. Belvalkar to approach, among others, Lord Ronaldshay, the late Governor of Bengal, who in a previous Convocation address had discoursed so ably on the aims of Indian Philosophy, for sympathy in the cause of the History of Indian Philosophy, which was then only recently projected. It was the encouragement that we received from Lord Ronaldshay, as well as the keen interest which Sir George Lloyd, the late Governor of our Presidency, took in our work that enabled us to approach the University of Bombay to extend their kind patronage to our projected scheme for a History of Indian Philosophy, and we are glad to point out that our University came forth, in the first instance, with a generous grant for three Volumes in the Series, which will be brought out under their patronage in course of time. Two of these Volumes, out of a total number of sixteen that have been projected, are now in the Press, and may see the light of day before long.

9. *The "Constructive Survey" and the "Creative Period".*—The mention of the grant of the University of Bombay to three volumes in the History of

Indian Philosophy makes it necessary for the present writer to say here a few words in regard to the relation that subsists between the present volume on the "Constructive Survey of Upanishadic Philosophy" and the Volume on the "Creative Period of Indian Philosophy" in the H. I. P. Series, which latter, it is hoped, may be published before long. The "Creative Period" discusses the contribution that was made by the Brāhmaṇas, the Āraṇyakas, the Upanishads, and the Post-Upanishadic period to the development of Indian Thought, and so far as the Upanishads are concerned, as befits a volume in the History of Indian Philosophy, undertakes a full discussion of the Upanishads one after another in their chronological and stratificatory order, paying attention to the analytical study of Upanishadic thought. The "Constructive Survey," on the other hand, focusses its attention only on the Upanishads, groups the various problems of Upanishadic thought under suitable headings, and takes a synoptic view of Upanishadic Philosophy. The one is an entirely analytical study, the other a thoroughly synthetic one. The relation that exists between these volumes can be made clear, if we give a parallel from Greek philosophy. The "Dialogues of Plato," to which the Upanishads might best be compared, could be discussed either analytically or synthetically; that is to say, we could either undertake an analytical investigation of the various Dialogues one after another in their chronological and stratificatory arrangement, or else we might take a synoptic view of the philosophical doctrines of Plato as advanced in the various Dialogues together. There is the same relation between the "Creative Period" and the "Constructive Survey", as there is, for example, between Gomperz's analytical survey of Plato's Dialogues, and

Zeller's synthetic presentation of Plato's philosophy, the one looking at the Dialogues *seriatim*, the other *in toto*. It is needless to add that for the student of Upanishadic thought, both the volumes are equally indispensable, the one only supplementing and not at all supplanting the other.

10. *The method followed in this Volme.*—The method followed in this presentation of Upanishadic Philosophy is, as the name implies, a method of construction through a systematic exposition of all the problems that emerge from the discussion of Upanishadic thought in their manifold bearings. As the alternative title of this work suggests, it is also a systematic Introduction to the problems of Indian Metaphysics. We have already pointed out how a systematic study of the Upanishads may serve as an excellent introduction to the Systems of Indian Philosophy. For long the necessity has been felt of an adequate text-book for introduction in the curricula of our Indian Universities on the subject of Indian Philosophy, and it is hoped that this work may supply the long-felt want. The aim of the present writer has been to group together all the different theories that have been advanced in the Upanishads under suitable headings such as Cosmogony, Psychology, Metaphysics, Ethics, and Mysticism in their logical sequence, and to make an attempt at envisaging his own point of view through a developmental exposition of these problems. The writer is only too aware of the value attaching to an objective presentation of philosophical problems, and it is for this reason that his own point of view has never been deliberately stated throughout the Volume; but anybody who will take the trouble of following the full sequence of the logical argument of the volume will see what elements of constructive thought the writer has to offer. Such a method of presentation is not new to Western Scholars, and has been ably illustrated in Pringle-Pattison's "Idea of God" published during recent years. The aim of the present writer, as may become apparent from a study of the work, has been to prepare the way for a deliberate formulation of his own thought on the problems of Metaphysics, which, God willing, he hopes to achieve in a forthcoming publication of the Academy on "The Pathway to God".

11. *Thanks.*—To Dr. Brajendranath Seal, Vice-Chancellor of the University of Mysore, I must express my most heartfelt thanks for the very kind trouble he took in reading through the typescript of this volume at his usual lightning speed, and in making important suggestions. To Prof. K. N. Dravid, M. A., of the Willingdon College, Sangli, I am most indebted for reading the whole volume with me before it was sent to the Press, as well as for suggesting improvements. Dr. S. K. Belvalkar has laid me under deep obligations by allowing me to quote in this work a passage or two from our joint Volume on the Creative Period of Indian Philosophy, as well as for help in other respects. I am also indebted to my friend Prof. R. Zimmermann, S. J., of St. Xavier's College, Bombay, for having looked through this Preface, as well as in having checked the Bibliographical Note which occurs at the end of the volume. I must express my most heartfelt thanks to my nephew, Prof. N. G. Damle, M. A., of Fergusson College, Poona, who has helped me much by looking through a larger part of the proofs of this volume. I must also thank my young friend, Mr. R. D. Wadekar, B. A., for his very conscientious help in discussing the Upanishadic Bibliography with me, as well as in looking through certain proofs of the Volume. Also, I must express my obligations to my former pupils, and now Professors, V. S. Gogate, M. A., and K. V. Gajendragadkar, M. A., of the Arts College, Nasik, for having helped me in the General Index and the Upanishad Index respectively. The untiring efforts of my pupil and friend, Mr. G. K. Sane, M. A., in the preparation and final disposition of the General Index deserve all commendation. The constant, day-to-day, cheerful help which my stenographer Mr. S. K. Dharmadhikari has extended to me, as well as his indefatigable diligence and resolve to stick to his guns through thick and thin, can never be adequately praised. The zealous and constant interest which Dr. N. G. Sardesai, Manager of the Oriental Book Agency, Poona, has evinced in this work cannot be praised too highly. Mr. Nanasaheb Gondhalekar, the Proprietor of the Jagaddhitechu, Press, Poona, has not spared himself, his Press, and his men for turning out this Volume in the fashion in which it is offered to the public. There are also a few other persons to be thanked. But as their interest in this Volume is spiritual, it behoves me, in the manner of the Kenopanishad, to leave their names unmentioned. " To gild refined gold, to paint the lily, To throw a perfume on the violet.... Is wasteful and ridiculous excess ".

R. D. RANADE.

TABLE OF CONTENTS

CHAPTER I

THE BACKGROUND OF UPANISHADIC SPECULATION

CHAPTER II

THE DEVELOPMENT OF UPANISHADIC COSMOGONY

CHAPTER III

VARIETIES OF PSYCHOLOGICAL REFLECTION

I. Empirical Psychology.

II. Abnormal Psychology.

III. Rational Psychology.

CHAPTER IV

ROOTS OF LATER PHILOSOPHIES

CHAPTER V

PROBLEM OF ULTIMATE REALITY IN THE UPANISHADS

I. The Cosmological Approach.

CHAPTER VI

THE ETHICS OF THE UPANISHADS

I. Theories of the Moral Standard.

II. Theories of the Moral Ideal.

III. Practical Ethics.

CHAPTER VII

INTIMATIONS OF SELF-REALISATION

CHAPTER I

THE BACKGROUND OF UPANISHADIC SPECULATION.

The Significance of the Study of the Upanishads.

1. In the History of Indian Thought, every revival of the study of the Upanishads has synchronised with a great religious movement. When, about two thousand four hundred years ago, the author of the Bhagavadgītā tried for the first time to synthesise the truths of Upanishadic philosophy in that immortal Celestial Poem, it was evidently with the desire of giving a new impulse to religious thought and thus laying the foundations of a truly mystical religion which should prove the guiding light of all mystical activities for ages to come. Then, about twelve hundred years later, when for a second time the architectonic builders of Vedāntic philosophy came to construct their Systems of Reality out of the material placed at their disposal by the Upanishadic Seers, there was again witnessed a phenomenon of a new religious revival, this time the religious revival taking the shape more of an intellectual than of a purely mystical religion. In the twentieth century to-day, after the lapse of another twelve hundred years, under the impact of Western civilisation and Western culture, supported by the infinite progress of modern science and an all-round study of the philosophies and religions of the world, we in India, who are the inheritors of a great spiritual past that has been left to us by our Upanishadic ances-

tors, stand face to face with a very difficult problem, namely, that of reconciling mysticism with intellectualism in such a way that any thought-construction that we might put forth on the basis of the eternal truths of Ātmanic experience suggested to us by the Upanishads, might harmoniously synthesise the claims of Science and Philosophy and Religion, so that our philosophical view of reality may not be disturbed but may only be supported by the advance of modern science, and both our scientific and philosophic views be made to redound in such a way to the glory of God that "the highest link of Nature's chain may only be seen to be tied to the foot of Jupiter's chair." The present writer believes that the Upanishads are capable of giving us a view of reality which would satisfy the scientific, the philosophic, as well as the religious aspirations of man ; because they give us a view which may be seen to be supported by a direct, first-hand, intuitive, mystical experience, which no science can impeach, which all philosophy may point to as the ultimate goal of its endeavour, and which may be seen at once to be the immanent truth in the various forms of religion which only quarrel because they cannot converge.

The Upanishads and the Rigveda.

2. It would be interesting to trace in a very brief outline the relation of these "Mystical texts" called the Upanishads to the earliest poetry of the Aryan race, namely the Rigveda, which must be regarded as having preceded them by a period of over a thousand years. In the first place, we must note that the Rigveda is a great hymnology to the personified forces of nature, and thus represents the earliest phase in the evolution of religious consciousness, namely, the objective phase of religion. The Upanishads, on the other hand, mark the subjective phase

CHAPTER I

THE BACKGROUND OF UPANISHADIC SPECULATION.

The Significance of the Study of the Upanishads.

1. In the History of Indian Thought, every revival of the study of the Upanishads has synchronised with a great religious movement. When, about two thousand four hundred years ago, the author of the Bhagavadgītā tried for the first time to synthesise the truths of Upanishadic philosophy in that immortal Celestial Poem, it was evidently with the desire of giving a new impulse to religious thought and thus laying the foundations of a truly mystical religion which should prove the guiding light of all mystical activities for ages to come. Then, about twelve hundred years later, when for a second time the architectonic builders of Vedāntic philosophy came to construct their Systems of Reality out of the material placed at their disposal by the Upanishadic Seers, there was again witnessed a phenomenon of a new religious revival, this time the religious revival taking the shape more of an intellectual than of a purely mystical religion. In the twentieth century to-day, after the lapse of another twelve hundred years, under the impact of Western civilisation and Western culture, supported by the infinite progress of modern science and an all-round study of the philosophies and religions of the world, we in India, who are the inheritors of a great spiritual past that has been left to us by our Upanishadic ances-

tors, stand face to face with a very difficult problem, namely, that of reconciling mysticism with intellectualism in such a way that any thought-construction that we might put forth on the basis of the eternal truths of Ātmanic experience suggested to us by the Upanishads, might harmoniously synthesise the claims of Science and Philosophy and Religion, so that our philosophical view of reality may not be disturbed but may only be supported by the advance of modern science, and both our scientific and philosophic views be made to redound in such a way to the glory of God that "the highest link of Nature's chain may only be seen to be tied to the foot of Jupiter's chair." The present writer believes that the Upanishads are capable of giving us a view of reality which would satisfy the scientific, the philosophic, as well as the religious aspirations of man ; because they give us a view which may be seen to be supported by a direct, first-hand, intuitive, mystical experience, which no science can impeach, which all philosophy may point to as the ultimate goal of its endeavour, and which may be seen at once to be the immanent truth in the various forms of religion which only quarrel because they cannot converge.

The Upanishads and the Rigveda.

2. It would be interesting to trace in a very brief outline the relation of these "Mystical texts" called the Upanishads to the earliest poetry of the Aryan race, namely the Rigveda, which must be regarded as having preceded them by a period of over a thousand years. In the first place, we must note that the Rigveda is a great hymnology to the personified forces of nature, and thus represents the earliest phase in the evolution of religious consciousness, namely, the objective phase of religion. The Upanishads, on the other hand, mark the subjective phase

of religion. There are no hymns to gods or goddesses of nature in the Upanishads, but on the contrary, they contain a scientific search for the Substratum underlying the phenomenal forces of nature. There are neither any offerings of prayers to gods in the Upanishads, nor is there visible, throughout the Upanishadic period, any inordinate fear of the wrath of these natural forces personified as gods. In other words, we may say that as we go from the Vedic period to the Upanishadic period, there is visible at every stage the process of a transference of interest from God to Self. When the individual Self has become the universal Self, when, in short, the Ātman has been realised, whom and what may anybody fear? For whom and what may any offerings be made? For whom and what may anybody pray to divinity? In a word, we may say, that as we pass from the Vedas to the Upanishads, we pass from prayer to philosophy, from hymnology to reflection, from henotheistic polytheism to monotheistic mysticism. Then, secondly, we must not fail to notice the progress that was already being made towards the conceptions of cosmogony even in certain hymns of the Rigveda itself. If we just take into account such a hymn as Rigveda x. 88, where the seer inquires what was the "hylē" out of which the heavens and the earth were built eternally firm and what it was upon which the Creator stood when he upheld the worlds, or yet again hymns like x. 5 and x. 27, where the conceptions of Being and Not-being in a cosmological sense are being already broached, or even that famous agnostic hymn of creation x. 129, where the primal existent is declared as being superior to both Being and Not-being and where the cognisant activity of the Creator himself is called in question, we may say that a beginning was made even at this Rigvedic period of the real philosophical impulse which passing through the Brāhmaṇic period was to gather force at the beginning of the Upanishadic period. Thirdly, from the psychological point of view, we may say that while the Rigveda may be regarded as a great work of emotion and imagination, the Upanishads may be regarded as a work of thought and reason. There are many passages in the Rigveda, especially in the hymns to Varuṇa, which have a close analogy to the devotional psalms of the Bible both in point of language and ideas—passages which are rarely to be met with in the literature of the Upanishads; on the other hand, in the Upanishads, we have more or less the coolness of intellectual argument exhibiting itself in a systematic search after the Ultimate Reality. Thus it happens that while there are to be met with in the Rigveda many hymns which express the meek submission of the suppliant devotee asking for gracious forgiveness from a divinity which is the creation of his own imagination, the Upanishads say in bold terms: "Seek not favour from any such divinity; reality is not the divinity which you are worshipping—*nedam yad idam upāsate*; the guardian of order is not outside; natural and moral order does not come from without; it springs from the Ātman, who is the synthesis of both outside and inside, who is veritably the ballast of nature, who is the unshakable bund that prevents the stream of existence from flowing recklessly as it lists."

The Upanishads and the Atharvaveda.

3. When we pass from the age of the Rigveda to the age of the Atharvaveda, we pass from the universe of hymns to the universe of incantations. Goblins, ghosts, sorcerers, witches, diseases and death, take the place of the god of thunder, the god of rain, the god of celestial and terrestrial fire, the god and goddess of light. The

Atharvaveda is veritably a store-house of the black art of the ancients. There is no doubt some relieving feature to the Mantraśāstra of the Atharvaveda, when auspicious charms take the place of destructive charms. But the general impression which the Atharvaveda leaves upon our mind is that of the blood-sucking activity of the ghoulish demon which saps the fountains of both devotion and reason, and leaves us in the arid wastes of witcheries and incantations. It is a far cry from the Atharvaveda to the Upanishads. The two are almost as poles apart. No doubt there can be found in the Atharvaveda some sort of philosophical reflection as in the hymns to Kāla xix. 53-54, nor can we say that the Upanishads contain no trace whatsoever of the Atharvic influence so far as incantations and charms are concerned, but the general distinction is quite clear, that when we pass from the Atharvaveda to the Upanishads, we pass from the domain of incantations to the domain of philosophy. We must not forget, however, to mention the few blemishes on Upanishadic thought that are to be found in the Bṛihadāraṇyaka and the Kaushītaki, which show the influence of a degraded order of customs even in the reign of philosophy. When as in Bṛihadāraṇyaka vi. 4 we read of helps towards securing the love of a woman, or the destruction of the lover of a wife, or the fulfilment of the desire for procreation, or yet again when in Kaushītaki ii, we read of means for the magical obtainment of a rich treasure, or securing the love of any man or woman, or yet again of charms which may prevent the death of children during one's life-time, or finally of the "Daiva Parimara" taught in that Upanishad by means of which the enemies die round about us as the effect of the charms exercised against them, we have to remember that these are the only specimens of blemishes on an age otherwise wholly devoted to philosophical and mystical reflection, and that, as the poet expresses it, instead of marring the beauty of Upanishadic thought, like spots on the face of the moon they only heighten the beauty of the philosophic reflection—*malinam api himāṁśor lakshma lakshmīṁ tanoti.*

The Upanishads and the Brahmanas.

4. When we come to the age of the Brāhmaṇas, we come to an age of ceremonialism and ritualism. As the chief topic of the Atharvaveda is incantation, similarly the chief topic of the Brāhmaṇas is sacrifice. It passes one's understanding how the original purity of the hymnology of the Rigveda should have been so much sullied in the age of the Brāhmaṇas, which only try to foist a superstructure of meaningless ceremonialism upon the hymnology of the Veda, and press into their service passages and texts from the Vedas which they utilise in such a way as to support the not-very-glorious life of the sacrificer. Curious indeed are the ways in which the Brāhmaṇa passages mingle together legends, exegeses, dogmas, philological and philosophical speculations so as to exhibit the efficacy of the Mantras for the practical life of the sacrificer. It is a pitiful phenomenon to notice how at the time of the Brāhmaṇas so much intellect should have been wasted on the formulation of the details of the various sacrificial rites : it only reminds one of the wheels within wheels of the scholastic interpretations of Christian dogma in the Middle Ages. The spirit of the Upanishads is, on the other hand, barring a few exceptions here and there, entirely antagonsitic to the sacrificial doctrine of the Brāhmaṇas. The halting attitude of the Muṇḍaka in regard to the efficacy of Brāhmaṇic ritualism is an exception to the general Upanishadic reaction in favour of philosophical thought

against the barren and empty formalism of the Brāhmaṇa literature. While, in one passage, the Muṇḍaka tells us that the only way towards securing the goal of human life consists in blindly following the routine of sacrificial and ritualistic works enjoined upon us by our ancestors (S. I. a), in another passage closely following upon the one which we are discussing, we are told that "Sacrifices are like those unsteady boats on the ocean of life which may take one at any time to the bottom of the sea. Those who regard sacrifices as the highest good of human life, go again and again from old age to death. Living in the midst of darkness, these *soi disant* wise men move about to and fro like blind men led by the blind. They regard themselves as having reached the goal of their life even while living in the midst of ignorance. Full of desire, they fall down from their places in the heavens as soon as their merit is exhausted. Thinking that sacrifice is the highest end of human life, they cannot imagine that there is any other end. Having enjoyed in the heavens the reward of their good works, they descend down to this world, or to a lower world still. It is only those who practise penance and faith in a forest, who tranquil their passions, lead the life of knowledge and live on alms,—it is only these that go to the immortal Ātman by the door-way of the Sun" (S. I. b). The Upanishads which stand for knowledge as against the Brāhmaṇical philosophy of works very rarely exhibit even this halting attitude towards ritualism to be met with in the Muṇḍaka. Their general tone is to try to find out the philosophical end of human life. Even so early as at the time of the Chhāndogya, the efficacy of the "inner sacrifice" had come to be definitely recognised : "Our real sacrifice consists in making oblations to the Prāṇa within us. One who does not know this inner sacrifice, even if he were to go in for a formal sacrifice, throws oblations merely on ashes. On the other hand, he who knows this inner sacrifice is relieved of his sins as surely as wool is burnt in a flame of fire. Knowing this inner sacrifice, even if a man were to do acts of charity for a Chāṇḍāla, he may verily be regarded as having sacrificed to the Universal Soul " (S. 2. a). The Kaushītaki again tells us definitely, referring probably to the custom at the time of the Āraṇyakas to perform acts of mental sacrifice, that " the ancient sages did not go in for a formal sacrifice knowing that an endless sacrifice was going on all the while within themselves " (S. 2. b). We thus see how the Brāhmaṇical idea of sacrifice comes to be modulated in the days of the Upanishads so as ultimately to be entirely transformed into a new conception of sacrifice altogether—that of a mental sacrifice—which is helpful to the process of the acquisition of spiritual knowledge. On the whole, it may not be untrue to say that the futility of works was definitely recognised at the time of the Upanishads which tried to substitute a philosophy of knowledge for the Brāhmaṇical philosophy of works.

Meaning of Revelation.

5. The Vedas, the Brāhmaṇas and the Upanishads have all of them been recognised from times immemorial as "Śruti" or Revelation. Let us try to find out what the real meaning of this expression is. It has been customary among all religious to regard their basal works as being revealed to them by God. Some regard their religious works as having been revealed to them in the midst of light and thunder, either from without or within. Others regard them as having been delivered to them in the form of significant sounds. In this way have the Bible and the Koran, like the Vedas and the Upanishads, been regarded as revelations of

God to man. The real meaning of Revelation seems to the present writer to be not any external message delivered to man from without, but a divine afflatus springing from within, the result of inspiration through god-intoxication. It was for this reason that St. Paul said that it was not he but God that spoke through him. It was for this reason that Jesus Christ advised his disciples to take no thought as to what they were going to speak, but that they should speak straightway and then God would speak through them. It was for this reason likewise that Plato explained in his *Ion* the origin of poetical composition through the afflatus of god-intoxication : " The authors of those great poems do not attain to excellence through the rules of any art, but they utter their beautiful melodies of verse in a state of inspiration, and, as it were, possessed by a spirit not their own. Thus the composers of lyrical poetry create those admired songs of theirs in a state of divine insanity......Thus every rhapsodist or poet......is excellent in proportion to the extent of his participation in the divine influence, and the degree in which the Muse itself has descended on him. ....And thus it appears to me....that these transcendent poems are not human, as the work of men, but divine, as coming from God." This passage gives us a very good account of the way in which all poetry, and likewise, all philosophy worthy of the name comes to be produced. It was in this way that we may say that the Vedic seers composed their hymns, and the Upanishadic philosophers set forth intellectual arguments. It is futile to discuss, as the Naiyāyikas and the Mīmāṁsakas later discussed, as to whether the Vedas and the Upanishads are " apaurusheya " or " paurusheya." The Naiyāyikas maintained that these works were " paurusheya", that is, composed by God. The Mīmāṁsakas, on the other hand, believing in the eternity of sound, said that they were "apaurusheya", that is, they were composed neither by man nor by God, but that, in the form of sounds in which they have come down to us, they existed from all eternity. As contrasted with both these schools, the Vedāntins maintain that the Vedas and the Upanishads are "apaurusheya", in the sense that they were inspired by God—*purushaprayatnam vinā prakaṭībhūta*. This last meaning of the word "apaurusheya" comes quite close to the meaning which we have tried to assign to the word Revelation; and thus we may see how the Vedas and the Upanishads must, like the basal literature of all other religions, be regarded as having been composed by seers in a state of god-intoxication.

The Upanishadic view of Revelation.

6. Let us see what the Upanishads themselves have got to say on the question of the meaning that we have assigned to the term Revelation. The Bṛihadāraṇyaka tells us that "the Ṛigveda, the Yajurveda, the Sāmaveda and the Atharvāṅgirasa have all of them been breathed forth by that great Primeval Being; likewise also have all history, all mythology, all sciences, all Upanishads, all poems, all aphorisms and all the commentaries thereon been breathed forth by that Great Divinity" (S. 3.). It is important to remember that this Upanishadic passage classes the Vedas and the Upanishads on the one hand, with History and Mythology on the other, as being breathed forth by God. Now nobody has regarded the Histories and the Mythologies as "Śruti" or Revelation, even though the Vedas and the Upanishads have been so regarded, and yet the Upanishadic passage classes the two together as being the result of the breathing forth of God. The only meaning, it seems to us, that we can assign to the above passage

is that all these great works, whether we take the Vedas and the Upanishads on the one hand, or History and Mythology on the other, may be regarded as having been due to the inspirational activity of God in the minds of those who composed them. It was not the writers of these works that were the authors of them, but it was the Divinity within them that was responsible for their production. We thus have the Upanishadic view of the Upanishads as the result of the inspirational activity of God, the philosophers to whom they are attributed having served merely as instruments for the display of this activity. This is a sort of a new Upanishadic Occasionalism, where the Seer or the Sage serves merely as an occasion for the creative activity of God. Thus, when the sage Śvetāśvatara said, that the Upanishad, which is named after him, was revealed to him through the power of his penance and the grace of God (S. 4. a), and yet again when the sage Triśaṅku uttered his *vedānuvachana*, which expression might be understood to mean either a "post-illuminational" discourse, or one which was "in consonance with his mystical illumination" (S. 4. b), they are supporting the view of the meaning of Revelation which we have taken above. There is yet again a second view which implies more or less a human participation in the transmission, if not in the composition, of these revealed texts, when, as in the Īśa and the Kena Upanishads, we are made aware of a continuity of philosophical tradition which had come down to the days of the Upanishads (S. 5. a). In the Chhāndogya Upanishad, likewise, we are told that Sages of old were careful to learn spiritual wisdom from their Teachers, for fear that when these Teachers had departed, there would be nobody living who would tell them "what could not be otherwise heard, what could not be otherwise thought, what could not be otherwise known" (S. 5. b). Finally, we have in the Bṛihadāraṇyaka a strange view of the genesis of Revelation, when we are told that the Ṛigveda, the Yajurveda and the Sāmaveda were all of them produced by the God of Death, who having coupled himself with a wife of his own creation, namely Speech, produced the above-mentioned Vedas along with all men and cattle from his union (S. 6)—a view which is quixotic enough for philosophical purposes, unless we understand it as having an anthropologic value, and as being the remnant of an old mythological way of thought which is to be found in plenty in most Brāhmaṇical as well as in some Upanishadic literature. On the whole, it may not be untrue to say that the Upanishads are regarded by the Upanishads themselves as being the work of the inspirational activity of God in the human mind.

Chronological arrangement of the Upanishads.

7. Having cleared the Upanishadic view of revelation, let us try to arrange in a chronological order the Upanishads which are going to be the subject-matter of the present Volume. It must be remembered at the outset that we must make a clear division between the Old Upanishads and the New Upanishads, the Old batch comprising the Thirteen Upanishads to be enumerated presently, while the New Upanishads contain such of the remaining Upanishads as can be proved to be authentic by higher literary criticism. The four Upanishads which Dr. Schrader has discovered recently, namely, the Bāshkala, the Chhāgaleya, the Ārsheya and the Śaunaka will not concern us in the present Volume, because their authenticity has not yet been universally accepted. The Mahānārāyaṇopanishad has also been recently proved to be obviously of a later date, and hence it cannot be included in our Older batch of

the Upanishads. The Thirteen Upanishads, which will be the subject-matter of the present Volume, may be arranged according to the order of the Muktika canon as Īśa, Kena, Kaṭha, Praśna, Muṇḍaka, Māṇḍukya, Taittirīya, Aitareya, Chhāndogya, Bṛihadāraṇyaka, Śvetāśvatara, Kaushītaki and Maitri. This, however, is an order which does not take the chronological sequence of the Upanishads into account, and it thus becomes necessary in the light of modern literary criticism and a historico-philological evaluation of the Upanishads to arrange them in proper chronological perspective. The problem has been so thoroughly treated by us elsewhere that it would be redundant to go over once more into the problem of the chronological arrangement of these Upanishads. We shall merely content ourselves with mentioning the conclusions that have been arrived at. Considering the Upanishadic age to have been placed somewhere between 1200 B. C., and 600 B. C., it becomes necessary to distribute the Upanishadic literature into chronological periods within the general limits that have been so fixed. Various tests have been employed as to the chronological arrangement of these Upanishads. (1) The language, the style, the vocabulary, the inflection and other grammatical peculiarities are one obvious test for determining the age of an Upanishad; but this cannot be a final test, because an old Upanishad may have been written in a fairly lucid style, while a newer Upanishad may have been composed in an almost archaic style. (2) Nor is the distinction between prose and verse a sufficient criterion for the chronological arrangement of the Upanishads. It seems to have been taken for granted by critics like Deussen that the oldest of these Upanishads were written in prose, that others which followed them were written in verse, and that a few others that remained came to be written in prose again. This is a gratuitous assumption which in the light of modern criticism does not seem to hold much water. (3) A third test, namely that of a successive elaboration of detail, is a fairly good test though it is not absolutely conclusive. Thus it may not be entirely incorrect to find the chronological order of certain Upanishads according to the elaboration of detail of the story of the "War of the Senses" as found in them. This story occurs in the Chhāndogya, the Bṛihadāraṇyaka, the Aitareya, the Kaushītaki and the Praśna Upanishads, and it must be legitimate to argue for the precedence or sequence of any of these Upanishads according to the elaboration of the detail of the story. (4) A fourth and a more difficult test, namely that of a regular ideological development, is not without its use. Thus, for example, the development of the idea of the relation of the "Two Souls," the Individual Soul and the Universal Soul, which occurs in the Kaṭhopanishad, the Muṇḍakopanishad and the Śvetāśvataropanishad could be regarded as a legitimate test for the chronological sequence of these Upanishads in that order, inasmuch as in the story of the Kaṭhopanishad the two Souls are regarded as being on a par with each other as enjoying equally the fruits of their action, while in the Muṇḍaka only one is described as tasting of the fruits of action, the other being described simply as an on-looker, while finally in the Śvetāśvatara an addition is made to the conception in the Muṇḍaka, namely that of the unborn Prakṛiti, consisting of the three qualities, the red, the white and the black, which the Individual Soul enjoys, but which the Universal Soul leaves off (S. 7). (5) A fifth test, which is only a particular case of the last test, but which deserves separate mention on account of the importance it has attained at the hands of certain modern writers, especially Prof. Keith, centres itself round the development of the idea of Transmigration in the Upanishads. Just as a similar attempt has been made in regard to the chronological arrangement of the Dialogues of Plato on the basis of the development of the doctrine of Ideas as found in them, similarly, an attempt is here made to find out the chronological sequence of the Upanishads on the basis of the development of the idea of Transmigration. It must be remembered, however, that this test comes very often to base itself upon negations, instead of positive assertions. Absence of the idea of Transmigration does not necessarily prove the priority of an Upanishad, because, it may be, that the idea may not form the subject-matter of that Upanishad, while the Upanishad itself may not be amenable to the postulation of that idea. Prof. Keith has argued, and many others have followed him in saying, that the Aitareya Āraṇyaka, especially in its older portion, must be regarded as very old indeed, because the idea of Transmigration does not occur in it. These writers seem to argue in a circle, because they hold that the older portion of the Āraṇyaka must be separated from the newer portion on account of the absence of the idea of Transmigration in it, and then they say that the idea of Transmigration must be regarded as late because it does not occur in the older portion. Now even supposing that we can succeed in making a division between the older portion and the newer portion of the Aitareya Āraṇyaka, the absence of the idea of Transmigration in the older portion can be regarded as no argument for its chrnonological severance from the newer portion ; while it is necessary to remember that the Fifth Chapter of the Second Section of the Aitareya Āraṇyaka does definitely assert the fact of Transmigration when it describes a man as veritably coming to life after death—a fact which it calls his "third birth". (6) Finally, the only test which may be regarded as being absolutely definite about the chronological arrangement of the Upanishads is that of inter-quotation. Thus we may say that the Taittirīya is definitely later than the Bṛihadāraṇyaka, inasmuch as the Taittirīya refers to the Bṛihadāraṇyaka in the very words in which this latter Upanishad states the doctrine of "quintuple existence" (S. 8). But this test can have no universal significance because we find only few definite inter-quotations among the Upanishads. Moreover, if we just take into account the different strata of composition in the various Upanishads, and divide each of the Upanishads according to the sub-units of which it may be composed, the problem of a general chronological arrangement of these sub-units becomes a hard one indeed ; but if we make all the allowance that we can for the existence of these strata in the Upanishads, and judge of the Upanishads as a whole, we may say that the Thirteen Upanishads, which we have mentioned above and which will form the theme of our present Volume, may be classed together into the following five different groups :—

I. Bṛihadāraṇyaka and Chhāndogya.
II. Īśa and Kena.
III. Aitareya, Taittirīya and Kaushītaki.
IV. Kaṭha, Muṇḍaka and Śvetāśvatara.
V. Praśna, Maitri and Māṇḍukya.

A study of the Bṛihadāraṇyaka and the Chhāndogya may easily lead us to regard them as belonging to the oldest group of the Upanishads. Even though they may be seen to consist of several sub-units, on the whole we may say that they belong to the oldest group. The Upanishads in group II, namely Īśa and Kena, it is customary to relegate to a comparatively late period; but the language, the sentiment and the archaic tone of the Īśa, especially the common material it has with the Bṛihadāraṇyaka and the Kena, which latter may be placed almost in the same category with it, may be regarded as constituting the second group. Of group III, the Aitareya must be regarded as an old Upanishad, but not necessarily as the oldest simply for the reason that has been adduced, namely, that it belongs to the earliest Veda, the Ṛigveda. The Taittirīya goes in the same group with the Aitareya, while the Kaushītaki, even though it may be regarded as on the whole an unoriginal Upanishad, still in the parts which belong to it properly, may be classed along with the Aitareya and the Taittirīya to constitute group III. Group IV is quite definite. The Muṇḍaka comes after the Kaṭha, and the Śvetāśvatara comes after the Muṇḍaka, and even though there is an evident archaism in the Śvetāśvatara and a clear sub-division of it into the first chapter on the one hand, and the other chapters on the other, on the whole it may be said to bring up the rear among these great poetical Upanishads. Of group V, the Praśna which forms quite a pre-conceived unity entirely unlike the other Upanishads, must be regarded as belonging to the latest group; the Maitri whose vocabulary is quite peculiar to itself and which has evidently two or more definite strata in it, must, on account of its mythological and astronomical references, be regarded as coming quite near to the time when the Paurāṇika tradition began; while the Māṇḍukya, which may be said to develop the thought of the Maitri itself in certain respects, namely, in postulating three and a half *moræ*, while the Maitri postulates only three, of the symbol Om, as well as on account of its aphoristic method of thought-presentation, may be regarded as being the last of the Older batch of the Upanishads. It would be hard to determine the exact date of the composition of any of these Upanishads; but the upward and the lower limits of the whole Upanishadic period may be fixed without much difficulty as being between 1200 and 600 B.C., and the later Upanishads of the above canon may be seen to be dovetailed into that next period of Indian Thought, when Buddhism was germinating in India, when the Sāṁkhya and the Yoga were being systematised, and when the Bhagavadgītā was being composed to finally hush the voice of the materialist and the atheist by synthesising the points of theistic significance in the Sāṁkhya and the Yoga, and by gathering together the red-letter pieces of Upanishadic philosophy and welding them all up together into a theistic-mystic poem—the pattern of many similar imitations in days to come.

The Brihadaranyaka.

8. It would be necessary for us to review briefly the contents of the various Upanishads as arranged chronologically in the above outline, and to set forth in a brief way the main points of interest in those Upanishads from the philosophical point of view. A full analysis of the Upanishads is neither possible nor desirable in this place, but we refer our readers to our History of Indian Philosophy Vol. II. for a full account of the contents of them. In order, however, that our readers may understand and appreciate the problem-by-problem treatment of the Upanishads in the succeeding chapters of this work, it would be necessary for us to introduce them briefly to the contents of the various Upanishads. We may begin by an analysis of the Bṛihadāraṇyaka. This Upanishad contains six chapters, of which the second, the third and the fourth are alone of philosophical consequence, the others containing philosophical matters interspersed with much

miscellaneous reflection. In the first chapter, we have a good description of the Cosmic Person considered as a sacrificial horse; then we pass to the theory of Death as the "archē" of all things; and then we have a parable in proof of the supremacy of Prāṇa, which is followed by a number of creationist myths put together at random. In the second chapter, we have the famous conversation between Gārgya, the proud Brahmin, and Ajātaśatru, the quiescent Kshatriya king. It is in this chapter likewise that we are introduced for the first time to the great sage Yājñavalkya, who is making a partition of his estate between his wives, as well as to the sage Dadhyach Ātharvaṇa whose philosophical teaching we shall consider at a later stage in this chapter. The sage Yājñavalkya, to whom we are introduced in chapter two, becomes the prominent figure of chapters three and four, and just as in chapter two we see him discoursing with his wife Maitreyī, similarly in chapter three we see him discoursing with a number of philosophers in the court of king Janaka, and in chapter four with king Janaka himself. The philosophical teachings of Yājñavalkya we shall consider somewhat later; but it would be necessary for us here to say something about his personality. An irascible philosopher by nature, as may be seen from the fate to which he subjects Śākalya who was disputing with him in the court of king Janaka, he seems nevertheless to possess the kindness of human feelings, especially in his relations with his wife Maitreyī. Given to bigamy, he nevertheless maintains a strict spiritual relation with Maitreyī, while Kātyāyanī, his other wife, he regards merely as a woman of the world and prizes accordingly. Adumbrating as he does his doctrine of immanence to Gārgī when she torments him with question after question, and wanting in chivalry as he seems to us as he proceeds without much ceremony to check her philosophic impudence, he nevertheless appears to be a shrewd man, who, when pressed by the sage Jāratkārava to some deepest questions, takes him by the hand out of the assembly and discourses with him on the topic of *Karman*, and a prudent man likewise who gives *ad hoc* answers to his controversialists, as may be seen from the way in which he ritualistically disposes of the ritualistic questions of Āśvala. A eudæmonist by nature, who supposes that the acceptance of presents is not incompatible with the imparting of philosophical knowledge, and therein maintaining rather the Sophistic view of wisdom, than the Socratic view that a great spiritual teacher must never contaminate himself with the acceptance of presents, Yājñavalkya is, undoubtedly, the greatest philosopher of the Upanishadic times, who, by his consistent philosophical Idealism and by his thoroughgoing practical Ātmanism, may give lessons to many a thinker of the present day. King Janaka, who seems to be an ardent lover of philosophical and spiritual wisdom, falls prostrate at the feet of this great philosopher, offering him his kingdom and his possessions, which the philosopher scarcely avails himself of. This king Janaka figures largely in the third and fourth chapters of this Upanishad, in the third chapter being only a spectator of the great controversy in his court, and in the fourth taking the liberty to learn personally from Yājñavalkya himself. It is this king likewise who is also introduced for a while in the fifth chapter of this Upanishad, which contains many other things besides, such as a number of miscellaneous reflections on ethical, cosmological and eschatological matters; while the sixth and the final chapter of the Upanishad contains the celebrated parable of the senses, and we are introduced to the philosopher Pravāhaṇa Jaivali whose celebrated doctrine of "Five Fires" we shall notice below. This last chapter, as has been pointed out above, ends with certain superstitious Brāhmaṇical practices, and contains, among other things, a statement of the genealogical tradition of the Upanishad which may be taken for what it is worth.

The Chhandogya.

9. The Chhāndogya, which belongs like the Bṛihadāraṇyaka to our group I, is an Upanishad which does not rise to such high literary or philosophical eminence as the Bṛihadāraṇyaka, even though it is quoted and referred to oftener by the later author of the Vedānta-sūtras. Chapters six, seven and eight alone are of philosophical importance, the others not coming up to that level at all. The first and the second chapters are merely a Brāhmaṇism *redivivus*, and if we just want to point to portions of the Upanishads in which the Brāhmaṇical liturgy and doctrine exercise the greatest amount of influence, we may point to the first and second chapters of this Upanishad. There is a small cosmological argument here and a little philosophical disquisition there; on the whole, these two chapters contain only such subjects as the significance of Om, the meaning, the kind and the names of Sāman, and the genesis and function of Om. There is, however, one very good satirical piece towards the end of the first chapter of this Upanishad which is worth remarking. It concerns the singing of the Mantras with a material end in view. We are told how, once upon a time, Baka Dālbhya, or as he was also called, Glāva Maitreya, had gone to a retired place to recite his Veda, how a white dog appeared before him, how a number of other dogs came to this dog and begged of it to chant certain hymns because they said they were hungry and by its chants the white dog might procure food for them, how the white dog told the

other dogs that they might come to it the next morning, how Baka Dālbhya, who was intent upon seeing what this canine recitation of hymns would be like, waited next morning to watch the dogs meet together, how the dogs, as previously settled, came together the next morning, each holding the tail of another in its mouth, as the priests do when they walk in procession at the time of sacrifice each holding the gown of the fore-going priest in his hand, how when they sat down, they began to sing "Hiṁ ! Om, let us eat, Om, let us drink, Om, let the gods procure food for us, O Lord of food, bring food to us, bring it to us, Om." This seems to us to be a ridicule poured upon the Mantra-singers who went in for their business with the desire of obtaining some material end. It seems to us that this Canine Chant—the Śauva Udgītha as it has been called—may be regarded as a good invective against the Brāhmaṇical belief in externalism, in the interest of the assertion of the supremacy of the spiritual end to any material end whatsoever. The third chapter of this Upanishad contains the famous description of the Sun as a great bee-hive hanging in space. It also contains a description of the Gāyatrī Brāhmaṇa-wise, the *bon mots* of Śāṇḍilya, a description of the world as a huge chest, the all-too disconnected instruction of Āṅgirasa to Kṛishṇa who was the son of Devaki, and finally a piece of heliolatory, with the myth of the emergence of the Sun out of a huge egg. In the fourth chapter we have the philosophy of Raikva, the story of Satyakāma Jābāla and his mother, and the story of Upakosala who in his turn obtains philosophical wisdom from his teacher Satyakāma Jābāla. The fifth chapter contains the eschatological teaching of Jaivali, which is identical in substance with the account to be found in the Bṛihadāraṇyaka, while it also contains the famous synthesis of thought effected by Aśvapati

Kaikeya out of the six cosmological doctrines advanced by the six philosophers who had gone to learn wisdom from him. The sixth chapter is evidently the best of all the chapters of the Chhāndgoya, and we have here the highly-strung "identität" philosophy of Āruṇi, who establishes an absolute equation between individual and universal spirit, for whom, in other words, there is no difference between the two at all. Āruṇi is the outstanding personality of the Chhāndogya, as Yājñavalkya is of the Bṛihadāraṇyaka. The Śatapatha Brāhmaṇa tells us that Āruṇi was a very renowned sage of anitiquity, and that Yājñavalkya was a pupil of Āruṇi. The philosophy which Āruṇi advances in the 6th chapter of the Chhāndogya does really entitle him to that position. So far so good: but it seems to us that when once the reputation of Āruṇi as a great philosopher had been established, other Upanishads felt no scruple in utilising him for the development of their own doctrine and we find Āruṇi playing quite a subordinate and unimportant rôle even in such an admittedly late Upanishad as the Kaushītaki. It is unfortunate that authors should feel the necessity of reviving the memory of a great man and turning it to bad account. A Falstaff reborn, as Shakespearian readers know, loses all the interest which he originally had when he first appeared. Even likewise with Āruṇi. He did play a great part, indeed, in the Chhāndogya; but later writers had no scruple in utilising his name, as we have said above, for very unimportant purposes. The seventh chapter of the Chhāndogya contains the famous discourse between Nārada and Sanatkumāra, the main points of which we shall discuss at a later stage of this chapter. Finally, the eighth chapter of this Upanishad contains some very excellent hints for the practical realisation of the Ātman, as well as the famous myth of Indra and Virochana which we shall have occasion duly to notice in a later chapter of this work.

The Isa and the Kena Upanishads.

10. The Īśa and the Kena Upanishads, which form our group II, are both named after the initial words of these treatises, just as the ancient chronicles of Scandinavia are named "Heimskringla" after their opening words. The Īśopanishad is quite a small Upanishad, and yet it contains many hints which show an extraordinarily piercing insight. Within the short compass of 18 verses, it gives us a valuable mystical description of the Ātman, a description of the ideal Sage who stands unruffled in the midst of temptations and sorrows, an adumbration of the doctrine of Karmayoga as later formulated, and finally a reconciliation of the claims of knowledge and works. The most valuable idea that lies at the root of the Upanishad is that of a logical synthesis which it attempts between the two opposites of knowledge and works, which are both required according to that Upanishd to be annulled in a higher synthesis. It is this idea of the logical synthesis of opposites which is an unconscious contribution which the Sage of the Upanishad makes to the development of Indian Thought.

The Kenopanishad which consists of four sections, two balancing against two, the first two being composed in verse, the last two in prose, exhibits also the division of the subjective and objective approaches to the proof of Ātman, namely, the psychological and the cosmological. The verse part of the Upanishad gives us a psychological argument for the existence of Ātman as the inspirer of the various sense-functions; it also breaks the idols, literally and metaphorically, in favour of the worship of Ultimate Reality conceived as Ātman; and finally it makes an essay in spiritual agniology telling us in a paradoxical fashion that those who know really do not know, and those who do not know may alone be said to know the ultimate reality. The prose part of the Upanishad gives us the famous myth of Indra and the Damsel and advances a cosmological argument for the proof of the Immeasurable Power which lies at the back of the forces of Nature. It teaches us a lesson of humility, inasmuch as it tells us that no man who is not humble may hope to come into the presence of this Power ; while it lays the moral foundation for this "esoteric doctrine" when it tells us that austerity, restraint and action are its ποῦ στῶ, the Vedas its limbs, and Truth its shelter. The Upanishad also advises us to find the same reality in objective as well as subjective existence, in the flash of the lightning as in the motion of the mind.

The Aitareya, the Taittiriya, and the Kaushitaki Upanishads.

11. The Aitareya Upanishad, properly so-called, is only a part of the larger Aitareya Āraṇyaka beginning with the fourth section of the second chapter of the Āraṇyaka and going to the end of that chapter. There are three chapters of the Upanishad itself, all of which are important. The first is given to a description of the creation of the world by the primeval Ātman through the intermediary Virāj. The second contains the famous philosophy of "Three Births" probably belonging to the sage Vāmadeva, a Vedic sage mentioned in Ṛigveda IV. 27. 1, whose opinions are cited with approval in the present Upanishad, and whose example is held up before the eyes of one who is desirous of gaining immortality. We shall discuss the philosophy of Vāmadeva at a later stage in this chapter ; but we cannot forbear from remarking here that the idea of life after death is definitely introduced in this chapter. Finally, the last chapter of this Upanishad is a very bold statement of the fundamental doctrine of idealistic philosophy that all psychical and cosmical existences must be regarded as the expression of a common principle, namely, intellect.

The Taittirīya is divided into three chapters. In the first chapter occurs the famous physiological description of the "nipple-like" gland which hangs downwards in the brain, and which is regarded as the seat of the Immortal Being. In this chapter likewise occur two famous ethical descriptions, as well as the mystical utterances of Triśaṅku. The second chapter is a collection of miscellaneous points containing, among other things, the first mention of the so-called "Doctrine of Sheaths", as well as a description of the Beatific Calculus. The third chapter takes up the question of the Sheaths from the second chapter and exhibits these as a ladder of metaphysical existences, and ends with that famous mystical monologue in which subject and object and the subject-object relation are all described as being ultimately one.

The Kaushītaki is divided into four chapters, of which the first is merely an enlarged variant on the description of the path of the Gods and the path of the Fathers, as occurring in the Chhāndogya and the Bṛihadāraṇyaka Upanishads, and the last is again a repetition of the story of Bālāki and Ajātaśatru as occurring in the Bṛihadāraṇyaka. It is only the second and the third chapters of this Upanishad which may be said to belong to the Kaushītaki proper. The second chapter is a collection of quite disconnected units and contains the doctrines of the four philosophers, namely, Kaushītaki who is described as "Sarvajit", or an all-conquering sage, as well as Paiṅgya, Pratardana and Śushkabhṛiṅgāra. Moreover, it contains a description of a number of social customs of the time, which are superstitious and which may therefore be regarded as irreligious. In the third chapter, Pratardana is described as imbibing the principles of philosophy from Indra. Now Indra is only a mythological name, a name of Vedic repute, and we may say that the points of philosophy contained in this chapter belong to Pratardana himself rather than to Indra. Nevertheless, we must consider the story as it is, and take into account the references that are freely made here to Indra's exploits as found in the Ṛigveda. Indra tells Pratardana that the only good for mankind here below is to know Him ; that He it was who had killed the three-headed son of Tvashṭṛi ; that He it was who had delivered over the Aruṇmukhas to the jackals ; that having broken many a treaty, He it was who killed the sons of Pralhāda in the heaven, the Paulomas in the inter-mundane regions, and the Kālakañjas on earth ; and that even though He had done these deeds, not a hair of His body was injured ; and that finally any one who understands Indra to be of this nature, and to have performed these exploits, never suffers, even though he may kill his mother or father, or go in for a theft, or destroy an embryo ; nor does the bloom ever depart from his face. It is in this conversation also between Indra and Pratardana that Prāṇa comes to be understood first as the principle of life, then as the principle of consciousness, and then is equated with Ultimate Reality, namely the Ātman, and we are told that it is this Ātman who is the cause of all good and evil actions in this world, and that all human beings are merely instruments in His hands.

The Katha, the Mundaka, and the Svetasvatara Upanishads.

12. ✓The Kaṭha, the Muṇḍaka and the Śvetāśvatara Upanishads which form our fourth group are related to each other as no three of the other Upanishads are. They all aim at envisaging the highest philosophical truths in a poetic manner, and thus become the chief sources from which the Bhagavadgītā

and other philosophical poems later freely borrow, the only difference between the Upanishads being that the Kaṭhopanishad is more or less a metaphysical work) the Muṇḍaka an emotional work, and the Śvetāśvatara a commixture of philosophy and mysticism. All the three Upanishads seem, moreover, to have been written at a time when the Sāṁkhya and the Vedānta had not yet parted ways. Of these the Kaṭha has its natural termination at the end of the first Adhyāya, as may be seen from the repetition of words at the end of the Adhyāya, as well as the "phalaśruti" which is also given at the same place. The second Adhyāya thus seems to be tacked on to the original redaction of the Upanishad, and even though this latter Adhyāya seems to furnish a sequel to the Nachiketas-Death story as may be seen from the last verse of that Adhyāya, as well as from the repetition of words even here, still, as may be seen by reference to Kaṭhopanishad II. 5. 6, Yama seems at this place just to be supplying an answer to the query of Nachiketas in I. i. 29, which suggests that all the intervening portion is a later addition. The Kaṭha, like the Muṇḍaka and the Śvetāśvatara, will be so often quoted in this work that it would be needless for us to discuss its contents at any length. Two of the most prominent features of the Kaṭha are the description of the "Chariot of the Body", and the death and dream approaches to the problem of reality. The whole of the Kaṭha is surcharged with lofty ideas about the Immortality of the Soul, as well as suggestions for the practical attainment of Ātman. In one passage, the Kaṭha brings out a distinction regarding the realisation of Ātman in the various worlds. While we are dwelling in this body on earth, we can visualise the Ātman only as in a mirror, that is contrariwise, left being to the right and right being to the left. In the world of the fathers, we visualise the Ātman as in a dream, the image leaving a psychical impression indeed, but being unreal. In the world of the Gandharvas, we are told, we see Him as one sees a pebble under water, the image being true but refracted. It is only in the Brahman-world, we are told, that we can distinguish the Ātman from the non-Ātman as light from shade, that is, we can see the Ātman as in broad day-light. This is a valauable contribution which the Kaṭhopanishad makes to Upanishadic thought.

The Muṇḍakopanishad is, as the name implies, an "Upanishad addressed to Shavelings," and may be classed according to its subject-matter along with the later Samnyāsa Upanishads. Its eclecticism is apparent on the face. The position it takes in regard to ritualism is halting . Its cosmology is suffused both by Sāṁkhya and Vedāntic ideas. Its metaphysics is squarely based on Vedic ideas and has a ritualistic tinge. While as a work which can incite to mystic thought, it has no parallel in the whole literature of the Upanishads.)

The Śvetāśvatara seems to have been written in the interests of Śaivism. It seems to have had its natural termination at the close of the first chapter, as may be seen from the repetition of the words at the end of it. The other chapters seem to have been added at a later stage. In the first chapter, we have suggestions for a good criticism of contemporary doctrines, including even Ātmanism, in favour of a Śaivite trinitarian monism. The second chapter contains a classical description of Yoga. The third, the fourth and the fifth chapters are devoted to a discussion of Śaivite and Sāṁkhya philosophies, and invite a discussion as to the meaning of the word " kapila " which has been mentioned in V. 2 ; while the last chapter is the only unsectarian portion of the Upanishad which gives us a purely theistic view of the Godhead, and introduces the idea of Bhakti to Guru as to God. As in the case of its compeer Upanishads, the Śvetāśvatara was written at a time when the Sāṁkhya and the Vedānta were yet intermixed. "The Sāṁkhya had not yet lost its God who is described as ruling the Pradhāna (VI. 10), while the Vedānta had not yet definitely had its Māyā, a mere metamorphosis of the Sāṁkhya Prakṛiti. The three Guṇas as in IV. 5 were yet the common property of both the Sāṁkhya and the Vedānta, having had their origin so far back as the Chhāndogya VI. 4. Nor had the Sāṁkhya yet laid an emphasis on the subjectivity of sense-perception, which was primarily responsible for the parting of the ways between the Sāṁkhya and the Vedānta. The doctrine of creation in the sense of evolution was mooted V. 5, but its full implications had not been yet thought out. The psychology and the metaphysics of the Sāṁkhya were yet in the making, and had not yet been sundered from those of the Vedānta as with a hatchet. It is for all these reasons that we say that the Śvetāśvatara, in which lie embedded side by side the Sāṁkhya and the Vedāntic doctrines of cosmology, psychology and metaphysics, is a very valuable Upanishad for the genetic study of the parting of the ways between the two great systems."

The Praśna, the Maitri and the Mandukya Upanishads.

13. The Praśnopanishad, which evidently belongs to a very late date in the history of Upanishadic literature, is a preconceived systematic unity, as almost no other Upanishad is. The six Sages, who are mentioned as going to Pippalāda to learn wisdom, ask each of them a question of Pippalāda in such a way that the person last mentioned asks his question first, and the order of their questions is such that they educe an evolving philosophy from Pippalāda, which we shall consider later. The nature, the style and the manner of presentation of the argument in the Praśnopanishad are also comparatively modern.

The Maitri is a very important Upanishad in the history of Upanishadic literature, inasmuch as its vocabulary and its many references are peculiar to itself. It can be divided into two different strata, the first four chapters constituting the first stratum, and the last three constituting the second. We may even say that the first four chapters of this Upanishad may be taken to be a comparatively early redaction, and, therefore, alone relevant for our purposes. The last three chapters contain references to such astrological names as Śani, Rāhu and Ketu (VIII. 6), Bṛihaspati, the author of a heretical philosophy (VII. 9), and a six-fold Yoga (VI. 18), which is the pattern of the later eight-fold Yoga. For the purposes of the present work which considers only the old Upanishadic philosophy, therefore, we may even restrict our attention to the first four chapters of this Upanishad. Under the spell of the Sāṁkhya and Buddhistic doctrines, king Bṛihadratha is introduced in this Upanishad as giving vent to a pessimistic mood, which is unusual in Upanishadic literature. This king goes to Śākayanya and begs of him to teach him the secret of philosophy. Śākayanya tells him what he has himself learnt from the sage Maitri, who may thus be regarded as the promulgator of the doctrines of this Upanishad. The first point in his philosophy is a description of the pure noumenal Self who "arising from the body shines in his own greatness," and the second is a description of the phenomenal Self called the Bhūtātman who is subject to the influence of actions good and bad, and who therefore undergoes transmigration. We do not know how far to regard the description of the Rājasa and the Tāmasa qualities in this Upanishad as a harbinger of the later doctrine of the Bhagavadgītā on that head; but it is worth while remarking that this Upanishad mentions among Tāmasa qualities such qualities as infatuation, fear, dejection, sleep, sloth, hurt, age, grief, hunger, thirst, niggardliness, anger, atheism, ignorance, jealousy, pitilessness, folly, shamelessness, roguery, haughtiness and changeability; and among Rājasa qualities such qualities as desire, affection, passion, covetousness, injury, love, a longing eye, activity, rivalry, restlessness, fickleness, instability, greed, partiality to friends, the support of those who are round about us, aversion for the undesirable, and attachment to the desirable (III. 5). It is interesting to note that while the pure noumenal Self is regarded as the Mover of the Body, under whose direction the Body goes round like a wheel driven by a potter, the sensory organs being the rein, the motor organs the horses, the body the chariot, the mind the charioteer, and the temperament the whip (II. 9), the phenomenal Self is declared to be like a beast chained by the fetters of good and evil, bound like one in prison, subject to terror as one in the hands of death, deluded by pleasure like one intoxicated by liquor, rushing headlong like one possessed by an evil spirit, bitten by adversity as by a great serpent, blinded by passion as by night, filled by Māyā as by sleight-of-hand, false like a dream, unsubstantial like the pith of the Banana tree, changing its dress like an actor, and falsely delighting the mind like a painted wall (IV. 2). So far about the earlier portion of the Maitri. In the later portion we have a heliotheism bordering upon pantheism, a number of astronomical speculations (VI. 14-16), the doctrine of the Word and the non-Word, non-Word being even superior to

Word, an exhortation to avoid the company of those who always live in a state of hilarity, those who beg, those who live on handicraft, those who perform sacrifices for the unworthy, the Śūdras who learn scriptures, the rogues who wear knotted hair, dancers, mercenaries, prize-fighters, mendicants, actors, those who have been dismissed from king's service, those who pretend to allay the evil influence of sprites and goblins, those who wear red-dress, ear-rings and skulls, and finally those who by their sophisms shake the faith of the people in the Vedas (VII. 8). We have also an adumbration of the later Haṭhayoga practices such as those of pressing the tongue against the palate, and conveying the breath through the Sushumnā (VI. 18-21), and finally a description of the seven mystical sounds which are heard in the process of contemplation, namely, those of a river, a bell, a brazen vessel, a wheel, the croaking of frogs, the pattering of rain, and finally a voice which comes from a place of seclusion (VI. 22).

The Māṇḍukya which is the last of the early great Upanishads—we may almost call it " the Last of the Romans "—is noticeable as laying once for all the foundations of the later Vedāntic philosophy. It partitions the symbol Om in three different *moræ* and adds a fourth mora-less part, corresponding to which there are different states of consciousness, corresponding to which, again, are different kinds of Soul. The great originality of the Māṇḍukya consists in positing the four states of consciousness, namely, wakefulness, dream, sleep, and a fourth un-nameable state of consciousness; while it teaches that there is an aspect of the Godhead corresponding to these states of consciousness, the last alone being ultimately real. The Absolute of philosophy surpasses even such a theological conception as that of God.

The Methods of Upanishadic Philosophy.

14. After having taken a brief review of the contents of the Upanishads, we shall pass on to a discussion of the various methods that have been employed by the Upanishadic philosophers. There is not one method alone which is adopted by the Upanishadic philosophers: various methods have been resorted to by them at different times according to the necessities of discussion.

(i) In the first place, we must note the *enigmatic* method which occurs from time to time in these Upanishads. When Śāṇḍilya said that reality was "tajjalān," he was adopting a cryptic way for saying how God could be regarded as the origin, the end, and the life of all things. When the philosopher of the Īśāvāsyopanishad introduced the Vidyā and Avidyā, and the Saṁbhūti and Asaṁbhūti triplets, he was also taking recourse to the same method, pointing to a synthesis of opposites underlying the apparent contradictions involved in the formulation of the two riddles. The best illustration, however, of the *enigmatic* method is to be found in the Śvetāśvataropanishad, where we are told that reality is like a great circumscribing felly, whose tyres are the three Guṇas, whose ends are the sixteen Kalās, whose spokes are the fifty Bhāvas or conditions of Sāṁkhya philosophy, whose counter-spokes are the ten Senses and their ten Objects, whose six sets of eights are the eights such as the Dhātus, the Gods, the eight-fold Prakṛiti and so on, whose single rope is the Cosmic Person, whose three paths are the Good, the Bad and the Indifferent, or yet again, the Moral, the Immoral, and the A-moral, and finally which causes the single infatuation of the Ignorance of Self on account of the two causes, namely, Good and Bad works (S. 9. a). The philosopher of the Śvetāśvatara again tells us that he contemplates

Nature which is like a vast expanse of water contributed to by the five different streams of the Senses, whose springs are the five Elements which make it fierce and crooked, whose waves are the five Prāṇas, whose fount is the Antaḥkaraṇapañchaka, whose whirl-pools are the five Objects of sense which entangle a man into them, whose five rapids are the kinds of grief caused by Generation, Existence, Transformation, Declination and Decay, which diverts itself into the fifty channels of the Bhāvās of Sāṁkhya philosophy, and finally, which has the five tides of periodic overflow namely, at Birth, in Childhood, in Manhood, in Old age and at Death (S. 9. b). Philosophy would be arid and dry, if it did not occasionally contain such *enigmatic* riddles. Even Plato describes how a man and no-man, seeing and not-seeing a bird and no-bird on a tree and not-tree, killed it and did not kill it, with a stone and no-stone.

(ii) Then, there is the *aphoristic* method as employed in the Māṇḍukya, which is the pattern of the later Sūtra literature of the various Systems of philosophy. This method has the advantage of compressing all the material of thought in short pregnant sentences, while leaving the commentator to scratch his head as best he may on the interpretation of them. It is for this reason probably that the same Vedānta-sūtras, for example, came to be interpreted in such different fashions by the various commentators on them. To translate from the Māṇḍukya, we are told how "the syllable Om is verily all that exists. Under it is included all the past, the present and the future, as well as that which transcends time. Verily all this is Brahman. The Ātman is Brahman. This Ātman is four-footed. The first foot is the Vaiśvānara, who enjoys gross things......in the state of wakefulness. The second foot is the Taijasa, who enjoys exquisite things......in the state of dream. The third is the Prājña, who enjoys bliss......in the state of deep-sleep......The fourth is the Ātman, ...who is alone, without a second, calm, holy and tranquil". This passage has been verily the basis upon which all the later systems of Vedāntic philosophy have come to be built.

(iii) We have next the *etymological* method which was adopted in many places by the Upanishadic seers under the spell of Brāhmaṇism, which had not yet ceased to influence the formulation of thought. In the Chhāndogya we are told how "svapiti" means "satā sampanno bhavati," or "svamapito bhavati," that is, becomes one with himself; how "aśiśishati" means "apa eva tadaśitam nayante," or water is leading off all that is eaten; how "pipāsati" means "teja eva tatpītam nayate," that is how heat is drying up what is drunk (S. 10. a). The Bṛihadāraṇyaka tells us that "purusha" is really "puriśaya", that is inhabiting the citadel of heart (S. 10. b). Finally even such a late Upanishad as the Māṇḍukya tells us that the first letter A of the syllable Om is equivalent to Āpti or attainment, because it possesses the property of Ādimattva or beginningness; the letter U means Utkarsha or exaltation, because it signifies Ubhayatva or intermediateness; and the third letter M means Miti or Apiti, because it signifies measurement or destruction (S. 10. c). But we may put it to the credit of the Upanishadic philosophers that such word—puzzles are to be met with only occasionally in Upanishadic literature.

(iv) The fourth is what we may call the *mythical* method which is resorted to very often in the Upanishads. This method is adopted in the first place for the purpose of conveying a moral lesson, as for example, in the Kenopanishad, where the parable of Indra and the Damsel is introduced to convey the lesson of humility, to show, in other words, that nobody can attain Brahman unless he is humble at heart. In the second place, the myth introduced may have an aetiological purpose, as for example, the myth of the Sun as coming out of the huge World-egg, the myth being serviceable here to mark the course of the generation of the world-system from a Primeval Egg, which itself originally came from Being, and Being from Not-Being. Thirdly, the transcendental myth itself is not wanting, when, for example, we are told, as in the Aitareya, how the Ātman entered the human skull and became individualised as the human soul, from which place again he looked back at his origin, and convinced himself that he was the Ātman. Or, finally, we may have a myth introduced even for the sake of parody, as for example, the Canine Chant which we have already had the occasion to notice in a previous section of this chapter.

(v) Then, again, we have the *analogical* method, which is to be found employed in many places by the Upanishads. When, for example, the sage Yājña-valkya introduces the analogy of the drum, the conch or the lute in order to explain the process of the apprehension of the Self, or when again Āruṇi introduces the analogy of the juices, which in constituting honey cease to be different from it, or yet again of the rivers that flow into the ocean and become merged in it, or of salt which becomes one with water when it is poured into it—all these illustrations serving to show the non-difference of the Individual Soul from the Universal Soul—we have the analogical method which tries to envisage by images what cannot be explained by the rigour of logic.

(vi) Then, sixthly, we have the *dialectic* method which is the stock-in-trade of the Upanishadic argument, and could be seen employed at every stage of the development of Upanishadic philosophy. We must take care to understand the word "dialectic" here in its root sense, as the method of the dialogue, instead of in the Platonic or the Hegelian sense in which it may otherwise be understood. The dialogue occasionally takes the form of a severe disputation as at the Symposium in king Janaka's court, which unfortunately became a tragedy on account of the imprecation uttered by Yājñavalkya on his last disputant, namely, Śākalya. In short, unless the superiority of the leading philosopher is implicitly acknowledged, a discourse very often takes the form of wrangling, and may end tragically, as it did at the Symposium we are referring to.

(vii) As contrasted with the dialectic method, we have what we may call the *synthetic* method of philosophy. Here an attempt is made not to destroy, but to fulfil, as may be seen by the synthesis of thought effected by Aśvapati Kaikeya out of the doctrines of the six cosmological philosophers in the Chhāndogya, or by Pippalāda out of the six psycho-metaphysical questions propounded to him by the six seers in the Praśnopanishad, or finally by Yājñavalkya out of the six metaphysical points of view suggested to him by King Janaka in Bṛihadāraṇyaka IV. There is neither a *tu quoque* argument here, nor any indifferent and precise cutting of the knot, but a sympathetic inclusion of the points of view suggested by others in a higher synthesis.

(viii) As against the dialectical and the synthetic methods, we have what we may call the *monologic* method, the method of soliloquy. The Upanishadic philosophers are generally very chary of imparting spiritual wisdom ; but it so happens occasionally that when they have given the right answer to their questioners' problem, they overhit themselves in their exposition, and lose themselves in a soliloquy in the midst of many. Thus it was that Yājñavalkya at the Symposium, after he had answered the question propounded to him by Uddālaka, lost himself into a reverie, and began to think aloud on the universal immanence of God in the famous passage which has been known as the Antaryāmi-Brāhmaṇa. Thus was it also that Yājñavalkya poured himself out in his conversation with Janaka on the immutable nature of Ātman in the Bṛihadāraṇyaka IV. 3-4. Finally, even though Yama, in the Kaṭhopanishad, was unwilling to impart wisdom to Nachiketas on the third question which was asked him by Nachiketas, when once he began to speak, he spoke in a philosophical monologue which absolutely overhit the bounds of the original question. The truth is, that in the case of these Upanishadic philosophers, it does not generally rain; but when it does rain, it pours profusely.

(ix) We have next the *ad hoc* or temporising method which is also a noticeable feature of Upanishadic philosophising. Very often the philosophers are absolutely pertinent, and never illuminate on any topic except the one which is immediately before them, and according to the capacity of the learner. In the celebrated Indra-Virochana myth, their preceptor Prajāpati tells them the secret of philosophy not all at once, but only when either of them has prepared himself for receiving the wisdom to be imparted. It thus happens that Virochana is completely satisfied with the first answer of Prajāpati, but Indra is not, and presses his Master again and again for the solution of his difficulties, Prajāpati disclosing the secret of his philosophy only ultimately. It thus comes to pass that the Ātman is successively proved to be no longer a mere bodily double, or as identical with the Self in the states of dream or deep-sleep, but with the Self as-identical-with-itself. Prajāpati only gives what his pupils need, and thus supplies us with an excellent example of the *ad hoc* method employed in Upanishadic philosophy.

(x) Finally, we have the *regressive* method which takes the form of many successive questions, every new question carrying us behind the answer to the previous question. Thus it was that when Janaka asked Yājñavalkya what was the light of man, Yājñavalkya said it was the Sun. Janaka went behind answer after answer, carrying Yājñavalkya from the Sun to the Moon, from the Moon to the Fire, from the Fire......to the Ātman, which exists behind them all as the Light-in-itself (Bṛi. IV. 3). Thus it was also how Gārgī took Yājñavalkya from question to question, asking him what was the support of water and Yājñavalkya answering it was air, asking again what was behind air and Yājñavalkya answering it was the intermundia, and so on, until from behind the intermundia, the world of the Sun, the world of the Moon, the world of the Stars, the world of the Gods......Gārgī carried Yājñavalkya to the region of Brahman. But when Gārgī asked again what lay behind the world of Brahman itself, she exhibited the inordinate curiosity of the female kind, especially when given to philosophy, which leads necessarily to a regress *ad infinitum*, Yājñavalkya checking the progress of the *questionnaire* in the only appropriate way—" Thy head shall fall off if thou inquirest again " (S. 11).

The Poetry of the Upanishads.

15. There is a branch of the Upanishadic method of philosophising which calls for treatment under a separate section. It is what we may call the poetical method of philosophy. This method does really suffer from the defect, that what is suggested under the garb of poetry can never be regarded as the rigorous truth of philosophy. The poetical method is applicable to philosophy where an emotion is to be created about the nature of reality, or when this reality becomes a fact of mystical apprehension. When such is the case, the seer gives no heed to the principles of metrification, and the metre he employs is wild and irregular, though at the same time pleasing by its wildness. "Like the Corybantes, who lose all control over their reason in the enthusiasm of the secret dance, and during this supernatural possession are excited to the rhythm and harmony which they communicate to men, these poets create their admired songs in a state of divine insanity." And thus, as we may naturally expect, the Upanishadic poetry is mystical, moral, or metaphysical, rather than heroic, or lyrical, or given to the description of nature or love. It may be remembered that the moral tone of Upanishadic poetry is strictly subservient to its metaphysical implications, and it does not rise, as in the case of the hymn to Varuṇa in Ṛigveda VII. 88, to an expression of the innermost feelings of the human heart, to a confession of sin, or to a prayer for gracious atonement to divinity. The poetry of the Īśopanishad is a commixture of moral, mystical and metaphysical elements ; that of the Kenopanishad is psycho-metaphysical ; that of the Kaṭhopanishad has as its chief topic the teaching about the Immortality of the Soul and the practical way to the realisation of Ātman ; the poetry of the Śvetāśvatara rises in the sixth chapter to a theistic description of God, and a representation of Him as *causa sui* ; it is only in the Muṇḍakopanishad that we find the highest emotion of which the Upanishads are capable. This of course is not yet of the highest order, but we may say that never elsewhere in the Upanishads do we find the stage of emotionalism that is reached in the Muṇḍaka. There are, however, a number of passages in the Upanishads which are couched in prose, and yet are highly poetic in sentiment. They are what a modern writer has called "conflagrations of prose-poetry". Thus for example, as a piece of sustained imaginative composition in prose, we may take the passage from the Chhāndogya which tells us that "the heaven must be regarded as the supporting beam from which the intermundane region hangs like a bee-hive. The Sun is the honey of the gods as preserved in this bee-hive. The rays which the Sun spreads in different quarters, namely, the eastern, the southern, the western, the northern and the upward directions are the different honey-cells looking in the various directions. The hymns of the four Vedas are the bees which work on the bee-hive from the various sides. The different colours of the Sun are the different kinds of nectar on which the various gods live", and, we are told, these gods live on them not by the ordinary processes of drinking or eating, but by merely "looking" at them (S. 12. a)—an expression which gives us an insight into the θεωρία of the Upanishadic gods. As an example of allegory in the Upanishads, we may take the eschatological passage from the Kaushītaki which speaks of "the river of agelessness, the hall of omnipresence, the couch of grandeur, the damsel of mind, the hand-maid of vision, the flowers of the worlds which these are intent on weaving, the passage of the Soul through the river merely by the motion of the mind, the haven of safety which it reaches by the assertion of its identification with the highest Brahman—a fit concatenation of circumstances that befall the Soul which is described as the Child of the Seasons." We have said above that the Upanishads do not contain either nature-poetry or love-poetry, and hence the beautiful does not much fall within the scope of Upanishadic thought ; but the Upanishads deal nevertheless with the sublime in nature, or with the sublime in the region of mind, or even in the transcendental sphere. As an example of the sublime in nature, we may take the passage from the Bṛihadāraṇyaka which tells us that " by the command of the imperishable Brahman, the sun and the moon stand in their places ; by the command of that Brahman, the heaven and the earth stand apart ; by the command of that Brahman, the moments and the hours, the days and the nights, the half-months and the months, the seasons and the years, all stand apart ; by the command of that Brahman, some rivers flow out to the east from the White Mountains, and others to the west or some other quarter " (S. 12. b.). As an example of sublimity in the subjective sphere, we may quote the passage from the Chhāndogya in which we are told that the city within is exactly like the city without, that the heart is the citadel of Ātman as the universe itself is, that just as in the outer world there is that unending space which contains within it the heaven and the earth, the fire and the wind, the sun and the moon, the lightning and the stars, similarly, even here, within this little citadel, are they to be equally found (S. 12. c). Finally, as an example of sublimity in the transcendental sphere, we have the passage from the Chhāndogya which tells us that " Infinity alone is bliss..... When one sees nothing else, hears nothing else, understands nothing else, that is the Infinite......The Infinite is above, below, behind, before, to the right and to the left......I am above, I am below, I am behind, I am before, I am to the right and to the left...... The Self is above, the Self is below, the Self is behind, the Self is before, the Self is to the right and to the left. He who knows this truly attains Swarājya " (S. 12. d).

The Philosophers of the Upanishadic period.

16. Let us now turn to a brief discussion of the doctrines of the great philosophers that lived and thought in the Upanishadic period. We shall be considering the doctrines in detail in the later chapters of this work, where they would be found distributed according to problems. At this place, we have to content ourselves with merely a concise statement of them for fear of repetition of the material in the later chapters. It is also necessary for us to introduce our readers to the names of the great philosophers, each of whom made some contribution to the development of Upanishadic thought, and, in the case of the metaphysical philosophers especially, to exhibit the logical link between their doctrines in order to indicate the lines for a fuller and systematic study of them. We shall severely exclude from our present conspectus the names of unhistorical or mythological personages. The dialogue between Indra, Virochana and Prajāpati, for example, merely serves to bring out certain philosophical conceptions, without enabling us to attribute them to historical personages. Indra, Virochana and Prajāpati are all of them mythological personages, and hence we can attribute to neither of them the doctrines that have been advanced in that great story. It is unfortunate that the author of that story should have entirely hidden himself behind it. Similarly, in the dialogue between Indra and Pratardana in the Kaushītaki, between Bhṛigu and Varuṇa in the Taittirīya, and between Nachiketas and Yama in the Kaṭha, Indra, Varuṇa and Yama seem respectively to be unhistorical persons. Nachiketas may have been a historical personage; while there is not much objection to regard Pratardana and Bhṛigu as historical. Then, again, it must be remembered, that many of the doctrines of the Upanishads are entirely untraceable

to their authors. Thus, for example, the doctrines of the Muṇḍaka cannot be traced to any particular author. The author must have been a great eclectic indeed; but it is unfortunate that we cannot trace his personality. The doctrines of the Śvetāśvatara, on the other hand, could be definitely attributed to the sage Śvetāśvatara, whose name has been mentioned towards the end of that Upanishad (VI. 21). While, therefore, we shall notice in the following short survey the names of the persons, which, without objection, may be regarded as historical, it is necessary to remember that there must have been many a philosopher who lived, and thought, and died unknown. His work has remained, though his personality has been lost.

Mystical, Moral and other philosophers.

17. Of the mystical philosophers, Triśaṅku seems indeed to have been a man of great insight, as may be seen from the little scroll that he has bequeathed to us in the Taittirīya Upanishad. Nor must we forget that Maitri himself, the promulgator of the Maitri Upanishad, was a great God-realiser, as may be seen from his description of "the Ātman as realised" in that Upanishad. Rāthītara, Pauruśishṭi and Nāka Maudgalya has each of them left to us the virtue which he regarded as of supreme importance, namely, Truth, Penance, and the Study of the Vedas. Mahīdāsa Aitareya seems to have been a philosopher interested in eugenics. His problem was the prolongation of human life, even though he tried to realise it ritualistically (S. 13. a). Āruṇi must have witnessed, if not practised, the fasting philosophy of ancient times (S. 13. b). The sage Kaushītaki was the inventor of the doctrine of Prāṇa as Brahman. He seems to have been an ancient "satyāgrahin," and to have practised the virtue of non-begging. He was the author of the doctrine of the "Three Meditations," namely on the Sun;

the Full moon, and the New moon, for the fulfilment of some specific desires. Paiṅgya seems to have been the henchman of Kaushītaki in his doctrine that Prāṇa was the lord of the Senses as well as the Mind. Pratardana was a free-thinker of antiquity, disbelieving in the efficacy of external ritualism, advocating the doctrine of the inner sacrifice which is always going on within us, and contributing to thought, probably, the doctrine of Prajñātman, a bio-psycho-metaphysical conception. Śushkabhṛiṅgāra seems to have taught that if a man regarded the Ṛigveda as supreme, all beings would worship him (archante); if he regarded the Yajurveda as supreme, all would join (yujyante) to prove his supremacy; and that if he regarded the Sāmaveda as supreme, all would bow down to him (saṁnamante). This is a philologico-philosophical contribution of Śushkabhṛiṅgāra made under Brāhmaṇic influence. Finally, the sage Jaivali seems to have held that the Universe exhibits at every stage the principle of sacrifice. "When we cast our glance at the sky, he said, we see that the heaven is a great altar in which the sun is burning as fuel, his rays being the smoke, the day being the light of the sacrificial fire, the quarters the coals, and the intermediate quarters the sparks of the fire; from the oblation that is offered in this sacrifice, namely Śraddhā, rises the Moon. If we look at the sky again, we see that "parjanya" is the great altar in which the year is burning as fuel, the clouds being the smoke, the lightning being the light of the sacrificial fire, the thunderbolt the coals, and the rumbling of the clouds the sparks of the sacrificial fire; from the oblation offered in this sacrifice, namely the Moon, rises Rain. Then again, the whole world is a great altar in which the earth burns as fuel, fire being the smoke, night being the light, the moon being the coals, and the stars the sparks of the fire; from the oblation offered in this sacrifice, namely Rain, rises Food. Fourthly, man himself is a great altar in which the opened mouth is the fuel, the breath the smoke, the tongue the light, the eyes the coals, the ears the sparks; from the oblation offered in his sacrifice, namely Food, rises Seed. Finally, woman herself is a great altar, in which Seed being offered as an oblation, rises Man. In this very peculiar way does Jaivali's philosophy connect the Śraddhā libation with the Moon, the Moon with Rain, the Rain with Food, the Food with Seed, and finally the Seed with Man. This is his celebrated Doctrine of Five Fires. Finally, when a Man is cremated, from out of the fire of cremation which serves as altar, a lustrous person arises, who goes either to the World of the Gods, or to the World of the Fathers, as his qualifications enable him to proceed".

Cosmological and Psychological philosophers

18. Of the cosmological philosophers, a passage from the Chhāndogya (V. 11) tells us that while Uddālaka held that the earth was the substratum of things, Prāchīnaśāla held that it was the heaven which was so, while Buḍila, Śārkarākshya, and Indradyumna held that water, space and air were respectively the substrata of things, and Satyayajña said that the substratum was the Sun—the celestial fire. In this passage we have the names of the persons who held that the elements were the ultimate substrata of things, even though in many other Upanishads these doctrines have been left untraced to philosophers. Raikva alone is elsewhere described as having held with Indradyumna that air was the substratum of all things. Aśvapati Kaikeya, who adopts the synthetic method, is described in the Chhāndogya as having incorporated these views into his doctrine of the Universal Ātman, the Ātman Vaiśvānara, who is "prādeśamātra" and "abhivimāṇa "—expressions whose meaning we shall determine later on—the heaven constituting the head of the Ātman, the sun his eye, the air his breath, space his body, water his bladder, and the earth his feet (Chhān. V. 18). A transition is made from cosmology to physiology when Satyakāma Jābāla teaches Upakosala that reality is to be found not in the sun, or the moon, or the lightning, but in the person in the eye (Chhān. IV), and from cosmology and physiology to psychology, when Gārgya thinks that the physical categories such as the sun, the moon, and the wind, and physiological categories such as the eye are the ultimate reality, and Ajātaśatru, his instructor, tells him that reality is to be found in the deep-sleep-consciousness (Bṛi. II). The very much greater interest that is taken in psychology rather than in cosmology by the Upanishadic philosophers is evident from the way in which they always ask questions about psychological matters. Of the interlocutors of Pippalāda in the Praśna Upanishad, the first, namely, Kabandhī Kātyāyana alone seems to be interested in cosmology when he asks—From what primal Being are all these things created?—while the others are interested in some kind of psychological question or other. Bhārgava Vaidarbhi is interested in physiological psychology, and asks—What sense is the lord of all the others? Kausalya Āśvalāyana is interested in the metaphysics of psychology, and asks the question—From what being Prāṇa, the lord of the senses, was born? Sauryāyaṇi Gārgya is an abnormal psychologist, taking interest in the problem of dreams. Śaibya Satyakāma is interested in mysticism, and asks the question about the efficacy of meditation on Om; while Sukeśī Bhāradvāja is again interested in the metaphysics of psychology, when he asks the question about the nature of the Person with

Sixteen Parts. The philosophy of Pippalāda emerges in the answers that he gives to these seers. Pippalāda is a great psycho-metaphysician of antiquity, advocating the doctrine of Rayi and Prāṇa, which is equivalent to the Aristotelian doctrine of Matter and Form, as well as the doctrines of the supremacy of the vital breath above the senses and the primary emergence of the vital breath from the Ātman. He regards the state of dream as one in which the mind of man has free play, bodying forth the forms of things inexperienced as well as experienced, and the state of deep sleep as one in which the light of the man is overpowered by the light of the Self. Pippalāda also teaches that by meditation on Om till the time of death, one goes to the celestial regions where one learns from Hiraṇyagarbha to see the all-pervading Person, while in regard to the doctrine of the Person with Sixteen Parts, he prepares the way for the later Sāṁkhya and Vedāntic doctrine of the Liṅga-śarīra. Bhujyu and Uddālaka, who are mentioned in the Bṛihadāraṇyaka are both of them interested in psychical research. The curious personality of Vāmadeva which appears for the first time in Ṛigveda IV. 26, 27, is introduced again in the Bṛihadāraṇyaka I. 4. 10, where he declares himself as having been Manu and the Sun in a previous birth, as well as in the Aitareya II. 4, where the philosophy of "Three Births" is declared to have been in consonance with his teaching. This sage, who seems to have been intensely interested in the question of rebirth, declares that "while yet in embryo he tried to know all the births of the gods. A hundred iron citadels tried to hold him; but a hawk that he was, with swiftness he came down to the earth. In embryo indeed did Vāmadeva speak in this manner." Vāmadeva seems to have held that there were three births of man: the first birth of a man occurs when

7

the spermatozoon combines with the ovum; his second birth occurs when a child is born to him; his third birth takes place when he is himself reborn after death. Bhṛigu, who is mentioned in the Taittirīya, was a great metaphysical psychologist, who held that food, life-breath, mind, intellect and bliss constituted, in the order of gradation, the expressions of Ātman. Finally, we are introduced in Bṛihadāraṇyaka IV to the doctrines of certain psycho-metaphysicians, when we are told that Jitvan Śailini held that speech was the highest reality; Udaṅka Śaulbāyana that breath was the highest reality; Varku Vārshṇa, Gardabhī-vipīta Bhāradvāja, Satyakāma Jābāla and Vidagdha Śākalya held respectively that the eye, the ear, the mind and the heart constituted the ultimate reality; while Yāñjavalkya, following the synthetic method, found a place for each of these doctrines in his final synthesis.

Metaphysical philosophers.

19. Of the metaphysical philosophers, Śāṇḍilya, Dadhyach, Sanatkumāra, Āruṇi and Yājñavalkya are the most prominent, the last being the greatest of them all.

Sandilya.

(i) The complete philosophy of Śāṇḍilya is preserved for us in that small section of the Chhāndogya, namely, III. 14, where Śāṇḍilya formulates for us the main doctrines of his philosophy. In the first place, he gives us the cosmological proof of the Absolute which he calls "Tajjalān", that from which things are born, to which they repair and in which they live. Secondly, he teaches the doctrine of *Karman* and says that fate alone betakes a man in the next world for which he has paved the way by his works in this life. In the third place, he gives us a characterisation of Ātman in thoroughly positive terms. This stands against the later negative theology of Yājñavalkya. Fourthly, he tells us that the Ātman is both great and small; greater than the great, and smaller than the small; infinite and infinitesimal. Lastly, he tells us that the end of human life consists in being merged in the Ātman after death, a consummation, which, he is sure he will reach.

Dadhyach.

(ii) The sage Dadhyach who, like Vāmadeva, is a sage of Vedic repute, as referred to in Ṛigveda I. 116. 12, is also a sage who occupies a prominent place in Bṛihadāraṇyaka II. The "Madhuvidyā" referred to in the Ṛigveda is in this Upanishad expounded in great detail. As regards his personal history, we are told in the Ṛigveda that he knew the secret of the "Madhuvidyā," and that he had been enjoined upon by Indra, on pain of capital punishment, not to disclose the secret to anybody. The Aśvins wanted to learn that wisdom from Dadhyach, and, because they were convinced that Indra would fulfil his threat, they first cut off the head of Dadhyach themselves, and substituted on his trunk the head of a horse. Dadhyach thereupon spoke by the horse's head to the Aśvins, and taught them the "Madhuvidyā." Indra was very wroth to see that the secret had been imparted by Dadhyach, and so he cut off the head from the body of Dadhyach, upon which, the Aśvins re-substituted the original head, and Dadhyach became whole again! It was this sage Dadhyach who is introduced in the Bṛihadāraṇyaka as having held the doctrine of the mutual interdependence of things, because all of them are indissolubly connected in and through the Self. To quote from the History of Indian Philosophy Volume II, "all things are in *mutuum commercium*, because they are bound together by the same *vinculum substantiale*, namely, the Self. The earth, says Dadhyach, is the honey of all beings, and all beings are the honey of the earth, just because the same 'lustrous,' 'immortal' Self inhabits them both. The fire is the essence of all things, and all things are the essence of fire, just because the immortal self is the essence of both. Similarly, are the wind, the sun, the space, the moon, the lightning, the thunder, the ether, and even law, truth, and humanity the essence of all things whatsoever, and all things are the essence thereof, inasmuch as the same law, the same element, the same indissoluble bond connects them both. Finally, the individual Self is itself the essence of all things, and all things are the essence of the individual Self, inasmuch as both of them are held together by the same Universal Spirit. It is this Universal Spirit which is the lord and king of all things. As all the spokes are contained between the axle and felly of a wheel, all things and all selves are connected in and through the Supreme Self. It is on account of the Supreme Self, that all things stand related together. All things appear on the back-ground of this eternal curtain. 'Nothing exists that is not covered by the Supreme Self. He becomes like unto every form, and all the forms are only partial revelations of Him. The Lord appears many through his magic power'. Thus does Dadhyach teach the doctrine of the supreme existence of the one, and the apparent existence of the many."

Sanatkumara.

(iii) The third philosopher who invites our attention is the sage Sanatkumāra of the Chhāndogya, the preceptor of Nārada. Leaving aside his sorites of psychological, physical and metaphysical categories which is of little consequence for philosophy, let us note here the points of value in his philosophy. In the first place, Sanatkumāra seems to teach a spiritual hedonism. Happiness—and, in Sanatkumāra's hands, happiness becomes the equivalent of spiritual happiness—is the spring of all action; action is the cause of faith; faith, of belief; when a man believes, he thinks; when he thinks, he knows; and when he knows, he reaches the truth. In this way, happiness, action, faith, belief, thought, knowledge and truth constitute, in Sanatkumāra's hands, a moral ladder to realisation (VII. 17-22). Secondly, it is Sanatkumāra who teaches the doctrine of Bhūman. "Bhūman" is that infinite happiness which arises by the vision of the divinity all around. When anything else is seen, that is "Alpa." Thus all possessions in the shape of cows and horses, elephants and gold, servants and wives, lands and palaces, are of little consequence as contrasted with Bhūman (VII. 23-24). Thirdly, the realisation of Bhūman occurs when an experience such as is implied in the expression "Sohamātmā" is attained (VII. 25). Lastly, Sanatkumāra teaches that Ātman is the source of all things whatsoever. From Ātman spring hope and memory; from Ātman spring space, light and waters; from Ātman everything unfolds, in Ātman everything hides itself. Ātman is the source of all power, all knowledge, all ecstasy (VII. 26).

Aruni.

(iv) Āruṇi, the greatest of the Upanishadic philosophers, barring of course Yājñavalkya, though he has been reported to be the latter's philosophical teacher—as may be seen also from a number of points of resemblance between Āruṇi and Yājñavalkya, especially in regard to their theories of Sleep and Dream on the one hand, and of Monistic Idealism and Doctrine of Appearance on the other—is a philosopher, who, like his other compeers of the Upanishadic period, is a great psycho-metaphysician. In regard to his psychological theories, we must remember that he advances the "Fatigue" theory of sleep (VI. 8. 2), and tells us that in the state of sleep, the individual Self becomes one with the Ātman (VI. 8. 1)—points which have become the current coin of Upanishadic thought. In regard to departing consciousness, he teaches that, while a man is dying, his speech first becomes merged in the mind, then his mind becomes merged in breath, then breath becomes merged in light, and finally light becomes merged in the deity (VI. 15)—a theory which Yājñavalkya later borrows and expatiates upon. In regard to his metaphysical doctrines, he views Substance from the cosmological point of view, regarding it as the final substratum of all things, in fact as the material cause of the universe, just as iron is the material cause of all iron-weapons, and gold of gold-ornaments (VI. 1. 4-6). Secondly, he tells us that this underlying Substance is "alone real", all else is merely a name. Āruṇi is an extreme nominalist who paves the way for the Doctrine of Illusion (VI. 1. 4-6). Thirdly, he tells us that what thus exists as the primal hypostasis cannot be regarded as Not-being, for from Not-Being nothing can come. Hence the hypostasis is Being (VI. 2. 1-2). This Being produces from itself first fire, then water, then the earth, in that order (VI. 2. 3-4). Interpreted generally, the Sanskrit words he uses, namely Tejas, Ap, and Anna, could be interpreted as meaning respectively the energizing principle, liquid existence, and solid existence. Fourthly, all things that exist in this world, animate as well as inanimate, are made up of these elements by the process of Trivṛitkaraṇa, a doctrine which Āruṇi first enunciates. Things are unreal; the Elements alone are real; and more than the Elements, Being, which is the root of them all (VI. 3-4). Next Āruṇi teaches that it is this Being which is also the Self in man. "That art Thou" is the recurring instruction of Āruṇi to his son Śvetaketu (VI. 8 ff).

The spirit in nature is thus at the same time the spirit in man. It is interesting to note the parallel of Āruṇi's idea with Green's. Cosmologically, this Being is the subtle essence which underlies phenomena, and which can be grasped only by faith (VI. 12), and by apt instruction from the teacher (VI. 14). Biologically, it is the supreme life-principle which gives life to the universe. The branches may die and yet the tree lives; but when the tree dies, the branches die also. Similarly, the universe may vanish, but God remains; but God cannot vanish, and hence the latter alternative is impossible (VI. 11). Psychologically, it annihilates all individualities. Do not juices lose their individuality in honey, asks Āruṇi (VI. 9)? Do not the rivers lose their individuality in the ocean (VI. 10)? Even likewise do all souls lose their individuality in the Ātman. Viewed from the moral point of view, the Ātman is truth. One who makes alliance with truth, makes alliance with Ātman also (VI. 16). Metaphysically, the Ātman pervades all. As salt may pervade every particle of water into which it is put, the Ātman fills every nook and cranny of the universe. There is nothing that does not live in Ātman (VI. 13). We thus see how Āruṇi boldly postulates an idealistic monism in which there is no room for difference even from within.

Yajnavalkya.

(v) Yājñavalkya, like his teacher Āruṇi, is a great psycho-metaphysician. We shall consider the points of his metaphysics first, and then go on to the consideration of his psychological doctrines. In fact, Yājñavalkya's philosophy would be so much called upon in our later Chapters, that we can only indicate it here very briefly and for the purpose of giving a synoptic view of his philosophy. We shall not consider the points of Yājñavalkya's philosophy in the order in which he answers the questions of his wife, and of the philosophers that meet him in King Janaka's court, and of King Janaka himself in the second, third and fourth chapters respectively of the Bṛihadāraṇyaka. We shall consider them only logically. In Chapter III of the Bṛihadāraṇyaka, he had, no doubt, a formidable number of intellectual adversaries to grapple with. Aśvala and Śākalya were interested more or less in ritualism and theology, and so they could be easily disposed of; but Jāratkārava, who was interested in eschatology Bhujyu, whom we have already met with as a psychical researcher, Ushasta, who was interested in the nature of Ultimate Reality, Kahola, who wanted to know the practical way to the realisation of Ātman, Gārgī and Uddālaka, who were both interested in the problem of immanence, the one dynamically, the other statically, were, in any case, a formidable list of opponents. The philosophy of Yājñavalkya which emerges in his conversation with these adversaries as well as his wife and king Janaka, may be briefly set down as follows. He teaches that all objects are centred in the Self, as all thoughts are centred in the mind, as all touches in the skin, as all waters in the ocean (II. 4. 11). The Ātman pervades all. Yājñavalkya also uses the simile of the immanence of salt in water (II. 4. 12), borrowing it probably from his teacher Āruṇi. Secondly, Yājñavalkya teaches that all things exist for the Self; if we do not so regard them, they would vanish for us (II. 4. 6). Thirdly, he tells us that all things are dear for the sake of the Self. In every act of mental affection, the Ātman is calling unto Ātman. The realisation of Ātman is the end of all endeavour (II. 4. 5). Fourthly, Yājñavalkya says that this Ātman alone is real; all else is "ārtam" —a mere tinsel-show (III. 4. 2 and III. 5. 1). Yājñavalkya then proceeds to characterise the Ātman in negative terms ; the Ātman is neither large nor small, neither short nor long ; he is flavourless, eyeless, odourless, and quality-less (III. 8. 8). Contrast this negative theology of Yājñavalkya with the positive theology of Śāṇḍilya. As a proof of the existence of Ātman, Yājñavalkya draws upon the argument from order : Ātman is the " bund " of all existence : our very hours and days are measured by this Ātman (III. 8. 9). The Ātman is universally immanent. He is the inner controller of all things. We are merely like little dolls, and throw out our hands and feet according as the great Thread-puller, Ātman, wishes to make us dance (III. 7). The Ātman is the ultimate light of man ; all other lights are lights by sufferance. When Ātman is realised as the light of man, one reaches self-consciousness (IV. 3. 1-6). The Ātman alone is the ultimate hearer, seer, thinker : there is no thinker beside Him (III. 4. 2). The Ātman perceives himself. Only when there is a duality, then one may see another ; but when One alone is, processes of perception and thought are alike impossible, and we are reduced to a state of solipsism (II. 4. 14). But Yājñavalkya takes care to say that the organs of perception of the percipient do not cease to function. That, from the epistemological side, is the relieving feature of his solipsism (IV. 3. 23-30). In psychology, Yājñavalkya teaches, like other Upanishadic philosophers, that when the state of dream occurs, the Ātman spreads out his own light (IV. 3. 9). The Ātman in this state moves out from his nest, guarding it nevertheless with breath (IV. 3. 12). It must be remembered, however, that the Ātman only seems to move, or only seems to imagine in the state of dream, and does not really move or imagine (IV. 3. 7). Yājñavalkya advises that when a man is dreaming, let no one wake him up suddenly, for fear, apparently, that the Soul may depart (IV. 3. 14). A father in that state is not a father; a mother, a mother; a thief a thief; a murderer, a murderer; a Chāṇḍāla, a Chāṇḍāla; and analogically, a Brahmin a Brahmin (IV.3.22). As regards the state of sleep, he advocates, like Āruṇi, the fatigue theory (IV.3.19). He tells us, furthermore, that sleep is a twilight condition, where one sees this world as well as the other world (IV.3.99). As regards departing consciousness, Yājñavalkya tells the story of the process of death in such a realistic fashion that we cannot but regard him as an exceedingly shrewd observer of nature. At the time of death, the corporeal self is mounted on by the intelligent self, the Śārīra Ātman by the Prājña Ātman, and it moves along groaning like a heavy-laden cart (IV. 3. 35). Before death occurs, the person in the eye first turns away (IV. 4. 1). The end of the heart is lighted, and by that light, the soul departs either by the way of the eye, or the head, or any other part of the human body (IV. 4. 2). His "Karman" alone accompanies him: it is the guardian of his destiny (IV. 4. 5). It is probably this doctrine of "Karman" that, we may say, Yājñavalkya imparted to Jāratkārava in III. 2. 13, and thus silenced him. According to Yājñavalkya, it seems that only when the Ātman has prepared another abode for himself that he leaves the body. Not unless it finds another blade to rest upon would a caterpillar leave its original blade (IV. 4. 3). Yājñavalkya says also that the newer existence must be even a brighter existence: does not the goldsmith create from the old gold a newer and brighter form (IV. 4. 4)? If the Self has left any desires in him while yet he lives in his body, he returns from his sojourn to this existence again; if no desires be left in him, he becomes one with Brahman (IV. 4. 6). At that time no consciousness remains. Consciousness is merely a "fleeting" phenomenon due to the entry of the Ātman in the elements which produce the bodily form (II. 4. 12). Yājñavalkya's wife was really frightened at the pass to which Yājñavalkya's philosophy had led, but we, who understand Yājñavalkya's absolute idealism may not wonder if, from that point of view, he regarded even transmigration as a delusion. If we may be allowed to use Yājñavalkya's own manner of philosophising, we may well ask, when the Ātman alone is, at all places and at all times, from what would he transmigrate, and to what? But all this is only implied in Yājñavalkya. For fear of disturbing the ordinary routine of thought, of which his wife supplies us with an illustration, Yājñavalkya hastily excuses himself from the *impasse* to which his doctrine had led him, by saying that sufficient for the nonce was the wisdom he had imparted (II. 4. 13).

General social condition.

20. Let us now examine somewhat the social condition in which these philosophers lived and made their speculations. (i) It seems the castes did evidently exist at the time of the Upanishads. We have the formulation of the caste system so far back as at the time of the Purusha-sūkta, which must be, in any case, considered anterior to the Upanishads. In the Bṛihadāraṇyaka, there is a very unorthodox theory about the origin of castes. This Upanishad does not argue, like the Bhagavadgītā at a later date, that the castes were created by God according to "qualities and works." On the other hand, we are told in the Bṛihadāraṇyaka that Brahman was the first to exist; but because it was alone, it did not fare well, and therefore it produced a better form, namely Kshatriya-hood. It was thus that from the original Brahman were created such heavenly deities as Indra, Varuṇa, Soma, Rudra, Parjanya, Yama, Mṛityu and Īśa. These constitute the warrior caste in the heavenly kingdom. Furthermore, after having created even Kshatriya-hood, Brahman did not fare well; and therefore it created Vaiśya-hood in the heavenly kingdom, namely the Vasus, the Rudras, the Ādityas, the Maruts and the Viśvedevas. But even then it thought it was deficient, and therefore, it created the Śūdra order, represented in the heavenly kingdom by the god Pūshan. In order to give itself completeness, again, Brahman created Dharma or Law, which probably binds all these castes together. Finally, Brahman assumed the form of Agni who was the Brahmin of the gods, and then we are told that the castes on the earth were created after the pattern of the castes in the heaven (S. 14). In this unorthodox theory, we have the origin of the earthly caste system on the pattern of a heavenly caste system almost in the manner in which the ectypes in Plato's theory of Ideas are merely replicas of the archetypes. Then, again, as regards the existence of Āśramas at the time of the Upanishads, we learn from the Taittirīya Upanishad that those of the student and the householder did definitely exist (S.15. a); while we have to conclude from other passages where one is advised "to leave the world as soon as one becomes weary of it" that the order of the recluses did also exist; and finally, from such Upanishads as the Muṇḍaka as well as the mention of Saṁnyāsa elsewhere, that the order of the Saṁnyāsins came last and was the completion of the three previously mentioned. In the Chhāndogya we have all the four orders enumerated deliberately. The householders are advised to give themselves up to sacrifice, study and charity; the recluses to penance; and the students to a life of celibacy with the master and extreme emaciation in his service. All these verily reach the holy worlds after death; but we are told that he alone who lives in Brahman, referring probably to the life of the Saṁnyāsin, attains to immortality (S. 15. b). When we rearrange these orders, we find that the foundations of the future Āśrama system are already to be found firmly laid even in such an old Upanishad like the Chhāndogya. So far about castes and orders at the time of the Old Upanishads.

(ii) Now about the position of women in society in the Upanishadic times. In the Upanishads, we meet with three chief different types of women : Kātyāyanī, the woman of the world, who is only once mentioned in the Bṛihadāraṇyaka ; Maitreyī, the type of a spiritual woman, a fit consort to the philosopher Yājñavalkya ; and Gārgī, the Upanishadic suffragette, who, fully equipped in the art of intellectual warfare, dares to wrangle with Yājñavalkya even at the court of King Janaka where a number of great philosophers are assembled, and declares that she would send two missiles against her adversary, Yājñavalkya, and that if he succeeds in shielding himself against those missiles, he may certainly be declared to be the greatest of the philosophers that had assembled. Bold and sturdy, she presses Yājñavalkya to a *regressus ad infinitum*, and had not Yājñavalkya checked her impudence by an appeal to the *argumentum ad caput*, she would have succeeded in nonplussing Yājñavalkya. But, even though she was to all appearances vanquished, she appears again a second time with two more moderate questions, and elicits from Yājñavalkya his doctrine of dynamic immanence (S. 16).

(iii) As regards the relations of the Brahmins and the Kshatriyas, the Bṛihadāraṇyaka declares that a Brahmin ought to take his seat below a Kshatriya at the Rājasūya sacrifice, thus giving him the honour that he deserves. On the other hand, the Kshatriya must remember that because Kshatrahood has been born from Brahminhood, therefore, even though he may attain to the highest state, he must rest upon the Brahmin as his source, that is, must live under the control and guidance of the Brahmins (S. 17. a). In the Chhāndogya we are told by Jaivali that Āruṇi was the first man in the Brahmin circle to receive spiritual wisdom, and that therefore it was the Kshatriya caste that reigned supreme (S. 17. b). In the Bṛihadāraṇyaka, we are told that it was only when Āruṇi went with the desire of living like a pupil to Jaivali, whom he regarded as superior to himself, that Jaivali could be prevailed upon to impart to him his spiritual wisdom (S. 17. c); and yet again in the Kaushītaki King Chitra Gārgyāyaṇi complimented Āruṇi who had gone to him, fuel in hand, upon having approached him in an humble manner and therefore having been really worthy of Brahminhood, whereupon he proceeds to instruct him in spiritual knowledge (S. 17. d). All these passages indicate both the earthly and the spiritual supremacy of Kshatriyahood to Brahminhood. On the other hand, in certain passages as in the Bṛihadāraṇyaka and Kaushītaki, where Gārgya, the proud Brahmin, had gone to King Ajātaśatru to learn wisdom, we read that Ajātaśatru told him that it was against the " usual practice " that a Kshatriya should instruct a Brahmin in spirituality, but that Ajātaśatru in the course of his conversation with Gārgya felt his superiority so much that he could not be prevented from imparting his higher wisdom to Gārgya, when, fuel in hand, the latter approached him in an humble manner (S. 18). It would seem from the above passage that the Brahmins were usually superior to Kshatriyas in spiritual knowledge, but that occasionally a Kshatriya might be superior to a Brahmin in that respect. Finally, in certain passages from the Upanishads, especially in the Bṛihadāraṇyaka and the

Maitri, we find that certain Brahmin sages stood very much superior to Kshatriya kings, who learnt wisdom from their Brahmin masters. "Here, O Yājñavalkya, is my kingdom," said King Janaka when he stood astonished at the great intellectual and spiritual wisdom of the Sage, "and here am I at your service" (S. 19. a). In the Maitri Upanishad we read that King Bṛihadratha, filled with repentance and remorse, went to the Sage Śākāyanya, and implored him to help him out of the world of existence, as one would help out a frog from a waterless well (S. 19. b). From these passages, it would seem that the Brahmins did very often maintain their intellectual and spiritual superiority. It must be remembered, however, that occasionally a Kshatriya, and occasionally a Brahmin, would be the intellectual and spiritual head of his age according to his abilities and powers, and that no charter was given either to Brahmin-hood or Kashatriya-hood that it alone should be the repository of intellectual and spiritual wisdom, and that, therefore, it would be ridiculous to argue, on the one hand, that the Brahmins alone, or on the other, that the Kshatriyas alone, were the custodians of spiritual culture, and thus, as in modern times, even a man belonging to the lowest order of society could, if he possessed the necessary ability and means, be in the vanguard of those who knew.

The Problems of Upanishadic philosophy.

21. It is only in the fitness of things that we should close this introductory chapter with a statement of the chief problems that emerge out of a consideration of the doctrines of the Upanishadic philosophers, as well as exhibit their inter-relation. Wonder, as Plato said, was the roof of philosophy in Greec as in India. The Upanishadic philosophers, we have seen, ceased to understand the forces of nature as certain heavenly deities before whom they had to bow down their heads in unconscious awe. From the Ṛigveda to the Upanishads we find the same transition as we find in the History of Greek Philosophy from Homer and Hesiod to Thales and Anaximander. Natural forces cease to be personified, and a definite attitude comes to be taken which is worthy only of speculative thinkers. "What is that," asked the Upanishadic philosophers, "which being known, everything else becomes known" (S. 20)? In short, they wanted to know the "archē" of knowledge. They first tried to find this in the cosmological sphere; but having failed to find it therein, they began to search after it in the psychological domain. What is it, they asked, which persists when the body is dead? What is it, again, which lives and persistently creates, even though the body may go into a state of sleep (S. 21)? Not without reason did Yājñavalkya stand victorious in the intellectual arena in Janaka's court when he appealed to the transmundane problem of the persistence of the Self after death. What is the real root, he asked, from which the tree of life springs again and again, even though knocked and cut down by that Dark Cutter, Death (S. 22)? We may well imagine how Janaka, who saw in the elephant, on which he was riding, a former sage, namely Buḍila, must have been regarded as a very wise man of the day (S. 23). Eschatological knowledge was regarded as the most precious of all. But even then, the desire of man to know the Ultimate could not be finally quenched. He must know the answer to the most central problem—What is the Real, What is the Ātman, What intellectual construction could he make about it? An attempt to solve this problem would lead the Upanishadic philosopher into the very heart of metaphysics, and when a certain intellectual solution was arrived at, the next problem would be how practically to attain to that knowledge, what should be the norm of conduct following which one may hope to " appropriate the God-head." As the culmination of this practical endeavour would come in the mystical attitude, which would complete the moral endeavour, which, without it, would be like the *Hamlet* with Hamlet out. Mysticism was the culmination of Upanishadic philosophy, as it is the culmination of all philosophies, and one who does not understand that the cosmology and the psychology, the metaphysics and the ethics of the Upanishads are merely a propaedeutic to their mystical doctrine can scarcely be said to have understood the spirit of Upanishadic philosophy.

SOURCES I

1 (*a*) तदेतत्सत्यं मंत्रेषु कर्माणि कवयो यान्यपश्यंस्तानि त्रेतायां बहुधा संततानि । तान्याचरथ नियतं सत्यकामा एष वः पंथाः सुकृतस्य लोके ॥ —मुं. I. 2. 1.

(*b*) प्लवा ह्येते अदृढा यज्ञरूपा अष्टादशोक्तमवरं येषु कर्म । एतच्छ्रेयो येऽभिनंदन्ति मूढा जरामृत्युं ते पुनरेवापि यन्ति ॥ अविद्यायामन्तरे वर्तमानाः स्वयं धीराः पंडितं मन्यमानाः । जंघन्यमानाः परियन्ति मूढा अंधेनैव नीयमानाः यथांधाः ॥ अविद्यायां बहुधा वर्तमाना वयं कृतार्था इत्यभिमन्यन्ति बालाः । यत्कर्मिणो न प्रवेदयन्ति रागात्तेनातुराः क्षीणलोकाश्च्यवन्ते ॥ इष्टापूर्तं मन्यमाना वरिष्ठं नान्यच्छ्रेयो वेदयन्ते प्रमूढाः । नाकस्य पृष्ठे ते सुकृतेऽनुभूत्वेमं लोकं हीनतरं वा विशन्ति ॥ तपःश्रद्धे ये ह्युपवसन्त्यरण्ये शान्ता विद्वांसो भैक्षचर्यां चरन्तः । सूर्यद्वारेण ते विरजाः प्रयान्ति यत्रामृतः स पुरुषो ह्यव्ययात्मा ॥

मुं. I. 2. 7–11.

2 (*a*) प्राणाय स्वाहा । व्यानाय° । अपानाय° । समानाय° । उदानाय° । स य इदमविद्वानग्निहोत्रं जुहोति यथांगारानपोह्य भस्मनि

जुहुयात्।... । यथैषीकातूलमग्नौ प्रोतं प्रदूयेत एवं हास्य सर्वे पाप्मानः प्रदूयन्ते य एतदेवं विद्वानग्निहोत्रं जुहोति । तस्मादु हैवंविद्यद्यपि चण्डालायोच्छिष्टं प्रयच्छेदात्मनि हैवास्य तद्वैश्वानरे हुतं स्यात्। छां. V. 19–24.

(b) अथातः सांयमनं प्रातर्दनमान्तरमग्निहोत्रमित्याचक्षते यावद्वै पुरुषो भाषते न तावत्प्राणितुं शक्नोति प्राणं तदा वाचि जुहोति यावद्वै पुरुषः प्राणिति न तावद्भाषितुं शक्नोति वाचं तदा प्राणे जुहोत्येतेऽनन्तेऽमृते आहुतीर्जाग्रच्च स्वपंश्च संततमव्यवच्छिन्नं जुहोत्यथ या अन्या आहुतयोऽन्तवत्यस्ताः कर्ममय्यो भवन्त्येतद्ध वै पूर्वे विद्वांसोऽग्निहोत्रं न जुहवांचक्रुः ।

कौ. II. 5.

3 एवं वा अरेऽस्य महतो भूतस्य निःश्वसितमेतद्यदृग्वेदो यजुर्वेदः सामवेदोऽथर्वाङ्गिरस इतिहासः पुराणं विद्या उपनिषद् श्लोकाः सूत्राण्यनुव्याख्यानानि अस्यैवैतानि सर्वाणि निःश्वसितानि ।

बृ. II. 4. 10.

4 (a) तपःप्रभावाद्देवप्रसादाच्च ब्रह्म ह श्वेताश्वतरोऽथ विद्वान् ।
अत्याश्रमिभ्यः परमं पवित्रं प्रोवाच सम्यगृषिसंघजुष्टम् ॥

श्वे. VI. 21.

(b) अहं वृक्षस्य रेरिवा । कीर्तिः पृष्ठं गिरेरिव । ऊर्ध्वपवित्रो वाजिनीव स्वमृतमस्मि । द्रविणं सवर्चसम् । सुमेधा अमृतोऽक्षितः । इति त्रिशंकोर्वेदानुवचनम् । तै. I. 10.

5 (a) अन्यदेवाहुर्विद्ययान्यदाहुरविद्यया । इति शुश्रुम धीराणां ये नस्तद् विचचक्षिरे ॥ ई. 10.

अन्यदेव तद्विदितादथो अविदितादधि । इति शुश्रुम पूर्वेषां ये नस्तद्विचचक्षिरे ॥ के. I. 3.

(b) एतद्ध स्म वै तद्विद्वांस आहुः पूर्वे महाशाला महाश्रोत्रिया न नोऽद्य कश्चनाश्रुतममतमविज्ञातमुदाहरिष्यतीति ह्येभ्यो विदांचक्रुः । छां. VI. 4. 5.

6 सो (मृत्युः) ऽकामयत द्वितीयो म आत्मा जायेतेति । स मनसा वाचं मिथुनं समभवत् ।...। स तया वाचा तेन आत्मना इदं सर्वमसृजत यदिदं किंच ऋचो यजूंषि सामानि छंदांसि यज्ञान् प्रजाः पशून् । बृ. I. 2. 4-5.

7 ऋतं पिबन्तौ सुकृतस्य लोके गुहां प्रविष्टौ परमे परार्धे ।

छायातपौ ब्रह्मविदो वदन्ति पंचाग्नयो ये च त्रिणाचिकेताः ॥
क. I. 3. 1.

द्वा सुपर्णा सयुजा सखाया समानं वृक्षं परिषस्वजाते । तयो-
रन्यः पिप्पलं स्वाद्वत्ति, अनश्नन्न्यो अभिचाकशीति ॥
मुं. III. 1. 1.

अजामेकां लोहितशुक्लकृष्णां बह्वीः प्रजाः सृजमानां सरूपाः ।
अजो ह्येको जुषमाणोऽनुशेते जहात्येनां भुक्तभोगां अजोन्यः ॥
श्वे. IV. 5.

8 पृथिव्यंतरिक्षं द्यौर्दिशोऽवांतरदिशाः । अग्निर्वायुरादित्यश्चंद्रमा
नक्षत्राणि । आप ओषधयो वनस्पतय आकाश आत्मा । इत्य-
धिभूतम् । अथाध्यात्मम् । प्राणो व्यानोऽपान उदानः समानः ।
चक्षुः श्रोत्रं मनो वाक् त्वक् । चर्म मांसं स्नावास्थिमज्जा । एत-
दधिविधाय ऋषिरवोचत् । पांक्तं वा इदं सर्वं पांक्तेनैव पांक्तं
स्पृणोतीति । तै. I. 7.

स एष पांक्तो यज्ञः पांक्तः पशुः पांक्तः पुरुषः पांक्तमिदं सर्वं
यदिदं किंच । बृ. I. 4. 17.

9 (*a*) तमेकनेमिं त्रिवृतं षोडशान्तं शतार्धारं विंशतिप्रत्यराभिः ।
अष्टकैः षड्भिर्विश्वरूपैकपाशं त्रिमार्गभेदं द्विनिमित्तैकमोहम् ॥
श्वे. I. 4.

(*b*) पंचस्रोतोंबुं पंचयोन्युग्रवक्रां पंचप्राणोर्मिं पंचबुद्ध्यादिमूलाम् ।
पंचावर्तां पंचदुःखौघवेगां पंचाशद्भेदां पंचपर्वामधीमः ॥
श्वे. I. 5.

10 (*a*) उद्दालको हारुणिः श्वेतकेतुं पुत्रमुवाच स्वप्नान्तं मे सोम्य विजा-
नीहीति । यत्रैतत्पुरुषः स्वपिति नाम सता सोम्य तदा संपन्नो
भवति तस्मादेनं स्वपितीत्याचक्षते । ....अशनायापिपासे मे
सोम्य विजानीहीति । यत्रैतत्पुरुषोऽशिशिषति नाम अप एव
तदशितं नयन्ते । ...यत्रैतत्पुरुषः पिपासति नाम तेज एव
तत्पीतं नयते । छां. VI. 8. 1-3.

(*b*) स वा अयं पुरुषः सर्वासु पूर्षु पुरिशयो नैनेन किंचनानावृतं
नैनेन किंचनासंवृतम् । बृ. II. 5. 18.

(*c*) अकारः प्रथमा मात्रा आप्तेरादिमत्त्वाद्वा ।...उकारो द्वितीया
मात्रा उत्कर्षादुभयत्वाद्वा । ...मकारस्तृतीया मात्रा मितेरपी-
तेर्वा । मां. 9–11.

11 अथ हैनं गार्गी वाचक्नवी पप्रच्छ याज्ञवल्क्येति होवाच यदिदं सर्वमप्स्वोतं च प्रोतं च कस्मिन्नु खल्वाप ओताश्च प्रोताश्चेति वायौ गार्गीति। कस्मिन्नु खलु वायुरोतश्च प्रोतश्चेत्यन्तरिक्ष-लोकेषु गार्गीति। कस्मिन्नु खल्वन्तरिक्षलोका ओताश्च प्रोता-श्चेति गंधर्वलोकेषु गार्गीति। कस्मिन्नु खलु गंधर्वलोका ओताश्च प्रोताश्चेत्यादित्यलोकेषु गार्गीति। कस्मिन्नु खल्वादित्य-लोका ओताश्च प्रोताश्चेति चंद्रलोकेषु गार्गीति। कस्मिन्नु खलु चंद्रलोका ओताश्च प्रोताश्चेति नक्षत्रलोकेषु गार्गीति। कस्मिन्नु खलु नक्षत्रलोका ओताश्च प्रोताश्चेति देवलोकेषु गार्गीति। कस्मिन्नु खलु देवलोका ओताश्च प्रोताश्चेतींद्रलोकेषु गार्गीति। कस्मिन्नु खल्विंद्रलोका ओताश्च प्रोताश्चेति प्रजापतिलोकेषु गार्गीति। कस्मिन्नु खलु प्रजापतिलोका ओताश्च प्रोताश्चेति ब्रह्मलोकेषु गार्गीति। कस्मिन्नु खलु ब्रह्मलोका ओताश्च प्रोता-श्चेति स होवाच गार्गि मातिप्राक्षीर्मा ते मूर्धा व्यपप्तदनति-प्रश्न्यां वै देवतामतिपृच्छसि गार्गि मातिप्राक्षीरिति ततो ह गार्गी वाचक्नव्युपरराम। —बृ. III. 6. 1.

12 (*a*) असौ वा आदित्यो देवमधु तस्य द्यौरेव तिरश्चीनवंशोऽन्त-रिक्षमपूपो मरीचयः पुत्राः। तस्य ये प्रांचो रश्मयस्ता एवास्य प्राच्यो मधुनाड्य ऋच एव मधुकृत ऋग्वेद एव पुष्पं ता अमृता आपस्ता वा एता ऋचः।...अथ येऽस्य दक्षिणा रश्म-यस्ता एवास्य दक्षिणा मधुनाड्यो यजूंष्येव मधुकृतो यजुर्वेद एव पुष्पं ता अमृता आपः।...अथ येऽस्य प्रत्यंचो रश्मयस्ता एवास्य प्रतीच्यो मधुनाड्यः सामान्येव मधुकृतः सामवेद एव पुष्पं ता अमृता आपः।...अथ येऽस्योदंचो रश्मयस्ता एवास्यो-दीच्यो मधुनाड्योऽथर्वांगिरस एव मधुकृत इतिहासपुराणं पुष्पं ता अमृता आपः।...अथ येऽस्योर्ध्वा रश्मयस्ता एवास्यो-र्ध्वा मधुनाड्यो गुह्या एवादेशा मधुकृतो ब्रह्मैव पुष्पं ता अमृता आपः।...अथ तत ऊर्ध्व उदेत्य नैवोदेता नास्तमेतैकल एव मध्ये स्थाता तदेष श्लोकः। न वै तत्र न निम्लोच नोदि-याय कदाचन। देवास्तेनाहं सत्येन मा विराधिषि ब्रह्मणेति। न ह वा अस्मा उदेति न निम्लोचति सकृद्दिवा हैवास्मै भवति य एतामेवं ब्रह्मोपनिषदं वेद। छां. III. 1-11.

(*b*) एतस्य वा अक्षरस्य प्रशासने गार्गि सूर्याचंद्रमसौ विधृतौ तिष्ठत एतस्य वा अक्षरस्य प्रशासने गार्गि द्यावापृथिव्यौ

विधृते तिष्ठत एतस्य वा अक्षरस्य प्रशासने गार्गि निमेषा
मुहूर्ता अहोरात्राण्यर्धमासा मासा ऋतवः संवत्सरा इति
विधृतास्तिष्ठन्त्येतस्य वा अक्षरस्य प्रशासने गार्गि प्राच्यो-
ऽन्या नद्यः स्यंदन्ते श्वेतेभ्यः पर्वतेभ्यः प्रतीचोऽन्याः ।

बृ. III. 8. 9.

(c) अथ यदिदमस्मिन्ब्रह्मपुरे दहरं पुंडरीकं वेश्म दहरोऽस्मिन्न-
न्तराकाशस्तस्मिन्यदंतस्तदन्वेष्टव्यम् । तद्वाव विजिज्ञासितव्य-
मिति । तं चेद् ब्रूयुर्यदिदमस्मिन्ब्रह्मपुरे दहरं पुंडरीकं वेश्म
दहरोऽस्मिन्नंतराकाशः किं तदत्र विद्यते यदन्वेष्टव्यं यद्वाव
विजिज्ञासितव्यमिति । स ब्रूयाद्यावान्वा अयमाकाशस्तावा-
नेषोऽन्तर्हृदय आकाश उभे अस्मिन्द्यावापृथिवी अन्तरेव समा-
हिते उभावग्निश्च वायुश्च सूर्याचंद्रमसावुभौ विद्युन्नक्षत्राणि
यच्चास्येहास्ति यच्च नास्ति सर्वं तदस्मिन्समाहितमिति ।

छां. VIII. 1. 1-3.

(d) यो वै भूमा तत्सुखं...यत्र नान्यत्पश्यति नान्यच्छृणोति नान्य-
द्विजानाति स भूमा...स एव अधस्तात्स उपरिष्टात्स पश्चात्
स पुरस्तात् स दक्षिणतः स उत्तरतः स एवेदं सर्वमिति ।
अथातोऽहंकारादेशः...। अथात आत्मादेश एवात्मैवाधस्ता-
दात्मोपरिष्टादात्मा पश्चादात्मा पुरस्तादात्मा दक्षिणत आत्मो-
त्तरत आत्मैवेदं सर्वमिति स वा एष एवं पश्यन्नेवं मन्वान एवं
विजानन्नात्मरतिरात्मक्रीड आत्ममिथुन आत्मानंदः स स्वराड्
भवति ॥ छां. VII. 23-25.

13 (a) पुरुषो वाव यज्ञः । तस्य यानि चतुर्विंशतिवर्षाणि तत्प्रातः-
सवनम् ।...। अथ यानि चतुश्चत्वारिंशद्वर्षाणि तन्माध्यंदिनं
सवनम् ।...।अथ यान्यष्टाचत्वारिंशद्वर्षाणि तत्तृतीयं सवनम् ।
एतद्ध स्म वै तद्विद्वानाह महिदास ऐतरेयः स किं म एतदुपत-
पसि योहमनेन न प्रेष्यामीति । स ह षोडशं वर्षशतं अजी-
वत् प्र ह षोडशं वर्षशतं जीवति य एवं वेद ।

छां. III. 16.

(b) षोडशकलः सोम्य पुरुषः । पंचदशाहानि माशीः । काममपः
पिब । अपोमयः प्राणो न पिबतो विच्छेत्स्यत इति ।

छां. VI. 7. 1.

14 ब्रह्म वा इदमग्र आसीत् एकमेव तदेकं सन्न व्यभवत् । तच्छ्रेयो
रूपं अत्यसृजत क्षत्रं यान्येतानि देवता क्षत्राणि इंद्रो वरुणः

सोमो रुद्रः पर्जन्यो यमो मृत्युः ईशान इति । स नैव व्यभवत् स विशमसृजत वसवो रुद्रा आदित्याः विश्वेदेवाः मरुत इति । स नैव व्यभवत् स शौद्रं वर्णमसृजत पूषणं, इयं वै पूषा, इयं हीदं सर्वं पुष्यति । स नैव व्यभवत् तच्छ्रेयो रूपमत्यसृजत धर्मम् । तदेतद्ब्रह्म, क्षत्रं, विद्, शूद्रः देवेषु । अग्निनैव देवेषु ब्रह्माभवत्, ब्राह्मणो मनुष्येषु, क्षत्रियेण क्षत्रियो, वैश्येन वैश्यः, शूद्रेण शूद्रः ।

बृ. I. 4. 11-15.

15 (*a*) वेदमनूच्याचार्योऽन्तेवासिनमनुशास्ति... आचार्याय प्रियं धनमाहृत्य प्रजातंतुं मा व्यवच्छेत्सीः । तै. I. 11. 1.

(*b*) त्रयो धर्मस्कंधाः यज्ञोऽध्ययनं दानमिति प्रथमः, तप एव द्वितीयो, ब्रह्मचार्याचार्यकुलवासी तृतीयो अत्यंतमात्मानमाचार्यकुलेऽवसादयन् । सर्व एते पुण्यलोका भवन्ति, ब्रह्मसंस्थोऽमृतत्वमेति । छां. II. 23. 1.

16 यथा काश्यो वा वैदेहो वा उग्रपुत्रः उज्ज्यं धनुरधिज्यं कृत्वा द्वौ बाणवन्तौ सपत्नौ अतिव्याधिनौ हस्ते कृत्वा उपोत्तिष्ठेद् एवमेवाहं त्वा द्वाभ्यां प्रश्नाभ्यां मुपोदस्थां तौ मे ब्रूहीति ।

बृ. III. 8. 2.

17 (*a*) तस्मात्क्षत्रात्परं नास्ति । तस्माद्ब्राह्मणः क्षत्रियमधस्ताद् उपास्ते राजसूये... सैषा क्षत्रस्य योनिर्यद्ब्रह्म तस्माद्यद्यपि राजा परमतां गच्छति ब्रह्मैव अंततः उपनिश्रयति ।

बृ. I. 4. 11.

(*b*) यथेयं न प्राक् त्वत्तः पुरा विद्या ब्राह्मणान् गच्छति, तस्मादु सर्वेषु लोकेषु क्षत्रस्यैव प्रशासनमभूदिति ।

छां. V. 3. 7.

(*c*) स (आरुणिः) होवाच प्रतिज्ञातो म एष वरो यां तु कुमारस्यांते वाचमभाषथास्तां मे ब्रूहीति । स (जैवलिः) होवाच दैवेषु वै गौतम तद्वरेषु मानुषाणां ब्रूहीति । स होवाच विज्ञायते हास्ति हिरण्यस्यापात्तं गोअश्वानां दासीनां प्रवाराणां परिदानस्य मा नो भवान् बहोरनंतस्यापर्यंतस्याभ्यवदान्यो भूदिति स वै गौतम तीर्थेनेच्छासा इत्युपैम्यहं भवन्तमिति वाचा ह स्मैव पूर्व उपयन्ति स होपायनकीर्त्योवास ।

बृ. VI. 2. 5-7.

(*d*) स (आरुणिः) ह समित्पाणिः चित्रं गाङ्ग्यायनिं प्रतिचक्रमे उपायानीति । तं होवाच ब्रह्मार्होऽसि गौतम यो मां उपागाः । एहि त्वा ज्ञपयिष्यामीति । कौ. I. 1.

18 स होवाचाजातशत्रुः प्रतिलोमं चैतद् यद् ब्राह्मणः क्षत्रियमुपेयाद् ब्रह्म मे वक्ष्यतीति । व्येव त्वा ज्ञपयिष्यामीति तं (गार्ग्यं) पाणावादाय उत्तस्थौ । बृ. II. 1. 15.

अथ ह वै गार्ग्यो बालाकिरनूचानः संस्पष्ट आस । सोऽयमुशीनरेषु संवसन्, मत्स्येषु, कुरुपंचालेषु, काशीविदेहेष्विति । स हाजातशत्रुं काश्यमेत्योवाच ब्रह्म ते ब्रवाणीति । तं होवाचाजातशत्रुः सहस्रं दद्मस्त एतस्यां वाचि । स होवाच बालाकिर्य एवैष आदित्ये पुरुषस्तमेवाहमुपास इति । °चंद्रमसि °विद्युति °स्तनयित्नौ °वायौ °आकाशे °अग्नौ °अप्सु °आदर्शे °छायायां °प्रतिश्रुत्कायां °शब्दे °शरीरे °दक्षिणेऽक्षिणि °सव्येऽक्षिणि । तत उ ह बालाकिस्तूष्णीमास । तं होवाचाजातशत्रुरेतावन्नु बालाका ३ इति एतावद्धीति होवाच बालाकिः । तत उ ह बालाकिः समित्पाणिः प्रतिचक्रम उपायानीति तं होवाचाजातशत्रुः प्रतिलोमरूपमेव तन्मन्ये यत् क्षत्रियो ब्राह्मणमुपनयेत । एहि व्येव त्वा ज्ञपयिष्यामीति । कौ. IV. 1–19.

19 (*a*) याज्ञवल्क्य, यो नो भगवन् अभयं वेदयसे, नमस्तेऽस्तु, इमे विदेहा, अयमहमस्मि । बृ. IV. 2. 4.

(*b*) बृहद्रथो वै नाम राजा विराज्ये पुत्रं विधापयित्वेदमशाश्वतं मन्यमानः शरीरं वैराग्यमुपेतोऽरण्यं निर्जगाम । स तत्र परमं तप आस्थायादित्यमुदीक्षमाण उर्ध्वबाहुस्तिष्ठति । अन्ते सहस्राहस्य अन्तिकमाजगाम अग्निरिवाधूमकस्तेजसा निर्दहन्निवात्मविद् भगवान् शाकायन्यः । उत्तिष्ठोत्तिष्ठ वरं वृणीष्वेति राजानमब्रवीत् । स तस्मै नमस्कृत्योवाच । भगवन्नाहमात्मवित् । त्वं तत्त्ववित् शुश्रुमो वयम् । स त्वं नो ब्रूहीति । शिरसास्य चरणावभिमृशमानो राजेमां गाथां जगाद ।... अन्धोदपानस्थो भेक इवाहमस्मिन्संसारे, भगवंस्त्वं नो गतिः त्वं नो गतिः । मै. I. 1–7.

20 कस्मिन्नु खलु भगवो विज्ञाते सर्वमिदं विज्ञातं भवति ।
मुं. I. 1. 3.

21 अस्य विस्रंसमानस्य शरीरस्थस्य देहिनः । देहाद्विमुच्यमानस्य

किमत्र परिशिष्यते ॥ एतद्वै तत् ॥...॥ य एष सुप्तेषु जागर्ति कामं
कामं पुरुषो निर्मिमाणः । तदेव शुक्रं तद्ब्रह्म तदेवामृत-
मुच्यते ॥ एतद्वैतत् ॥ क. II.5. 4–8.

22 तान् हैतैः श्लोकैः पप्रच्छ । यथा वृक्षो वनस्पतिस्तथैव पुरुषो-
ऽमृषा । तस्य लोमानि पर्णानि त्वगस्योत्पाटिका बहिः ।
त्वच एवास्य रुधिरं प्रस्यंदि, त्वच उत्पटः । तस्मात्तद् आतृण्णा-
त्प्रैति, रसो वृक्षादिवाहतात् ॥ मांसान्यस्य शकराणि, किनाटं
स्नाव तत्स्थिरम् । अस्थीन्यंतरतो दारुणि, मज्जा मज्जोपमा
कृता ॥ यद् वृक्षो वृक्णो रोहति मूलान्नवतरः पुनः । मर्त्यः
स्विन्मृत्युना वृक्णः कस्मान्मूलात्प्ररोहति ॥
बृ. III. 9. 28.

23 एतद्ध वै तज्जनको वैदेहो बुडिलमाश्वतराश्विमुवाच यन्नु
हो तद्गायत्रीविदब्रूथा अथ कथं हस्तीभूतो वहसीति मुखं
ह्यस्याः सम्राण्न विदांचकारेति होवाच तस्या अग्निरेव मुखं
यदि ह वा अपि बह्विवाग्नावभ्यादधति सर्वमेव तत् संदह-
त्येवं हैवैवंविद्यद्यपि बह्विव पापं कुरुते सर्वमेव तत्संप्साय
शुद्धः पूतोऽजरोऽमृतः संभवति । बृ. V. 14. 8.

CHAPTER II

THE DEVELOPMENT OF UPANISHADIC COSMOGONY

Search after the Substratum.

1. When Sir Henry Maine said that except the blind forces of nature nothing moves in this world which is not Greek in its origin, he should have at least excluded from the scope of his assertion the Upanishadic philosophy, and more particularly, the Upanishadic cosmogony. The hey-day of Upanishadic philosophy was that great millenium before ever the earliest Greek philosophers, Thales and Anaximander, began to speculate, and as in Greek philosophy, so in Upanishadic philosophy, the primary impulse to thought came from cosmologic, and more particularly from cosmogonic, speculation. The starry heavens above, the regularities of the moving seasons, the roaring of wind in the firmament, the conflagrations of the all-powerful fire, the periodical inundations of waters, in general, the settled recurrence of all happenings in nature, must have filled the natural inquirer with an impulse to find out the real meaning of all these phenomena ; and it is no wonder that as in Greek philosophy, so in Upanishadic philosophy, the primary search was after the φύσις of things. What is that which abides in the midst of changes ? What is that, which as the Upanishad puts it, may be called the "Tajjalān"? What is that from which all things spring, into which they are resolved, and in which they live and have their being ? (S. I. a) ? From the Taittirīyopanishad we learn that "that alone might be regarded as the Ultimate

Reality of things, from which all these beings were born, by which they live when born, to which they repair and into which they are finally resolved" (S. I. b). This is very much like the way in which Aristotle tells us the early Greek cosmologists conceived of their primary substance: ἐξ οὗ γάρ ἔστιν ἅπαντα τὰ ὄντα, καὶ ἐξ οὗ γιγνεται πρῶτον καὶ εἰς ὅ φθείρεται τελευταῖον.... τοῦτο στοιχεῖον καὶ ταύτην ἀρχὴν φασιν εἶναι τῶν ὄντων. Then again, when the Sage of the Śvetāśvataropanishad asks in wonder at the very beginning of his treatise, "From whom are we born, in whom do we live and have our being?" (S. I. c), we are put in mind of a similar remark of Hesiod at the opening of his "Theogony" when he asks "Who made all this, and how did he make them?". The search after the ultimate cause of things, the substratum, the φύσις of things, is as characteristic of the early Upanishadic cosmogony, as it is of the later Greek cosmogony; and even though, as we may see in the sequel of this chapter, there is no justification for saying that Greek cosmogony was derived from the Upanishadic, still on account of the universally acknowledged, and definitely proved, priority of the Upanishadic speculation, he must be a bold man indeed who dares to say that all things except the blind forces of nature have come from Greece!

Progress of the Chapter.

2. Coming to the details of Upanishadic cosmogony, even though it may not be impossible for us to trace the probable historical evolution of the different theories held on the subject of the genesis of the universe by the Upanishadic seers, based upon a more or less final chronological stratification of the different passages in the Upanishads,—a task which has been attempted by us elsewhere,—the necessities of methodology require that in a work like the present which professedly takes a synoptic view of the problems of Upanishadic thought, we should re-arrange the theories in such a way as to enable us to institute a comparison between those theories and the theories held on the subject in a country like Greece. We may thus at once proceed to divide the theories of Upanishadic cosmogony into two main groups : the impersonalistic and the personalistic. Among the impersonalistic theories may be included the theories which regard either or all of the elements as the substratum of things, or even such abstract conceptions as not-Being, or Being, or Life-force as lying at the root of all things whatsoever. Among the personalistic theories are theories which try to account for the origin of creation from the Ātman or God, and insist in various ways either on the dualistic aspect of creation, or the emanatory, or even the highly philosophic aspect implied in Theism proper. When the Upanishadic Sages regard the elements as the source of things, we must take them to mean what they say, and not, as certain later commentators under the spell of their theological idea have done, regard those elements as equivalent to deities. Thus for example, when it is said that either fire or water or air is the source of things, we have to understand the Upanishadic sages to imply that it is the elements that go by those names that are to be regarded as responsible for the unfoldment of creation. All theological commentators on the Upanishads such as Śaṅkara and Rāmānuja have understood these elements as meaning deities and not the elements proper. But if we just consider for a while the naiveté with which the theories were ushered into being, it may seem impossible for us to doubt that the Upanishadic seers meant by the elements the elements proper, and not the deities corresponding to those elements. It is true that the word "divinity" is, on certain occasions, used in the case of these elements, but it must be remembered that a similar word θεός was used in the case of their elemental substrata even by Greek philosophers, and it is not without reason that Aristophanes should call such apotheosisers of elements by the name of ἄθεοι. Then again, the idea of creation *ex nihilo* seems to be generally repugnant to the Upanishadic mind, and as in Greece, so in India we have the firm belief of the Upanishadic sages in the impossibility of the generation of anything from out of Nothingness, or Not-Being. When, again, it seems to have been felt impossible by the Upanishadic seers that either the elements, or such abstract conceptions as Not-Being or Being could be held responsible for the explanation of creation, they felt the necessity of explaining that genesis from Life-force or Cosmic-force. Finally, when even this could not be regarded as a sufficient explanation of creation, they were obliged to take recourse to the idea of the Person, by whom the creation could be said to have been brought into being. We must also note that there is not much room for the idea of creation in an absolutistic system of metaphysics, which would try to explain away all creation as being only an illusion or appearance. We shall take this aspect of the problem of creation also into account before we proceed, at the end of the Chapter, to say what the theistic idea of creation in the Upanishads was, especially in the account given by the Śvetāśvataropanishad.

Water as the Substratum.

3. To begin with the elements as constituting the φύσις of things, we have first to take into account the theory in the Bṛihadāraṇyakopanishad which tells us almost in Thalesian fashion that water was the source of all things whatsoever: " In the beginning, verily, the

Waters alone existed; from the Waters was born Satya or Truth; Satya produced Brahman, Brahman gave birth to Prajāpati, and from Prajāpati were born the gods; these gods worship Satya alone" (S. 2. a). In this passage we are told not that the Ātman or any personal Being existed originally, but that the waters were the first to exist, and that everything later came from them. It is curious to note also that Brahman is here declared to have been created from Satya, which means that we have not to understand the word Brahman in the sense of primal reality as we understand it later. Then, again, when it is said that Satya was born from Water, we have to understand by Satya the ultimate "concrete" existent. We are also told that the Satyam consists of three syllables: the first is Sa, the second is Ti, and the third is Yam, the first and the last being real, and the second unreal (S. 2. b). Freely interpreted, this passage would mean that unreality is enclosed on both sides by reality: the present moment which is evanescent is enclosed on both sides by an eternity which is real: we move from eternity to eternity, halting for a short while in the caravansary of the present; and it is wonderful to notice that the whole of the "Satyam" has been supposed to have come out of the primeval waters. This is almost Thalesian, for Thales regarded water as the origin of all things and his philosophy did not need the hypothesis of a God as responsible for the creation of Water, unlike the Genesis which required the spirit of God to move upon the face of the primeval waters, or unlike Manu who said that water was only the first existence that was created by God. The Bṛihadāraṇyakopanishad, like Thales, regards Water as the origin of all things whatsoever, disposing of a belief in God as the creator of the Water itself.

Air.

4. After water comes air. Raikva, who holds the theory of air as the final "absorbent" of things, and therefore probably as the origin of them, has an interesting story connected with him. Once upon a time, we are told, king Jānaśruti was wandering in a forest when he happened to overhear the conversation between two swans. One of these swans said to the other, just as all the lower throws of dice merge in the highest throw, that is, pass to the winner, similarly all the good things that people do in the world pass to the sage Raikva, the philosopher with the car. Now Jānaśruti was so astonished at the conversation, that he at once sent his attendant to inquire and return to him with the knowledge as to where this sage Raikva dwelt. The attendant, after having visited different places, found out Raikva who was scratching his itch beneath a car, and then returned to his master to tell him that he had found out Raikva. King Jānaśruti went to Raikva with a number of cows, a gold necklace and a chariot drawn by a she-mule, and prayed to the Sage to teach him what god he worshipped. The sage Raikva replied that he had no business with the cows, the necklace and the chariot of the Śūdra king, and advised him to return. King Jānaśruti returned, but went back again to the Sage with the cows, the golden necklace, the chariot, as well as his beautiful daughter; whereupon, the sage Raikva seemed to be satisfied, and having lifted the beautiful daughter's face towards himself, said, "Verily, O Śūdra, you are making me speak on account of this face," and then he imparted to the king the knowledge which he possessed, namely that he believed that the Air was the final absorbent of all things. "When fire is extinguished it goes to the air, when the sun sets it goes to the air, when the moon sets it goes to

the air, when the waters dry up, they go to the air: thus verily is Air the final absorbent of all things whatsoever" (S. 3). In this way did the sage Raikva with his car, who reminds us singularly of Diogenes with his tub, tell king Jānaśruti that Air was the end of all things. The logical conclusion from such a position is that if air be the end of all things, it may also be regarded as the beginning of them. In fact, Raikva's philosophy is like that of Anaximenes, the Greek philosopher, who taught that air was both the beginning and the end of all things: only Raikva does not say definitely that air is the φύσις, but only leaves us with the remark that air is the end of all things. This is indeed a very crude conception and has not much scientific value, because Raikva does not explain the actual process of the absorption of all things into air, as Anaximenes later explained both the origin and the end of all things in air by the processes of rarefaction and condensation. We must, however, praise Raikva for having had the boldness to regard Air as the final absorbent of all things, more particularly, of both Water and Fire, which according to other philosophers of his time, were regarded as constituting the φύσις of all things whatsoever.

5. The theory of fire as the origin of all things is not maintained very explicitly in the Upanishads; but there is a passage in the Kaṭhopanishad whcih tells us that Fire, having entered the universe assumed all forms (S. 4. a), which is almost equivalent to the Heracleitean formula that Fire is exchanged for all things and all things for Fire. On the other hand, in the Chhāndogyopanishad, we are told that Fire was the first to evolve from the primeval Being, and that from fire came water, and from water the earth (S. 4. b). It

Fire.

is interesting to note that in this passage the Heracleitean idea of the Way Up and the Way Down is also brought in, inasmuch as it is maintained that from fire is born water and from water earth, while, counter-logically, at the time of dissolution, the earth may be dissolved in water, the water in fire, and the fire in the Primeval Being. It is rather difficult for any philosopher to hold the opinion that fire is the origin of all things, inasmuch as it seems evident that fire burns up all, and is therefore a fit instrument for the process of a general ἐκπύρωσις, and it is not difficult to deduce from the theory advanced in the Chhāndogyopanishad the idea of a periodic conflagration of things. The difference, however, between the Chhāndogyopanishad and Heracleitus is that while Heracleitus regards Fire as the very origin of all things, the Chhāndogyopanishad makes Fire the first evolute from the primeval Being; while the Chhāndogyopanishad does not insist upon the idea of change, of which Fire seems to be the very type to the change-loving mind of the Ephesian philosopher.

Space.

6. When we come to Pravāhaṇa Jaivali's doctrine of space as the origin of all things, we come to a much higher conception than has yet been reached in the schemes of the foregoing philosophers. Even in Greek philosophy, the conception of space as the "archē" of things came very late in the development of thought. With Thales, Anaximenes, Heracleitus and Empedocles we meet with the conceptions of water, air, fire, earth, either individually or collectively. It is only when we come to the time of Philolaus, that, according to Aristotle's evidence, we get to the notion of space as the "archē" of all things. Fire, air, water and earth are more or less tangible; but "space" to be regarded as the "archē" of all things requires a higher philosophical imagination. When Pravāhaṇa Jaivali was asked what was the final habitat of all things, he answered it was Space. "All these beings emerge from space and are finally absorbed in space; space is verily greater than any of these things; space is the final habitat" (S. 5. a). This passage from the Chhāndogyopanishad is corroborated by another passage from the same Upanishad in which we are told that "space is really higher than fire. In space are both the sun and the moon, the lightning and the stars. It is by space that man is able to call......In space and after space are all things born. Meditate upon Space as the highest reality" (S. 5. b). According to these passages from the Chhāndogyopanishad, then, we must regard space as a higher entity than any of the conceptions that have been hitherto reached.

Not-Being.

7. There are certain passages in the Upanishads which teach that Not-Being, τό ὄν, was the primary existent. The Taittirīyopanishad tells us that "at the beginning of all things what existed was Not-Being. From it was born Being. Being shaped itself of its own accord. It is thus that it is called well-made or self-made" (S. 6). Commentators on this passage who do not want a privative conception like not-Being to be the "archē" of all things, rightly understand this passage to signify that at the very beginning of things it was "as if" nothing existed and not that not-Being was verily the first concrete existent, and that it was from such a semblance of non-existence that Being was created. We could very well conceive how philosophers like Śaṅkarāchārya who believe in an Ultimate Being would explain such a passage; but it must be remembered that in this agnostic conception of a primal non-

existent, the Taittirīyopanishad is anticipated by that famous Sūkta in the Ṛigveda, which is called after its opening words, the Nāsadīya Sūkta, which tells us that at the beginning of all things, there was neither Being nor not-Being, but that what existed was only an ocean of Night (RV. X. 129). It must be remembered that the conception of a primary Void or Night is to be met with even in Greek philosophy in the theory of Epimenides. A passage from the Bṛihadāraṇyakopanishad also tells us that "in the beginning of all things, verily nothing was existent but that everything was covered by Death or Hunger, for Hunger is verily Death. Death made up his mind, let me have a Self, and thus worshipping, he began to move. From his worship were born the waters. The froth of the waters solidified, and became the earth. Death toiled on the earth, and as a result of his toil, fire was produced" (S. 7). Here we have the origin of the elements water, earth, and fire from primeval Not-Being, call it either Death or Hunger, or equate it, if you please, with the Void or Night of Greek philosophy. In any case, it seems to be implied in such passages that there is a stage in the development of human thought, when finding it impossible to grapple with any concrete existence, it is compelled to take recourse to a privative logical conception like Not-Being, from which even positive Being comes to be later explained. Even in such highly developed systems of philosophy as those of Plato and Aristotle, we have the recognition of a Not-Being, and it cannot be gainsaid that at least for the purposes of logic the existence of Not-Being has to be taken account of even in positive constructions of philosophy. When, on the other hand, philosophers like Gorgias try to prove that there is a real Not-Being as contrasted with the Being of Parmenides, we must suppose that they are doing so merely for the purposes of eristic; for by what other name shall we call that process by which from the equational fact of Not-Being *being* Not-Being, they deduce the existence of Not-Being, from which, contrariwise, they try to prove that Being does not exist? We need not be concerned with such an eristic philosophy like that of Gorgias, but we must needs take into account the recognition of Not-Being in philosophies of positive construction like those of Plato and Aristotle. It was in this sense, it seems to us, that the passages from the Taittirīyopanishad and the Bṛihadāraṇyakopanishad are to be explained, and by Not-Being we must understand not absolute Not-Being but only relative Not-Being, the primal semblance of existence as contrasted with later concrete existence.

Not-Being and the Egg of the Universe.

8. There is however, an interesting side to the theory of Not-Being as the "archē" of all things. The Chhāndogyopanishad connects the philosophy of Not-Being with the myth of the Universal Egg. We are told in the Upanishad that "what existed in the beginning was Not-Being. It then converted itself into Being. It grew and became a vast egg. It lay in that position for the period of a year, and then it broke open. Its two parts were, one of gold and the other of silver. The silvery part became the earth, and the golden part became the heaven. The thick membrane of the egg became the mountains; the thin membrane became the clouds; the arteries of the egg became the rivers of the world; the fluid in its interior became the ocean; while what came out of the egg was the Sun. When the Sun was born, shouts of hurrah arose" (S. 8). Readers of comparative mythology need scarcely be reminded as to how similar the myth from the Chhāndogyopanishad is to corresponding myths in Babylonian, Egyptian, Phœnician, Persian, and Greek mythologies. In Greece, we know, how in the Orphic cosmogony, Chronos and Adrastea produced a gigantic egg which divided in the midst, and with its upper half formed the sky, and with the lower the earth, and how out of the egg came Phanes, the shining God, containing within himself the germs of all the other gods. It is interesting to note that behind Chronos and Adrastea, as we have them in this myth, are ideas of time and necessity respectively. The word Αδράστεια occurs in Greek literature so far back as the 8th century B.C.; and it is customary to derive it from διδράσκω and take it as signifying "that which is not inclined to run away." May we venture to make a suggestion that the word Adrastea seems very much to be the Greek counterpart of the Sanskrit "Adṛishṭa" which also signifies necessity? One does not know how, but it seems probable that, the idea of Adṛishṭa was conveyed to the Greek people at a time when the Greek and the Indian Aryans lived together. To return to our argument, however, the myth of the Sun coming out of the egg has parallels in the mythologies of many ancient peoples; but the creation of this egg from a primeval Non-existent seems to be peculiar to the Indian myth as we have it in the Chhāndogyopanishad. We must notice also that just as the universe was regarded by the Upanishadic sages as a huge egg, similarly it also came to be regarded as "a huge chest with the earth as its bottom and the heavens as its upper lid, the sky as its inside and the quarters as its corners, containing in its inside a rich treasure" (S. 9). We are noting here this alternative conception of the universe regarded as a huge cubical chest merely for the purpose of contrasting it with the universe regarded as a great spherical egg, though it has got nothing to do with the philosophy of Not-Being.

Being.

9. After the conception of Not-Being as the "archē" of things we come to the conception of Being. A passage from the Chhāndogyopanishad tells us directly that Being alone existed at the beginning of things. It takes to task those who suppose that the primeval Existent must be regarded as Not-Being, and that Being must be regarded as having been produced therefrom. " How could it possibly be so," asks the Upanishad, " how could Being come out of Not-Being, existence from non-existence ? It is necessary for us to suppose that at the beginning verily all this was Being, and it was alone and without a second. This Primeval Being reflected, let me be many, let me produce ; having bethought thus to itself, it produced fire. Fire thought, let me be many, let me produce ; and it produced water. Water thought, let me be many, let me produce ; and it produced the Earth (food or matter) " (S. 10. a). " The Primeval Being then thought, verily I am now these three deities. Let me enter into them by my Self, and unfold both Name and Form. Let me make each of them three-fold and three-fold " (S. 10. b). " It thus comes about that what we call the red colour in a flame belongs really to fire. Its white colour is that of water and its black colour belongs to the earth. Thus does vanish the flame-ness of a flame. The flame is indeed only a word, a modification and a name, while what really exists is the three colours. What we call the red colour in the Sun, is really the colour of fire, its white colour is the colour of water, its black colour is the colour of the earth. Thus verily vanishes the sunness of the Sun. The Sun is only a word, a modification and a name. What really exists is the three colours. Thus likewise does depart the moon-ness of the moon, and the lightning-ness of the lightning. What really exists is the three colours only" (S. 10. c). It is interesting to note in these passages, in the first place, that the primeval existent is regarded as Being, and is described as being one without a second. In the second place, we see how from this primeval Being is produced the three-fold Prakṛiti which we might call "tejobannātmikā" Prakṛiti, that is consisting of fire, water, and earth. Then, thirdly, it must be noted that the Chhāndogyopanishad teaches us definitely the doctrine of "trivṛitkaraṇa" which is the Upanishadic prototype of the "pañchīkaraṇa" of later Vedānta. Just as in the Vedāntic theory of pañchīkaraṇa, out of the five original elements, fire, air, water, earth, and space, half of each element was regarded as being kept intact, while the other half was regarded as being divided into four equal different parts, four such parts from the different elements one after another going to make up a half, which in combination with the half of the original element made up one transformed evolute of the original element, similarly, in the case of the Upanishadic trivṛitkaraṇa each of the three original elements namely fire, water and earth is to be regarded as being divided into two equal portions, one half being kept intact, while the other half is divided into two equal portions, the two quarters of the two other elements in combination with the one-half of the original element making up a transformed evolute of the original element. This idea of the mixture of the elements in the Upanishads is a very interesting one from the point of view of its analogy with a similar idea in the philosophy of Anaxagoras who taught that there was a portion of everything in everything, and thus that the elements came to be mixed with each other and gave rise to transformed products. Then, fourthly, we must remember that the Chhāndogyopanishad tells us that there are three different colours belonging to the three different elements namely the red, the white and the black, which it must be noted were later borrowed by the Sāṁkhya philosophy and made to constitute the three different colours corresponding to the three different qualities of the Sāṁkhya Prakṛiti. Finally, the Chhāndogyopanishad tells us that what really exists is the three different colours, or the three different elements, while all such objects of nature as, the sun, the moon, and the lightning, which are constituted out of the three original elements or colours are merely words or names or modificatory appearances of the original elements. In the spirit of an extreme nominalism, the Chhāndogyopanishad tries to reduce all later products to mere semblance or appearance, while it keeps the door open for the real existence of the three elements alone, all of them having been born from the Primeval Being—a sort of a philosophical trinitarian monism !

Prana.

10. When we come to the conception of Prāṇa as the φύσις of things, we rise to a higher conception than was reached in Greek philosophy. Prāṇa originally meant breath ; and as breath seemed to constitute the life of man, Prāṇa came to signify the life-principle ; and just as the life-principle in man came to be called Prāṇa, similarly the life-principle in the universe came also to be designated Prāṇa. By Prāṇa is thus meant either life-force or cosmic-force. When Ushasti Chākrāyaṇa was asked in the Chhāndogyopanishad what might be regarded as the ultimate substratum of all things, he said it was Prāṇa : for " verily it is into

Prāṇa that all these beings enter and it is from Prāṇa that they originally spring" (S. 11. a). Of the same import is the doctrine of Raikva in the Chhāndogyopanishad when he tries to bring out a correspondence between the macrocosm and the microcosm, and when he says that just as air is the life-principle of the universe—a theory which we have already noticed—similarly breath is the life-principle in man. "Prāṇa is verily the final absorbent; for when man sleeps, his speech is reduced into Prāṇa, his eye and his ear and his mind are all absorbed in Prāṇa. It is Prāṇa which is the final absorbent of all these things" (S. 11. b). "We may thus say," says Raikva, "that there are these two absorbents; one in the macrocosm and the other in the microcosm, the one being Air, and the other being Prāṇa" (S. 11. c). Having recognised this supremacy of Prāṇa, the Chhāndogyopanishad, in the doctrine which Sanatkumāra imparts to Nārada, has no difficulty in maintaining that, "just as all the spokes of a wheel are centred in its navel, similarly all these beings, and in fact, everything that exists is centred in Prāṇa" (S. 12. a). Prāṇa may thus be regarded as the very navel of existence. The philosopher Kaushītaki tells us that "Prāṇa is the ultimate Reality, the mind being its messenger, the eye the protector, the ear the informant, and the speech the tire-woman. To this Prāṇa as the Ultimate Reality, all these beings make offerings, without Prāṇa having ever sought them" (S. 12. b). We thus see in a general way how Prāṇa comes to be recognised as superior to all the organs of sense in the human system.

The Controversy between Prana and the Organs of Sense.

11. There are, however, one or two classical passages in the Upanishads which tell us in the language of myth the supremacy of Prāṇa. It was once resolved, we are told in the Chhāndogyopanishad, by the senses of man to decide which of them was supreme, and for that reason they went to Prājāpati, their Creator. The Creator replied that that sense might be regarded as the soverign of them all, which after departing leaves the body powerless and in a pitiable condition, upon which the senses resolved to run the race for supremacy. Speech was the first to go out of the body, and having lived outside for a year, came back and wondered how the body could exist in spite of its absence. It was told that the body lived like a dumb man not speaking, but breathing with the breath, seeing with the eye, hearing with the ear, and thinking with the mind, upon which speech returned. Then the organ of vision departed, and having lived outside for a year, came back and wondered how the body could live in spite of its absence. It was told that the body lived like a blind man not seeing, but breathing with the breath, speaking with the mouth, hearing with the ear, and thinking with the mind, upon which the eye re-entered. Then the organ of audition departed, and having lived outside for a year, came back and wondered how the body could still exist in spite of its absence. It was told that the body lived like a deaf man not hearing, but breathing with the breath, speaking with the mouth, seeing with the eye, and thinking with the mind, upon which the ear returned. Then the mind went out, and having lived outside for a year, returned and wondered how the body could still exist in spite of its absence. It was told that the body lived like a child without mind, but breathing with the breath, speaking with the mouth, seeing with the eye, and hearing with the ear, upon which the mind re-entered. Then, finally, when the breath was on the point of departing, it tore up the other senses as a well-bred horse might tear up the pegs to which it is tethered. Then the organs of sense assembled together and said to Prāṇa, 'Sir, thou art our lord; depart not from us'; and the tongue said to the Prāṇa, 'if I am richest, it is really thou that art richest'; and the eye said, 'if I am the support, it is really thou that art the support'; and the ear said, 'if I am wealth, it is really thou that art wealth'; and the mind said, 'if I am the final abode, it is really thou that art the final abode'. It is for this reason that people have declared the primacy not of the organs of sense, of the speech, or the eye, or the ear, or the mind, but of breath. For the breath is verily all these" (S. 13. a). This passage in the Chhāndogyopanishad is probably the earliest and the most classical as illustrating the controversy between the organs of sense and Prāṇa, and the resulting supremacy of Prāṇa over the organs. With a little variation, the same story occurs in the Kaushītaki Upanishad also (II. 14), which, being so much the later, we are not much concerned with as merely repeating for us the story of the Chhāndogyopanishad. But there are one or two points in the story of the controversy of the Senses and Prāṇa in the Praśnopanishad which we cannot leave unnoticed. There, in the first place, the elements namely space, wind, fire, water, and earth join hands with the organs of sense, namely, speech, mind, eye and ear in the controversy with Prāṇa. In the second place, we must note the two similies employed in the Praśnopanishad. The body is there called Bāṇa, which, as Max Müller suggests, may well be taken to mean a harp, and the elements as well as the organs of sense contend that they have the power to uphold this harp and to modulate it. Incidentally, it is interesting to notice the description of the body in the Praśnopanishad as a harp, which is almost Pythagorean or Platonic. Then again when Prāṇa wants to go out, it is compared to the queen-bee, which, when it goes out, is accompanied by all the bees that move after it, and which, when it comes back, is likewise followed by the bees that return forthwith. Thirdly, there is an almost henotheistic worship of Prāṇa by the organs of sense in the Praśnopanishad where it is regarded not merely as the sovereign of the organs of sense, but also as the sovereign of the deities of the universe. It is thus that Prāṇa comes to be identified with Agni, with Sūrya, with Parjanya, with Vāyu, with Being, as well as Not-Being ; and in the spirit of the prayer offered in the Chhāndogyopanished, here also the Prāṇa is requested not to move out, as it is the Prāṇa which informs, and is immanent in, the organs of sense, such as speech and hearing and vision, as well as mind (S. 13. b).

Prana, a bio-psycho-metaphysical conception.

12. In the account of Prāṇa which we find in the Kaushītaki Upanishad there are certain noticeable features which do not oocur either in the Chhāndogyopanishad or the Praśnopanishad. In the first place, Prāṇa is directly identified with life (Āyuḥ). This is as much as to say that life exists so long as Prāṇa exists and life departs as soon as Prāṇa departs. Then again, Prāṇa is identified with consciousness (Prajñā). It is interesting to note that consciousness is here distinguished from life as the higher category of existence. There may be forms of life without consciousness ; but wherever there is consciousness there must be life ; and the Kaushītaki Upanishad seems to recognise this difference and describes Prāṇa not merely as the principle of life but as the principle of consciousness also. Then, thirdly, the Upanishad identifies Prāṇa with the Ātman itself, the Ultimate Reality which is ageless and immortal, which does not increase by good actions nor diminish by bad actions (S. 14). It thus comes about that Prāṇa is life from the biological point of view, consciousness from the psychological point of view, and Ātman from the metaphysical point of view. This is verily a philosophical apotheosis of Prāṇa.

The idea of a Creator, and the creation of mythological and philosophical dualities.

13. We now come to the personalistic theories of creation. Hitherto we have discussed theories which regard either or all of the elements, namely fire, air, water, earth and space, or even such privative conceptions as Not-Being or Night or Hunger or Death, or even such an abstract metaphysical conception as Being, or finally the highly developed bio-psycho-metaphysical conception of Prāṇa, as the φύσις of things. We must note that in all these theories of creation, no creator with a personal existence is brought in for the purposes of creation. We have a more or less naturalistic account of cosmogenesis. On the other hand, in the theories which we are now about to discuss, we shall have to take account of the personal element in creation. In the Praśnopanishad we are told by Pippalāda that at the beginning of creation, the creator became desirous of creating, and, with that end in view, practised penance, and after having practised penance, first created a pair namely Rayi and Prāṇa, corresponding respectively to matter and spirit, with the intention of creating all existence whatsoever from them. While we must give credit to Pippālada for having conceived the notion of a duality of primary existences, Rayi and Prāṇa, almost in the spirit of Aristotle's Matter and Form, the application which Pippalāda makes of his twofold principle is rather amusing. The moon is matter, he says, while the sun is spirit; the path of the fathers is matter, while the path of the gods is spirit; the dark half of the month is matter, while the bright half is spirit; night is matter, while day is spirit. It was in this way that the Creator was able to create all the dual existence whatsoever in the world (S. 15. a). In a similar spirit does the Taittirīyopanishad tell us that "the Creator at the beginning of things practised penance, and having practised penance, created all things that exist, and having created them entered into them, and having enered into them, became himself both the manifest and the unmanifest, the defined and the undefined, the supported and the unsupported, the conscious and the unconscious, the true and the false" (S. 15. b). Though the Taittirīyopanishad agrees with the Praśnopanishad in positing a Creator who at the beginning of things was required to practise penance, still it differs from it in substituting the philosophical duality of the defined and the undefined, the conscious and the unconscious, the true and the false, instead of the mythological duality of the Praśnopanishad, namely, the dark half of the month and the bright half of the month, the path of the fathers and the path of the gods, night and day, the moon and the sun, and the rest. But it is evident that in the two passages we have been considering, we have the idea of a Creator introduced, which enables us to say that these passages logically mark an advance over the earlier ones which give merely an impersonalistic account of creation.

The Atman, and the creation of the duality of sex.

14. Another explanation of the duality of existence, this time of the duality of sex, occurs in the Bṛihadāraṇyakopanishad, where we are told that "the Ātman alone existed in the beginning of things and he had the form of man......He first said to himself, I am He, and it was for this reason that he came to be called I. It is for this reason also that when a man is asked who he is, he first replies it is I, and then he gives out his name......This Ātman was afraid; it is for that reason that when a man is alone, he fears. Then the Ātman began to reflect, why should I fear if there is nothing existing beside me, of which I might be afraid ; it was thus that all fear departed from him......It is said verily that fear proceeds only from a second. But the Ātman could not still find satisfaction ; for that reason it is that when a man is alone, he does not find satisfaction. The Ātman therefore wished for a second,......and having divided himself into two halves, became both the husband and the wife, man as well as woman. The woman began to reflect, 'how having generated me from himself, he seeks intercourse with me?' 'Let me hide myself' she said, and so she became a cow ; the Ātman, however, became a bull and had intercourse with her. ......She became a mare, while he became a horse. She became a she-ass, and the other became a he-ass and had intercourse with her. It was thus that both the male and the female creatures were created by the Ātman up to the very ants. All these were created by him" (S. 16). It must be noted, as we have pointed out above, that this passage gives us an explanation of the generation of the duality of sex from the Ātman in the organic world, but it yet leaves the inorganic generation entirely unexplained.

Creation by Atman through the Intermediary Person.

15. A very much more elaborate explanation of the generation of all the objects in the universe is offered in the Aitareyopanishad, which we might very well regard as giving us the fullest account of the fact of creation in the Upanishads. We are told there, that in the beginning the Ātman alone existed, and that there was no other blinking thing whatoever. The Ātman thought to himself, let me create the worlds; whereupon he created the four worlds, namely those of the super-celestial region of waters, the heavens with their celestial lights, the mortal earth, and the subterranean region of waters. It was thus that the heaven and the earth were encompassed on the upper and the nether sides by regions of water. After these worlds were created, the Ātman proceeded to create first a World-Person—an intermediate entity subsisting between the Ātman, the primary reality, and the Universe, the object of later creation—whom he fashioned out of waters, and breathed into his nostrils the breath of life. It is interesting to note in passing that this is the only analogue in the Upanishadic cosmogonies to the conception of Logos in Greek or Christian philosophy, but it must be remembered that this Logos in the Upanishadic philosophy plays quite a subservient and secondary part to the Ātman. The Ātman then brooded upon this World-Person, and as a result of his brooding, created first his various organs of sense, then the functions corresponding to them, and lastly the deities or the world-governors corresponding to such functions in the Cosmos.

"He first created the Mouth from which proceeded Speech, and from Speech, Fire.

He created the Nostrils from which proceeded Breath, and from Breath, Air.

He created the Eyes from which proceeded Sight, and from Sight, the Sun.

He created the Ears from which proceeded Hearing, and from Hearing, the Quarters.

He created the Skin from which proceeded Hair, and from Hair, the Herbs and Trees.

He created the Heart from which proceeded Mind, and from Mind, the Moon.

He created the Navel from which proceeded the Down-Breath, and from Down-Breath, Death.

Finally, he created the Generative Organ from which proceeded Semen, and from Semen, Water."

It is interesting to note that in this explanation of the creation of various categories of existence, the function always follows the structure in the microcosm of the intermediary Person, but always precedes it in the macrocosm of the Universe. Thus the organs of sense, such as the mouth, the nostrils, the eye and the ear were created in the Person before their functions namely, speech, breath, sight, and hearing, which having been created were the cause of the creation of objective existences such as fire, air, the sun and the quarters in the macrocosm of the Universe. The Ātman thereupon attacked the Person with Hunger and Thirst, which, in the Aitareyan cosmogony, reminds us of Love and Hate in Empedoklean cosmology. Hunger and Thirst said to the Ātman, find us places in this creation. The Ātman replied to them that he would find them places in the deities themselves, and thus he made them co-partners with them. It is for this reason that whenever any offerings are made to a deity, Hunger and Thirst are always allotted a share in those offerings. After the creation in this fashion of the Worlds, the Cosmic Person, the World-governors, and Hunger and Thirst, the Ātman next proceeded to create Matter as food for them all, ...which being created, the Ātman finally proceeded to create the Soul in the human body. 'How shall this body live without me ?', he thought to himself, 'but how may I enter this ?' Having thus bethought himself, he rent open the place where the hair are made to part, and entered by that door. This is called the " door of division ". This also is the " place of rejoicing ". It is at that place that women part their hair. It is at that place that on the skulls of children we see a hole. It is on that spot that when a Saṁnyāsin dies, a cocoanut is broken with the purpose of releasing his pent-up Soul. To come to our argument, when the Ātman entered the body by the door of division, and was so born as the individual Soul, he began to be subject, so the Aitareyopanishad tells us, to the three states of consciousness, namely, the waking, the dreaming and the deep-sleep state of consciousness. After having been born, the individual Soul began to look about himself at all things to see whether they proclaimed a ἕτερος, but to his great astonishment only saw the supreme Brahman spread everywhere. It is for the reason that the individual Soul saw (drā) the Brahman (Idam) spread everywhere that he is called Idandra, which by contraction has become Indra, a mysterious name given to the Godhead by the mystery-loving gods (S. 17). We thus see how the individual Soul was the last object to be created by the Ātman and how ultimately there is a metaphysical identity between the individual Soul and the supreme Soul.

Atman and the theory of Emanation.

16. So far we have had more or less mythological explanations of the creation of objects from the primeval Ātman. We have said at the beginning of the chapter that there are a few descriptions in the Upanishads which come very near to full-fledged theories of creation. But before we proceed to these accounts, we must consider briefly how in the

Taittrīyopanishad we have an emantaory theory of cosmogony where we are told that "from the Ātman, in the first instance, proceeded space, from space air, from air fire, from fire water, and from water the earth" (S. 18). This is a complete enumeration of the five different Elements which are described as having proceeded one after another from the primeval Ātman, who, to all intents and purposes, is described in the passage as not playing any very active part in creation. It is important to remember that the expression that is used in the passage to designate the fact of emanation is Sambhutiḥ. From the Ātman emanated Space, and from Space in the course of progressive generation the rest of the Elements. We are not told that the Ātman "created" Space, and from Space created Air, and so on. It is also important to notice in this passage the ὁδὸς ἄνω and the ὁδὸς κάτω. At the time of the origin of the universe, from the Ātman proceeded space, and from space air, from air fire, from fire water and from water the earth: this is the Way Down. At the time of destruction, counter-logically, the earth would be resolved in water, water in fire, fire in air, air in space, and space in the eternal Ātman: this is the Way Up. In general, we may say that the passage from the Taittirīyopanishad which we are discussing is very significant for us, first, as enumerating most definitely for the first time in the whole region of Upanishadic literature the five different Elements; secondly, for having introduced the Heracleitean conception of the Way Up and the Way Down; thirdly, for the theory of emanation as apposed to creation implied in it; and lastly, for the realistic trend of its argument which has been a standing crux to all absolutistic interpreters of Upanishadic philosophy, who would try to reduce everything except the Ātman to an appearance or illusion.

The Personal-Impersonal theory of creation in Mundaka.

17. The Muṇḍakopanishad offers a connecting link between such an emanatory theory of creation and a theistic theory as in the Śvetaśvatara which we shall presently discuss by suggesting a personal-impersonal theory of the origin of the universe and telling us that "at the beginning of creation, there existed a heavenly Formless Person who was unborn, without a mind, lustrous, and super-immutable. From him were born life, mind, senses, space, air, light, water, and earth, which last is the basis of the universe......From him also were born gods of various descriptions, angels, men, beasts, and birds. From him were born rice and barley, penance and faith, truth, celibacy, and religious law ......He was likewise the source of all the oceans and mountains, the rivers which run to and fro, the herbs and trees, and the essence which runs through them, by which verily the inner Soul holds them all together" (S. 19). In this way were all earthly and celestial existences, all organic and inorganic nature, all moral and psychological qualities born from the primeval Person, who is yet described as formless and beyond even what we call the immutable. Even this account of the origin of the universe from the primeval Person is not entirely untainted by mythological considerations; but it stands much higher than any of the afore-discussed theories, and approaches the truly theistic theory of creation which accounts for the creation of all sorts of existences by the primeval Person. The truly theistic tinge, however, is yet lacking, because the passage from the Muṇḍakopanishad which we are discussing describes the Person as impersonal and speaks of emanation (Syandante) or generation (Jāyate) instead of creation proper.

18. This entirely personal setting for the supreme Godhead is to be found in the Śvetāśvataropanishad. It is true that the Śvetāsvataropanishad was written in the interest of a Śaivite theory of theism; but if we just divest our minds of this sectarian aspect and equate the god Śiva of the Śvetāśvataropanishad with the supreme Godhead, which has, in fact, been done in many places by the Śvetāśvataropanishad itself, we may see how the Śvetāśvataropanishad tries philosophically to account for the creation of the world by the Godhead by the method of construction through criticism of the various extant opinions on the subject of the origin of the world. The passage from the Śvetāśvataropanishad I. 2 makes a classical enumeration of the various opinions held at the time of the Upanishad on the subject of the origin of the world. "Some people say", says the Upanishad, "that it is Time, others Nature, others Necessity, others Chance, others the Elements, others yet the Person, still others the Combination of these, and yet a few others the Ātman, which is the cause of all things whatsoever" (S. 20. a). The Śvetāśvataropanishad in the course of its chapters criticises all these theories and puts forth a constructive programme of Śaivite theism in explanation of the origin of the universe. We cannot say, says the Śvetāśvataropanishad, that Time is the origin of all things, for, is not God, it asks, the very Time of Time, or as another Upanishad puts it, Death to the very God of Death? (S. 20. b). We cannot try to explain the origin of the world from Nature, says the Śvetāśvataropanishad; for is not Nature itself brought to maturity by the presence of God inside it? (S. 20. c). Nor can we say that Necessity and Chance are the origin of things: they are either too fatalistic or too unphilosophical ways for the explanation of creation. The Ele-

The Theistic theory of Creation in Svetasvatara.

ments cannot be regaded as the "archē" of things, for the elements are merely the garment of God, and it is due to His supreme skill in work that earth, water, fire, air and space were created (S. 20. d). Nor can we say that the Combination of all these elements is a veritable "archē," because for these to be combined, we must have an eternal Being who is the primal cause of their combination (S. 20. e). Nor can we finally say that either the Purusha of the Sāṁkhyas, who is too free from creation to be ever regarded as responsible for it, or the Ātman of the Vedāntins, who is really a powerless Being if we just consider that he is the cause of happiness as well as of sorrow, can be regarded as responsible for creation. Rudra alone who rules the world by his powers, who stands before every being at the time of destruction, and creates the universe at the time of its origin, can be regarded as the Creator of all things that exist. He is the supreme Godhead, to whose power is due the whirling round of the wheel of the universe (S. 20. f). He is the supreme cause, the lord of all Souls; of him there is neither generator nor protector; he is the self-subsisting mover of the unmoving manifold, and causes the one primal seed to sprout in infinite ways (S. 20. g). In this manner does the Śvetāśvataropanishad advance a truly philosophic theory of creation, in which all power is ultimately due to a personal Godhead who causes the whole universe to move round his finger—"Im Kreis das All am Finger laufen liesse."

The Theory of Independent Parallelism as an explanation of the analogies of Upanishadic and Greek philosophies.

19. We have hitherto considered both the impersonalistic and the personalistic theories of creation, pointing out incidentally the analogies which subsist between the Upanishadic and the Greek theories of cosmogony. Even though, however, the similarities have been pointed out, they have not yet been explained. The problem of the relation of Greek and Indian cosmogonies, and in general, of Greek and Indian philosophies, is a very interesting problem, and it may just be worth our while to attempt a brief solution of it. The problem of the relation of the two philosophies is only a branch of the general Græco-Indian problem of the relation of the two cultures. In an analysis of the two cultures in the various departments, we may say that there are three theories which can be advanced to explain their extraordinary similarities. (1) The Theory of Borrowal either by Greece from India or by India from Greece could find historical justification only after the date of Alexander. Just as Greece left a mark upon Indian progress in the departments of sculpture and numismatics after Alexander's invasion, similarly, India left a deep impression upon the Platonists of Alexandria as seen especially in the all-to Yogic ecsatasy of the Neo-Platonists, and their borrowal of the three qualities πνευματικοί, ψυχικοί, ὑλικοί from Sāṁkhya philosophy. But the far more important question in the general Græco-Indian problem is how the two cultures were related before the invasion of Alexander. Diogenes, the biographer of Greek philosophers, and Jamblichus, the Neo-platonist, narrate to us stories of the visit to Brahmins of early Greek philosophers, among them philosophers like Thales and Pythagoras. But this fact has yet to be historically proved. The absence of a single reference in Plato to Indian philosophy forbids the truth of such a statement. (2) Thus, in order to explain the many analogies of Comparative Mythology and Comparative Philology, we have to take recourse to a second theory, namely the Theory of Common Origin. The story for example. of the Universal Being as an egg-like sphere, and Phanes, the shining god, coming out of its two lids, namely, the earth and the sky; the bi-partition of the primeval Ātman into two portions, the man and the wo-man, with its analogy in Hebrew literature; and the similar descriptions of the Aśvattha in the Kaṭhopanishad and the Igdrasil in Scandinavian mythology, may all be traced to a time when the European and the Indian Aryans lived together. Similarly, about Comparative Philology. The present writer has proved in his essay on "the Comparative Study of Greek and Sanskrit" that the many great analogies of the entire grammatical structure of the two languages could hardly be explained except on the theory of a continued stay together of the two peoples, thus reinforcing from an altogether different point of view the truth of the Theory of Common Origin in certain departments of the two cultures. (3) Finally, there is the Theory of what we may call Independent Parallelism, which is of especial value to us in explaining the analogies of philosophical concepts. We have already noticed how the definitions of the primary substance in the two philosophies are identical; how the query of Hesiod at the beginning of his work corresponds almost exactly to the query at the beginning of the Śvetāśvataropanishad; how the conception of water as the "archē" in the Bṛihadāraṇyakopanishad has its counterpart in the theory of Thales; how the doctrine of air as the final absorbent in the Chhāndogya has its analogue in the theory of Anaximenes; how the Heracleitean conception of the exchange of fire for all things is to be met with in the Kaṭhopanishad; how the earth as the basis of the cosmos as we find it in the Muṇḍakopanishad is echoed in Hesiod; how the conception of Space as the fifth element recognised in the Taittirīyopanishad has its parallel in the theory of Philolaos; how the conceptions of Not-Being and

Being in the Taittirīya and the Chhāndogya Upanishads have their parallels in the theories of Gorgias and Parmenides; how the Way Up and the Way Down in Taittirīyopanishad are repeated in the theory of Heracleitus; how, finally, the conception of Trivṛitkaraṇa in the Chhāndogya Upanishad has its analogue in the Anaxagorian doctrine of there being a portion of everything in everything. So far about the cosmological resemblances proper. Nor are the extra-cosmological resemblances of the two philosophies less interesting. The Pythagorean doctrine of Transmigration and its Indian analogue dating so far back as the days of the Ṛigveda, the Phaedrus myth of the Charioteer and the Horses and an exactly similar myth in the Kaṭhopanishad, the representation of the idea of the Good in Plato as the Sun of the world of ideas having its counterpart in the description in the Kaṭhopanishad of the Ātman as verily the Sun who is the eye of the world and is free from all imperfections, the μὴ ὄν of Plato corresponding phonetically, philologically and even philosophically to the Māya of the Vedānta, Parmeides's attack in Plato against the Universality of the Idea represented to a word in the famous criticism by Śaṅkara of the Naiyāyika idea of the Universal, the analogy of the Vāk in Ṛigveda to the Logos in Heracleitus, the Stoics, and Greek philosophy generally—all these could not be said to be less interesting specimens of the analogies of Greek and Indian Thought. How may we explain these cosmological, and extra-cosmological, analogies? Not by the Theory of Borrowal, for this cannot be historically proved. Nor by the Theory of Common Origin, because, in spite of the similarities, the philosophical concepts of the two lands are placed in a setting all their own, the Pythagorean theory of Numbers and the Platonic theory of

Ideas being as peculiar to Greek thought, as the Upanishadic doctrine of the Turīya and the Mimāṅsaka doctrine of the Sphoṭa are peculiar to Indian thought. We must needs take the help of the Theory of the Independent Parallelism of Thought, where no borrowing or common origin could be historically proved. The Gīta conception of God as the A of the Indian alphabet and the Gospel conception of God as the Alpha and Omega of things, and the Kālidasian description of the stream of love as raging all the more on account of hindrances in its path finding its echo in the Shakespearean description of love in the "Two Gentlemen," are instances how imagination may work absolutely alike in regions of poetry or philosophy. There is nothing to prevent the flights of genius from achieving the same ends wherever it may be placed. Neptune might be discovered by Adams and Leverrier at the same time. Darwin and Wallace might simultaneously discover the principle of Natural Selection. Scott and Amundsen might reach the North Pole at the same moment. What might prevent Philosophers from grasping the same point of view, even though separated by Time and Place ?

SOURCES II

1 (*a*) तज्जलानिति शान्त उपासीत । छां. III. 14. 1.

(*b*) यतो वा इमानि भूतानि जायन्ते, येन जातानि जीवन्ति, यत्प्रयन्त्यभिसंविशन्ति तद्विजिज्ञासस्व तद्ब्रह्मेति ।

तै. III. 1.

(*c*) किं कारणं ब्रह्म कुतः स्म जाता जीवाम केन क्व च संप्रतिष्ठाः।

श्वे. I. 1.

2 (*a*) आप एवेदमग्र आसुस्ता आपः सत्यमसृजन्त, सत्यं ब्रह्म,

ब्रह्म प्रजापतिं, प्रजापतिर्देवान् । ते देवाः सत्यमेवोपासते ।
बृ. V. 5. 1.

(b) तदेतत् त्र्यक्षरं सत्यमिति । स इत्येकमक्षरम् । तीत्येकमक्षरम् ।
यमित्येकमक्षरम् । प्रथमोत्तमे अक्षरे सत्यम् । मध्यतोऽनृतम् ।
तदेतदनृतमुभयतः सत्येन परिगृहीतं सत्यभूयमेव भवति ।
बृ. V. 5. 1.

3 वायुर्वाव संवर्गो यदा वा अग्निरुद्वायति वायुमेवाप्येति
यदा सूर्योऽस्तमेति वायुमेवाप्येति यदा चन्द्रोऽस्तमेति
वायुमेवाप्येति ॥ १ ॥ यदाप उच्छुष्यन्ति वायुमेवापियन्ति
वायुर्ह्येवैतान्सर्वान्संवृङ्क्त इत्यधिदैवतम् ॥ २ ॥
छां. IV. 3. 1-2.

4 (a) अग्निर्यथैको भुवनं प्रविष्टो रूपं रूपं प्रतिरूपो बभूव ।
क. II. 5.

(b) एवमेव खलु सोम्य अन्नेन शुंगेनापोमूलमन्विच्छ, अद्भिः
सोम्य शुंगेन तेजोमूलमन्विच्छ, तेजसा सोम्य शुंगेन
सन्मूलमन्विच्छ । सन्मूलाः सोम्येमाः सर्वाः प्रजाः सदा-
यतनाः सत्प्रतिष्ठाः ॥ छां. VI. 8. 4.

5 (a) अस्य लोकस्य का गतिरित्याकाश इति होवाच । सर्वाणि
ह वा इमानि भूतान्याकाशादेव समुत्पद्यन्ते, आकाशं
प्रत्यस्तं यन्ति । आकाशो हि एव एभ्यो ज्यायान् । आकाशः
परायणम् । छां. I. 9. 1.

(b) आकाशो वाव तेजसो भूयान् । आकाशे वै सूर्याचंद्र-
मसावुभौ । विद्युन्नक्षत्राण्यग्निः । आकाशेनाह्वयति...आकाशे
जायते । आकाशमभिजायते । आकाशमुपास्स्वेति ।
छां. VII. 12. 1.

6 असद्वा इदमग्र आसीत् । ततो वै सदजायत । तदात्मानं
स्वयमकुरुत । तस्मात्तत्सुकृतमुच्यत इति ।
तै. II. 7.

7 नैवेह किंचनाग्र आसीन्मृत्युनैवेदमावृतमासीत् । अशना-
यया । अशनाया हि मृत्युः । तन्मनोऽकुरुत । आत्मन्वी
स्यामिति । सोऽर्चन् अचरत् । तस्यार्चत आपोऽजायन्त ।...।
तद्यदपां शर आसीत्तत्समहन्यत । सा पृथिव्यभवत् । तस्या-
मश्राम्यत् । तस्य श्रान्तस्य तप्तस्य तेजो रसो निरवर्तताग्निः ।
बृ. I. 2. 1-2.

8 आदित्यो ब्रह्मेत्यादेशः । तस्योपव्याख्यानम् । असदेवेदमग्र आसीत् । तत्सदासीत् । तत्समभवत् । तदाण्डं निरवर्तत । तत्संवत्सरस्य मात्रामशयत् । तन्निरभिद्यत । ते आण्ड-कपाले रजतं च सुवर्णं चाभवताम् । तद्यद्रजतं सेयं पृथिवी । यत्सुवर्णं सा द्यौः । यज्जरायु ते पर्वताः । यदुल्बं स मेघो नीहारः । या धमनयस्ता नद्यः । यद्वास्तेयमुदकं स समुद्रः । अथ यत्तदजायत सोऽसावादित्यः । तं जायमानं घोषा उलूलवो अनूदतिष्ठन् ।

छां. III. 19. 1-3.

9 अन्तरिक्षोदरः कोशो भूमिबुध्नो न जीर्यति । दिशो ह्यस्य स्रक्तयो द्यौरस्योत्तरं बिलम् । स एष कोशो वसुधानः तस्मिन्विश्वमिदं श्रितम् ॥

छां. III. 15. 1.

10 (a) सदेव सोम्येदमग्र आसीदेकमेवाद्वितीयम् । तद्ध एक आहुरसदेवेदमग्र आसीदेकमेवाद्वितीयं तस्मादसतः सज्जायत । कुतस्तु खलु सोम्य एवं स्यादिति होवाच कथमसतः सज्जायेतेति । सत्त्वेव सोम्येदमग्र आसीत् एकमेवाद्वितीयम् । तदैक्षत बहु स्यां प्रजायेयेति । तत्तेजो-ऽसृजत । तत्तेज ऐक्षत बहु स्यां प्रजायेयेति तदपोऽसृ-जत...। ता आपः...अन्नमसृजन्त ।

छां. VI. 2. 1-4.

(b) सेयं देवतैक्षत हन्त अहमिमास्तिस्रो देवता अनेन जीवेन आत्मना अनुप्रविश्य नामरूपे व्याकरवाणि । तासां त्रिवृतं त्रिवृतं एकैकां करवाणीति । छां. VI. 3. 2–3.

(c) यदग्ने रोहितं रूपं तेजसस्तद्रूपं, यच्छुक्लं तदपां, यत्कृष्णं तदन्नस्य अपागादग्नेरग्नित्वं, वाचारंभणं विकारो नामधेयं, त्रीणि रूपाणि इत्येव सत्यम् । यदादित्यस्य° यच्चंद्रमसो° यद्विद्युतो° । छां. VI. 4. 1–4.

11 (a) कतमा सा देवतेति । प्राण इति होवाच सर्वाणि ह वा इमानि भूतानि प्राणमेवाभिसंविशंति, प्राणमभ्युज्जिहते। छां. I. 11. 5

(b) अथाध्यात्मं प्राणो वाव संवर्गः स यदा स्वपिति प्राणमेव वागप्येति, प्राणं चक्षुः, प्राणं श्रोत्रं, प्राणं मनः, प्राणो ह्येवैता-न्सर्वान्संवृंक्त इति । छां. IV. 3. 3.

(c) तौ वा एतौ द्वौ संवर्गौ वायुरेव देवेषु प्राणः प्राणेषु।
छां. IV. 3. 4.

12 (a) अथ वा अरा नाभौ समर्पिता एवमस्मिन्प्राणे सर्वं सम-
र्पितम्। छां. VII. 15. 1.

(b) प्राणो ब्रह्मेति ह स्माह कौषीतकिः। तस्य ह वा एतस्य
प्राणस्य ब्रह्मणो मनो दूतं, चक्षुर्गोप्तृ, श्रोत्रं संश्रावयितृ,
वाक्परिवेष्ट्री। तस्मै वा एतस्मै प्राणाय ब्रह्मण एताः सर्वा
देवता अयाचमानाय बलिं हरन्ति। कौ. II. 1.

13 (a) अथ ह प्राणा अहंश्रेयसि व्यूदिरेऽहं श्रेयानस्म्यहं श्रेयान-
स्मीति। ते ह प्राणाः प्रजापतिं पितरमेत्योचुर्भगवन्को
नः श्रेष्ठ इति तान्होवाच यस्मिन्व उत्क्रान्ते शरीरं पापिष्ठ-
तरमिव दृश्येत स वः श्रेष्ठ इति। सा ह वागुच्चक्राम सा
संवत्सरं प्रोष्य पर्येत्योवाच कथमशकतर्ते मज्जीवितुमिति
यथा कला अवदन्तः,प्राणन्तः प्राणेन पश्यंतश्चक्षुषा,शृण्वन्तः
श्रोत्रेण, ध्यायन्तो मनसैवमिति प्रविवेश ह वाक्। चक्षुर्होच्-
चक्राम तत्संवत्सरं प्रोष्य पर्येत्योवाच कथमशकतर्ते मज्जी-
वितुमिति यथांधा अपश्यन्तः, प्राणन्तः प्राणेन, वदन्तो वाचा,
शृण्वन्तः श्रोत्रेण, ध्यायन्तो मनसैवमिति प्रविवेश ह चक्षुः।
श्रोत्रं होच्चक्राम तत्संवत्सरं प्रोष्य पर्येत्योवाच कथमशकतर्ते
मज्जीवितुमिति यथा बधिरा अशृण्वन्तःप्राणंतः प्राणेन, वदन्तो
वाचा, पश्यन्तश्चक्षुषा, ध्यायन्तो मनसैवमिति प्रविवेश ह
श्रोत्रम्। मनो होच्चक्राम तत्संवत्सरं प्रोष्य पर्येत्योवाच कथ-
मशकतर्ते मज्जीवितुमिति यथा बाला अमनसः, प्राणन्तः
प्राणेन,वदन्तो वाचा, पश्यन्तश्चक्षुषा, शृण्वन्तः श्रोत्रेणैवमिति
प्रविवेश ह मनः। अथ ह प्राण उच्चिक्रमिषन्स यथा सुहयः
पड्वीशशंकून्संखिदेदेवमितरान्प्राणान्समखिदत्तं हाभिसमे-
त्योचुर्भगवन्नेधि त्वं नः श्रेष्ठोऽसि मोत्क्रमीरिति। अथ हैनं
वागुवाच यदहं वसिष्ठोऽस्मि त्वं तद्वसिष्ठोऽसीत्यथ हैनं
चक्षुरुवाच यदहं प्रतिष्ठास्मि त्वं तत्प्रतिष्ठासीति। अथ हैनं
श्रोत्रमुवाच यदहं संपदस्मि त्वं तत्संपदसीत्यथ हैनं मन
उवाच यदहमायतनमस्मि त्वं तदायतनमसीति। न वै
वाचो न चक्षूंषि न श्रोत्राणि न मनांसीत्याचक्षते प्राणो
ह्येवैतानि सर्वाणि भवति॥ छां. V. 1. 6-15.

(b) भगवन्कत्येव देवाः प्रजां विधारयन्ते कतर एतत्प्रकाशयन्ते

कः पुनरेषां वरिष्ठ इति । तस्मै स होवाचाकाशो ह वा एष
देवो वायुरग्निरापः पृथिवी वाङ्मनश्चक्षुः श्रोत्रं च । ते
प्रकाश्याभिवदन्ति वयमेतद्बाणमवष्टभ्य विधारयामः । तान्व-
रिष्ठः प्राण उवाच मा मोहमापद्यथाहमेवैतत्पंचधात्मानं
प्रविभज्यैतद्बाणमवष्टभ्य विधारयामीति तेऽश्रद्दधाना
बभूवुः । सोऽभिमानादूर्ध्वमुत्क्रमत इव तस्मिन्नुत्क्रामत्य-
थेतरे सर्व एवोत्क्रामन्ते तस्मिंश्च प्रतिष्ठमाने सर्व एव
प्रतिष्ठन्ते । तद्यथा मक्षिका मधुकरराजानमुत्क्रामन्तं सर्वा
एवोत्क्रामन्ते तस्मिंश्च प्रतिष्ठमाने सर्वा एव प्रतिष्ठन्त एवं
वाङ्मनश्चक्षुः श्रोत्रं च ते प्रीताः प्राणं स्तुवन्ति । एषोऽग्नि-
स्तपत्येष सूर्य एष पर्जन्यो मघवानेष वायुरेष पृथिवी रयि-
र्देवः सदसच्चामृतं च यत् ।...। या ते तनूर्वाचि प्रतिष्ठिता
या श्रोत्रे या च चक्षुषि । या च मनसि संतता शिवां तां
कुरु मोत्क्रमीः । प्र. II. 1–12.

14 आयुः प्राणः प्राणो वा आयुः ।...। अस्ति त्वेव प्राणानां
निःश्रेयसमिति । जीवति वागपेतो मूकान्हि पश्यामो, जीवति
चक्षुरपेतोऽन्धान् हि पश्यामो, जीवति श्रोत्रापेतो बधि-
रान्हि पश्यामो, जीवति मनोऽपेतो बालान्हि पश्यामः ।
यो वै प्राणः सा प्रज्ञा, या वा प्रज्ञा स प्राणः सह ह्येताव-
स्मिञ् शरीरे वसतः, सहोत्क्रामतः । ... यथाग्नेर्ज्वलतः
सर्वा दिशो विस्फुलिंगा विप्रतिष्ठेरन् एवमेवैतस्मादात्मनः
प्राणाः यथायतनं विप्रतिष्ठन्ते, प्राणेभ्यो देवाः, देवेभ्यो
लोकाः । ... तद्यथा रथस्यारेषु नेमिरर्पितो, नाभावरा
अर्पिता एवमेवैता भूतमात्राः प्रज्ञामात्रास्वर्पिताः प्रज्ञामात्राः
प्राणेऽर्पिताः । स एष प्राण एव प्रज्ञात्मा आनंदोऽजरोऽ
मृतो न साधुना कर्मणा भूयान्भवति, नो एवासाधुना
कनीयान् । कौ. III. 2–9.

15 (*a*) भगवन् कुतो ह वा इमाः प्रजाः प्रजायन्त इति । तस्मै स
होवाच । प्रजाकामो वै प्रजापतिः । स तपोऽतप्यत । स
तपस्तप्त्वा । स मिथुनमुत्पादयते । रयिं च प्राणं चेतौ मे
बहुधा प्रजाः करिष्य इति । आदित्यो ह वै प्राणो रयिरेव
चंद्रमाः... संवत्सरो वै प्रजापतिः तस्य अयने दक्षिणं
चोत्तरं च ... एष ह वै रयिः यः पितृयानः... मासो वै
प्रजापतिः तस्य कृष्णपक्ष एव रयिः शुक्लः प्राणः.... अहो-

रात्रो वै प्रजापतिः तस्य अहरेव प्राणो रात्रिरेव रयिः।
प्र. I. 3-13

(*b*) सोऽकामयत बहु स्यां प्रजायेयेति । स तपोऽतप्यत। स
तपस्तप्त्वा इदं सर्वं असृजत यदिदं किंच। तत्सृष्ट्वा तदे-
वानुप्राविशत्। तदनुप्रविश्य सच्च त्यच्चाभवत्। निरुक्तं
चानिरुक्तं च। निलयनं चानिलयनं च। विज्ञानं चाविज्ञानं
च। सत्यं चानृतंच। तै. II. 6.

16 आत्मैवेदमग्र आसीत् पुरुषविधः..... । सोहमस्मीति अग्रे
व्याहरत्। ततोऽहंनामाभवत्। तस्मादप्येतर्हि आमंत्रितो
अहमयमित्येवाग्र उक्त्वा अथ अन्यन्नाम प्रब्रूते.... । सोऽ
बिभेत्। तस्मादेकाकी बिभेति। स हायमीक्षांचक्रे यन्मदन्य-
न्नास्ति कस्मान्नु बिभेमीति तत एव अस्य भयं वीयाय....
द्वितीयाद्वै भयं भवति। स वै नैव रेमे तस्मादेकाकी न
रमते। स द्वितीयमैच्छत्...। स इममेवात्मानं द्वेधाऽपात-
यत्ततः पतिश्च पत्नी चाभवताम्.... । सा हेयमीक्षांचक्रे
कथं नु मात्मन एव जनयित्वा संभवति, हन्त तिरोऽ-
सानीति सा गौरभवत् वृषभ इतरस्तां समेवाभवत्.... ।
वडवा इतराभवत् अश्ववृष इतरो। गर्दभी इतरा गर्दभ
इतरस्तां समेवाभवत्....। अजायन्त एवमेव यदिदं किंच
मिथुनमापिपीलिकाभ्यः, तत्सर्वमसृजत। बृ. I. 4. 1-4.

17 आत्मा वा इदमेक एवाग्र आसीन्नान्यत्किंचन मिषत्। स
ईक्षत लोकान्नु सृजा इति। स इमांल्लोकानसृजत अंभो,
मरीचीः, मरं, आपः.... । स ईक्षतेमे नु लोका लोकपा-
लान्नु सृजा इति। सोऽद्भ्य एव पुरुषं समुद्धृत्यामूर्च्छयत्
तमभ्यतपत्तस्याभितप्तस्य मुखं निरभिद्यत यथांडं मुखा-
द्वाग्वाचोऽग्निर्नासिके निरभिद्येतां नासिकाभ्यां प्राणः
प्राणाद्वायुरक्षिणी निरभिद्येतामक्षिभ्यां चक्षुश्चक्षुष आदित्य
कर्णौ निरभिद्येतां कर्णाभ्यां श्रोत्रं श्रोत्राद्दिशस्त्वङ् निर-
भिद्यत त्वचो लोमानि लोमभ्य ओषधिवनस्पतयो,हृदयं निर-
भिद्यत हृदयान्मनो मनसश्चंद्रमा, नाभिर्निरभिद्यत नाभ्या अ-
पानोऽपानान्मृत्युः,शिश्नं निरभिद्यत शिश्नाद्रेतो रेतस आपः।
तमशनापिपासाभ्यामन्ववार्जत्...। तं (आत्मानं) अश

नापिपासेऽब्रूतां अभिप्रजानीहीति । तेऽब्रवीदेतास्वेव वां देवतासु आभजामि, एतासु भागिन्यौ करोमीति । तस्माद्यस्यै कस्यै च देवतायै हविर्गृह्यते भागिन्या एव अस्यां अशनापिपासे भवतः ॥ स ईक्षतेमे नु लोकाश्च लोकपालाश्च, अन्नमेभ्यः सृजा इति ।.... स ईक्षत कथं नु इदं मदृते स्यादिति । स ईक्षत कतरेण प्रपद्या इति ...। स एतमेव सीमानं विदार्य एतया द्वारा प्रापद्यत । सैषा विदृतिर्नाम द्वाः । तदेतन्नांदनम् । तस्य त्रय आवसथाः त्रयः स्वप्नाः अयमावसथोऽयमावसथो ऽयमावसथ इति । स जातो भूतान्यभिव्यैख्यत् किमिहान्यं वावदिषदिति । स एतमेव पुरुषं ब्रह्म ततमपश्यत् । इदं अदर्शमिती ३ । तस्मादिदंद्रो नाम .... तमिदंद्रं संतं इन्द्र इत्याचक्षते परोक्षेण । । परोक्षप्रिया इव हि देवाः । परोक्षप्रिया इव हि देवाः । ऐ. I. 1–3.

18 तस्माद्वा एतस्मादात्मन आकाशः संभूतः । आकाशाद्वायुः, वायोरग्निः, अग्नेरापः, अद्भ्यः पृथिवी । तै. II. 1.

19 दिव्यो ह्यमूर्तः पुरुषः सबाह्याभ्यंतरो ह्यजः । अप्राणो ह्यमनाः शुभ्रो ह्यक्षरात्परतः परः ॥ एतस्माज्जायते प्राणो मनः सर्वेंद्रियाणि च । खं वायुर्ज्योतिरापः पृथिवी विश्वस्य धारिणी । .... तस्माच्च देवा बहुधा संप्रसूताः साध्या मनुष्याः पशवो वयांसि । प्राणापानौ व्रीहियवौ तपश्च श्रद्धा सत्यं ब्रह्मचर्यं विधिश्च ॥ ... अतः समुद्रा गिरयश्च सर्वेऽस्मात्स्यंदन्ते सिंधवः सर्वरूपाः । अतश्च सर्वा ओषधयो रसश्च येनैष भूतैस्तिष्ठते ह्यंतरात्मा ॥ मुं. II.1.2–9.

20 (*a*) कालः स्वभावो नियतिर्यदृच्छा भूतानि योनिः पुरुष इति चिंत्यम् । संयोग एषां न त्वात्मभावादात्माप्त्यनीशः सुखदुःखहेतोः ॥ श्वे. I. 2.

(*b*) येनावृतं नित्यमिदं हि सर्वं ज्ञः कालकालो गुणी सर्वविद्यः । श्वे. VI. 2.

स विश्वकृद्विश्वविदात्मयोनिर्ज्ञः कालकालो गुणी सर्वविद्यः । श्वे. VI. 16.

अहमन्नमन्नमदन्तमाद्मि । तै. III. 10. 6.

(*c*) यच्च स्वभावं पचति विश्वयोनिः । श्वे. V. 5.

(*d*) तेनेशितं कर्म विवर्तते ह पृथिव्यप्तेजोऽनिलखानि चिन्त्यम् ।
श्वे. VI. 2.

कर्माध्यक्षः सर्वभूताधिवासः । श्वे. VI. 11.

(*e*) आदिः स संयोगनिमित्तहेतुः परस्त्रिकालादकलोऽपि दृष्टः ।
श्वे. VI. 1.

(*f*) एको हि रुद्रो न द्वितीयाय तस्थुः य इमांल्लोकान् ईशत ईशनीभिः । प्रत्यङ्जनास्तिष्ठति संचुकोपान्तकाले संसृज्य विश्वा भुवनानि गोपाः ॥ श्वे. III. 2.

स्वभावमेके कवयो वदन्ति कालं तथान्ये परिमुह्यमानाः ।
देवस्यैष महिमा तु लोके येनेदं भ्राम्यते ब्रह्मचक्रम् ॥
श्वे. VI. 1.

(*g*) स कारणं करणाधिपाधिपो न चास्य कश्चिज्जनिता न चाधिपः । श्वे. VI. 9.

एको वशी निष्क्रियाणां बहूनामेकं बीजं बहुधा यः करोति ।
श्वे. VI. 12.

CHAPTER III

VARIETIES OF PSYCHOLOGICAL REFLECTION

Empirical, Abnormal and Rational Psychology.

1. If we were to consider the date at which the Upanishadic seers lived in India, we would be surprised to find that they could have to their credit such an amount of psychological reflection. The Upanishadic seers were foremost in their age in philosophical reflection in general, and psychological reflection in particular. The three departments of their speculation in the field of Psycholcgy may be classified as the Empirical, the Abnormal, and the Rational; and even though their Empirical Psychology was less developed than the Abnormal, and the Abnormal less than the Rational, we would have to take account of their speculation in all these fields before we could adjudge the value of their psychological reflection as a whole.

I—EMPIRICAL PSYCHOLOGY

The relation of Mind to Alimentation.

2. We must, however, bear in mind that Empirical Psychology is a science of recent growth, and thus we must not expect to find a full-fledged empirical investigation of mental science in the days of the Upanishads. We must, on the contrary, be content with what little information is supplied to us under that head in the various Upanishads. The Upanishadic philosophers believed that the mind for its formation was dependent upon alimentation. The mind was supposed to be manufactured out of the food that we take (S. I. a). "The food that we eat",

says a passage, "is transformed in three different ways: the heaviest part of it becomes the excrement, that of medium density is transformed into flesh, and the subtlest part goes to form the mind" (S.1.b). "Just as in the churning of curds, the subtlest part rises up and is transformed into butter, so when food is eaten, the subtlest part rises up and is transformed into mind" (S. 1. c). Later, even in the days of the Bhagavadgītā, we find that the three different mental temperaments, the Sāttvika, the Rājasa, and the Tāmasa were supposed to be due to the different kinds of food that we eat (XVII.8-10). When once it was believed that the qualities of the food consumed formed the quality of the mind of the consumer, it was natural to insist, in the interest of the highest morality, upon a kind of *katharsis* in alimentation. "When the food is pure," says a passage (S. 2), "the whole nature becomes pure; when the nature becomes pure, memory becomes firm; and when a man is in possession of a firm memory, all the bonds which tie a man down to the world become unloosed. It was because he (Nārada) had his impurity destroyed, that the venerable Sanatkumāra pointed out to him the way beyond darkness". The way which leads us beyond darkness, therefore, must be sought for in purity of alimentation, which involves in its train the purity of mind.

Attention involves suspension of breath.

3. One of the acute observations which these ancient seers made concerns the fact that in the process of attention we always hold our breath, and seem neither to breathe out nor to breathe in. When we speak, we neither expire nor inspire (S. 3. a). When we do an action which involves voluntary effort, as, for example, "producing fire

by rubbing two sticks together, or running a race, or bending a bow and stringing it, we neither exhale, nor inhale" (S. 3. b). Our attention in such acts is concentrated on the action itself, and it cannot be diverted to such subsidiary processes as those of breathing out and breathing in. This is what in the Kaushītaki Upanishad is called the "inner sacrifice", which goes after the name of its discoverer, the sage Pratardana, and is called the Prātardana sacrifice. Pratardana said, that while a man is speaking, he is not able to breathe, and therefore may be said to sacrifice his breath in his speech; on the contrary, while a man is breathing, he is not able to speak, and may be said to sacrifice his speech in his breath. "These two endless and immortal oblations," said Pratardana, "man offers always, whether waking or sleeping. All other oblations have an end, for they consist of works. Knowing this, the ancient sages did not offer the ordinary sacrifice" (S. 3. c). In this passage, a justification is found for not performing the ordinary sacrifice when one knows that an inner sacrifice is ever going on inside him.

Analysis of fear.

4. Another curious observation which these seers made may be mentioned in passing. This concerns the analysis of the emotion of fear. It is only when a feeling of otherness gains lodgment in us (S. 4. a) that we come to entertain the emotion of fear. The primeval Ātman feared, as he was alone; but "on finding out that there was no other person whom he should fear, he became fearless; for it is only from (the idea or existence of) a second that fear proceeds" (S. 4. b). It is in this way that all feeling of fear departs from a man who recognises his own true Self, because

this recognition implies that beside his own true Self there is no other entity which might cause fear.

The claim of Will for primacy.

5. Another very important point in connection with the psychology of the Upanishads is the conflict manifested in the Chhāndogya Upanishad beween the respective claims for primacy of the Will or the Intellect. Here we have in brief the indication of a future quarrel between Voluntarism and Intellectualism. The following passage most eloquently describes the stress which the seer first lays on Will as the primary reality: "All these therefore......centre in will, consist of will, abide in will. Heaven and earth willed, air and ether willed, water and fire willed. Through the will of heaven and earth, rain falls; through the will of rain, food wills; through the will of food, the vital airs will; through the will of the vital airs, the sacred hymns will; through the will of the sacred hymns, the sacrifices will; through the will of the sacrifices, the world wills; through the will of the world, every thing wills. This is Will. Meditate on Will. He who meditates on Will as Brahman......he is, as it were, lord and master as far as Will reaches—he who meditates on Will as Brahman" (S. 5). The seer of this Upanishad is evidently imbued with the all-pervading power of Will. It seems that this passage among others must have influenced the philosophy of that admirer of the Upanishads, Schopenhauer, who laid so much stress on Will as the *Ding-an-sich*. We may compare the following passage from The World as Will and Idea (Book I). "If we observe the strong and unceasing impulse with which the waters hurry to the ocean, the persistency with which the magnet turns ever to the north pole, the readi-

ness with which iron flies to the magnet, the eagerness with which the electric poles seek to be reunited, and which, like human desire, is increased by obstacles ; if we see the crystal quickly take form with such wonderful regularity of construction,......if we observe the choice with which bodies repel and attract each other,.....if we observe all this, I say, it will require no great effort of the imagination to recognize, even at so great a distance, our own nature. That, which in us pursues its ends by the light of knowledge, but here, in the weakest of its manifestations, only strives blindly and dumbly in a one-sided and unchangeable manner, must yet in both cases come under the name of Will. " According to the doctrine which is common to this Upanishad and Schopenhauer, the whole world seems to be filled with the force of will ; and "what appears as *motivation* in human beings is the same as what appears as *stimulation* in the vegetative life and as *mechanical process* in the inorganic world"—motivation, stimulation, and mechanical process being different manifestations of the same force of Will.

The claim of Intellect for primacy.

6. As against this primacy of Will, the seer of the Chhāndogya Upanishad goes on in the very next section of that work to affirm the primacy of Intellect. The affirmation of Will is the thesis, to which the seer opposes the affirmation of Intellect as the antithesis : "Intellect is better than Will. For it is only when a man thinks that he wills..... All these centre in Intellect, consist of Intellect, abide in Intellect. Therefore, if a man does not think, even if he knows much, people say of him, he is nothing......But if a man thinks, even though he knows little, people indeed desire to listen to him.

Intellect is the centre, Intellect is the self, Intellect is the support of all these. Meditate on Intellect. He who meditates on Intellect as Brahman .... he is, as it were, lord and master as far as Intellect reaches—he who meditates on Intellect as Brahman" (S. 6. a). The seer of this Upanishad is here definitely asserting the supremacy of Intellect over Will: Voluntarism here makes way for Intellectualism. This conclusion is supported by another passage from the Maitri Upanishad, where the writer speaks of the mind in its reflective aspect as being the fount and source of all mental modifications whatsoever: "He (man) sees by the mind alone; he hears by the mind; and all that we call desire, will, doubt, belief, disbelief, resolution, irresolution, shame, thought, and fear,—all this is but mind itself" (S. 6. b).

Classification of mental states.

7. This intellectualistic way of thought finds its culmination in the Aitareya Upanishad, where, by a bold stroke of genius, the seer of that Upanishad makes a noteworthy classification of the various mental functions, at the basis of which, he says, lies Intellection. This passage is remarkable as being the earliest contribution to a classification of mental states: "Sensation, perception, ideation, conception, understanding, insight, resolution, opinion, imagination, feeling, memory, volition, conation, the will-to-live, desire, and self-control, all these are different names of Intellection" (S. 7). It is remarkable that the seer not merely mentions the different levels of intellectual experience such as sensation, perception, ideation, and conception, as different from one another, but also recognises the other two characteristic forms of experience, feeling and volition; makes a distinction between volition which need not involve

the idea of activity, and conation which does; as well as recognises the processes of imagination and memory. Finally, the intellectualistic trend of thought in the seer is apparent from the way in which he makes Intellect the fount and source of all mental activity whatsoever.

Intellectualistic Psychology and Idealistic Metaphysics.

8. It is no wonder if this intellectualistic psychology makes room for an idealistic metaphysics. The intellectualistic seer of the Aitareya Upanishad is an idealist as well. In the very section that follows the one we have quoted, the author goes on to point out how Intellect is the backbone, not merely of psychical functions, but of reality itself: "This god Brahmā, and this god Indra,.........these five great elements (earth, air, ether, water, fire),.........creatures born from the egg, from the womb, and from perspiration, sprouting plants, horses, cows, men, elephants, whatsoever breathes whether moving or flying, and in addition whatsoever is immovable—all this is led by Intellect and is supported on Intellect. The world is led by Intellect. Intellect is the support. Intellect is the final reality" (S. 8. a). This is as outspoken an Idealism as Idealism can be. The author says that all the movable and immovable objects in this world, all those creatures which walk or fly, all the elements and gods exist by virtue of intellect and in intellect. This is in the very spirit of Berkeley who says in his "Treatise," "All the choir of heaven and furniture of the earth, in a word, all those bodies which compose the mighty frame of the world have not any subsistence without a mind; that their being is to be perceived or known; that consequently so long as they are not actually perceived by me, or do not exist in my mind

or that of any other created spirit, they must either have no existence at all, or else subsist in the mind of some Eternal Spirit:—it being perfectly unintelligible and involving all the absurdity of abstraction to attribute to any single part of them an existence independent of a Spirit". Of like import is the passage from the Maitri Upanishad which tells us that it is the inner self which governs "external" existence, that, in short, the inner Prāṇa is the source of the existence of the Sun—a knowledge, which, the passage says, is given only to a few (S. 8. b).

II—ABNORMAL PSYCHOLOGY

The problem of death in Chhandogya.

9. We now pass on to consider the aspects of Abnormal Psychology as developed in the Upanishads. The question as to what becomes of a man's soul after the death of the body recurs time after time in the Upanishads. Not content with a discussion of man's life here below, the seers of the Upanishads make the eschatological question assume quite an extraordinary importance. The question is very often asked—what must be considered the root of human life? "The tree, if hewn down, springs anew from the previous root; what must be the root of a man's life in order that it may spring up again, even though hewn down by (the great cutter) Death" (S. 9. a). It is supposed, moreover, that eschatological knowledge is the highest kind of knowledge. Let nobody call himself wise unless he knows what becomes of a man after death. It was thus that the Sage Jaivali accosted Śvetaketu, the son of Āruṇi, and proved to him that even though he reckoned

himself wise, he was after all merely an ignoramus :—

"Boy, has your father instructed you ?" "Yes, Sir."

"Do you know where all the creatures go to from hence ?" "No, Sir."

"Do you know how they return again ?" "No, Sir."

"Do you know where the path of the gods and the path of the fathers diverge ?" "No, Sir."

"Do you know why that (the other) world never becomes too full ?" "No, Sir."

"Then, why did you say that you had been instructed? How can a man, who does not know these (simple) things, say that he has been instructed ?" (S. 9. b).

The problem of death in Katha.

10. The most important passage, however, where eschatological knowledge is regarded as the "highest good" occurs in the celebrated dialogue in the Kaṭha Upanishad between Nachiketas and Yama, the God of death, where Nachiketas, being offered three boons by Yama, and having chosen two already, declines to choose for the third boon anything short of the knowledge of the soul's existence after the death of the human body:—

N: "There is this doubt in the case of a dead man; some say that he is, others say he is not. I would like to be instructed by thee in this matter. This do I choose for my third boon."

Y: "Even the gods have formerly entertained doubt about this matter. Nor is this matter easy of comprehension, being a subtle one. Choose another boon, O Nachiketas, press me not, and let me alone on this point."

N: "Verily, the gods themselves have entertained doubt about this matter; and thou hast thyself said that this matter passes comprehension. It is impossible for me to find another instructor in that subject beside thyself, nor do I find that any other boon would be equal to this."

Y: "All those desires which are impossible to be satisfied in this world of mortals, ask me for them if you so wish: these damsels with chariots and musical instruments, such as are indeed impossible for men to obtain—be waited upon by these, which I shall present to you; but, Nachiketas, do not ask me about death."

N: "All these, O God of death, are but ephemeral objects, and wear out the vigour of the senses. Moreover, life itself would be short (for their full enjoyment); keep them unto thyself—these horses, these dances, and these songs. What mortal would delight in a long life, after he has contemplated the pleasures which beauty and enjoyment afford? No. That which has become a matter of doubt and inquiry, O Death, speak to me about that great Hereafter. Nachiketas chooses no other boon than that which concerns this great secret." (S. 9. c).

The problem of Sleep: the Fatigue and Puritat theories.

11. After the question of the nature of death, comes the question of the nature of sleep, which is only a palliated form of death. On this subject we find very interesting theories advanced by those seers of antiquity. One passage proclaims unmistakably an explanation of the nature of sleep given by modern physiology—the 'Fatigue' theory of sleep: "As a falcon or any other bird, after having flown in the sky, becomes tired, and folding his wings repairs to his nest, so does this person hasten to that state where, when asleep, he desires no more desires, and dreams no more dreams." (S. 10). But beyond this proper physiological explanation of sleep, we find very curious theories held on this point by the sages of the Upanishads. The seer of the Praśna Upanishad holds that sleep is caused by the senses being absorbed in that highest 'sensorium,' the mind: "as all the rays of the Sun, O Gārgya, become collected into the bright disc at the time of sunset, and emerge again from it at the time of sunrise, so do all the senses become collected into that highest sensorium—the mind: that is the reason why (in deep sleep) man is not able to hear, nor to see, nor to smell. People say about him that he has slept." (S. II. a). This same seer qualifies his statement a little further, and says that the reason of the deep sleep is that the mind is merged into an ocean of light: "and when he is overpowered by light, then does this god (Soul) see no dreams, and at that time great happiness arises in the body." (S. II. b). Another theory which is advanced in the Chhāndogya Upanishad is, that sleep is caused by the soul getting lodgment in the arteries: "When a man is fast asleep, and being happy knows no dreams, then his soul has moved in the arteries." (S. II. c). This same idea is elaborated in the Bṛihadāraṇyaka Upanishad, where a physiological explanation, which in the light of modern science appears almost a mythological explanation, is offered according to the ancient ideas. It was imagined that the heart sent forth about 72,000 arteries to the 'Purītat', which Deussen translates as 'perikardium', and which Max Müller, following the commentator, wrongly translates by 'the surrounding body'. This Purītat corresponds to the pineal gland of Descartes, so far as function is concerned; but it differs from it in its anatomical location. The Purītat must be considered as meaning a kind of membraneous sac round the heart. It was imagined by those ancient seers, that in deep sleep the soul moved from the heart by means of the arteries and got lodgment inside the Purītat, whence sleep followed. This same idea was later developed in the Nyāya philosophy where sleep was explained as being due to the moving of the soul right inside the Purītat, the state of dream being explained as due to the soul's position just on the threshold of the Purītat—the soul knocking for entrance inside it,—while it was imagined that during the waking state the soul kept moving from the heart to the Purītat. The origin of this doctrine in the Nyāya philosophy is to be traced to the passage in the Bṛihadāraṇyaka which we are at present discussing: "When a man is fast asleep and when he is not conscious of anything, his soul moves by means of the arteries, called Hitāḥ, which are 72,000 in number, and which are spread from the heart to the Purītat; there he sleeps like a youth, or a great king, or a great Brahmin who has reached the summit of happiness." (S. II. d).

The problem of sleep: the Prana and Brahman theories.

12. Another explanation of the phenomenon of sleep is offered by the seer of the Chhāndogya Upanishad when he says that sleep occurs when the mind is merged in Prāṇa, that is breath or energy: "As a bird when tied by a string flies first in every direction, and finding no rest anywhere, settles down at last on the very spot where it is fastened, exactly in the same manner, my Son, the mind, after flying in every direction, and finding no rest anywhere, settles down on breath; for indeed, my Son, mind is fastened to breath" (S. II. e). The next explanation of sleep occurs in the Bṛihadāraṇyaka Upanishad where we are told that sleep occurs when the soul goes to rest in the 'space' inside the heart. In order to prove this to Gārgya an experimental inquiry was undertaken by Ajātaśatru. He took Gārgya by the hand and came to a place where a man was sleeping. He then called out to him by these names, "Thou, Great one, clad in white raiment, Soma, King of all", and (yet) he did not rise. Then he rubbed him with his hand, (struck him with a stick—Kau.,) and he got up. Then said Ajātaśatru "when this man was asleep, where then was this Person full of intelligence, and from whence did he return?" Gārgya did not know the answer. Thereupon, Ajātaśatru said "when this man was asleep, then the Person full of intelligence (i.e. the Soul) lay in the space which is in the heart." (S. II. f). The last explanation offered of the phenomenon of sleep is the very curious explanation, that, in deep sleep, the Soul is at one with Brahman! This is like saying that when one has no explanation to give, one might excuse himself with the Absolute! A passage from the Praśna Upanishad, again, tells us that in deep sleep "the mind, which is the sacrificer, is carried every day to Brahman," which is corroborated by another passage from the Chhāndogya, which says "when a man sleeps, then, my dear son, he becomes united with the True, he is gone to his own (Self). Therefore they say, 'svapiti', he sleeps, because he is gone (apīta) to his own (sva)." (S. II. g). The idea was that in deep sleep the Soul was at one with Brahman, and thus deep sleep was likened to the state of ecstasy. There is, in fact, as much likeness, or as little, between sleep and ecstasy, as there is, as Spinoza would have said, between God and Dog: the same letters, but what an important difference! It seems that this difference was later appreciated even in the Upanishads when it was said that even though the soul was at one with Brahman in deep sleep, it still did not know this, was not cognisant of it: "as people, who do not know a field, walk again and again over a golden treasure that is hidden somewhere in the earth, and yet are not able to discover it, thus do all these creatures day after day become merged in Brahman, and yet do not discover it, because they are carried away by untruth." (S. 11. h).

The Dream Problem.

13. The next question to consider is the analysis which the Upanishadic philosophers make of the dream-state of consciousness in reference to the state of sleep. A famous passage in the Bṛihadāraṇyaka Upanishad tells us how, at the end of sleep, the soul "moves away from his nest" wherever he likes; "guarding with breath the lower nest, the immortal one moves away from his nest, to where he can roam at will—That golden person, the lovely bird! Going hither and thither at the end of sleep, the God creates manifold forms for himelf, either rejoicing with women, or eating, or seeing terrible sights." (S. 12. a). The same passage tells us how the states of sleep and dream constitute an intermediate state between consciousness and unconsciousness: "there are two states for that person, the one here in this world, the other in the other world, and there is an intermediate third state (which we may call the twilight state of consciousness), consisting of the states of dream and sleep; remaining in this third state, he sees both those states which belong to this and the other world." We are also told how the soul in this state resembles a fish moving from bank to bank: "as a large fish moves along both the banks, the nearer and the farther, so does this person move along both these states, the state of sleeping and the state of waking." And it is also said how the soul puts forth a great deal of creative activity in this state: "And there are no chariots, nor horses, nor any roads, but he himself creates the chariots and the horses and the roads; there are no joys, nor pleasures, nor any blessings, but he creates the joys and the pleasures and the blessings; there are no ponds, or lakes, or rivers, but he creates the ponds and the lakes and the rivers—because he is indeed the Maker." We see here what a great stress is laid on the constructive activity of the soul in the state of dream. Finally, we are told in a passage of the Praśna Upanishad, how dreams, even though they are usually a mere replica of actual waking experience, also occasionally involve absolutely novel construction: "There that god experiences greatness in sleep. What is seen over and over again, he sees once more (in the dream); what is heard over and over again, he hears once again (in the dream)...... ...What is seen and not seen, what is heard and not heard, what is enjoyed and not enjoyed, he experiences all, because he is the All." (S. 12. b). This must indeed be regarded as a very subtle analysis of dream-experience.

Early psychical research.

14. As the Upanishadic philosophers made this acute study of the sleeping and dreaming states of consciousness, they were not slow to take into account the aberrations of consciousness as manifested especially in the phenomena of mediumships and possessions. If we might say so, they conducted their own psychical research, however rudimentary, and however noiseless, it might have been. We have a definite illustration of this kind to show that the problem of psychical research had attracted their attention even in those old days. For example, we are informed in a passage of the Bṛihadāraṇyaka Upanishad (S. 13) how the sage Bhujyu, the son of Lāhyāyana, in his student days, went to the Madra country and came to the house of Patañchala, the son of Kapi. This Patañchala had a daughter who was possessed by a Gandharva, an aerial spirit, and who thus served as a medium. Bhujyu asked the spirit who he (the spirit) was, and received the answer that he was Sudhanvan, the son of Aṅgiras. On knowing this, Bhujyu asked the spirit two more questions: one was as to the actual extent of the world, and the other as to where the sons of Parīkshit were, who, by the bye, at that time, must have been regarded as historical personages. What answer Bhujyu received to these questions we are not told; but we see definitely how Bhujyu must, on account of these questions, be regarded as an occultist who worked according to his own lights in his days on the lines of modern Psychical Research.

The Power of Thought.

15. Finally, we must notice the very great stress that is laid in various passages of the Upanishads on what the New Psychology calls "Thought-power". "He who knows and meditates on the foot of Brahman, consisting of the four quarters as resplendent, becomes (himself) endowed with splendour in this world;" "he who meditates on the Brahman as lustre becomes himself illustrious, reaches the illustrious and bright worlds;" "when the Sun was born, all sorts of shouts rose round about him......; he who knows this, and meditates on the Sun as Brahman, him shall reach pleasant shouts from all sides, and shall continue, yea, shall continue;" "if one meditates on Brahman as support, he himself will find support; if as greatness, he himself will become great; if as mind, he himself will receive honour; if as the *parimara* of Brahman, round about (*pari*) him shall die (*mṛi*) all the enemies who hate him"; and lastly "he who meditates on Brahman as Not-Being, shall himself cease to exist; he, on the other hand, who will meditate on Brahman as Being shall (always) exist; this is what they know" (S. 14). We recommend these passages to all those who believe in the thaumaturgy of thought.

III—RATIONAL PSYCHOLOGY

No psychology "ohne Seele."

16. Modern writers on Psychology give no attention to Rational Psychology; they consider it either useless or metaphysical. As Prof. James Ward points out, modern psychologists vie with each other in writing a psychology *ohne Seele.* The ancient conception of Soul has evaporated, and in its place we find a self, which is regarded as a "centre of interest," and which is supposed to be generated when a new interest springs up and destroyed as soon as the interest terminates. The *impasse* into which such a view brings the Psychologists may be realised at a glance when we consider that some of them have been forced to recognise the continuance of such a bloodless self even after the death of the body, and in place of the old-world view of an immortal Soul we find the idea of a "centre of interest" which survives (!) after the death of the body when the interest is not fulfilled in the person's life-time. The old-world view, as in Plato so in the Upanishads, planted itself squarely on the recognition of the Soul as an entity which was free to take on a body, as it was also free to go away and transmigrate. Whatever the limitations of such a view, it was a view which one could at least understand; but the modern notion of an anæmic "centre of interest," which could continue to exist after the death of the body, passes absolutely beyond the comprehension of anybody except a metaphysician who makes such concessions to naturalism as to make an entire farrago of his philosophical ideas.

The question of the seat of the soul.

17. The first question with which a Rational Psychology may be concerned is the question of the seat of the soul. And when this question is asked, it is not unusual to answer it by taking a spatial view of the habitation of the soul. It is likely to be ignored that the soul is an unextended entity, and that as such it is bereft of all spatial connotation. And yet, Rational Psychology has concerned itself with a discussion of the part or parts of the body with which the soul comes more directly into contact. Prof. James says: "In some manner our consciousness is present to everything with which it is in relation. I am *cognitively* present to Orion whenever I perceive that constellation, but I am not *dynamically* present there, I work no effects. To my brain, however, I am dynamically present, inasmuch as my thoughts and feelings seem to react upon the processes thereof. If, then, by the seat of the mind is meant nothing more than the locality with which it stands in immediate dynamic relations, we are certain to be right in saying that its seat is somewhere in the cortex of the brain."[1] The views that have been held in regard to this question have been many and various. I. H. Fichte, as we know, supposed that the soul was a space-filling principle. Descartes imagined that the seat of the soul was the pineal gland, while Lotze maintained that the soul must be located somewhere in the "structureless

[1] *Principles of Psychology* I. 214.

matrix of the anatomical brain-elements, at which point....all nerve-currents may cross and combine." We have already seen the opinion of Prof. James that if the soul's activity is to be referred to one part of the body more than to any other, it ought to be referred to the cortex of the brain. Aristotle supposed that the seat of the soul was in the heart; and he came to this conclusion by observing "(1) that the diseases of the heart are the most rapidly and certainly fatal, (2) that psychical affections, such as fear, sorrow, and joy cause an immediate disturbance of the heart, (3) and that the heart is the part which is the first to be formed in the embryo."[1] The Upanishadic psychology agrees with the Aristotelian in locating the soul in the heart. We have already seen how important a part the "pericardium" plays in the Upanishadic psychology of sleep. The Upanishadic philosophers felt no difficulty in locating the soul in the heart; and it is not till we reach a later era in the evolution of Indian thought that we find that the seat of consciousness is transferred from the heart to the brain. It is only in the Yogic and the Tāntric books[2] that the cerebro-spinal system comes to be recognised, and it is there that consciousness comes to be referred to the brain instead of to the heart.

The heart and the brain as seats.

18. In one important Upanishadic passage, however, we already find an incipient transition from the one view to the other. Though in the Upanishads as a whole we find that the heart is regarded as the seat of the soul, in a passage of the Taittirīya Upanishad, in a very cryptic style and with a good deal of prophetic insight, the Upanishad-seer gives his reflections as to the way in which the soul in the heart

1 Hammond, *Aristotle's Psychology* p. xxiii.

2 Vide Seal's *Positive Sciences of the Ancient Hindus* pp. 218-219.

moves by a passage through the bones of the palate right up to the skull where the hairs are made to part, and on the way greets the Brahman who is his lord and master. It is important to remember that while the soul in the heart is characterised as the *manomaya purusha*, the Brahman that resides in the brain is called *manasaspati*, the soul's overlord. "What we know as the space inside the heart, therein is this immortal golden being, namely mind (or soul). What we know as hanging like a nipple between the bones of the palate, through it is the entrance to the Lord[1] on the passage right up to the skull where the hairs are made to part. *Bhūḥ*.. *Bhuvaḥ*....*Suvaḥ*......*Mahaḥ*—when these (mystic) words are uttered, the soul moves right up to Brahman. The soul gains autonomy, joins the Ruler of mind (or soul), becomes the lord of speech, the lord of sight, the lord of hearing, the lord of knowledge, becomes (in short) the Brahman who bodies himself forth in space" (S. 15). A great deal of difficulty has been experienced in the interpretation of this passage. The passage no doubt tells us that the sense-centres as well as the intellect-centre are to be referred to the brain, inasmuch as it says that the soul can obtain mastery over these only by moving to the brain from the heart; yet, the actual path which has been indicated in the above passage cannot be traced without difficulty. What is the "nipple-like" appearance of which the Upanishad speaks? Is it the uvula, or the pituitary body? Deussen and Max Müller have both understood it to be the uvula. Are we then to understand that the Upanishad-philosopher was so struck

1 Indra, elsewhere paraphrased as Idandra, ***breaking through the skull***; cf. तस्मादिदन्द्रो नामेदन्द्रो ह वै नाम तमिदन्द्रं संतमिन्द्र इत्याचक्षते परोक्षेण परोक्षप्रिया इव हि देवाः । ऐ. I. 3.14.

by the inexplicably hanging uvula that he regarded it to be the door to the overlord of soul, and are we to understand that Deussen and Max Müller took into account the experiences of the mystic who regards the uvula as the medium by which he comes to taste the nectar which oozes in the state of ecstasy from the ventricles of the brain into the pharynx ? Or, are we to suppose that the Upanishad-philosopher was so fortunate as to witness a skull dissected open and to observe that the pituitary body is situated just above the pair of bones of the hard palate, and then to be able to suppose that the soul in the heart could travel along the course of the sympathetic nerves to the pituitary body, and through it move further to its overlord in the lateral ventricle, around which, in the grey matter, are situated the various special sense-centres ? The latter interpretation is not improbable ; but one does not know whether the Upanishad-philosopher knew anatomy enough to trace the actual path, or was interested in occultism enough to see the path with his mental eye !

The relation of the body and the soul.

19. However this may be on the physiological side, we may say that the Upanishadic philosophers definitely raised the psychological question of the relation between body and soul. The Maitri Upanishad, though it is a late Upanishad, raises the question of an efficient cause, and in Platonic fashion endows the soul with the power of motion. It tells us that there were certain sages in ancient times called the Vālakhilyas who went to the Prajāpati Kratu and asked him who was the driver of the chariot of the body : " The body, venerable Sir, is verily like an unmoving cart ; may your Honour be pleased to tell us if you know who is the mover of it." And the Upanishad tells us that the answer which they elicited from the Prajāpati was that the mover of the body-chariot was the soul, "the pure tranquil, imperishable, unborn entity who stands independently in his own greatness" (S. 16. a). Moreover, the Kaushītaki Upanishad tells us that the soul must be regarded as the master of all bodily faculties, the lord of all sense-functions: "As a razor is placed in the razor-case, or fire in the fire-hearth, similarly does this conscious self pervade the body up to the very hairs and nails. These senses depend upon the soul as the relatives upon the rich man. As the rich man feeds with his kinsmen, and as the kinsmen feed on the rich man, even so does this conscious self feed with the senses and the senses feed on the self" (S. 16. b). This passage tells us how the various bodily senses are dependent on the self and how the self is immanent in the whole body.

The history of the spatial extension of the soul.

20. The passage quoted above leads to the view that the soul fills the whole of the body, a doctrine which is not unlikely to have led to the Jaina doctrine that as large as the body is, even so large is the soul,—that the soul of the elephant is as large as the body of the elephant, while the soul of the ant is only as large as the body of the ant—"*hastipudgalam prāpya hastipudgalo bhavati, pipīlikāpudgalam prāpya pipīlikāpudgalo bhavati.*" This is the *reductio ad absurdum* of a belief in the extended nature of soul, which will not allow us to think of the soul except under spatial limitations. The history of the doctrine of the space-filling nature of the soul as advanced in the Upanishads is a very interesting one. In the Bṛihadāraṇyaka Upanishad we are told that "the intelligent luminous self in the heart is as small as a grain of rice or barley, and yet it is the ruler o all and lord of all, overruling all this and whatsoever else exists" (S. 17. a). In a passage of the Kaṭha Upanishad, as well as elsewhere, we find that the soul is no longer conceived as of the size of a mere grain of rice or barley, but is thought to be of the size of a thumb —an idea which plays a very important part in the Upanishads: "The soul, who is the lord of all things that have been and that are to be, and is therefore over-awed by none of them, is of the measure of a thumb and dwells in the midpart of the body (that is, in the heart)" (S. 17. b). In a passage of the Chhāndogya Upanishad, the soul is understood as not of the size of a thumb, but of the measure of a span (S. 17. c). The soul is here called "prādeśamātra" and "abhivimāna." These words have occasioned a very great difficulty to the commentators. Śaṅkarāchārya, who understands the soul as all-pervading, cannot bring himself to be reconciled to the statement that the soul should be merely a span long, prādeśamātra.[1] Now the word prādeśa is really an important word. In the Amarakosha,[2] it is understood as meaning a span, as also in the Medinīkosha.[3] Śaṅkarāchārya himself knew that the word prādeśa was "elsewhere" used in the sense of a span,[4] which his scholiast Ānandagiri explains as being the meaning of the word in Jābālaśruti. According to Śaṅkara, the word prādeśa elsewhere signified not merely a span's length but

1 This is the reason why he explains the expression as द्युमूर्धादिभिः पृथिवीपादांतैर्विशिष्टमेकं प्रादेशमात्रम् ।

2 प्रादेशतालगोकर्णास्तर्जन्यादियुते तते । II. 6. 83. The Commentator explains प्रादेश by saying that it means तर्जन्यादिसहितविस्तृतांगुष्ठः ।

3 प्रादेशो देशमात्रे स्यात्तर्जन्यंगुष्ठसंमिते ।

4 शाखांतरे तु मूर्धादिश्चिबुकप्रतिष्ठ इति प्रादेशमात्रं कल्पयंति । इह तु न तथाऽभिप्रेतम् । C. on छां V. 18. 1.

the span's length from the forehead to the chin. This is a very significant fact as we shall presently see. In the Mahābhārata,[1] Bhīmasena has been described as being a span's length taller than his younger brother Arjuna. In the Maitri Upanishad,[2] the word prādeśa has manifestly the same meaning. Under these circumstances it is but natural that the word prādeśa in the passage which we are discussing may be taken to mean a span, especially, as Śaṅkara points out, *the* span's length between the forehead and the chin. The word "abhivimāna" has also caused a great deal of difficulty. The interpretation which Śaṅkarāchārya has put upon it, and with which Deussen, Max Müller and Rajendralal Mitra have all agreed, seems after all to be an unnatural interpretation. Thus Śaṅkara[3] explains the word as meaning one who knows himself—the Kantian "I am I"—an interpretation which does not come out of the expression "abhivimāna." Deussen[4] translates the whole passage in a way which only supports the meaning of Śaṅkara so far as the word "abhivimāna" is concerned: "Wer aber diesen Ātman Vaiśvānara so [zeigend] als eine Spanne gross auf sich selbst (*abhi*) bezogen (*vimāna*) verehrt, der isst die Nahrung in allen Welten, in allen Wesen, in allen Selbsten." Max Müller[5] translates "abhivimāna" as, "identical with himself," while Rajendralal Mitra[6] says it means "the principal object indicated by the pronoun I." All these interpretations err in under-

1 प्रमाणेन भीमसेनः प्रादेशेनाधिकोऽर्जुनात् । म. भा. V. 51. 19.

2 शरीरप्रादेशांगुष्ठमात्रमणोरप्यण्व्यं ध्यात्वा अतः परमतां गच्छति । मै. VI. 38.

3 प्रत्यगात्मतयाऽभिविमीयतेऽहमिति ज्ञायत इत्यभिविमानः । C. on छां. V. 18. 1.

4 Sechzig Upanishad's pp. 150-151.

5 Sacred Books of the East Vol. I. p. 88

6 Twelve Principal Upanishads by Tukaram Tatya p. 578.

standing too much by the preposition *abhi*. By no manipulation, however clever, could the meaning of "self" be extracted out of it as Deussen and others have tried to do. Would it not be much more natural to understand "abhivimāna" as meaning simply "measuring"? The expression "prādeśamātram abhivimānam" could then be understood as equivalent to "measuring the span's length from the forehead to the chin," and the interpretation of the whole passage becomes easy: "He who worships the Self as measuring the span's length from the forehead to the chin, and as existing in all men, he enjoys food in all worlds, in all beings, and in all selves." In fact, we are asked in this passage to worship the Soul who resides in the span's distance between the forehead and the chin, and who is therefore the master of the head, which by a consensus of opinion is recognised in Hindu thought as the "uttamāṅga" or the best part of the body. No wonder that Prof. James could trace the feeling of Self in certain cephalic movements of his, and say that "the Self of selves, when carefully examined, is found to consist mainly of the collection of these peculiar motions in the head, or between the head and the throat."[1]

The soul, both infinitely large and infinitely small.

21. We have hitherto seen some of the stages in the logical, not necessarily historical, evolution of the idea of the extension of the soul. Being first regarded as merely of the size of a grain of rice or barley, it was then regarded as of the size of a thumb, and later of the size of a span, while we have also seen that the Kaushītaki Upanishad speaks of the soul as filling the whole extent of the body and being hidden in it as the razor is hidden in a razor-case. We now come to treat of

1 Principles of Psychology I. 301.

the idea of the soul as not being restricted to any part of the body, but being verily infinite and occupying all space. The Muṇḍaka Upanishad speaks of the "eternal, all-pervading, omnipresent, subtle, and imperishable Soul who is the origin of all beings, and whom the wise alone can perceive," and the Kaṭha Upanishad lends its support to this statement by saying that "the wise man ceases to grieve when he has known this great all-pervading Soul" (S. 17. d). The Maitri Upanishad, not being able to choose between the rival theories about the size of the soul, offers an easy eclecticism by combining all of them together in a promiscuous statement. It tells us that a man "reaches the supreme state by meditating on the soul, who is smaller than an atom, or else of the size of the thumb, or of a span, or of the whole body" (S. 17. e). In this promiscuous statement it is difficult to make out which theory this Upanishad advocates. An alternative interpretation of the passage can also be offered, as it has been offered by Cowell and Max Müller, following the commentator Rāmatīrtha, but to say as Rāmatīrtha says that the soul is "of the size of a thumb in the span-sized heart in the body" does not lessen difficulties. That the Upanishadic philosophers felt the necessity of reconciling such contrary statements as that the soul is only of the size of a grain of rice or barley, and that it is all-pervading and omnipresent, may be seen from a passage in the Kaṭha Upanishad which asks us to believe the contradiction that "the soul of the living being is subtler than the subtle, and yet greater than the great, and is placed in the cavity of the heart,"—a statement which, with equal seeming contradiction, is corroborated by the philosopher of the Chhāndogya Upanishad who says: "My soul in the heart is smaller than a grain of rice or barley, or a mustard or a canary seed; and yet my soul, which is pent up in the heart, is greater than the earth, greater than the sky, greater than the heaven, greater than all these worlds" (S. 17. f). The Nemesis of the theory which attributes a spatial extension to the soul lies just in these contradictions, and there is no way out of the difficulty except on the supposition that the soul transcends all spatial limitations.

Analysis of the states of consciousness.

22. And yet, so far as the soul comes to inhabit the body, it must be recognised as passing through certain psychical states; and the analysis which the Māṇḍūkya Upanishad makes of the four states of consciousness must be regarded as very acute, and considering the date of its production, wholly extraordinary. The credit which a modern psychologist gives to Swami Vivekānanda for having introduced the conception of the "superconscious" in psychology must be rightfully given to the author of the Māṇḍūkya Upanishad. There are not merely the three obvious states of consciousness, says the philosopher of this Upanishad, but a fourth must also be recognised, which corresponds to what is usually called the "superconscious." But the word superconscious in our opinion is an unhappy word to designate this fourth state: to speak of a "superconscious state of consciousness" is to utter a solecism. And so, we here propose to use the word "self-conscious" to designate this fourth state. The soul, then, according to the Upanishad, experiences four chief states, namely, those of wakefulness, dream, deep sleep, and pure self-consciousness: "This soul is four-footed (that is, has four conditions). The first condition is that of wakefulness, when the soul is conscious only of external objects and enjoys the gross things, and then it is to be called Vaiśvānara. The second condition is that of dreaming, when the soul is conscious of internal objects and enjoys the subtle things, and then it is called Taijasa. When the person in sleep desires no desires, and dreams no dreams, that state is to be called the state of sound sleep. Thus, the third condition of the soul is that of sound sleep, when being centred in itself and being full of knowledge and bliss, it feeds on bliss : it is then called Prājña. The fourth state of the soul is that of pure self-consciousness, when there is no knowledge of internal objects nor of external ones, nor of the two together ; when the soul is not a mass of intelligence, transcending as it does both consciousness and unconsciousness ; when it is invisible, uncommunicable, incomprehensible, indefinable ; when it is beyond thought and beyond the possibility of any indication, being virtually the quintessence of self-intuition, in which all the five kinds of sensation are finally resolved ; when it is tranquil and full of auspiciousness and without a second : it is then to be called Ātman" (S. 18).

The microcosm and the macrocosm.

23. This recognition of the four chief states of individual consciousness, the waking, the dreaming, the sleeping, and the self-conscious, as well as the names which are assigned to the soul in these states, namely those of Vaiśvānara, Taijasa, Prājña, and Ātman, have played a very large part in the later more systematized Vedānta. This is the reason why the Māṇḍūkya Upanishad has been regarded as a late Upanishad. But it is to be noted that the Upanishad does not make mention of the corresponding four states of the consciousness of the Cosmic Self. In later Vedānta, the Cosmic Self as it passes through *its* four states comes to be called the Virāj, Hiraṇyagarbha, Īśa and Brahman respectively. Corresponding to the four aspects of the microcosm, there come to be recognised the four aspects of the "makranthropos," a decidedly better word to use than "macrocosm". The Cosmic consciousness comes to be regarded as corresponding state by state to the Individual consciousness, and what is in the Individual comes to be found also in the World. Even though this idea is not fully brought out in the Upanishads, we already trace in them an incipient tendency towards that view. Leibnitz's theory of representation is already present in the Chhāndogya Upanishad : "Within this city of Brahman (this body), there is a small lotus-like place (the heart), and within it a small internal space; that which is within this small space is worthy of search and understanding....Of the very kind as this outer space is, of the same kind is this internal space inside the heart; both heaven and earth are contained within it, both fire and air, both the sun and the moon, both the lightning and the stars" (S. 19). Here we see the root of the theory that the individual is to be regarded as the world in miniature, and the world only the individual writ large, and that the individual object serves as a mirror in which the whole of reality is reflected—a theory to which Leibnitz gives expression when he says : "In the smallest particle of matter, there is a world of creatures, living beings, animals, entelechies, souls. Each portion of matter may be conceived as like....a pond full of fishes."[1]

24. Another interesting problem in connection with the Upanishadic psychology is the problem of the so-called sheaths or bodies of the soul. We all know what importance has been attached to the conception of these "bodies of man" by modern Theoso-

The "sheaths" of the soul.

1 Monadology 66–67.

phists. Corresponding to these bodies, they have also recognised seven different planes, on which, according to them, the several bodies of man keep functioning. Thus, the various planes which they recognise may be said to be respectively the physical, the astral, the mental, the intuitional, the spiritual, the monadic, and the divine. Let us see what justification there can be for such a view in the light of the theory which the Upanishads advance. In fact, the only Upanishad where we find mention of a theory of this kind is the Taittirīya Upanishad. In the second chapter of this Upanishad, we are told that "within this physical body which is made up of food, is another body which is made up of vital air; the former is filled with the latter, which is also like the shape of man. More internal than the body which is made up of vital air is another body which consists of mind; the former is filled with the latter, which is again like unto the shape of man. More internal still than the mental body is another body which is full of intelligence; the former is filled with the latter, which is again like unto the shape of man. Finally, still more internal than this body of intelligence is another body consisting of bliss; the former is filled with the latter, which still is like the shape of man" (S. 20. a). Here we are told that various bodies are pent up within this physical body,—as if the physical body were like a Pandora's box,—that the wise man is he who knows that there are what may be called by sufferance the physical, astral, mental, intuitional, and beatific "bodies" of man, that every internal body is enclosed within an external one, and, finally, that all these bodies have the shape of man. It was possibly such a passage as this which has been responsible for spreading such a notion as that of the "pañcha-kośas" or the five bodies of man.

Limitations of a modern interpretation.

25. Among modern Theosophists, this theory has assumed quite an extraordinary importance. The etheric double, they say, is exactly like the shape of the human body, that it lingers a few days after the death of the physical body, that the etheric double of a child lingers only for three days after its death but that in the case of an adult it may linger for a sufficiently long time to allow for the period of mourning, that in dreams while we are having the curious experience of flying like a bird in mid-air or swimming like a fish in the seas[1] it is our etheric double which by a kind of endosmosis is transmitting its experience into the physical body, that the scheme of the five bodies mentioned in the Upanishads is only a description of the " manifest " bodies of man, and that over and above these, there are two more "unmanifest" bodies which may be called the Monadic and the Divine, the Anupādaka and the Ādi, or in Buddhistic terminology, the Parinirvāṇa and the Mahāparinirvāṇa. So far as we apprehend it, the general mistake of this theory consists in taking words for things, in refusing to see that what are by sufferance called the " bodies " of man in the Upanishads are nothing more than mere allegorical representations of certain psychological conceptions. Man is made up of a physical body, of vital air, of mind and intellect, and of the faculty which enables him to enjoy an ecstatic θεωρία. This only is what is meant by the passage in question. To ignore its mere psychological aspect and to proceed to erect an occultist philosophy upon the doctrine is hardly justifiable. The great Śaṅkara did recognise the " kośas," but he understood them as having merely an ideal existence. We have to dis-

1 The Spencerians would explain these experiences as being due to a remnant of racial experience that may have been transmitted to the individual,

criminate in thought (*viveka*),[1] he says the five different kośas, and to find our true Self beyond the physical body, beyond the ψυχή or vital principle, beyond the mind and intellect, and beyond even our beatific consciousness. He wavers,[2] however, in deciding as to whether we should identify the Brahman with beatific consciousness, or whether we should even penetrate beyond it to find the Brahman ; but in any case, he insists that the kośas or sheaths have no real existence, and that a theory which is built upon the conception of the sheaths is a theory which is " built upon ignorance."

The problem of Sheaths, at bottom the problem of Substance.

26. That the words " anna, prāṇa, manas, vijñāna, and ānanda " are not to be understood as meaning veritable *sheaths* may be seen by reference to a celebrated passage in the third chapter of the same Taittirīya Upanishad, where the author is discussing what should be regarded as the φύσις of things ; and he rules out of order the theories that "matter," "life," " mind," or " intellect " could be regarded as the principle of things, and comes to the conclusion that " intuitive bliss " alone deserves to be regarded as the source of reality. The seer of that Upanishad makes Bhṛigu approach his father Varuṇa, and ask him about the nature of ultimate reality. The father directs

[1] अन्नप्राणमनोमयविज्ञानानंदपंचकोशानाम् ।
एकैकांतरभाजां भजति विवेकात्प्रकाश्यतामात्मा ॥ स्वात्मनिरूपणम्

[2] Contrast his C. on Taittirīya III. 6 एवं तपसा विशुद्धात्मा (अन्न) प्राणादिषु साकल्येन ब्रह्मलक्षणमपश्यन् शनैः शनैरन्तरनुप्रविश्य अन्तरतममानंदं ब्रह्म विज्ञातवान् तपसैव साधनेन भृगुः with C. on Taittirīya II. 2 अन्नमयादिभ्य आनंदमयांतेभ्य आत्मभ्योऽभ्यंतरतमं ब्रह्म विद्यया प्रत्यगात्मत्वेन दिदर्शयिषुः शास्त्रमविद्याकृतं पंचकोशापनयनेन अनेकतुषकोद्रववितुषीकरणेनेव तदन्तर्गततण्डुलान् प्रस्तौति ।

him to practise penance and learn the truth for himself ; he only gives him the hint that the ultimate principle should be one " from which things spring, in which they live, and into which they are finally resolved." The boy after practising penance returns to his father and tells him that food (or matter) may be regarded as the principle of things. The father is not satisfied, and asks him to practise penance again. The son comes back with the answer that vital air may be regarded as the principle, and so on. The father is not satisfied with the successive answers which his son brings him, namely, that the ultimate reality may be regarded as vital air, mind, or intellect, and when the son finally brings the answer that it may be beatific consciousness which may be regarded as the source of all things whatsoever, the Upanishad breaks off, and we have no means of knowing whether the father was satisfied with the final answer. We are only told that this piece of knowledge shall be forever mysteriously known as the Bhārgavī Vāruṇī Vidyā and that this is " exalted in the highest heaven " (S. 20. b), meaning thereby that it is honoured even amongst the gods.

The Idea of Transmigration, an Aryan Idea.

27. We now pass on to discuss the question of Transmigration in the Upanishads, but we cannot understand its full significance unless we see it on its background, namely the form which it takes in pre-Upanishadic literature. The question of Transmigration may fitly be regarded as the crux of Early Indian Philosophy. We have been often told that the idea of Transmigration is of a very late origin in Indian thought, that it did not exist at the time of the Ṛigveda, that it was an un-Aryan idea, that, as Professor Macdonell puts it, " it seems more probable that the Aryan settlers received the first impulse in this direction from the *aboriginal inhabitants* of India,"[1] that even though "the Aryan Indians borrowed the idea from the aborigines, they certainly deserve the credit of having elaborated out of it the theory of an unbroken chain of existences, intimately connected with the moral principle of requital." Having said that the idea of Transmigration is of un-Aryan origin and that it was received from the aborigines by the Indian Aryans, Professor Macdonell is obliged to account for the appearance of the same idea in Pythagoras by saying that the "dependence of Pythagoras on Indian philosophy and science certainly seems to have a high degree of probability......The doctrine of metempsychosis in the case of Pythagoras appears without any connection or explanatory background, and was regarded by the Greeks as of foreign origin. He could not have derived it from Egypt, as it was not known to the ancient Egyptians."[2] Since the appearance of Herr Rohde's book on *Psyche, Seelenkult* and *Unsterblichkeitsglaube der Griechen* in 1894, we have come to see that the real source of a belief in transmigration among any people, under certain circumstances, lies in their own ethno-psychological development, and not in an unproven or unprovable inter-influence from one country to another. It is upon this fruitful hypothesis that we can see the upspringing and the continuance of the idea of transmigration among the Greeks from Homer downwards through Orpheus to Pythagoras in their own native land; it is upon the same hypothesis that we can see the development of the same idea among the Indian Aryans from the Ṛigveda through the Brāhmaṇas to the Upanishads, without invoking the aid of any

1 History of Sanskrit Literature, p. 387.
2 Loc. cit. p. 422.

unwarrantable influence from the aborigines of India. And thus, the idea of transmigration, so far from being merely an un-Aryan importation in Aryan thought, appears clearly to devlop stage by stage in Aryan thought itself.

Transmigration in the Rigveda : the Xth Mandala.

28. It is quite true that in the major part of the Ṛigveda, the idea of Transmigration seems conspicuous by its absence. The cheerful and joyous attitude of the Indian Aryans made it impossible for them to think too much of the life after death. They believed in the world of the gods, and they believed in the world of the fathers, and they did not care to believe in anything else. It was sufficient for them to know that the godly men went to a Heaven which overflowed with honey,[1] and that the commonalty went to a world where Yama had the privilege first to go and to gather a number of men about him,—a not uncovetable place, it seems, " of which it was impossible that anybody could be robbed."[2] Even though, then, we grant that the idea of Transmigration is not very conspicuous in the greater portion of the Ṛigveda, it remains at the same time equally true that, in certain other places, an approach is being made to the idea of Transmigration. The first stage in the evolution of this idea consists in taking an animistic or hylozoistic view of the world. In a verse of the 16th hymn of the tenth Maṇḍala which is devoted to the description of a funeral occasion, the eye of the dead man

1 तदस्य प्रियमभि पाथो अश्यां नरो यत्र देवयवो मदन्ति ।
उरुक्रमस्य स हि बन्धुरित्था विष्णोः पदे परमे मध्व उत्सः ॥ ऋ. 1. 154. 5.

2 यमो नो गातुं प्रथमो विवेद नैषा गव्यूतिरपभर्तवा उ ।
यत्रा नः पूर्वे पितरः परेयुरेना जज्ञानाः पथ्या ३ अनु स्वाः ॥ ऋ. x. 14. 2.

has been asked by the Seer to move back to the Sun which is its analogue in the makranthropos, the *anima* to the wind which is its analogue, and the *animus* has been directed to go to the heaven or to the earth according to its qualities (*dharma*), or else to move even to the waters or the plants if it so suited it.[1] This verse instead of expressing transmigration proper may be said to be putting forth certain hints towards an animistic or hylozoistic view of the world ; but the word *dharma* which it introduces is a very significant word. It is the earliest trace of a theory of *karman*, especially as the soul is asked to go to heaven or to earth according to its qualities. But a still more definite passage is found in another hymn of the tenth Maṇḍala of the Ṛigveda, where a hylozoism is advocated with even greater stress. There we definitely know that the whole hymn[2] is addressed to a departed spirit, and the poet says that he is going to recall the departed soul in order that it may return again and live. The poet says that the spirit which has gone far away to the world of death he will recall and make live once more. The spirit, he continues, "which may have gone to heaven or earth or to the four-cornered globe, which may have been diffused in the various quarters or have taken resort in the waves of the sea or the beams of the light, which may have ensouled the waters or the herbs, or gone to the sun or the dawn, or rested on the mountains, or which may have spread through the whole universe and become identical with the past and the future"—that soul, says the poet, he will recall by means of his song, and make it take on a tenement.

1 सूर्यं चक्षुर्गच्छतु वातमात्मा द्यां च गच्छ पृथिवीं च धर्मणा ।
अपो वा गच्छ यदि तत्र ते हितं ओषधीषु प्रतितिष्ठा शरीरैः ॥ ऋ.
x. 16. 3.

2 Rigveda X.58.1—12.

Too great a belief in the power of song! But the fact remains that the whole hymn breathes an atmosphere of hylozoism, and the poet makes us feel that a soul is not wholly lost after bodily death, being mixed with the elements.

Transmigration in the Rigveda: the 1st Mandala.

29. But is hylozoism the final word of the Ṛigveda? By no means. We have one very characteristic hymn of the Ṛigveda which, we fear, has not been noticed with even a tithe of the attention which it really deserves. The meaning which Roth, and Böhtlingk and Geldner have found in at least two verses of the hymn has been strangely overlooked, and it is wonderful that people keep saying that the idea of Transmigration is *not* to be found in the Ṛigveda. The hymn we refer to is the great riddle-hymn of the Ṛigveda, i. 164. It consists of fifty-two verses and breathes throughout a sceptico-mystical atmosphere. It says that He who made all this does not himself probably know its real nature,[1] and it sets such a high price on the mystical knowledge which it glorifies that any one who comes to be in possession of this knowledge, so the hymn proclaims, may be said to be his father's father.[2] It is no doubt true that even though the hymn occurs in the first Maṇḍala of the Ṛigveda, it is not for that reason to be understood as belonging to the oldest part of the Ṛigveda. For example, it advocates a facile unity of godhood,[3] which is only a later development of thought. It quotes the

1 य ईं चकार न सोऽस्य वेद । ऋ. I. 164. 32.

2 कविर्यः पुत्रः स ईमा चिकेत यस्ता विजानात् स पितुष्पिता सत् । ऋ. I. 164. 16.

3 एकं सद्विप्रा बहुधा वदन्ति अग्निं यमं मातरिश्वानमाहुः ॥ ऋ. I. 164. 46.

very same verse[1] which we find in the celebrated Purushasūkta, which has been rightly recognised as one of the late productions of the Vedic period. It even contains the famous verse[2] on the "Two Birds" which later plays such an important part in the Muṇḍaka Upanishad. All these things point unmistakably to the fact that the hymn of the Ṛigveda which we are considering must be regarded as a late hymn of the Ṛigveda, even though it has the privilege of being included in the canon of the first Maṇḍala. Nevertheless, the fact remains that the very important revelations which it makes on the subject of the idea of transmigration have been strangely neglected. In spite of the Herakleitean style in which the whole hymn has been composed, in spite of the fact that it contains allusions to such various conceptions as those of the Fire, the Cow and the Calf, and the First-born of the Law, a psychological vein is ever present through the whole hymn, and among other things, the reference to the "Two Birds," namely the individual soul and the universal soul, makes it unmistakable that the poet is darkly expressing, in his own metaphorical way, his ideas about the nature of soul and the relation between the individual and universal souls. For example, the poet asks us, who has ever seen the precise mode in which the boneless soul, the very life-blood and informing spirit of the earth, comes to inhabit a bony tenement? And if a man did not know this himself, who has ever moved out of himself and gone to the wise man to receive illumination on it?[3] Then

1 यज्ञेन यज्ञमयजन्त देवास्तानि धर्माणि प्रथमान्यासन् । ऋ. I. 164. 59.

2 द्वा सुपर्णा सयुजा सखया समानं वृक्षं परिषस्वजाते ।
तयोरन्यः पिप्पलं स्वाद्वत्त्यनश्नन्न्यो अभिचाकशीति ॥ ऋ. I. 164. 17.

3 को ददर्श प्रथमं जायमानमस्थन्वंतं यदनस्था बिभर्ति ।
भूम्या असुरसृगात्मा क्वस्वित् को विद्वांसमुपगात् प्रष्टुमेतत् ॥ ऋ.
I. 164. 4.

the seer says categorically that this breathing, speedful, moving life-principle is firmly established inside these tenements of clay.[1] Moreover he tells us that the immortal principle, conjoined with the mortal one, moves backwards and forwards by virtue of its natural power ; but the wonder of it is, the poet goes on to say, that the mortal and immortal elements keep moving ceaselessly in opposite directions, with the result that people are able to see the one but are unable to see the other.[2] These two last verses were regarded by Roth and Böhtlingk and Geldner as against Oldenberg to have supplied sufficient evidence as to the proof of the existence of the idea of transmigration in the Ṛigveda, as they rightly thought that the verses tell us that the soul is a moving, speedful life-principle which comes and goes, moves backwards and forwards, comes in contact with the body and then moves from it in the opposite direction. Oldenberg is evidently wrong when he understands verse 38 to refer to the morning and evening stars, as he must acknowledge that the verse speaks of the mortal and immortal principles. But the culminating point of the whole doctrine is reached when the poet tells us that he himself saw (probably with his mind's eye) the guardian of the body, moving unerringly by backward and forward paths, clothed in collected and diffusive splendour, and that it kept on *returning frequently* inside the mundane regions.[3] That this "guardian" is no other than the soul may be seen

1 अनच्छये तुरगातु जीवमेजद् ध्रुवं मध्य आ पस्त्यानाम् । ऋ. I. 164. 30.

2 अपाङ् प्राङेति स्वधया गृभीतोऽमर्त्यो मर्त्येना सयोनिः ।
ता शश्वन्ता विषूचीना वियन्ता न्यन्यं चिक्युर्न निचिक्युरन्यम् ॥ ऋ.
I. 164. 38.

3 अपश्यं गोपामनिपद्यमानं आ च परा च पथिभिश्चरंतम् ।
स सध्रीचीः स विषूचीर्वसान आ वरीवर्ति भुवनेष्वन्तरिति ॥ ऋ.
I. 164. 31.

from the way in which verse 31 follows immediately on verse 30 which mentions the "breathing, speedful, moving life-principle"; moreover, the frequentative (*varīvarti*) tells us the *frequency* of the soul's return to this world. It was with this idea uppermost in his mind that the poet talks, in Herakleitean fashion, of those who come hither as those who are moving away, and those who are moving back as already returning hither,[1] as Herakleitos should talk of the gods being mortals and the men immortals.

The ethno-psychological development of the idea of Transmigration.

30. We have been obliged to make this long survey of the Vedic idea of life after death only in order to prove that the three chief moments in the idea of Transmigration, namely the passage of the soul from the body, its habitation in other forms of existence like the plants or the waters, and even its return to the human form, are all implicitly found even so far back as the times of the Ṛigveda; and when these are coupled with the incipient idea of the quality of action (*dharma*) which determines a future existence, we see that there is no reason why we should persist in saying that the idea of Transmigration is an un-Aryan idea, that the Indians borrowed it from the non-Aryan aborigines of India, and that in some inexplicable way the idea found entrance in other countries and cults beyond India. On the principles of ethnic psychology, almost every nation contains within it the possibility of arriving at the idea of Transmigration from within its own proper psychological development; and there is no more reason why we should say that Greece borrowed the idea of Transmigration from India than we might say that Egypt

1 येऽर्वाञ्चस्ताँ उ पराच आहुर्ये पराञ्चस्ताँ उ अर्वाच आहुः ॥ ऋ. I. 164. 19.

herself borrowed it from India. If Prof. Keith[1] acknowledges that the Egyptians themselves believed in the possibility of a dead man " returning to wander on earth, visiting the places he had loved in life, or again changing himself into a heron, a swallow, a snake, a crocodile or a girl," there is no justification for saying, as he does, that " this is indeed transmigration, but a different transmigration from either that of Greece or India." Whenever there is recognised the possibility of the soul coming to inhabit a body as a god-like principle from without, wherever it is supposed that the soul could likewise part from the body as it came, wherever it is thought that the soul after parting from the body could lead a life of disembodied existence, and wherever it is supposed to return again to the earth and inhabit any form of existence whatsoever, there is a kind of undying life conceived for the soul from which the step to actual Transmigration is not very far removed ; while the crowning idea in transmigration, namely, that of ἀνάμνησις is a product of very late growth, and even though it is found in Pythagoras and Plato and the Indian system of Yoga, we have no reason to attribute it definitely to the Vedic seers or to the Upanishadic philosophers, unless perhaps we scent it in the rather unconscious utterance of the sage Vāmadeva that he was in a former life " Manu or the Sun."[2]

Transmigration in the Upanishads: the Kathopanishad.

31. We now come to deal with the question of the idea of Transmigration in the Upanishads themselves. We have already tried to prove that the idea of Transmigration has been adumbrated in the great

1 R. A. S. Journal 1909 p. 569 seq : " Pythagoras and transmigration."

2 अहं मनुरभवं सूर्यश्च । बृ. I. 4. 10.

riddle-hymn of the Ṛigveda. In the Upanishads, on the other hand, the idea has been most explicitly advanced. When the father of Nachiketas told him that he had made him over to the God of Death, Nachiketas replied by saying that it was no uncommon fate that was befalling him : " I indeed go at the head of many to the other world ; but I also go in the midst of many. What is the God of Death going to do to me? Look back at our predecessors (who have already gone); look also at those who have succeeded them. Man ripens like corn, and like corn he is born again" (S. 21. a). Nachiketas is anticipating the gospel, and saying more than the gospel of St. John : " Except a corn of wheat fall into the ground and die, it abideth alone ; but if it die, it bringeth forth much fruit."[1] The gospel never says that the corn of wheat is reborn ; but Nachiketas says that just as a corn of grain ripens and perishes and is born again, so does a man live and die to be born again.)

Transmigration in the Upanishads : the Brihadaranyaka Upanishad.

32. The *locus classicus*, however, of the idea of Transmigration is to be found in the Bṛihadāraṇyaka Upanishad, which goes into great details over the manner in which a man dies and is born again. We are first told how at the time of birth all the elements wait upon the approaching soul, their lord and king ; and then we are told, how these wait again upon the soul to give him a send-off when he is about to depart : " And as on the approach of a king, the policemen, magistrates, charioteers, and governors of towns wait upon him with food, and drink, and tents, saying 'he comes, he approaches,' similarly do all these elements wait on the conscious self, saying this Brahman comes, this Brahman approaches ; and again, as at the

1 St. John. 12.24.

time of the king's departure, the policemen, magistrates, charioteers, and governors of towns gather round him, similarly do all vital airs gather round the soul at the time of death" (S. 21. b). Then follows a very realistic description of the actual manner of death : " When the vital airs are gathered around him, the Self collecting together all the portions of light moves down into the heart ; and when the 'person in the eye' has turned away, then he ceases to know any forms. He becomes concentrated in himself, that is the reason why they say he is not able to see ; he becomes at one with himself, that is the reason why they say he is not able to speak, or hear, or know. Then the tip of his heart is filled with light, and, through that light the soul moves out either by the way of the eye, or the head, or any other part of the body. As the Self moves out, life moves after it ; and as the life moves, the various vital airs depart after it. Him follow[1] his knowledge, his works, and his former consciousness" (S. 21. c). It is important to notice that in this last sentence a doctrine of *karman* is being advanced, which becomes still more explicit almost immediately ; " And as a caterpillar, after reaching the end of a blade of grass, finds another place of support and then draws itself towards it, similarly this Self, after reaching the end of this body, finds another place of support, and then draws himself towards it. And as a goldsmith, after taking a piece of gold, gives it another newer and more beautiful shape, similarly does this Self, after having thrown off this body and dispelled ignorance, take on another, newer, and more beautiful form, whether it be

1 The verb *anvārabh* is understood by Max Muller and Deussen as meaning 'take hold of", *e.g.*, Deussen translates " Dann nehmen ihn das Wissen und die Werke bei der Hand und seine vormalige Erfahrung"—*Sechzig Upanishad's* p. 475.

of one of the Manes, or Demi-gods, or Gods, or of Prajāpati, or Brahman, or of any other beings. This Self, then, as his conduct and behaviour has been, so does he become. He whose works have been good becomes good; he whose works have been evil becomes evil. By holy works, he becomes holy; by sinful works, sinful. It is for this reason that they say that a person consists merely of desires; as his desire is so is his will; as his will, so his work; as his work, so his evolution" (S. 21. d). This passage is important from various points of view. It tells us in the first place that a Soul finds out its future body before it leaves its former one: in fact, it seems that the passage calls in question a "disembodied" existence. Then again, it tells us that the Soul is a creative entity, and in Aristotelian fashion, creates a body as a goldsmith creates an ornament of gold. Then again, the passage says that the Soul is like a Phœnix which at every change of body takes on a newer and more beautiful form. Next, it regards the Soul as amenable at every remove to the law of *karman*, and tells us that it receives a holy body if its actions have been good, and a sinful body if its actions have been bad. Further, the same passage tells us that "as to the man who has no desires left in him, who is desireless because he has all his desires fulfilled, his desires being centred only in the Self, the vital airs do not depart: such a man being Brahman (while he lived) goes to Brahman (after death). Of that import is this verse: 'when a man becomes free of all desires that are in his heart, mortal as he is, he nevertheless becomes immortal and obtains Brahman.' And as the slough of a snake might lie on an ant-hill, dead and cast away, even so does his body lie. Being verily bodiless he becomes immortal; his vital spirits are (merged in) Brahman, and become pure light" (S. 21. e).

33. Of this immortal existence, however, we shall have occasion to speak presently. Before we do this, we must explain what was supposed by the Upanishadic philosophers to be the fate of the ordinary soul, and especially of the bad soul. To speak of the latter first, there are various passages in the Upanishads, for example, in the Bṛihadāraṇyaka, Īsa, and Kaṭha Upanishads, which tell us that the Upanishadic philosophers believed that the wicked soul was destined to go to a "joyless" "demonic" region which was "enveloped in darkness." This conception—the belief in a Hades—the Upanishadic philosophers share with many other branches of the Aryan race. There is however, nothing on record in the Upanishads to show whether these bad souls had to suffer eternal damnation in this sunless region, or whether their stay in that region was only temporary. "Joyless indeed are the regions" says the Bṛihadāraṇyaka Upanishad "and also enveloped in pitchy darkness where ignorant and unenlightened men go after death." "Demonic[1] are the regions" says the Īśa Upanishad "and also enveloped in pitchy darkness, where those who have destroyed their souls are obliged to go." This same Upanishad adds that "those who worship what is not real knowledge enter into gloomy darkness," which idea is also elesewhere expressed by the Bṛihadāraṇyaka Upanishad. While the Kaṭha Upanishad tells us that "those who make a gift of barren cows which have drunk water and eaten hay and given their milk, themselves go to the joyless regions" (S. 22). These passages show us that the Upanishadic

The destiny of the evil soul.

1 Dr. R. G. Bhandarkar in an important article in the B. B. R. A. S. Journal makes the following interesting suggestion. The Sanskrit equivalent of the word demonic viz. "Asurya" may here refer to the Assyrian country, "Assyrian" and "Asuryan" being philologically identical, the y and the s being interchangeable as in Greek.

philosophers believed in a sunless region where the ignorant, the unenlightened, the self-murdering, and the pseudo-charitable were obliged to go after death.

Eschatology in the Bribadaranyaka.

34. As regards the other souls, a passage in the Bṛihadāraṇyaka Upanishad, which seems to be the oldest of its kind, tells us that a soul after death ascends through the regions of the wind and the sun and the moon, and comes at last to a region which is like the Platonic "Isles of the Blessed" and which is free from grief and snow, and there dwells through eternity: "When a man goes away from this world, he comes to the wind. There the wind opens for him a hole as large as the hole of a chariot-wheel. Through it he moves upward and comes to the sun. There the sun opens for him a hole as large as the hole of a 'Lambara'. Through it he moves upward and comes to the moon. There the moon opens for him a hole as large as the hole of a drum. Through it he ascends and comes to a world which is sorrowless and snowless and there remains for aye" (S. 23). This passage must be regarded as one of the oldest of eschatological passages in the Upanishads. In the first place, the passage, in itself or in its context, does not make it clear whether such a fate is reserved for all souls or for the good souls only: it speaks of souls without distinction. The eschatological passages in the Chhāndogya Upanishad, which we shall quote presently, must be regarded as of a later date, because that Upanishad goes into very great details over the respective fates of the ascetic or the householder, and consigns the one to the way of the Gods, and the other to the way of the Fathers. In fact, we find in that Upanishad a differential elaboration of the eschatological idea which is advanced in the passage from the Bṛihadāraṇyaka which we have already quoted. Secondly, it is remarkable that, as in the Upanishads generally, so in this Upanishad, the world of the moon is regarded as situated at a greater distance from us than the world of the sun. Thirdly, it is to be noticed that the Region of the Blessed of which the passage speaks is a region "without snow." Does this mean that the Upanishadic philosopher was tormented by too much cold in the region where he lived? And finally, the idea of "eternity" is already introduced in that important passage, and we are told that such a soul lives in these blessed regions for ever and ever.

Eschatology in the Chhandogya: the Two Paths.

35. In the Chhāndogya Upanishad, on the other hand, as we have pointed out, the eschatological idea undergoes a deal of transformation. There we are told that there are two ways open to the mortals, the bright way and the dark way, the "archirmārga" and the "dhūma-mārga," the "devayāna" and the "pitṛiyāṇa," the Way of the Gods, and the Way of the Fathers. It is these two paths which were later immortalised in the Bhagavadgīta[1] as they are already adumbrated in the hymns of the Ṛigveda[2].

1 अग्निर्ज्योतिरहः शुक्लः षण्मासा उत्तरायणम् ।
तत्र प्रयाता गच्छंति ब्रह्म ब्रह्मविदो जनाः ॥
धूमो रात्रिस्तथा कृष्णः षण्मासा दक्षिणायनम् ।
तत्र चांद्रमसं ज्योतिर्योगी प्राप्य निवर्तते ॥
शुक्लकृष्णे गती ह्येते जगतः शाश्वते मते ।
एकया यात्यनावृत्तिमन्ययाऽवर्तते पुनः ॥ भ. गी. VIII. 24-26.

2 The Devayāna which is mentioned in Rigveda X. 19. 1 has the same meaning as in the Upanishads:

परं मृत्यो अनु परेहि पंथां यस्ते स्व इतरो देवयानात् ।

The path which in the above verse is regarded as "different from" the Way of the Gods must be only the Way of the Fathers—Pitriyāṇa. The word Pitriyāṇa, however, in the Rigveda is often used with a sacrificial instead of a funeral connotation: of:

पंथामनु प्रविद्वान् पितृयाणं द्युमदग्ने समिधानो विभाहि । ऋ. X. 2. 7.

As regards those who practise penance and faith in a forest, says the Upanishad, whether after their death people perform their obsequies or not, their souls enter the path of light, and they move successively "from light to day, from day to the bright half of the month, from the bright half of the month to the six months during which the sun moves to the north, from these months to the year, from the year to the sun, from the sun to the moon, and from the moon to the lightning. There is a person not-human who carries them to Brahman. This path is known as the path of the Gods, or the path of Brahman. Those who proceed on this path never return to the cycle of human existences, yea never return" (S. 24. a). Over against this path, there is according to the same Upanishad another path reserved for those, who, living in towns, lead a life of charitable deeds and perform works of public utility. Such people do not indeed travel by the path of the Gods which is reserved only for the penance-performing ascetics of the forest. They travel by the path of smoke, "from smoke they go to night, from the night to the dark half of the month, from the dark half of the month to the six months during which the sun moves to the south, but they do not reach the year. From these months they go to the world of the fathers, from the world of the fathers to the sky, from the sky to the moon. There they dwell till the time comes for them to fall down. Thence they descend by this road: from the moon they come down to the sky, from the sky to the wind. Having become wind they become smoke; having become smoke they become mist; having become mist they become a cloud; having become a cloud they rain down. Then they are born as either rice or barley, herbs or trees, sesamum or beans. At this stage, verily the path is difficult to follow. Whoever eats the food or discharges the seed, like unto him do they become" (S. 24. b).

The moral backbone of Upanishadic eschatology.

36. It is not difficult to understand that these so-called paths are merely imaginary ways in which the primeval mind tried to express itself in regard to the eschatological idea; but they were not so understood for a great length of time, and dogmatic systematisers tried to justify them in one way or another, the most reasonable of these justifications being that the Sun and the Moon and the Smoke and the Night were regarded as presiding deities, and therefore the soul was understood as being given over in the charge of these deities who sent him whither he deserved. It is not difficult to see that the two paths which are spoken of in the above passage are merely mythological explanations of an insoluble problem. The great Rāmadāsa, the patron saint of the Deccan, said in his Dāsabodha that one does not need to believe in the two paths.[1] What becomes of the soul after death it is not given to man to understand; and if any credit is to be given to the author of the Upanishadic passage, it is not for having solved the problem but for having attempted the solution. Philosophically speaking, we are not much concerned with the actual stages of the ascent or descent of the soul, but only with the idea of ascent and descent. And looking at the problem in this way, one is filled with a great deal of surprise and admiration when one sees that the ideas of ascent or descent were placed on no less than a moral founda-

1 उत्तरायेण ते उत्तम । दक्षणायेन तें आधम । हा संदेहिं वसे भ्रम ॥ साधु तो निःसंदेह ॥ १३ ॥ शुक्लपक्ष उत्तरायेण । गृहीं दीप दिवा मरण अंती राहावें स्मरण । गती कारणें ॥ १४ ॥ इतकें नलगे योगियासी । तो आंताचि मुक्त पुण्यराशी । तिळांजुळी पापपुण्यासी । दिधली तेणें ॥ १५ ॥ दा. VII. 10.13-15.

tion. "According as a man's works are, so does he become." It is this moral backbone of the Upanishadic eschatology that gives it a great philosophical value. In the passage of the Chhāndogya Upanishad just next to the one we have discussed, we are told that those who have been of a "beautiful" character quickly attain to a covetable birth, that of a Brāhmaṇa or Kshatriya or Vaiśya, and those who have been of an "ugly" character speedily attain to a miserable birth, as that of a dog or swine or pariah (S. 24. c), which statement is made still more definite in the Kaushītaki Upanishad where the law of *karman* is explicitly mentioned, and a soul is said to take on the body of "a worm or a moth, a fish or a bird, a leopard or a lion, a serpent or a man, or any of these other creatures, according to his *karman* and knowledge" (S. 24. d.)

Upanishadic and Platonic eschatology.

37. We have seen hitherto that the philosophers of the Upanishads believed in a region like the Platonic Hades in which the incurables were possibly confined for ever; we have seen that they believed in a region like the Islands of the Blest, differing however from Plato inasmuch as they regarded life in this region as absolutely eternal; we have seen that they believed in the Path of the Gods which led stage by stage to the world of Brahman, whence they supposed there was no back-turning; while they also believed in the Path of the Fathers, which led the soul to supramundane regions where it lived so long as its merit was not exhausted, but when this came to an end, the soul had to descend in the shape of rain-drops and take on a body according to the remnant of its works. On the other hand, we do not find that anything like the conception of the Tartarus of Plato or the Purgatory of Dante was present to the mind of the Upanishadic

philosophers. This could be explained on the simple hypothesis that to the Upanishadic seers, as to the later Indian philosophers, the world itself was a grand purgatory where the effects of sin were to be wiped out by good action. On the other hand, we find that creatures low in the scale of evolution were " sundered as with a hatchet " from the rest of creation ; to them the Chhāndogya Upanishad denies the right to enter on the path of liberation, ordaining that they must for ever be fixed in the round of births and deaths. Neither on the path of the Gods, nor on the path of the Fathers, are these base creatures allowed to tread. They must keep up the round of coming and going : their rule is not " die to live " but " live to die." And it is wonderful that the Upanishad includes even " a tiger or a lion, a wolf or a boar," in the same category with " a worm or a moth, a gnat or a mosquito" (S. 24. e).

Variation in the conception of the Path of the Gods.

38. There is, however, a later phase in the development of the conception of the path of the Gods which we must not fail to notice. The Kaushītaki Upanishad makes a curious development in the conception of the Path of the Gods. It tells us that when a soul comes to the Path of the Gods, " he first goes to the world of Fire, then to the world of Wind, then to the world of Varuṇa, then to the world of the Sun, then to the world of Indra, then to the world of Prajāpati, and finally to the world of Brahman." It does away with the relays recognised in the Bṛihadāraṇyaka Upanishad or the Chhāndogya Upanishad and substitutes new ones. Instead of such unmeaning conceptions as the " world of day," or " the world of the bright half of the month," or " the world of the six months during which the sun is moving towards the

summer solstice," or finally "the world of the year," it substitutes "the worlds of deities" which are recognised as properly deities. Then it tells us, that "when such a soul has reached the world of Brahman, Brahman directs his attendants to run towards the soul and receive him with all the glory which is due to himself alone. He says that as the soul has reached the Ageless river, he can never become old. Upon the command, five hundred celestial damsels move towards the soul—a hundred with fruits, a hundred with ointments, a hundred with garlands, a hundred with clothes, and a hundred with perfumes ; and they decorate the soul with all the ornaments which are due to Brahman. Being so decorated, the soul knowing Brahman, moves towards Brahman. He comes to the Ageless river which he crosses merely by the motion of the mind. He then shakes off his good deeds as well as his bad deeds. His beloved relatives partake of the good deeds, and unbeloved of the bad deeds. And as a man driving fast in a chariot looks down on the revolving wheels, so does the soul look at day and night, good and bad, and all the contrary pairs. Being free from good and free from evil, knowing Brahman, he moves towards Brahman" (S. 24. f).

Idea of Immortal Life.

39. The culminating point, however, of the Upanishadic psychology is reached when we come to the treatment of the idea of Immortal Life. This is one of the crucial points in the interpretation of Upanishadic doctrine, and expert opinion has been divided on this point for the simple reason that every dogmatic philosopher has wished to find nothing but his own doctrine in the Upanishads. We, who stand for no dogma in particular, know how to understand the

Upanishadic passages on this head, because we want to take a merely historical survey of the doctrine, and not to press the passages into the service of any particular view to which we may be committed. Looking at the Upanishads from this point of view, we see that there is a systematic evolution that could be traced through them of the ideas that were held on the subject of Immortality. We are told in a passage of the Chhāndogya Upanishad that the best kind of eternal life that may be conceived for anybody is that he should be "lifted to the region of the deity" whom he has loved and worshipped during life, and that he should partake of all the happiness that is possible in that region (S. 25. a). Another passage from the Muṇḍaka Upanishad tells us that the best kind of eternal life should be regarded rather as the "companionship" of the highest God with whom the soul should be liberated at the time of the great end (S. 25. b). Not satisfied with a mere companionship, another passage declares that eternal life consists in attaining to an absolute "likeness" to God and enjoying life of personal immortality, a view which plays so large a part in the theology of Rāmānuja (S. 25. c). On the other hand Śaṅkarāchārya would be satisfied with nothing short of an "absorption in divinity" and a life of impersonal immortality. As rivers which flow into the sea disappear in the mighty waters and lose their name and form, even so does the wise soul become absorbed in the transcendent Person and lose its name and form. As when honey is prepared by the collection of various juices, the juices cannot discriminate from which tree they came, even so when the souls are merged in the Real they cannot discriminate from which bodies they came (S. 25. d). This is nothing short of a doctrine of impersonal immortality. Finally, an important passage from the Muṇḍaka Upanishad tells us that the soul of a man who has come to self-consciousness becomes mingled after death with the whole Universe (S. 25. e). Such a soul becomes a great diffusive power, whose voice is on the rolling air and who stands in the rising sun, and who may be seen in star or flower or wherever the eye may be cast[1]. Or else to express it in the words of a poet of rare imagination :

" He is made one with Nature : there is heard
His voice in all her music, from the moan
Of thunder to the song of the night's sweet bird ;
He is a presence to be felt and known
In darkness and in light, from herb and stone,
Spreading itself where'er that Power may move
Which has withdrawn his being to its own ;
Which weilds the world with never wearied love,
Sustains it from beneath, and kindles it above "[2].

SOURCES III

1 (a) अन्नमयं हि सोम्य मनः । छां. VI. 5. 4.
(b) अन्नमशितं त्रेधा विधीयते । तस्य यः स्थविष्ठो धातुस्त-त्पुरीषं भवति, यो मध्यमस्तन्मांसं, योऽणिष्ठस्तन्मनः ।
छां. VI. 5. 1.
(c) दध्नः सोम्य मथ्यमानस्य योऽणिमा स ऊर्ध्वः समुदीषति, तत्सर्पिर्भवति एवमेव खलु सोम्य अन्नस्याश्यमानस्य योऽणिमा स ऊर्ध्वः समुदीषति तन्मनो भवति ।
छां. VI. 6. 1-2.

2 आहारशुद्धौ सत्त्वशुद्धिः सत्त्वशुद्धौ ध्रुवा स्मृतिः स्मृतिलंभे सर्वग्रंथीनां विप्रमोक्षः । तस्मै (नारदाय) मृदितकषायाय तमसस्पारं दर्शयति भगवान् सनत्कुमारः ।
छां. VII. 26. 2.

3 (a) तस्मादप्राणन्ननपानन्वाचमभिव्याहरति । छां. 1. 3. 3.
(b) अतो यान्यन्यानि वीर्यवन्ति कर्माणि यथाग्नेर्मन्थनमाजेः

---

1 Tennyson, *In Memoriam* CXXX.

2 Shelley, *Adonais* XLII.

सरणं दृढस्य धनुष आयमनमप्राणन्ननपानंस्तानि करोति।

छां. I. 3. 5.

(c) अथातः सांयमनं प्रातर्दनं आंतरमग्निहोत्रमित्याचक्षते। यावद्वै पुरुषो भाषते, न तावत् प्राणितुं शक्नोति, प्राणं तदा वाचि जुहोति। यावद्वै पुरुषः प्राणिति, न तावद् भाषितुं शक्नोति, वाचं तदा प्राणे जुहोति। एते अनन्ते अमृते आहुतीर्जाग्रच्च स्वपंश्च सन्ततं जुहोति। अथ या अन्या आहुतयः अंतवत्यस्ताः कर्ममय्यो हि भवंति, तद्ध स्मैतत् पूर्वे विद्वांसोऽग्निहोत्रं न जुहवांचक्रुः।

कौ. II. 5.

4 (a) यदा ह्येवैष एतस्मिन् उदरं अंतरं कुरुते अथ तस्य भयं भवति। तै. II. 7.

(b) सोऽबिभेत् तस्मादेकाकी बिभेति यन्मदन्यन्नास्ति कस्मान्नु बिभेमीति तत एवास्य भयं वीयाय द्वितीयाद्वै भयं भवति। बृ. I. 4. 2.

5 तानि ह वा एतानि संकल्पैकायनानि, संकल्पात्मकानि, संकल्पे प्रतिष्ठितानि। समकल्पेतां द्यावापृथिवी, समकल्पेतां वायुश्चाकाशं च समकल्पंत आपश्च तेजश्च...स एष संकल्पः संकल्पमुपास्स्वेति।

छां. VII. 4. 2.

6 (a) चित्तं वाव संकल्पाद् भूयो यदा वै चेतयतेऽथ संकल्पयते। ...। तस्माद्यद्यपि बहुविदचित्तो भवति नायमस्तीत्येवैनमाहुः।...।अथ यद्यल्पविच्चित्तवान् भवति तस्मा एवोत शुश्रूषंते। चित्तं ह्येवैषामेकायनं, चित्तमात्मा, चित्तं प्रतिष्ठा चित्तमुपास्स्वेति। छां. VII. 5. 1.

(b) मनसा ह्येष पश्यति मनसा शृणोति, कामः संकल्पो विचिकित्सा, श्रद्धाऽश्रद्धा, धृतिरधृतिर्ह्रीर्धीर्भीरित्येतत्सर्वं मन एव। मै. VI. 30.

7 संज्ञानं आज्ञानं विज्ञानं प्रज्ञानं मेधा दृष्टिः धृतिः मतिः मनीषा जूतिः स्मृतिः संकल्पः क्रतुः असुः कामः वशः सर्वाण्येवैतानि प्रज्ञानस्य नामधेयानि भवंति।

ऐ. III. 2.

8 (a) एष ब्रह्मा, एष इन्द्रः... इमानि च पंच महाभूतानि.... अंडजानि च जारुजानि च स्वेदजानि च उद्भिज्जानि च

अश्वा, गावः, पुरुषा, हस्तिनो, यत्किंचेदं प्राणि जंगमं च पतत्रि च, यच्च स्थावरं, सर्वं तत्प्रज्ञानेत्रं प्रज्ञाने प्रतिष्ठितं। प्रज्ञानेत्रो लोकः प्रज्ञा प्रतिष्ठा। प्रज्ञानं ब्रह्म।

ऐ. III. 3.

(*b*) द्विधा वा एष आत्मानं बिभर्त्ययं यः प्राणो यश्चासावादित्यः असौ वा आदित्यो बहिरात्मा, अंतरात्मा प्राणोऽतो बहिरात्मक्या गत्याऽन्तरात्मनोऽनुमीयते गतिरित्येवं ह्याह। अथ यः कश्चिद्विद्वानपहतपाप्माऽक्षाध्यक्षोऽवदातमनास्तन्निष्ठआवृत्तचक्षुः सोऽन्तरात्मक्या गत्या बहिरात्मनोऽनुमीयते गतिरित्येवं ह्याह। मै. VI. I.

9 (*a*) यद् वृक्षो वृक्णो रोहति मूलान्नवतरः पुनः।
मर्त्यः स्विन्मृत्युना वृक्णः कस्मान् मूलात्प्ररोहति॥

बृ. III. 9. 28.

(*b*) श्वेतकेतुर्हारुणेयः पंचालानां समितिमेयाय तं ह प्रवाहणो जैवलिरुवाच कुमार अनु त्वा अशिषत् पिता इति। अनु हि भगव इति। वेत्थ यदितोऽधि प्रजाः प्रयंतीति, न भगव इति। वेत्थ यथा पुनरावर्तन्त इति, न भगव इति। वेत्थ पथोर्देवयानस्य पितृयाणस्य च व्यावर्तना इति, न भगव इति। वेत्थ यथाऽसौ लोको न संपूर्यत इति, न भगव इति। अथानु किमनुशिष्टोऽवोचथाः यो हीमानि न विद्यात्कथं सोऽनुशिष्टो ब्रुवीतेति।

छां. V. 3. I-4.

(*c*) येयं प्रेते विचिकित्सा मनुष्येऽस्तीत्येके नायमस्तीति चैके। एतद्विद्यामनुशिष्टस्त्वयाहं वराणामेष वरस्तृतीयः॥ देवैरत्रापि विचिकित्सितं पुरा न हि सुविज्ञेयमणुरेष धर्मः। अन्यं वरं नचिकेतो वृणीष्व मा मोपरोत्सीरति मा सृजैनम्॥ देवैरत्रापि विचिकित्सितं किल त्वं च मृत्यो यन्न सुविज्ञेयमात्थ। वक्ता चास्य त्वादृगन्यो न लभ्यो नान्यो वरस्तुल्य एतस्य कश्चित्॥ ये ये कामा दुर्लभा मर्त्यलोके सर्वान् कामांश्छंदतः प्रार्थयस्व। इमा रामाः सरथाः सतूर्या न हीदृशा लम्भनीया मनुष्यैः। आभिर्मत्प्रत्ताभिः परिचारयस्व नचिकेतो मरणं मानुप्राक्षीः। श्वोऽभावा मर्त्यस्य यदन्तकैतत्सर्वेन्द्रियाणां जरयंति तेजः। अपि सर्वं जीवितमल्पमेव तवैव वाहास्तव नृत्यगीते॥ अजीर्यताममृतानामु-

पेत्य जीर्यन्मर्त्यः कधस्थः प्रजानन् । अभिध्यायन् वर्णरति-प्रमोदानतिदीर्घे जीविते को रमेत ॥ यस्मिन्निदं विचिकित्सन्ति मृत्यो यत्साम्पराये महति ब्रूहि नस्तत् । योऽयं वरो गूढमनुप्रविष्टो नान्यं तस्मान्नचिकेता वृणीते ॥

क. I. 1. 20-29.

10 तद्यथास्मिन्नाकाशे श्येनो वा सुपर्णो वा विपरिपत्य श्रान्तः संहृत्य पक्षौ संलयायैव ध्रियत एवमेवायं पुरुषः एतस्मा अन्ताय धावति यत्र सुप्तो न कंचन कामं कामयते न कंचन स्वप्नं पश्यति । बृ. IV. 3. 19.

11 (*a*) यथा गार्ग्य मरीचयोऽर्कस्यास्तं गच्छतः सर्वा एतस्मिंस्तेजोमण्डल एकीभवंति ताः पुनः पुनरुदयतः प्रचरंत्येवं ह वै तत्सर्वं परे देवे मनस्येकीभवति । तेन तर्ह्येष पुरुषो न शृणोति, न पश्यति, न जिघ्रति, स्वपितीत्याचक्षते ।

प्र. IV. 2.

(*b*) स यदा तेजसाभिभूतो भवति अत्रैष देवः स्वप्नान्न पश्यत्यथ तदैतस्मिञ् शरीरे एतत्सुखं भवति ।

प्र. IV. 6.

(*c*) तद्यत्रैतत्सुप्तः संप्रसन्नः स्वप्नं न विजानाति, आसु तदा नाडीषु सृप्तो भवति । छां. VIII. 6. 3.

(*d*) अथ यदा सुषुप्तो भवति यदा न कस्यचन वेद, हिता नाम नाड्यो द्वासप्ततिसहस्राणि हृदयात् पुरीततमभिप्रतिष्ठंते, ताभिः प्रत्यवसृत्य पुरीतति शेते, स यथा कुमारो वा महाराजो वा महाब्राह्मणो वा अतिघ्नीमानंदस्य गत्वा शयीत एवमेवैष एतच्छेते । बृ. II. 1. 19.

(*e*) उद्दालको हारुणिः श्वेतकेतुं पुत्रमुवाच स्वप्नांतं मे विजानीहीति ।....स यथा शकुनिः सूत्रेण प्रबद्धो दिशं दिशं पतित्वा अन्यत्रायतनं अलब्ध्वा बंधनमेवोपश्रयते एवमेव खलु सोम्य तन्मनो दिशं दिशं पतित्वा अन्यत्रायतनं अलब्ध्वा प्राणमेवोपश्रयते प्राणबंधनं हि सोम्य मनः ।

छां. VI. 8. 1, 2.

(*f*) स होवाचाजातशत्रुः प्रतिलोमं चैतद् यद्ब्राह्मणः क्षत्रियमुपेयात् ब्रह्म मे वक्ष्यतीति, व्येव त्वा ज्ञपयिष्यामीति, तं (गार्ग्यं) पाणावादाय उत्तस्थौ तौ ह पुरुषं सुप्तमाजग्मतुः तं एतैर्नामभिरामंत्रयांचक्रे "बृहन् पांडरवासः सोम राजन्" इति, स नोत्तस्थौ, तं पाणिनापेषं बोधयांचकार

(*v. l.* यष्टया विचिक्षेप–कौ०) स होत्तस्थौ । स होवाचा-जातशत्रुःयत्रैष एतत्सुप्तोऽभूद्य एष विज्ञानमयः पुरुषः क्वैष तदाभूत् कुत एतदागादिति तदु ह न मेने गार्ग्यः । स होवाचाजातशत्रुर्यत्रैष एतत्सुप्तोऽभूद्य एष विज्ञानमयः पुरुषः....एषोऽन्तर्हृदय आकाशस्तस्मिञ्छेते ।

बृ. II. 15–17.

(*g*) मनो ह वाव यजमानः । इष्टफलमेवोदानः, स एनं यजमानं अहरहर्ब्रह्म गमयति । प्र. IV. 4.

यत्रैतत्पुरुषः स्वपिति नाम, सता सोम्य तदा संपन्नो भवति, स्वमपीतो भवति, तस्मादेनं स्वपितीत्याचक्षते ।

छां. VI. 8. 1.

(*h*) यथापि हिरण्यनिधिं निहितमक्षेत्रज्ञा उपर्युपरि संचरंतो न विंदेयुः एवमेवेमाः सर्वाः प्रजा अहरहर्गच्छन्त्यः एतं ब्रह्मलोकं न विंदंति अनृतेन हि प्रत्यूढाः । छां. VIII.3.2.

12 (*a*) तस्य वा एतस्य पुरुषस्य द्वे एव स्थाने भवत इदं च परलोकस्थानं च, सन्ध्यं तृतीयं स्वप्नस्थानं, तस्मिन् सन्ध्ये स्थाने तिष्ठन्नेते उभे स्थाने पश्यतीदं च परलोकस्थानं च ।..न तत्र रथा न रथयोगा न पन्थानो भवन्त्यथ रथान् रथयोगान् पथः सृजते, न तत्रानन्दा मुदः प्रमुदो भवन्त्यथानन्दान् मुदः प्रमुदः सृजते, न तत्र वेशान्ताः पुष्करिण्यः स्रवन्त्यो भवन्त्यथ वेशान्तान् पुष्करिणीः स्रवन्तीः सृजते स हि कर्ता ।....प्राणेन रक्षन्नवरं कुलायं बहिष्कुलायादमृतश्चरित्वा । स ईयतेऽमृतो यत्र कामं हिरण्मयः पुरुष एकहंसः ॥ स्वप्नान्त उच्चावचमीयमानो रूपाणि देवः कुरुते बहूनि । उतेव स्त्रीभिः सह मोदमानो जक्षदुतेवापि भयानि पश्यन् ॥ ....तद्यथा महामत्स्य उभे कूलेऽनुसंचरति पूर्वं चापरं च, एवमेवायं पुरुषः एतावुभावन्तावनुसंचरति स्वप्नान्तं च बुद्धान्तं च । बृ. IV. 3. 9–18.

(*b*) अत्रैष देवः स्वप्ने महिमानमनुभवति । यद्दृष्टं दृष्टमनुपश्यति, श्रुतं श्रुतमेवार्थमनुशृणोति....दृष्टं चादृष्टं च, श्रुतं चाश्रुतं च, अनुभूतं चाननुभूतं च, सच्चासच्च, सर्वं पश्यति, सर्वः पश्यति । प्र. IV. 5

13 अथ हैनं भुज्युर्लाह्यायनिः पप्रच्छ याज्ञवल्क्येति होवाच मद्रेषु चरकाः पर्यव्रजाम ते पतञ्चलस्य काप्यस्य गृहानैम तस्यासीद्दुहिता गन्धर्वगृहीता तमपृच्छाम कोऽसीति सोऽ

ब्रवीत्सुधन्वाऽऽङ्गिरस इति, तं यदा लोकानामन्तानपृच्छाम अथैनमब्रूम क्व पारिक्षिता अभवन्निति क्व पारिक्षिता अभवन्, स त्वा पृच्छामि याज्ञवल्क्य क्व पारिक्षिता अभवन्निति । बृ. III. 3. 1.

14 (*a*) स य एतमेवं विद्वान् चतुष्कलं पादं ब्रह्मणः प्रकाशवानित्युपास्ते प्रकाशवानस्मिँल्लोके भवति ।

छां. IV. 5. 3.

स यस्तेजो ब्रह्मेत्युपास्ते तेजस्वी वै स तेजस्वतो लोकान् भास्वतो अभिसिद्ध्यति । छां. VII. 11. 2.

(*b*) अथ यत्तदजायत सोऽसावादित्यस्तं जायमानं घोषा उलूलवोऽनूदतिष्ठंत....स य एतमेवं विद्वानादित्यं ब्रह्मेत्युपास्तेऽभ्याशो ह यदेनꣳसाधवो घोषा आ च गच्छेयुरुप च निम्रेडेरन्निम्रेडेरन् ।

छां. III. 19. 4.

(*c*) तत्प्रतिष्ठेत्युपासीत प्रतिष्ठावान् भवति । तन्मह इत्युपासीत महान् भवति । तन्मन इत्युपासीत मानवान् भवति ।... तद् ब्रह्मणः परिमर इत्युपासीत पर्येनं म्रियंते द्विषन्तः सपत्नाः । तै. III. 10. 3–4.

(*d*) असन्नेव स भवति असद् ब्रह्मेति वेद चेत् । अस्ति ब्रह्मेति चेद्वेद संतमेनं ततो विदुः ॥ तै. II. 6.

15 स य एषोऽन्तर्हृदय आकाशः । तस्मिन्नयं पुरुषो मनोमयः । अमृतो हिरण्मयः । अन्तरेण तालुके । य एष स्तन इवावलम्बते । सेन्द्रयोनिः । यत्रासौ केशान्तो विवर्तते । व्यपोह्य शीर्षकपाले । भूः.....भुवः...सुव...मह इति ब्रह्मणि । आप्नोति स्वाराज्यम् । आप्नोति मनसस्पतिम् । वाक्पतिश्चक्षुष्पतिः । श्रोत्रपतिर्विज्ञानपतिः । एतत्ततो भवति । आकाशशरीरं ब्रह्म ।

तै. I. 6. 1-2.

16 (*a*) अथ अपहतपाप्मानस्तिग्मतेजसा ऊर्ध्वरेतसो वालखिल्या इति श्रूयंते । अथ क्रतुं प्रजापतिमब्रुवन् । भगवन् शकटमिवाचेतनमिदं शरीरं....प्रचोदयिता वा अस्य यद् भगवन् वेत्सि तदस्माकं ब्रूहीति । तान् होवाचेति । यो ह खलु वाव शुद्धः...शांतः...शाश्वतोऽजः स्वतंत्रः स्वे महिम्नि तिष्ठति । अनेनेदं शरीरं चेतनवत् प्रतिष्ठापितं । प्रचोदयिता वैषोऽप्यस्येति । मै. II. 3–4.

(*b*) तद्यथा क्षुरः क्षुरधाने हितः, विश्वंभरो वा विश्वंभरकुलाये एवमेवैष प्रज्ञात्मा इदं शरीरमनुप्रविष्ट आ लोमभ्य आ नखेभ्यः । तमेतमात्मानं एत आत्मानोऽन्ववस्यन्ते यथा श्रेष्ठिनं स्वाः । तद्यथा श्रेष्ठी स्वैर्भुंक्ते यथा वा स्वाः श्रेष्ठिनं भुंजंति, एवमेवैष प्रज्ञात्मा एतैरात्मभिर्भुंक्ते एवमेवैत आत्मान एतमात्मानं भुंजंति । कौ. IV.20.

17 (*a*) मनोमयोऽयं पुरुषो भाःसत्यस्तस्मिन्नन्तर्हृदये यथा व्रीहिर्वा यवो वा स एष सर्वस्येशानः सर्वस्याधिपतिः सर्वमिदं प्रशास्ति यदिदं किंच । बृ. V. 6. 1.

(*b*) अंगुष्ठमात्रः पुरुषो मध्य आत्मनि तिष्ठति । ईशानो भूतभव्यस्य न ततो विजुगुप्सते ॥ क. II. 2. 12.

(*c*) तान्होवाचैते वै खलु यूयं पृथगिवेममात्मानं वैश्वानरं विद्वांसोऽन्नमात्थ यस्त्वेतमेवं प्रादेशमात्रमभिविमानमात्मानं वैश्वानरमुपास्ते स सर्वेषु लोकेषु सर्वेषु भूतेषु सर्वेष्वात्मस्वन्नमत्ति । छां. V. 18. 1.

(*d*) नित्यं विभुं सर्वगतं सुसूक्ष्मं तदव्ययं यद् भूतयोनिं परिपश्यंति धीराः । मुं. I. 1. 6.

महांतं विभुमात्मानं मत्वा धीरो न शोचति । क. I. 2. 21.

(*e*) शरीरप्रादेशांगुष्ठमात्रमणोरप्यण्व्यं ध्यात्वा अतःपरमतां गच्छति । मै. VI. 38.

(*f*) अणोरणीयान् महतो महीयानात्मास्य जंतोर्निहितो गुहायाम् । क. I. 2. 20.

एष म आत्माऽन्तर्हृदयेऽणीयान् व्रीहेर्वा यवाद्वा सर्षपाद्वा श्यामाकाद्वा श्यामाकतण्डुलाद्वा, एष म आत्माऽन्तर्हृदये ज्यायान् पृथिव्या ज्यायानन्तरिक्षाज्ज्यायान् दिवो ज्यायानेभ्यो लोकेभ्यः । छां. III. 14. 3.

18 सोयमात्मा चतुष्पात् । जागरितस्थानो बहिःप्रज्ञः स्थूलभुग्वैश्वानरः प्रथमः पादः ॥ स्वप्नस्थानोऽन्तःप्रज्ञः प्रविविक्तभुक् तैजसो द्वितीयः पादः । यत्र सुप्तो न कंचन कामं कामयते न कंचन स्वप्नं पश्यति तत्सुषुप्तम् । सुषुप्तस्थान एकीभूतः प्रज्ञानघन एव आनंदमयो ह्यानन्दभुक् प्राज्ञस्तृतीयः पादः ॥ .....॥ नान्तःप्रज्ञं न बहिःप्रज्ञं नोभयतःप्रज्ञं न प्रज्ञानघनं न प्रज्ञं नाप्रज्ञम् । अदृष्टमव्यवहार्यमग्राह्यम-

लक्षणमचिन्त्यमव्यपदेश्यमेकात्म्यप्रत्ययसारं प्रपंचोपशमं शांतं शिवमद्वैतं चतुर्थं मन्यन्ते स आत्मा ॥

मां. 2-7.

19 अथ यदिदमस्मिन् ब्रह्मपुरे दहरं पुण्डरीकं वेश्म दहरोऽस्मिन्नंतराकाशस्तस्मिन् यदन्तः स्तदन्वेष्टव्यं तद्वाव विजिज्ञासितव्यमिति । .....यावान् वा अयमाकाशस्तावानेषोऽन्तर्हृदय आकाश उभे अस्मिन् द्यावापृथिवी अन्तरेव समाहिते उभावग्निश्च वायुश्च सूर्याचन्द्रमसावुभौ विद्युन्नक्षत्राणि ।

छां. VIII. I. 1-3.

20 (*a*) तस्माद्वा एतस्मादन्नरसमयाद् अन्योऽन्तर आत्मा प्राणमयः तेनैष पूर्णः । स वा एष पुरुषविध एव ।..। तस्माद्वा एतस्मात्प्राणमयाद् अन्योन्तर आत्मा मनोमयः । तेनैष पूर्णः । स वा एष पुरुषविध एव ।...। तस्माद्वा एतस्मान्मनोमयाद् अन्योऽन्तर आत्मा विज्ञानमयः । तेनैष पूर्णः । स वा एष पुरुषविध एव ।...। तस्माद्वा एतस्माद्विज्ञानमयाद् अन्योऽन्तर आत्माऽऽनन्दमयः । तेनैष पूर्णः । स वा एष पुरुषविध एव ।

तै. II. 2-5.

(*b*) भृगुर्वै वारुणिः वरुणं पितरमुपससार । अधीहि भगवो ब्रह्मेति । तस्मा एतत्प्रोवाच ।.....। यतो वा इमानि भूतानि जायंते, येन जातानि जीवंति, यत्प्रयन्त्यभिसंविशन्ति । तद्विजिज्ञासस्व तद्ब्रह्मेति । स तपोऽतप्यत स तपस्तप्त्वा अन्नं ब्रह्मेति व्यजनात् । अन्नाद्ध्येव खल्विमानि भूतानि जायंते, अन्नेन जातानि जीवन्ति, अन्नं प्रयन्त्यभिसंविशन्तीति । तद्विज्ञाय पुनरेव वरुणं पितरमुपससार । अधीहि भगवो ब्रह्मेति । तं होवाच तपसा ब्रह्म विजिज्ञासस्व तपो ब्रह्मेति । स तपोऽतप्यत स तपस्तप्त्वा प्राणो ब्रह्मेति व्यजानात् ।......। स तपस्तप्त्वा विज्ञानं ब्रह्मेति व्यजानात् ।...। स तपस्तप्त्वा आनन्दो ब्रह्मेति व्यजानात् ।......। सैषा भार्गवी वारुणी विद्या परमे व्योमन् प्रतिष्ठिता ।

तै. III 1-6.

21 (*a*) बहूनामेमि प्रथमो बहूनामेमि मध्यमः ।
किंस्विद्यमस्य कर्तव्यं यन्मयाद्य करिष्यति ॥
अनुपश्य यथा पूर्वे प्रतिपश्य तथा परे ।

सस्यमिव मर्त्यः पच्यते सस्यमिवाजायते पुनः ॥
क. I. 1. 5–6.

(*b*) तद्यथा राजानमायांतमुग्राः प्रत्येनसः सूतग्रामण्योऽन्नैः पानै-रावसथैः प्रतिकल्पंतेऽयमायात्ययमागच्छतीत्येवं हैवंविदं सर्वाणि भूतानि प्रतिकल्पंत इदं ब्रह्मायातीदमागच्छतीति। तद्यथा राजानं प्रतियियासंतमुग्राः प्रत्येनसः सूतग्रामण्योऽभिसमायन्त्येवमेवेममात्मानमंतकाले सर्वे प्राणा अभिसमायन्ति। बृ. IV. 3. 37–38.

(*c*) स यत्रायमात्माऽऽबल्यं न्येत्य संमोहमिव न्येत्यथैनमेते प्राणा अभिसमायंति, स एतास्तेजोमात्राः समभ्याददानो हृदयमेवान्ववक्रामति, स यत्रैष चाक्षुषः पुरुषः पराङ् पर्यावर्ततेऽथारूपज्ञो भवति। एकीभवति न पश्यतीत्याहुः... एकीभवति न वदतीत्याहुरेकीभवति न शृणोतीत्याहुः... एकीभवति न विजानातीत्याहुस्तस्य हैतस्य हृदयस्याग्रं प्रद्योतते तेन प्रद्योतेनैष आत्मा निष्क्रामति चक्षुष्टो वा मूर्ध्नो वाऽन्येभ्यो वा शरीरदेशेभ्यः, तमुत्क्रामंतं प्राणोऽनूत्क्रामति, प्राणमनूत्क्रामन्तं सर्वे प्राणा अनूत्क्रामन्ति....तं विद्याकर्मणी समन्वारभेते पूर्वप्रज्ञा च। बृ. IV. 4. 1–2.

(*d*) तद्यथा तृणजलायुका तृणस्यांतं गत्वाऽन्यमाक्रममाक्रम्यात्मानमुपसंहरत्येवमेवायमात्मा इदं शरीरं निहत्य...अन्यमाक्रममाक्रम्यात्मानमुपसंहरति। तद्यथा पेशस्कारी पेशसो मात्रामुपादायान्यन्नवतरं कल्याणतरं रूपं तनुत एवमेवायमात्मा इदं शरीरं निहत्य अविद्यां गमयित्वाऽन्यन्नवतरं कल्याणतरं रूपं कुरुते, पित्र्यं वा गांधर्वं वा दैवं वा प्राजापत्यं वा ब्राह्मं वाऽन्येषां वा भूतानाम्। स वा अयमात्मा यथाकारी यथाचारी तथा भवति साधुकारी साधुर्भवति पापकारी पापो भवति पुण्यः पुण्येन कर्मणा भवति पापः पापेन। अथो खल्वाहुः काममय एवायं पुरुष इति स यथाकामो भवति तत्क्रतुर्भवति, यत्क्रतुर्भवति तत्कर्म कुरुते, यत्कर्म कुरुते तदभिसंपद्यते।

बृ. IV. 4. 3–5.

(*e*) अथाकामयमानो योऽकामो निष्काम आप्तकाम आत्मकामो न तस्य प्राणा उत्क्रामंति ब्रह्मैव सन् ब्रह्माप्येति। तदेष श्लोको भवति।

यदा सर्वे प्रमुच्यंते कामा येऽस्य हृदि श्रिताः ।
अथ मर्त्योऽमृतो भवत्यत्र ब्रह्म समश्नुत इति ॥
तद्यथाऽहिनिर्ल्वयनी वल्मीके मृता प्रत्यस्ता शयीत, एव-
मेवेदं शरीरं शेतेऽथ अयमशरीरोऽमृतः प्राणो ब्रह्मैव तेज
एव । बृ. IV. 4. 9-7.

22 अनंदा नाम ते लोका अंधेन तमसावृताः ।
तांस्ते प्रेत्याभिगच्छंत्याविद्वांसोऽबुधो जनाः ॥ बृ.IV. 4.11.
असुर्या नाम ते लोका अन्धेन तमसावृताः ।
तांस्ते प्रेत्याभिगच्छंति ये के चात्महनो जनाः ॥ ई. 3.
अंधं तमः प्रविशंति येऽविद्यामुपासते ॥
ई.9. and बृ. IV. 4. 10.

पीतोदका जग्धतृणा दुग्धदोहा निरिंद्रियाः ।
अनन्दा नाम ते लोकास्तान्स गच्छति ता ददत् ॥
क. I. 1. 3.

23 यदा वै पुरुषोऽस्माल्लोकात्प्रैति स वायुमागच्छति तस्मै स
तत्र विजिहीते यथा रथचक्रस्य खं स तेन स ऊर्ध्व आक्रमते
स आदित्यमागच्छति तस्मै स तत्र विजिहीते यथा लम्ब-
रस्य खं तेन स ऊर्ध्व आक्रमते स चन्द्रमसमागच्छति
तस्मै स तत्र विजिहीते यथा दुन्दुभेः खं तेन ऊर्ध्व आक्र-
मते स लोकमागच्छत्यशोकमहिमं तस्मिन्वसति शाश्वतीः
समाः । बृ. V. 10. 1.

24 (*a*) अथ यदु चैवास्मिञ् छव्यं कुर्वन्ति यदि च न, अर्चिषमे-
वाभिसंभवन्ति, अर्चिषोऽहः, अह्न आपूर्यमाणपक्षं, आपूर्य-
माणपक्षाद्यान् षडुदङ्ङेति मासांस्तान् , मासेभ्यः संवत्सरं,
संवत्सरादादित्यं, आदित्याच्चन्द्रमसं, चन्द्रमसो विद्युतं
तत्पुरुषोऽमानवः स एतान् ब्रह्म गमयत्येष देवपथो ब्रह्म-
पथ एतेन प्रतिपद्यमाना इमं मानवमावर्तं नावर्तन्ते नाव-
र्तन्ते । छां. IV. 15. 5-6.

(*b*) तद्य इत्थं विदुर्ये चेमेऽरण्ये श्रद्धा तप इत्युपासते तेऽर्चिष-
मभिसंभवन्ति......स एतान् ब्रह्म गमयत्येष देवयानः
पन्था इति । अथ य इमे ग्राम इष्टापूर्ते दत्तमित्युपासते ते
धूममभिसंभवंति, धूमाद्रात्रिं, रात्रेरपरपक्षं, अपरपक्षाद्यान्
षड् दक्षिणैति मासांस्तान्, नैते संवत्सरमभिप्राप्नुवंति ।
मासेभ्यः पितृलोकं, पितृलोकादाकाशं, आकाशाच्चन्द्रमसं

.....तस्मिन् यावत्संपातमुषित्वा अथ एतमेवाध्वानं पुनर्निवर्तन्ते, यथैतमाकाशमाकाशाद्वायुं, वायुर्भूत्वा धूमो भवति, धूमो भूत्वाऽभ्रं भवति, अभ्रं भूत्वा मेघो भवति, मेघो भूत्वा प्रवर्षति, त इह व्रीहियवा ओषधिवनस्पतयस्तिलमाषा इति जायन्तेऽतो वै खलु दुर्निष्प्रपतरं यो यो ह्यन्नमत्ति यो रेतः सिंचति तद् भूय एव भवति।

छां. V. 10. 1-6.

(c) तद्य इह रमणीयचरणा अभ्याशो ह यत्ते रमणीयां योनिमापद्येरन् ब्राह्मणयोनिं वा क्षत्रिययोनिं वा वैश्ययोनिं वा अथ य इह कपूयचरणा अभ्याशो ह यत्ते कपूयां योनिमापद्येरन् श्वयोनिं वा सूकरयोनिं वा चांडालयोनिं वा।

छां. V. 10. 7.

(d) ये वै के चास्माल्लोकात् प्रयंति चन्द्रमसमेव ते सर्वे गच्छन्ति ....एतद्वै स्वर्गस्य द्वारं यच्चन्द्रमाः। तं यत्प्रत्याह तमतिसृजते य एनं प्रत्याह तमिह वृष्टिर्भूत्वा वर्षति, स इह कीटो वा पतंगो वा मत्स्यो वा शकुनिर्वा शार्दूलो वा सिंहो वा परश्वान् वा पुरुषो वाऽन्यो वैतेषु स्थानेषु प्रत्याजायते यथाकर्म यथाविद्यम्। कौ. I. 2.

(e) अथैतयोः पथोर्न कतरेणचन तानीमानि क्षुद्राण्यसकृदावर्तीनि भूतानि भवन्ति। जायस्व म्रियस्वेत्येतत्तृतीयं स्थानं, तेनासौ लोको न संपूर्यते तस्माज्जुगुप्सेत। छां. V. 10. 8.

त इह व्याघ्रो वा सिंहो वा वृको वा वराहो वा कीटो वा दंशो वा मशको वा यद्यद्भवंति तदाभवंति।

छां. VI. 9. 3.

(f) स एतं देवयानं पंथानमासाद्य अग्निलोकमागच्छति, स वायुलोकं, स वरुणलोकं, स आदित्यलोकं, स इंद्रलोकं, स प्रजापतिलोकं, स ब्रह्मलोकं....तं ब्रह्म आह अभिधावत मम यशसा, विजरां वायं नदीं प्रापत्, न वाऽयं जिगीष्यतीति। तं पंचशतान्यप्सरसां प्रतियंति शतं फलहस्ताः शतं आंजनहस्ताः शतं माल्यहस्ताः, शतं वासोहस्ताः, शतं चूर्णहस्ताः...तं ब्रह्मालंकारेणालंकुर्वंति। स ब्रह्मालंकारेणालंकृतो ब्रह्म विद्वान् ब्रह्माभिप्रैति...स आगच्छति विजरां नदीं तां मनसैवात्येति, तत्सुकृतदुष्कृते धूनुते। तस्य प्रियज्ञातयः सुकृतमुपयंत्यप्रिया दुष्कृतम्। तद्यथा रथेन धावन् रथचक्रे पर्यवेक्षत एवमहोरात्रे पर्यवेक्षत एवं सुकृत-

धुनुते सर्वाणि च द्वंद्वानि। स एष विसुकृतो विदुष्कृतो ब्रह्म विद्वान् ब्रह्मैवाभिप्रैति। कौ. I. 4.

25 (a) स य एवमेतद्राजनं देवतासु प्रोतं वेद एतासामेव देवतानां सलोकतां सार्ष्टितां सायुज्यं गच्छति।

छां. II. 20. 2.

(b) वेदान्तविज्ञानसुनिश्चितार्थाः संन्यासयोगाद्यतयः शुद्धसत्त्वाः।
ते ब्रह्मलोकेषु परांतकाले परामृताः परिमुच्यंति सर्वे॥

मुं. III. 2. 6.

(c) यदा पश्यः पश्यते रुक्मवर्णं कर्तारमीशं पुरुषं ब्रह्मयोनिम्।
तदा विद्वान् पुण्यपापे विधूय निरंजनः परमं साम्यमुपैति॥

मुं. III. 1. 3.

(d) गताः कलाः पंचदश प्रतिष्ठाः देवाश्च सर्वे प्रतिदेवतासु।
कर्माणि विज्ञानमयश्च आत्मा परेऽव्यये सर्वे एकीभवंति॥
यथा नद्यः स्यंदमानाः समुद्रेऽस्तं गच्छंति नामरूपे विहाय।
तथा विद्वान्नामरूपाद्विमुक्तः परात्परं पुरुषमुपैति दिव्यम्॥

मुं. III. 2. 7.-8.

स यथेमाः नद्यः स्यंदमानाः समुद्रायणाः समुद्रं प्राप्यास्तं गच्छंति भिद्येते तासां नामरूपे समुद्र इत्येवं प्रोच्यते एवमेवास्य परिद्रष्टुरिमाः षोडशकलाः पुरुषायणाः पुरुषं प्राप्यास्तं गच्छंति भिद्येते तासां नामरूपे पुरुष इत्येवं प्रोच्यते स एषोऽकलोऽमृतो भवति। प्र. VI. 5.

यथा सोम्य मधु मधुकृतो निस्तिष्ठंति नानात्ययानां वृक्षाणां रसान् समवहारमेकतां रसं गमयंति ते यथा तत्र न विवेकं लभंतेऽमुष्याहं वृक्षस्य रसोऽस्म्यमुष्याहं वृक्षस्य रसोऽस्मीत्येवमेव खलु सोम्येमाः सर्वाः प्रजाः सति संपद्य न विदुः सति संपद्यामह इति।....इमाः सोम्य नद्यः पुरस्तात्प्राच्यः स्यंदंते पश्चात्प्रतीच्यस्ताः समुद्रात् समुद्रमेवापियंति समुद्र एव भवति ता यथा तत्र न विदुरियमहमस्मीति।

छां. VI. 6. 10.

(e) संप्राप्यैनमृषयो ज्ञानतृप्ताः कृतात्मानो वीतरागाः प्रशांताः।
ते सर्वगं सर्वतः प्राप्य धीरा युक्तात्मानः सर्वमेवाविशन्ति॥

मुं. III. 2. 5.

CHAPTER IV

ROOTS OF LATER PHILOSOPHIES

Introductory.

1. It has been customary among commentators of Upanishadic Philosophy to regard the variegated philosophical texts of the Upanishads as constituting one systematic whole. Thus the many great commentators on the Upanishads, such as those belonging to the schools of Pluralism, Qualified Monism, Monism, Pure Monism and others, have tried to utilise even those passages, whose import is manifestly against the particular doctrines which they are holding, as authoritative texts to prop up their own particular dogmas. The primary cause of such a handling of the Upanishads is a mistaken notion of the meaning of revelation. The Upanishads, like the Ṛigveda, having been regarded as a revelation from God, it seems impossible to these commentators that such a revelation should contain texts which are contradictory of each other. A second reason for the manifest attempt to press all the Upanishadic texts into the service of the particular dogma to which these philosophers are committed is the lack of a historico-critical spirit which refuses to see in the Upanishads the bubbling up of the thoughts of numerous sages of antiquity, each of whom tried to express as naively, as simply, and as directly as possible the thoughts which were uppermost in his mind, and which he regarded as fully descriptive of the view of reality which consciously or unconsciously had sprung up within him. As we shall see in the course of the chapter, the Upanishads supply us with various principles of thought, and may thus be called the Berecynthia of all the later sys-

tems of Indian Philosophy. Just like a mountain which from its various sides gives birth to rivers which run in different directions, similarly the Upanishads constitute that lofty eminence of philosophy, which from its various sides gives birth to rivulets of thought, which, as they progress onwards towards the sea of life, gather strength by the inflow of innumerable tributaries of speculation which intermittently join these rivulets, so as to make a huge expanse of waters at the place where they meet the ocean of life. It is thus that we see in the Upanishads roots of Buddhistic as well as Jain Philosophy, of Sāṁkhya as well as Yoga, of Mīmānsā as well as Śaivism, of the theistic-mystic philosophy of the Bhagavadgītā, of the Dvaita, the Viśishṭādvaita as well as the Advaita systems. Let no man stand up and say that the Upanishads advocate only one single doctrine. A careful study of the Upanishads, supplemented by a critico-historical spirit engendered by the study of Western thought, will soon reduce to nought all such frivolous notions that there is only one system of thought to be found in the Upanishads. For long the personal equation of philosophers has weighed with them in determining the interpretation of texts so as to suit their own particular dogmas. As against these, it shall be our business in the course of this chapter to point out how from the Upanishads spring various streams of thought, which gradually become more and more systematised into the architectonic systems of later Indian Philosophy.

The Upanishads and Buddhism.

2. We shall begin by a consideration of the sources of Buddhism as found in Upanishadic literature. It may be remembered that the end of the Upanishadic period and the beginning of the Bud-

histic period are contemporaneous, and that the one gradually and imperceptibly merges into the other. When the Chhāndogyopanishad said that in the beginning verily Not-Being alone existed, and that it was later that Being was born from it (S. I. a), we have to understand that a reference was made here to a doctrine which was to become full-fledged in the later denial of existence and the maintenance of a void in Buddhistic literature. When in his commentary on the above passage, Śaṅkarāchārya states that this may refer to the doctrine of the Buddhists, who said that "sadabhāva" alone existed before the creation of anything, he is right in referring it to the doctrine of the Buddhists. The metaphysical maintenance of Not-Being has its psychological counterpart in the maintenance of the theory of the denial of Soul. When the Kaṭhopanishad said, that when a man is dead, various people think variously about the spirit that inspired him, some saying that it still lives, others saying that it has ceased to exist (S. I. b), we have in embryo the "anattā-vāda" of the Buddhists, the theory of a denial of Soul, a theory which the Buddhists probably held in common with the Chārvākas with whom there was no soul except the body. Then again, the cry of Nachiketas—that everything that exists exists only for the nonce and never for the morrow, that objects of sensual enjoyment only wear away the vigour of the senses, that life is only as short as a dream, that he who contemplates the delights issuing from attachment to colour and sex may never crave for longevity (S. I. c)—all this may be taken to be equally well the cry of Buddhism, which is almost contemporaneous with the thoughts put into the mouth of Nachiketas, that everything in this world is full of sorrow, "sarvam duḥkham duḥkham," that every thing that exists is fleeting and evanescent, "sarvam kshaṇikam kshaṇikam." The injunction given in the Bṛihadāraṇyaka that a man who thus becomes disgusted with the world should rise from desires for progeny or wealth, and take to the life of a mendicant (S. I. d) is only too prophetic of the order of Bhikkus in Buddhism as well as Jainism. When again, the Aitareyopanishad said that all the existence in this world—the five great elements, all the beings that are born from the egg or the embryo or owe their existence to perspiration or germination from the earth, all horses and cattle and men, and finally everything that breathes or moves or flies or is stationary—all these are known by intellect and are based in intellect (S. I. e), we have here enunciated for us the root-principle of the metaphysics and the epistemology of the Vijñānavādins, when we remember that there is only an easy passage from the word "prajñāna" which is actually used in the quotation, to the word "vijñāna," which the Vijñānavādins use. Finally, when in the conversation between Jaratkārava and Yājñavalkya in the Bṛihadāraṇyaka, Jaratkārava pressed Yājñavalkya to the deepest issue, Yājñavalkya said that it behoved them to retire to a private place and discuss the merits of the question he had asked only in private, and we are told that what passed between Jaratkārava and Yājñavalkya was only a conversation about the nature of Karman, and that they together came to the conclusion that a man becomes holy by holy actions and sinful by sinful actions (S. I. f.)—a thought which was probably later reiterated in the Kaṭhopanishad where we are told that the souls take on a new body in inorganic or live matter according to their works and wisdom (S. I. g)—a passage where we have once for all laid down for us the principle of Karman which became the inspiration of Buddhistic as well as other systems of philosophy in India, but which appears with a peculiar moral force in Buddhistic as in no other system of philosophy. Thus we see that all the main rudiments of Buddhism are present in embryo in the Upanishads: the doctrine of Not-Being, the doctrine of Denial of Soul, a contempt of sense-pleasure bordering upon pessimism, the order of mendicants, the idealistic theory of knowledge, and finally the doctrine of Karman. It is true that with these rudiments Buddhism constructed a philosophy which seems to be fundamentally different from the philosophy of the Upanishads, but which as we have seen, found sufficient inspiration from them to be traceable to them as to a parent.

Samkhya in the Chhandogya, Katha and Prasna Upanishads.

3. Like Buddhism, Sāṁkhya was also a system of philosophy which was very early to come into existence. Its origin may certainly be traced to Upanishadic literature if not even earlier. It is true that the Sāṁkhya, along with its compeer system the Yoga, is mentioned by name only in such a late Upanishad as the Śvetāśvatara (S. 2. a); but the root-ideas of Sāṁkhya are to be found much earlier in Upanishadic literature. When in the Chhāndogya we are told that behind all things, there are really three primary colours, namely the red, the white, and the black, and that it is only these three colours which may really be said to exist, while all other things that are constituted out of them are merely a word, a modification and a name, we have the rudiments of the theory of three Guṇas of the later Sāṁkhya philosophy—a fact which was made use of in the description of the original Prakṛiti, made up of the red, the white and the dark colours by the Śvetāśvataropanishad (S. 2. b). We must remember, therefore, that for the origin of the three Guṇas in the Sāṁkhya philosophy we have to go to the concep

tion of the three colours in the Chhāndogyopanishad as repeated also in the Śvetāśvataropanishad. Then again, we have an interesting specimen of how Sāṁkhya philosophy was yet in the making at the time of the Kaṭhopanishad. When we are told in that Upanishad that above the Mind is Buddhi, above the Buddhi is the Mahat Ātman, above the Mahat Ātman is the Avyakta, above the Avyakta is the Purusha, and that beyond and above the Purusha there is nothing else (S. 3. a), and yet again, when we are told, just a little after the verse which we have considered above, that the Mind must be merged in the Jñāna Ātman, the Jñāna Ātman in the Mahat Ātman, and the Mahat Ātman in the Śānta Ātman (S. 3. b), we have evidently to equate the Buddhi of the one passage with the Jñana Ātman of the other, the Mahat Ātman of the one with the Mahat Ātman of the other, and the Purusha of the one with the Śānta Ātman of the other, only the Avyakta of the first passage which comes in between the Mahat Ātman and the Purusha having been elided in the second scheme for the sake of convenience, or even for the sake of metre. In any case it stands to reason that we may suppose that in these two passages we have enunciated for us Mind and Intellect, the Mahat, the Avyakta, and the Purusha,—categories which play such an important part in the later Sāṁkhya philosophy. Then also we have to note that the conception of the Linga-śarīra in the later Sāṁkhya philosophy is already adumbrated for us in the Praśnopanishad, which reiterates from time to time the nature of the Purusha with sixteen parts. In this body verily is that Being who is made up of sixteen parts, says one passage (S. 4. a); another goes on to enumerate the constituents of this Person which are breath, faith, space, air, light, water, earth, the senses, mind, food, power, penance, ritual, karman, the worlds, and the name (S. 4. b). It may be noticed that the sixteen parts that are here declared to constitute the Person are more or less mythological and fabulous in their nature ; but we are concerned here more with the *idea* of the Person with sixteen parts than with the *constituents* of the Person themselves. When the later Sāṁkhya Philosopher developed his conception of the Liṅga-śarīra consisting of seventeen parts, he must have had at the back of his mind this conception of the Person with sixteen parts from the Praśnopanishad, even though there is an amount of difference between the two conceptions. It is to be remembered, nevertheless, that the Prāṇas and the elements, the senses and the mind, which are enumerated in the Praśnopanishad as constituting the Person with sixteen parts, are also included in the conception of the Liṅga-śarīra in the later Sāṁkhya philosophy, which only elaborates these and makes the Liṅga-śarīra consist of the five elements, the five Prāṇas, the five senses, and the mind, all of which are included in the scheme of the Praśnopanishad, with the addition of intellect only. Finally, the relation of the sixteen parts in the Praśnopanishad to the Person himself is also noteworthy, as we are told that these parts are to the Person as rivers are to the Ocean, the former merging themselves into the real being of the latter, what exists really and ultimately being the Person in one case, and the Ocean in the other. "As the rivers which flow to the Ocean disappear after having reached the Ocean, their very name and form are destroyed, and they are simply called the Ocean, even so these sixteen parts tend towards the Person, and reaching him disappear, their very name and form are destroyed, and they are simply called the Person, who is himself without parts and immortal" (S. 4. c). Or, to take another metaphor, this time a realistic one, these parts are centred in the Person as spokes in the navel of a wheel (S. 4. d). In any case, it is noticeable that the conception of the Person with sixteen parts in the Praśnopanishad may safely be regarded as the precursor of the later Sāṁkhya conception of the Liṅga-śarīra, which was itself borrowed by the later Vedāntic philosophy.

Samkhya in the Svetasvatara Upanishad.

4. We have hitherto considered the traces of Upanishadic Sāṁkhya philosophy in the Chhāndogya, Kaṭha and Praśna Upanishads. The *locus classicus*, however, of Sāṁkhya philosophy is the Śvetāśvatara which gives us a fuller and more detailed account of Sāṁkhya philosophy as understood in those days. To begin with, it may be remembered that the Śvetāśvatara was written at a time when the Vedānta, the Sāṁkhya, and the Yoga were yet fused together. There was yet no definite line of cleavage between the Māyā of the Vedānta and the Prakṛiti of the Sāṁkhya, and the Sāṁkhya was, like its compeer system the Yoga, theistic in its metaphysical standpoint. The Śvetāśvataropanishad wavers between the theistic and the deistic view of the Godhead. In one place God is described as bringing to maturity Nature or Svabhāva, when he is said to preside over the process of development and to utilise the Guṇas as best he may (S. 5. a). He is also described as the Lord of Pradhāna or Prakṛiti, of individual Souls, as well as of Guṇas (S. 5. b). Like a spider that weaves a web out of the material from within itself, the one God-head unfolds himself by means of the qualities born of Prakṛiti (S. 5. c). The Prakṛiti is merely God's magic power, and God is the great magician (S. 6. a). With his powers, God is described as creating the world, while the other, namely the Indi-

vidual Soul, is described as bound in the chains forged for him by the Universal Soul (S. 6. b). In this way we get a theistic description of the Godhead, who is endowed with all activity, and the power of creation and government. On the other hand, there are other passages where God is described as living apart from Prakṛiti in a transcendent sphere, while the Individual Soul in the blindfoldment of his ignorance lies by the Prakṛiti and is caught in the meshes of her love (S. 7. a). In a true deistic spirit God is described as only the spectator of actions, as being absolutely free from the influence of qualities and as thus living apart from contamination with Prakṛiti (S. 7. b). We need not point too often that the Śvetāśvatara was written at the time of the parting of the ways between the Vedāntic, the Sāṁkhya and the Yoga Schools of Thought, which explains why we have not in the Śvetāśvatara cut-and-dry doctrines about Nature and God and their inter-relation That the Sāṁkhya and the Vedānta were merged together at the time of the Śvetāśvatara could also be proved by the way in which the Upanishad describes the tawny-coloured being (Kapila) as first created by the Godhead, who is described as looking upon him while he was being born (S. 8. a). Much controversy has arisen about the interpretation of the word "Kapila" in the above passage and doctrinaires are not wanting who hold that the Kapila referred to in the above passage was no other than the originator of the Sāṁkhya Philosophy. It need not be denied that the author of the Śvetāśvatara had no idea whatsoever at the back of his mind about the existence of Kapila, the originator of the Sāṁkhya Philosophy, but it is evident from the way in which two other passages from the same Upanishad tell us that the Kapila of the above passage is merely the equivalent of Hiraṇyagarbha, the Intermediary Person, the Logos of Indian Philosophy, who was the first to be created by God, and who was endowed by him with all powers (S. 8. b) ; while what doubt may still be lurking about such a Vedāntic interpretation of the word Kapila, which the author of the Upanishad must have had in mind, may finally be set at rest by the consideration of a last passage from the Śvetāśvatara, where we are told that it was Brahmā, the Creator, who was first created by the Godhead as intermediary between himself and creation (S. 8. c), thus placing beyond the shadow of a doubt the identity of the Kapila Ṛishi of Śvetāśvatara V. 2 with the Hiraṇyagarbha of Śvetāśvatara III. 4 and IV. 12, as well as the Brahmā, the Creator, of Śvetāśvatara VI. 18.

The Upanishads and Yoga.

5. As for the roots of the Yoga system, we must also turn to the Śvetāśvatara, which is its *locus classicus*. There is a passage of a very peculiar interest in the second chapter of the Śvetāśvatara which gives us the rudiments of the practice and philosophy of the Yoga doctrine as later formulated. It may be seen that in the first place it calls our attention to the posture of the body at the time of practising the Yoga. Anticipating the Bhagavadgītā, it tells us that we should hold the trunk, the neck, and the head in a straight line at the time of meditation. No elaborate scheme of Āsanas is yet furnished, which was to form the principal theme of the New Upanishads, especially those pertaining to Yoga which brought Rājayoga into line with Haṭhayoga. Then, secondly, we are advised to control our senses by means of mind, a process equivalent to the later Pratyāhāra. Thirdly, we are told to re-

gulate our breath, implying that it should be made rhythmical, which practice may be called the precursor of the later Prāṇāyāma. Fourthly, we are told that the environment in which one should practise meditation should be pure, and free from sand and fire, as well as sounds and water-pools, and that as far as possible, the meditation should be practised in the recesses of a cave. Fifthly, we are informed of the harbingers of a spiritul day-light to come, namely the forms of mist and smoke, the sun and the fire, as well as other appearances which will be discussed in the last chapter of this work. Sixthly, we are led into the secret of the physiological effects produced by the "fire of Yoga". We are told that one who practises Yoga becomes ageless and immortal; and that he feels his body to be light and completely healthy. Lastly, the Śvetāśvatara immediately carries us to the highest result secured by the practice of Yoga, namely, to the state of Samādhi, where the Individual Soul sees the Universal Soul and becomes one with him (S. 9. a), a fact adumbrated in the famous Yoga-Sūtra—*tadā drashṭuḥ svarūpe avasthānam.* The process of Dhāraṇā and Dhyāna as preparatory to Samādhi are not separately mentioned in this Upanishad for the reason that both of them may be seen to be parts of, and thus capable of being incorporated in, the highest state, namely, that of Samādhi. The Kaṭhopanishad, however, makes mention of Dhāraṇā and tells us that this consists in a continued equanimity of the senses, mind, and intellect, and calls it the highest state of Yoga (S. 9. b); while the Dhyāna is also mentioned in the Śvetāśvatara I. 14, where we are asked to meditate upon the Godhead and to bring him out of the recess of our heart (S. 9. c). We thus see that if we just add the Yama and the Niyama of later Yogic philosophy to the various elements of Yoga as mentioned in the old Upanishads, namely, the Āsana, the Prāṇāyāma, the Pratyāhāra, the Dhāraṇā and the Dhyāna, all as preparatory to Samādhi, we have the full-fledged eight-fold scheme of the Yoga, or the Way to Spiritual Realisation. Moreover, the deistic conception of God as advanced in the Yoga-Sūtras, especially in a Sūtra like *kleśakarmavipākāśayaiḥ aparāmṛishṭaḥ purusha-viśesha Īśvaraḥ*, is already present in the Upanishads when, as in the Muṇḍaka, we are told that the Universal Soul merely looks on, while the Individual Soul is engaged in the enjoyment of Prakṛiti, or, as in the Kaṭha, the Godhead is described as being beyond the reach of the sorrows of the world, just as the Sun, who is the eye of the world, is beyond the reach of the defects of vision (S. 9. d). Finally, the physiological basis of Yoga was being already discussed in the days of the Kaushītaki and the Maitri, when it seems an impetus was being given to physiological thought, which, as later advanced by the embryological and other discussions in the Garbhopanishad, was to pave the way for a physiology which was to be at the root of the systems propounded by Charaka, Agniveśa and others. Thus in the Maitri Upanishad an enumeration is made of the seven Dhātus : bone, skin, muscle, marrow, flesh, semen and blood ; of the four Malas, namely, mucus, tears, fæces, and urine ; and of the three Doshas, namely, wind, bile, and phlegm (S. 9. e); and in the Kaushītaki Upanishad we are told that the blood-vessels that go from the heart to the Purītat are as small as a hair divided thousand-fold, and that they are either tawny-coloured, or white,or dark, or yellow, or red (S. 9. f). With a little variation these blood-vessels were described, before the time of the Kaushītaki, in the Chhāndogya, as being tawny, white, blue, yellow and red (S. 9. g), and in the Bṛihadāraṇyaka as white, blue, tawny, green and red

(S. 9. h). Whatever we may say about the "white" blood-vessels or "yellow" blood-vessels and the rest, it is evident that the authors of these passages knew at least the distinction between the blue and the red blood-vessels, a fact of great physiological importance. It was the study of Yoga which was the cause of the rise of physiological science which was the precursor of the later full-fledged systems of medicine.

The Upanishads and Nyaya-Vaiseshika.

6. The mention of blood-vessels and the Purītat takes us to another subject, namely, the source of certain Nyāya-Vaiśeshika doctrines as found in the Upanishads. It may easily be seen that the Upanishads are in a sense entirely different in their tenor and argument from the systems that go under the names of Nyāya-Vaiśeshika. While the business of the Vaiśeshika philosophy is to make a catalogue of ultimate existences in Nature, and of Nyāya philosophy to discuss the nature of dialectic and its aberrations, the Upanishads aim at stating as simply as possible the metaphysical doctrine of Ātman. The only point of contact, it seems, between the Nyāya-Vaiśeshika on the one hand and the Upanishads on the other, so far as their metaphysics is concerned, is the conception of the *Summum Bonum* or Moksha which the Nyāya-Vaiśeshika systems derive from the Upanishads. Moreover the Nyāya-Vaiśeshika systems of philosophy require a highly developed stage of logical thought which would care more for the instrument of knowledge than for knowledge itself. Hence we do not find many traces of the Nyāya-Vaiśeshika doctrine in the Upanishads. But the doctrine of the Purītat as advanced in the Upanishads has been bodily taken by the Nyāya and Vaiśeshika systems of philosophy, and a change for the better has been also introduced in that

doctrine by those systems. While the Bṛihadāraṇyakopanishad tells us, probably for the first time in the history of Upanishadic Thought, that at the time of sleep, the Soul moves by the Nāḍis to the Purītat, in which it takes lodgment and causes the physiological action of sleep (S. 10. a), the Nyāya philosophy takes up this idea from the Bṛihadāraṇyaka, only substitutes Mind for Soul, and says that it is the Mind which thus moves through the arteries to the Purītat, and it is only when the Mind is lodged in the Purītat that sleep occurs. The principal reason for the change thus introduced by the Nyāya Philosophy seems to be, probably, that one could easily predicate sleep about the Mind, but could never predicate it about the Soul, which must be regarded as always un-sleeping! Secondly, the Vaiśeshika philosophy itself, particularly in its enumeration of the Dravyas, namely the five different Elements along with Kāla, Manas and Ātman, the Dik being included in the Ākāśa, is indebted to many passages from the Upanishads where the five Elements are mentioned along with other conceptions, as for example, to the passage in the Śvetāśvatara where we are told that the Ātman is the Time of Time, and that the Elements, namely, earth, water, fire, air and ether are merely his handiwork (S. 10. b). Finally, when the Chhāndogya Upanishad says that it is the Ākāśa or ether which is the carrier of sound,—for we are told, it is by Ākāśa that man calls, it is by Ākāśa that man hears, it is by Ākāśa that man is able to hear the echo of a sound (S. 10. c),—we are introduced to a conception which later played such an important part in the Naiyāyika philosophy when it defined Ākāśa by its principal mark, namely, that of being the carrier of sound. The Mīmānsā doctrine, on the other hand, it may be remembered by the bye, is more scientifically correct than the

Upanishadic-Naiyāyika doctrine when it tells us that it is the air which is the carrier of sound and not ether — a fact corroborated by modern science.

The Upanishads and Mimansa.

7. The Mīmānsā school of thought, by the very nature of its ritualistic problems, has not much in common with Upanishadic philosophy, whose business it is to consider the nature of the Ultimate. But there is one very important philosophical doctrine of the Mīmānsakas which has been advocated by the Īśāvāsyopanishad. This Upanishad tells us that " those who walk on the path of ignorance, namely, that of works, go to pitchy darkness ; while those who walk on the path of knowledge go to greater darkness still. Ignorance leads to the one result, while knowledge leads to the other. This is what we have heard from the Sages, who have told us about the nature of ignorance and knowledge. But he, who knows both the path of ignorance and the path of knowledge together, by his knowledge of the one is able to cross the bund of death, and by his knowledge of the other to attain to immortality " (S.11). This very important quotation from the Īśāvāsyopanishad tells us the way of synthesis out of the conflicting claims of works and knowledge. On the one hand, mere works are insufficient, on the other, mere knowledge is insufficient. The Pūrva Mīmānsā which advocates the one and the Uttara Mīmānsā which advocates the other may both be said to take partial views. As against both these the Īśāvāsyopanishad tells us that he who knows how to reconcile the claims of both works and knowledge is able to extricate himself from the evils inherent in either and to enjoy the advantages of both by going beyond both of them. We know how in later times there was a very great con-

flict between the schools of Prabhākara, Kumārilabhaṭṭa and Śaṅkara, the first maintaining that absolution could be attained only by means of works,—and knowledge itself he regarded as work,—the second maintaining that absolution could be attained only by a combination of knowledge and works, and the third maintaining that absolution must be attained only by knowledge. The Īśāvāsyopanishad puts forth an idea which supports neither the doctrine of Prabhākara on the one hand, nor the doctrine of Śaṅkara on the other, but only the doctrine of Kumārilabhaṭṭa that absolution is to be obtained by a combination of knowledge and works, while it even goes beyond Kumārilabhaṭṭa in asserting that both knowledge and works are to be negated in the higher synthesis of realisation. As Kumārilabhaṭṭa said a bird could not fly in the heaven merely by one wing, but only by means of both wings together, similarly, says the Īśāvāsya, man must reconcile the claims of both knowledge and works to be able to soar in the regions of the Infinite, the synthesis of soaring being even superior to the fact of equipoise. We thus see how the Īśāvāsyopanishad puts forth a theory which later became the pivot of the doctrine of the moderate Mīmānsakas, supporting as it does neither the doctrine of the ultra-Mīmānsakas, nor that of the ultra-Vedāntists.

The Upanishads and Saivism.

8. As for the roots of Śaivism in the Upanishads, we must turn again to the Śvetāśvatara. Even though Umā as a heavenly damsel is mentioned so far back as the Kenopanishad, still, for a detailed and systematic philosophy of Śaivism, we must necessarily turn to the Śvetāśvatara. It is true that the conception of Rudra-Śiva was being developed since the days of the Ṛigveda and the Atharvaveda;

but it is only when we come to the time of Śvetāśvatara that we find the doctrine of Śiva placed on a more or less philosophical foundation. We are told in this Upanishad that "it is the God Īśa who supports both the mutable and the immutable, the manifest and the unmanifest. As contrasted with Him is the powerless Ātman, who is bound on account of his being the enjoyer of the fruits of action; but that, when this Ātman knows the Īśa, he is relieved of his bonds, namely, the Pāśas" (S. 12. a). The philosophy of Paśu, Pati, and Pāśa is thus to be already seen in an embryonic stage in the Śvetāśvatara. "Rudra is the only Lord God. They do not maintain another God. He who rules these worlds by means of his powers, standing before every man's face, and destroying the created world in anger at the time of the Great End (S. 12. b)—He is the Lord Śiva, who, hidden in all beings, is the sole enveloper of the universe, who is like the very subtle film at the top of ghee, by the knowledge of whom alone comes freedom from the meshes of ignorance" (S. 12. c). "Verily does the God spread manifold the meshes in his hands, and move on the surface of this globe. He creates and recreates and maintains his sovereignty over all the worlds" (S. 12. d). In this fashion is the God Rudra, who is identified with Śiva or Īśa, magnified in the Śvetāśvatara as the only Lord God who is the Supreme Soul of Souls and who is the Governor of the universe, by the knowledge of whom alone the individual Soul, who is bound down in the meshes of ignorance, can attain absolution. This was the manner in which the Śvetāśvatara paved the way for later Śaivism, its theistic way of glorification, suffused with a trinitarian monism, becoming the pivot of the doctrines of Kāśmir Śaivism and Southern Śaivism.

Phraseological and Ideological identities between the Upanishads and the Bhagavadgita.

9. When we come to discuss the relation between the Upanishads and the Bhagavadgītā, we must observe at the outset that a full discussion of this problem cannot be attempted at the short space at our disposal in this chapter. The problem is so interesting and so wide that a full discussion of it could be attempted only in a separate treatise. It is necessary for us nevertheless to indicate the main lines of the relation between the Upanishads and the Bhagavadgītā at this place. There is an amount of truth in the famous verse which tells us that "the Upanishads are like a cow, Kṛishṇa like a milk-man, Arjuna like the calf that is sent to the udders of the cow before milking, and the Bhagavadgītā like the milk-nectar that is churned from the udders of the cow." As illustrations of the way in which the Bhagavadgītā borrows ideas, phrases and even sentences from the Upanishads, we have to note how the verse from the Kaṭhopanishad which tells us that "the Ātman is never born nor is ever killed, he never comes from anything, nor becomes anything, he is unborn, imperishable, eternal, has existed from all eternity, and is not killed even when the body is killed" (S. 13. a) is reproduced almost word for word in Bhagavadgītā II. 20; as well as that other verse from the Kaṭha which tells us that "when a killer thinks he is killing and when the killed thinks he is being killed, neither of them verily knows, for the Ātman is neither killed nor ever kills," (S. 13. b) is reproduced in those very words in Bhagavadgītā II. 19. Then again we see how a verse from the Kaṭhopanishad which tells us that "the Ātman is not even so much as heard of by many, that even hearing Him people do not know Him, that the speaker of the Ātman is a miracle, that the obtainer of Him must have exceed-

ing insight, that he who comes to know him after being instructed by such a wise man is himself a miracle" (S. 13. c) is paraphrased and adopted in Bhagavadgītā II. 29; while another verse from the same Upanishad "What word the Vedas declare, what word the penances busy themselves about, what word inspires the life of spiritual discipleship, that word, briefly I tell thee, is Om" (S. 13. d) is also reproduced almost word for word in Bhagavadgītā VIII. 13. Finally, the conception of Devayāna and Pitṛiyāṇa, the path of the Gods and the path of the Fathers (S. 13. e), which the Upanishads, as we have seen, themselves borrowed from the Vedas, was handed over by them to the Bhagavadgītā, which, in a very crisp description of the two paths (VIII. 24-25), tells us, in the very same strain as the Upanishads, that those who move by the path of the Gods move towards Brahman, while those who go by the path of the Fathers return by the path by which they have gone.

Development of the Bhagavadgita over the Upanishads.

10. So far we have considered the passages from the Bhagavadgītā and the Upanishads which are substantially idenical from the point of view of either phraseology or ideology. We shall now consider those passages and ideas from the Upanishads which the Bhagavadgīta has borrowed, transformed, and developed, so as to suit its own particular philosophy. The verse from the Īśāvāsyopanishad which tells us in a spirit of apparent contradiction that "a man should spend his life-time only in doing actions, for it is only thus that he may hope to be untainted by action" (S. 14. a), has supplied the Bhagavadgītā with an idea so prolific of consequences that the Bhagavadgītā has deemed it fit to erect a whole philosophy of Karmayoga upon it. As we may also point out in the chapter on the Ethics of the Upanishads, this passage supplies us with the means as well as the goal of moral life, without giving us the connecting link between them. As we shall see later, the principal theme of the Bhagavadgītā is to teach a life of activity coupled with the effects of actionlessness through the intermediate linkage of un-attachment to and indifference to the fruits of action. Secondly, when in the Muṇḍakopanishad we find the description of the Cosmic Person with fire as his head, the sun and the moon as his eyes, the quarters as his ears, the Vedas as his speech, air as his Prāṇa, the universe as his heart, and the earth as his feet (S. 14. b), we have in embryo a description of the Viśvarūpa which later became the theme of the famous Eleventh Chapter of the Bhagavadgītā on the transfigured personality of Kṛishṇa. It is true at the same time that the Muṇḍakopanishad probably borrows the idea from the Purushasūkta, but it is equally true to say that it supplies the Bhagavadgītā with a text upon which the latter enlarges, and evolves the conception of the Cosmic Person, who fills all, who is all-powerful, to whom the past and the future are like an eternal now, submission to whom and assimilation to whom constitute the ends of mortal endeavour. Then, thirdly, while the Kaṭhopanishad gives us a scheme of psychological and metaphysical existences mixed together in a famous passage where it declares that beyond the senses are the objects, beyond the objects is mind, beyond the mind is intellect, beyond the intellect is Mahat, beyond the Mahat is the Avyakta, and finally beyond the Avyakta is the Purusha, beyond whom and outside whom there is nothing else (S. 14. c), the Bhagavadgītā simplifies the scheme very much by retaining only the psychological categories and doing away with the metaphysical, for the simple reason that it understands the passage to have a psychological rather than a metaphysical significance. Thus, when the Bhagavadgītā in III. 42 tells us that beyond the senses is mind, that beyond the mind is intellect, and that beyond intellect is the Purusha, it drops out altogether the categories of the objective world,—the Mahat and the Avyakta,—retains only the psychological categories and simplifies the scheme immensely. Finally, the devotional impulse which beats in the heart of Nārada when he implores Sanatkumāra to initiate him into spiritual wisdom (S. 15. a), as well as the equally fervent emotional attitude of Bṛihadratha when he requests Śākāyanya to lift him out of the mire of existence like a frog from a waterless well (S. 15. b),—which emotional attitudes may be seen to be strangely in contrast with the otherwise generally dry intellectual argumentation of the Upanishads,—become later almost the foundation-stone for the theistic-mystic philosophy of the Bhagavadgītā, in which the dry intellectualism and the speculative construction of the Upanishads disappear, and we have the rare combination of poetry and philosophy which makes the "Upāsanā" of the Śvetāśvatara (S. 15. c), or "Bhakti" to God as to Guru (S. 15. d) the *sine quâ non* of a truly mystic life, whose end is the realisation of God.

The Aśvattha in the Upanishads and the Bhagavadgītā.

11. In one important respect, however, the Bhagavadgītā takes a position almost antagonistic to the position advanced in the Upanishads. In the Kaṭhopanishad, we have the description of "the eternal Aśvattha tree with its root upwards and branches downwards, which is the pure immortal Brahman, in which all these worlds are situated, and beyond which there is nothing else" (S. 16). In this passage we are told that the Aśvattha tree is the Brahman itself, and that it is imperishable. On the other hand, the Bhagavadgītā, at the opening of its 15th Chapter, tells us that "the Aśvattha tree has its root upwards and branches downwards. Its leaves are the Vedas. It sends out its branches both downwards and upwards, which are nourished by the Guṇas. The sensual objects are its foliage. Yet again, its infinite roots spread downwards in the form of action in the human world. It is not possible to have a glimpse of that tree here in this fashion. It has neither end, nor beginning, nor any stationariness whatsoever. After having cut off this Aśvattha tree, which has very strong roots, by the forceful weapon of unattachment, we should then seek after that celestial abode from which there is no return, and reach the primeval Person, from whom all existence has sprung of old" (XV. 1-4). We are not concerned here to discuss the merits or demerits of this description of the Aśvattha tree in the Bhagavadgītā. We shall not consider the contradictions that are introduced in this description, but we are concerned here only to find how far this description from the Bhagavadgītā agrees with the description in the Kaṭhopanishad. It may be noted at once that there is an agreement between the Upanishad and the Bhagavadgītā so far as the Aśvattha tree is regarded as having its root upwards and its branches downwards. But, while the Upanishad teaches that the Aśvattha tree is real, and identical with Brahman, and therefore impossible of being cut off, the Bhagavadgītā teaches that the Aśvattha tree must be regarded as unreal, and as identical with existence, and therefore that it is necessary to cut off this tree of existence by the potent weapon of non-attachment. The two descriptions seem to be almost at daggers drawn. It may be noticed by students of comparative mythology that the descriptions of the Aśvattha tree in the Upanishad and in the Bhagavadgītā have an analogue in the description of the tree Igdrasil in Scandinavian mythology. It is important to notice also that the description of the Igdrasil agrees with that of the Upanishads in making the tree identical with Reality, and therefore having a real concrete existence. On the other hand, it agrees with the Bhagavadgītā in making the actions, the motives, and the histories of mankind the boughs and branches of this tree of existence. We cannot do better than quote in this place Carlyle's famous description of the tree Igdrasil: "All Life is figured by them as a Tree. Igdrasil, the Ash-tree of Existence, has its roots deep down in the kingdoms of Hela or Death; its trunk reaches up heaven-high, spreads its boughs over the whole Universe; it is the Tree of Existence. At the foot of it, in the Death-kingdom, sit Three *nornas* Fates,—the Past, Present, Future; watering its root from the Sacred Well. Its 'boughs,' with their buddings and disleafings,—events, things suffered, things done, catastrophes,—stretch through all lands and times. Is not every leaf of it a biography, every fibre there an act or word? Its boughs are Histories of Nations. The rustle of it is the noise of Human Existence, onwards from of old. It grows there, the breath of Human Passion rustling through it;—or storm-tost, the stormwind howling through it like the voice of all the gods. It is Igdrasil, the Tree of Existence. It is the past, the present and the future; what was done, what is doing, what will be done; the infinite conjugation of the verb To do." It is unfortunate that the Scandinavian description should have placed the roots of the Ash tree deep down in the kingdoms of Hela or Death, and even though its trunk is described as reaching up heaven-high, it were much to be wished that its roots had come from the region of the life eternal. In that respect, both the Bhagavadgītā and the Upanishads have a distinct advantage over the Scandinavian mythology.

The Krishna of the Chhandogya and the Krishna of the Bhagavadgita.

12. We must not forget, however, to discuss the merits of a question which has assumed some importance at the hands of certain modern interpreters of the Bhagavadgītā and the Upanishads, especially because it seems to us that these interpreters have raised a dust and complain that they cannot see. In the Chhāndogya, there is the mention of a Kṛishṇa who was the son of Devakī, and these interpreters feel no difficulty in facilely identifying him with Kṛishṇa, the son of Devakī, who was the divine hero of the Mahābhārata. We shall see how futile such an identification is. But before we go on to this discussion, we must state first the meaning of the passage where the name of Kṛishṇa, the son of Devakī, occurs. In the third chapter of Chhāndogya, there is a passage which stands by itself, the purport of which is to liken a man to a sacrificer and thus institute a comparison between the human life and the sacrificer's life. What happens in the case of the life of a sacrificer ? When he undertakes to perform a sacrifice, he is first disallowed to take food, or to drink water, or in any way to enjoy. This constitutes his Dīkshā. Then, secondly, there are certain ceremonies called the Upasadas in that sacrifice, in which he is allowed to eat and drink and enjoy himself. Thirdly, when such a sacrificer wishes to laugh, and eat and practise sexual intercourse even while the sacrifice is going on, he is allowed to do so if he just sings the hymns of praise called the Stutaśastras. Fourthly, he must give certain

Daxiṇās or gifts to the sacrificial priests in honour of the sacrifice that he is performing. Fifthly, he pours out the Soma libation which is equivalent to a new birth of the sacrificer. Finally, the sacrificer takes the Avabhṛitha bath at the end of the sacrificial ceremony which puts an end to the sacrifice. These are the stages through which a sacrificer's life passes. Now we are told in the passage which we are discussing that Ghora Āṅgirasa, the reputed teacher of Kṛishṇa who was the son of Devakī, institutes a comparison between the life of a sacrificer and the life of a man in general. At the initial stage of a man's life, he has to serve merely as an apprentice, and cannot eat and drink and enjoy on certain occasions. Secondly, another stage opens before him, namely, when he can eat and drink and enjoy himself. Thirdly, when he grows a little older, he can laugh and eat and practise sexual intercourse. Fourthly, the price which he has to pay for leading a holy life is that he should cultivate the virtues, namely, penance, liberality, straightforwardness, harmlessness, and truthfulness. Fifthly, when he has procreated, we may say he is born again in his child. The final act of the human drama takes place when death lets down the curtain, and the man is on the point of departing from his life. At such a critical time, says Ghora Āṅgirasa to Kṛishṇa—and we are told that when this knowledge was imparted to Kṛishṇa he never thirsted again for further knowledge——man must take refuge in these three thoughts: Thou art the indestructible; Thou art the unchangeable; Thou art the very edge of life (S. 17). From this passage a number of modern critics have argued that the Kṛishṇa, the son of Devakī, who is mentioned in this passage, must be regarded as identical with Kṛishṇa, the son of Vasudeva, who, as we have pointed out, is the divine hero of the Mahābhārata. Mr.

Grierson in the "Encyclopædia of Religion and Ethics" points out in a very facile fashion, that "Kṛishṇa Vāsudeva, who was the founder of the new monotheistic religion, was the pupil of a sage named Ghora Āṅgirasa, who taught him so that he never thirsted again." In answer to such an identification of Kṛishṇa, the son of Vasudeva, and Kṛishṇa, the pupil of Ghora Āṅgirasa, we have to point out that this is merely an assertion without proof. It passes our understanding how for the simple reason that Kṛishṇa, the pupil of Ghora Āṅgirasa, was the son of Devakī as mentioned in the Chhāndogya, he could be identified with Kṛishṇa, the son of Devakī, of the Mahābhārata, where no mention is made whatsoever of Ghora Āṅgirasa who was the teacher of Kṛishṇa in the Chhāndogya. Such a fact cannot be easily ignored in a work like the Mahābhārata which is expected to give us everything about the divine warrior Kṛishṇa, and not leave the name of his teacher unmentioned. If the Kṛishṇa of the Chhāndogya is to be identified with the Kṛishṇa of the Mahābhārata, for that matter why should not we identify the Hariśchandra of the Aitareya Brāhmaṇa who had a hundred wives with the Hariśchandra of mythology who had only one wife? Mere similarity of name proves nothing. It fills one with humour that a new facile philosophy of identifications Brāhmaṇa-wise should have been instituted in modern times by a host of critics of no small calibre when they would raise a huge structure of mythico-imaginary identifications by rolling together the god Vishṇu of Vedic repute, Nārāyaṇa the Cosmic God, Kṛishṇa the pupil of Ghora Āṅgirasa, and Vāsudeva the founder of a new religion, and thus try to prove that the sources of the religion of the Bhagavadgītā are to be found in the teaching of Ghora Āṅgirasa! There would seem to be some meaning, however, in the attempted identification of the Kṛishṇa of the Chhāndogya with the Kṛishṇa of the Bhagavadgītā, when, in verse 4 of the passage we are discussing, we are told that the gifts which such a sacrificer should make to priests are those of the following virtues: Tapas, Dānam, Ārjavam, Ahinsā and Satyavachanam. This list is closely similar to the list of virtues enumerated in the Bhagavadgītā XVI.1-2, where the same virtues are enumerated along with a number of other virtues, and almost in the same order. But this fact also proves nothing, because, as we have pointed out in the preceding paragraphs, the Bhagavadgītā is a congeries of quotations, phrases, and ideas borrowed from the Upanishads, and it is only by accident, as we may say, that the five virtues mentioned above should have been enumerated in the Upanishadic passage where Kṛishṇa, the son of Devakī, is also mentioned. There is a story about the Delphic Oracle that a number of trophies were hung round about the temple in praise of the god who had saved so many souls at different times from shipwreck in the midst of waters. A philosopher went to the temple and asked, Yea, but where are those that are drowned? Similarly may we say about the virtues in the Chhāndogya passage which are identical with the virtues in the passage from the Bhagavadgītā. True, that the virtues enumerated in the Chhāndogya almost correspond to the virtues enumerated in the Bhagavadgītā; but, why, for the world, should not the essence of the teachings of Ghora Āṅgirasa have been incorporated into the Bhagavadgītā, when the Upanishad passage tells us that at the last moment of a man's life, he should take resort to these three thoughts: Thou art the indestructible, Thou art the unchangeable, Thou art the very edge of life? Why should not the Bhagavadgītā have profited by these three expressions: Akshita, Achyuta and Prāṇasaṁśita? Why should it have left us merely with the advice that a man should utter Om at the time of his death and meditate upon God? Finally, we may say that the burden of the proof of the identification of the two Kṛishṇas falls upon those who make the assertion, and so far as their arguments have gone, we do not think that they have, in any way, proved the identification at all.

The Upanishads and the Schools of the Vedānta.

13. The relation of the Upanishads to the Brahmasūtras is no less interesting and no less important than the relation of the Upanishads to the Bhagavadgītā. In fact, the whole of the philosophy of the Vedānta in its various schools has been based upon these three foundation-stones, namely, the Upanishads, the Brahmasūtras, and the Bhagavadgītā, and thus it may easily be expected that the interrelation of the Brahmasūtras to the Upanishads from which they were derived must constitute an equally important problem. Bādarāyaṇa, the author of the Brahmasūtras, borrows so frequently and so immensely from the Upanishads, in fact, all his aphorisms are so much rooted in the texts of the Upanishads, that it would be impossible either to understand or to interpret the Brahmasūtras without a perpetual reference to the texts of the Upanishads. As to whether he taught the dualistic Vedānta or the qualified monistic Vedānta, or the monistic Vedānta, it is not our business here to discuss; but it must be remembered that each of the three great schools of Vedāntic philosophy, namely, the schools of Madhva, Rāmānuja, and Śaṅkara, interprets the Brahmasūtras as well as the Upanishads in its own way. The Śuddhādvaita, the Dvaitādvaita and other interpretations of the philosophy of the Brahmasūtras and the Upanishads are merely varied combinations of the ultimate positions reached in these three main systems of philosophy. Hence, when we have discussed how far the Upanishads sanction the difference between the Dvaita, the Viśishṭādvaita and the Advaita schools of philosophy, we have exhausted all the different fundamental conceptions of the Vedānta, from whose permutation and combination all the other systems are derived. And even while we are discussing these three main schools of Vedāntic philosophy, a number of fundamental propositions arise, difference in the treatment of which constitutes difference in the systems themselves. Thus the main problems which these philosophers have to answer are these: What is the nature of God? Is He different from, included in, or identical with the Absolute? In other words, are the theological conception of God and the philosophical conception of the Absolute one and the same? What is the relation of the Individual to the Universal Soul in these systems? Do these systems maintain the reality of creation, or, do they suppose that, after all, creation is only an appearance and an illusion? What is the doctrine of Immortality in these systems? What do these systems say about the immanence and transcendence of God? How can we define the Absolute—in positive terms, in negative terms, in both, or in neither? The answer to these and other problems of the same kind constitutes the *fundamentum divisionis* of the systems themselves. We shall see how the three great schools of Vedāntic philosophy find answers for these problems according to their different lights in the texts of the Upanishads.

14. The dualistic school of philosophy initiated by Ānandatīrtha finds justification for its maintenance of the doctrine of the entire disparateness of the Individual and the Universal Souls in such a passage as the one from the Kaṭha, which tells us that "in this world there are two Souls which taste of the fruits of action, both of which are lodged in the recess of the human heart, and which are as different from each other as light and shade" (S. 18. a), corrected, as later, in the passage from the Muṇḍakopanishad which tells us that "there are two birds, companions and friends, both sitting on the same tree, of which one partakes of the sweet fruits of the tree, while the other without eating merely looks on" (S. 18. b). The difficulty in the passage from the Kaṭhopanishad which we have quoted above is—how can we regard the Universal Soul as enjoying the fruits of action? The enjoyment of the fruits of action could be predicated only about the Individual Soul and not about the Universal Soul which must be regarded as above such enjoyment. Hence, it was probable, that the Muṇḍaka Upanishad relieved the Universal Soul of the burden of the enjoyment of the fruits of such action, and laid the fact of enjoyment at the door of the Individual Soul. In any case, it is worth while noting that the Individual Soul is in the above two passages spoken of as being entirely distinct from the Universal Soul, and as being probably dependent upon it. These are the texts, which, like the later one from the Bhagavadgītā "there are two Persons in this world, the Mutable and the Immutable; the Mutable is all these beings, while the Immutable is the one who exists at the top of them" (XV. 16), have been quoted in support of their doctrine of the entire disparateness of the Individual and the Universal Souls by the followers of Madhva. Then, again, when they speak about

Madhvaism in the Upanishads.

the existence of a supreme God, who is the creator, the preserver and the destroyer of the universe, who exists as a personal Being, and as over-lord of all the Souls who are his servants, they have ample justification in passages like the one from the Śvetāśvatara which tells us that "there is a single God who is hidden in all beings, who pervades all, and who is the inner Soul of all Souls" (S. 19. a), as well as those others from the Śvetāśvatara itself which tell us that "beyond this universal God there exists nothing, than whom there is nothing subtler or greater, who stands motionless like a tree in the sky and fills every nook and cranny of the universe" (S. 19. b), or again like that last passage from Śvetāśvatara, which, in the spirit of Xenophanes, tells us that God is all eye and all ear—

οὖλος ὁρᾷ, οὖλος δέ νοεῖ, οὖλος δέ τ' ἀκούει

—with his face everywhere, his hands and feet everywhere, who creates the beings of the earth and the fowl of the air, and who brings into being both the heaven and the earth (S. 19. c). Such a theory of the sovereignty of the Lord over organic as well as inorganic nature brings in its train a realistic theory of creation which tells us that "all these beings were created from Him; they live and move and have their being in Him; and they are ultimately resolved in Him" (S. 20. a), as well as that all inorganic nature was created by Him, "space being the first to come out of Him, from which later were produced air and fire and water and earth, and the herbs and the trees and the food in the universe" (S. 20. b). We have already seen in our discussion of the theories of cosmogony in an earlier chapter that a realistic account of creation such as is implied in these passages is really an obstacle to those who try to make creation merely an appearance or an illusion, and that therefore these texts support the doctrine of the realistic theory of creation of

Madhva as of none else. It is true that Śaṅkara tries to explain the ablative implied in "yatovā" or "tasmādvā" as being Adhishṭhāna-pañchamī, Rāmānuja trying to explain it as merely Upādāna-pañchamī, while Madhva explains it truly as Nimitta-pañchamī. This is as much as to say, that while according to Śaṅkara the Ātman or the Ultimate Reality stands behind the universe as the support and substratum of all creation which merely appears on it, according to Rāmānuja, the Ātman is the material cause of the universe as gold of gold-ornaments or earth of earthen-ware in quite a realistic manner, while according to Madhva, the Ātman or the Supreme Soul is the creator of the universe or the instrumental cause of its unfoldment. Finally, so far as the doctrine of immortality is concerned, a passage like the one from the Chhāndogya which tells us that the worshipper is lifted up to the region of the deity whom he has worshipped in life (S. 21) supports the doctrine of Madhva that absolution consists not in being merged in the Absolute, nor even in being assimilated to Him, but in coming near his presence and participating in his glory so that the devotee may be lifted, according to the requirements of the doctrine of Kramamukti, along with the God whom he has worshipped, to the state of the highest absolution at the end of time.

The Triune Absolute of Ramanuja.

15. Rāmānuja agrees with Madhva in maintaining the utter separateness of the Individual Souls and God, the reality of Creation, as well as to a great extent the doctrine of Immortality; but he differs from him in regarding the Absolute to be of the nature of a Triune Unity,—a sort of a philosophic tripod,—of which Nature, the Individual Souls, and God form the feet. So far, again, as the relation between the Souls and God is concerned, he disagrees with Madhva in maintaining a qualitative monism, though he agrees with him in maintaining a numerical pluralism. For his doctrine of Triune Unity, Rāmānuja finds ample justification in the passages from the Śvetāśvatara which tell us that there are "three ultimate existences, all of them eternal and all together constituting the Absolute, namely, the powerless unknowing Soul, the powerful knowing God, and the eternal Prakṛiti, which exists for the enjoyment of the individual Soul, and from which he receives recompense for his works" (S. 22. a), and yet again that "man need but know the three entities which constitute the Absolute, namely, the enjoyer, the enjoyed, and the mover, and that when a man has known these three, nothing remains to be known" (S. 22. b). Thus we see that the Absolute of Rāmānuja consists of Nature, Soul and God, God being identical with the Absolute considered in his personal aspect, while there is only this difference between them that while God is the theological conception, the Absolute is the philosophical conception, of the Triune Unity. It thus comes about that God is as much the Soul of Nature as he is the Soul of Souls. This is the fundamental platform in the philosophy of Rāmānujāchārya, and we shall see what justification he finds for such views in the Upanishads themselves.

God, the Soul of Nature.

16. How is God the Soul of Nature? There is a passage in the Bṛihadāraṇyaka which tells us that God is the Antaryāmin of the universe: He lives inside and governs the universe from within. This doctrine of the Antaryāmin, which is advanced in that Upanishad in the conversation between Uddālaka Āruṇi and Yājñavalkya, constitutes the funda-

mental position in the philosophy of Rāmānuja when he calls God the the Soul of Nature. Uddālaka Āruṇi asked Yājñavalkya two questions. "Pray tell me," he said, "what is the Thread by which this world and the other world and all the things therein are held together?" "Pray tell me also," he continued, "who is the Controller of the Thread of this world and the other world and all the things therein?" These are the two celebrated questions propounded in the passage which we are discussing, namely, the doctrine of the Thread and the doctrine of the Thread-Controller. Yājñavalkya answered the first question by saying that Air might be regarded as the Thread by which this world and the other world and all the things therein are held together. The second question he answered by saying that He alone might be regarded as the inner Controller "who dwells in the earth and within the earth, whom the earth does not know, whose body the earth is, who from within controls the earth. He is thy Soul, the inner controller, the immortal. He who dwells in the waters and within the waters, whom the waters do not know, whose body the waters are, who from within controls the waters, He is thy Soul, the inner controller, the immortal." Thus Yājñavalkya went on to tell Uddālaka Āruṇi that the inner Controller is He who is immanent likewise "in fire, in the intermundia, in air, in the heavens, in the sun, in the quarters, in the moon, in the stars, in space, in darkness, in light, in all beings, in Prāṇa, in all things and within all things, whom these things do not know, whose body these things are, who controls all these things from within. He is thy Soul, the inner controller, the immortal. He is the unseen seer, the unheard hearer, the unthought thinker, the ununderstood understander; other than Him, there is no seer, other than Him there is no hearer, other than Him there is no thinker, other than Him there is no understander; He is thy Soul, the inner controller, the immortal. Everything beside Him is naught" (S. 23. a). In this wise does Yājñavalkya declare the immanence within, and the inner control of the universe by the all-pervading God. In the same fashion does the author of the Taittirīya tells us that "at the time of creation, God entered everything that he created, and after having entered, became both the This and the That, the Defined and the Undefined, the Supported and Supportless, Knowledge and Not-Knowledge, Reality and Unreality—yea, he became the Reality; it is for this reason that all this is verily called the Real" (S. 23. b). This passage also declares the immanence of God in all things whatsoever, even in contradictories, and tells us that what thus comes to exist is the Real. The whole of Nature, therefore, which is God's handiwork, as well as God's garment, is filled and inspired by God who is its inner Controller and Soul.

God, the Soul of Souls.

17. How is God the Soul of Souls? We are told in the Bṛihadāraṇyaka by the help of a simile which is oft repeated in the Upanishads that "just as the spokes of a wheel are held together in the navel and felly of a wheel, similarly in this Supreme Soul are centred all these beings, all gods, all worlds, all the individual souls—the Supreme Soul is the king of them all" (S. 24. a). In another passage, the same Upanishad tells us, by a change of metaphor, that "just as little sparks may come out of fire, even so from the Supreme Soul all prāṇas, all worlds, all gods, all beings come out. This is to be mystically expressed by saying that the Supreme Soul is the verity of verities; the prāṇas, as well as other things mentioned along with them, are verities, of whom the Universal Soul is the supreme verity" (S. 24. b). In these passages we are told how God may be regarded as the Soul of Souls, and we are also unmistakably told that the Supreme Soul is the Real of the Reals, the verity of verities, the individual souls and the world being themselves verities. This is corroborated by another passage of the Bṛihadāraṇyaka which tells us that God is the All—"both the formed and the formless, the mortal and the immortal, the stationary and the moving, the this and the that......He is the verity of verities, for all these are verities, and He is the supreme verity" (S. 24. c). Both the moving and the stationary are thus the forms of God ; this is as much as to say, that God is the Soul of organic as well as inorganic nature. He fills the Souls as he fills the Universe, and controls them both as their inner governor.

Ramanuja's Doctrine of Immortality.

18. What is the doctrine of Immortality corresponding to such a philosophic position ? Rāmānuja's main text in this matter is the passage from the Muṇḍaka which tells us that "when the devotee sees the golden-coloured Person who is the all-doer, the all-governor, and the source of the universe, he shakes off both sin and merit, and free from these, attains to divine likeness" (S. 25. a). We have already noticed to a certain extent in the concluding portion of the last chapter how this conception of the immortal life in Rāmānuja compares with the conceptions both of Madhva and Śaṅkara. While, to Madhva, beatitude consists in being lifted up to the region of the deity and coming into his presence, to Rāmānuja it consists in attaining to divine assimilation and in being like him though different from him, while to

Śaṅkara it consists in being finally atoned to Divinity and being absorbed in that Divine Life in such a way that no trace of personal existence remains. These conceptions of Immortality are the logical outcome of the philosophical positions advanced by these thinkers. We are not concerned here to discuss which of them seems to us to be philosophically sound, but we are only noting how each of these philosophers finds justification for his theory of the immortal life in the Upanishads themselves. There is a further point in which Madhva and Rāmānuja agree with each other and differ from Śaṅkara. In a passage from the Muṇḍaka we are told that "a man, who has attained to a perfect catharsis from evil, and has his intellect firmly rooted in the principles of the Vedānta, after death goes to the regions of Brahmā, with whom he attains to final absolution at the time of the great end" (S. 25. b). This passage preserves the personal immortality of the souls and keeps them from being absorbed in divinity. Such a "Kramamukti," as it is called, is not in line with the real philosophical position of Advaitism, which sees in man the possibility of being liberated even while he lives. According to Advaitism, it is possible for man to attain to "Jīvanmukti" as it is called, to become free while living and though living, to say nothing about the state of the soul after man's death. When a man has realised God, he becomes one with Him, and is absorbed in him. That is the Advaitic position. There is an end of the matter, and the help of no celestial god, however great, need be invoked for carrying such a devotee along with him to the state of liberation at the time of the Great End.

19. How does Śaṅkara's philosophy lead to such a view of the immortal life? What are the logical pre-

suppositions of such a doctrine? What, in other words, are the fundamental conceptions of Śaṅkara's philosophy which ultimately justify such a view of the absorption of the Individual into the Universal Soul? How does Śaṅkara answer the problems which have been mooted in the systems of Madhva and Rāmānuja? A full solution of these questions cannot be attempted here. We can only indicate the lines on which Śaṅkara answers the opposite points of view and constructs an Advaitic philosophy, which is all the while, according to him, based on the Upanishads themselves. From the point of view of the Absolute, *sub specie æternitatis*, Nature and Soul and God are all equally appearances. The Absolute alone is: and Nature and Soul and God are, only so far as they are, the Absolute. But, *sub specie temporis*, there is a Nature, there are the Souls, there is a God. Śaṅkara makes the great distinction between the Pāramārthika and Vyāvahārika views of reality as Kant makes the distinction between the noumenal and the phenomenal. It is from the phenomenal point of view that we may say that Souls are different from God; that Nature exists as a *heteros*; that God creates; but noumenally, the Absolute alone exists, and Nature, and Souls, and God are all merged in the Absolute. For him who sees the Ātman everywhere, what difference can ever remain, asks Śaṅkara? All difference vanishes for him. "Theologians may battle among themselves, but the Absolutist battles with none." It is from this point of view that the truths of the dualistic and the qualified-monistic systems of the Vedānta are both subsumed in the higher synthesis of the monistic. We shall see how Śaṅkara finds justification for such views in the Upanishads.

The fundamental propositions of Sankara's Philosophy.

The Absolute, the only Reality.

20. The fundamental platform of Śaṅkarite philosophy is that the universe is one: that there is no difference within it, or without it. From death to death does he go, says the Kaṭhopanishad, who sees difference in this world; non-difference can be perceived only by the highly trained intellect (S. 26. a). Brahman is alike throughout its structure, and the knowledge of any part of it is the knowledge of the whole. When Śvetaketu returned from his teacher's house, proud, self-satisfied, and thinking himself learned, his father asked him whether his teacher had taught him the knowledge of Ultimate Existence, "by hearing which everything that is not heard becomes heard, by thinking which everything that is not thought becomes thought, by knowing which everything that is not known becomes known." Śvetaketu plainly confessed ignorance and requested his father to tell him what that supreme instruction was. Then Āruṇi, his father, told him that, "just as by the knowledge of a lump of earth, everything that is made of earth comes to be known, all this being merely a word, a modification and a name, the ultimate substratum of it all being the earth; that just as by the knowledge of a piece of iron everything made of iron becomes known, all this being merely a word, a modification and a name, the ultimate substratum of it all being iron; that just as by the knowledge of a pair of nail-scissors, everything made of steel becomes known, all this being merely a word, a modification and a name, the ultimate substratum of it all being steel" (S. 26. b), similarly, when any part of Brahman is known, the whole of it is known, the ultimate substratum of it all being Brahman itself, which is self-identical, self-subsistent, and self-known. The implication of this passage is that everything that exists is Brahman.

This is corroborated also by a passage from the Bṛihadāraṇyaka when in his conversation with his wife Maitreyi, Yājñavalkya said "all this Brāhmaṇa-hood, all this Kshatriya-hood, all these worlds, all these gods, all these beings, in fact, everything that exists is Ātman. Just as when a drum is being beaten, one is not able to grasp the external sound, but by grasping the drum or the beater of the drum, the sound becomes grasped; just as when a conch-shell is being blown, one is not able to grasp the external sound, but by grasping the conch-shell or the blower of the conch-shell, the sound becomes grasped; that just as when a lute is being played, one is not able to grasp the external sound, but by grasping the lute or the player of the lute, the sound becomes grasped" (S. 26. c), similarly, in the case of the knowledge of the external world, if one is not able to grasp the external world as it is in itself, by grasping the Mind, or by grasping the Ātman, the external world becomes grasped. This latter statement, of course, is only implied in the above passage, and not explicitly stated; but it cannot be gainsaid that the Ātman is here compared to the lute-player or the drum-beater or the conch-blower, while the Mind by means of which the Ātman perceives is compared to the lute or the drum or the conch, while the external world is compared to the sounds that issue from these instruments. This is verily an idealistic monism in which the active part is attributed to the Ātman, while the Mind serves as the instrument for its activity. In another passage of the same Upanishad, Yājñavalkya tells Maitreyi that the Ātman is the only knower and that he could not be known by anyone except himself. "It is only when there seems to be a duality that one smells the other, that one sees the other, that one hears the other, that one speaks about the other, that one imagines about the other, that one thinks about the other; but where the Ātman alone is, what and whereby may one smell, what and whereby may one perceive, what and whereby may one hear, what and whereby may one speak, what and whereby may one imagine, what and whereby may one think? He who knows all this, by what may anybody know *Him*? He is the eternal knower, by what may *He* be known?" (S. 26. d). Such a doctrine takes Yājñavalkya perilously near the position of an absolute solipsism from which he tries to extricate himself in his conversation with king Janaka in a later chapter of the same Upanishad when he tells us that "when it is said that such a one does not see, the real truth is that he sees and yet does not see; for never is the vision of the seer destroyed, for that is indestructible; but there is nothing besides him, and outside him, which may be said to be seen by him. When it is said that such a one does not smell or taste or speak or hear or imagine or touch or know, he does all these things and yet does not do them, for never are the olfaction, the taste, the speech, the audition, the imagination, the touch and the knowledge of him destroyed, for they are indestructible; there is, however, nothing outside him and different from him which he may smell, or taste, or speak, or hear, or imagine, or touch, or think" (S. 26. e). In this way, does Yājñavalkya extricate himself from the absolutely solipsistic position in which his absolute monism has landed him. The outcome of these passages is, that for the Absolutist there is nothing different from or outside the Ātman, that knowledge of any part of him is the knowledge of the whole, that all causation is ultimately due to him, that everything beside him is an appearance, that he is the only eternal knower, and that it is only when he becomes entangled in the phenomenal acts of perception and knowledge that he may be said to perceive and know, and yet the truth is that he does not perceive and know. The Ātman is the only entity to exist, and there is naught beside him.

The negative-positive characterisation of the Absolute.

21. Even though metaphysical philosophy may require such a rigoristic conception of the Absolute, for the purposes of religion and for the explanation of the phenomenal existence of the world, a God has to be invented, who, in Māṇḍukyan fashion, should be the lord of all, the knower of all, the inner controller of all, the *fons et origo* of all, the final haven of all. Advaitism does not negate such a conception of God. It requires God just for the sake of the purposes above mentioned; but higher than God philosophically, it regards the conception of the Absolute. God to an Advaitist is the personal aspect of the Absolute, and the Absolute the impersonal aspect of God. It is in this spirit that the Māṇḍukyopanishad makes a distinction between the conceptions of God and the Absolute, and regards the latter conception as philosophically even a higher one. "The Absolute is neither inwardly cognisant, nor outwardly cognisant, nor on both sides together. It is not a cognition-mass. It is neither knower nor not-knower. It is unseen, unpracticable, ungraspable, indefinable, unthinkable, unpointable. It is the essence of the experience of self-identity; in it all this universe ceases. It is tranquil, blessed, and without a second" (S. 27. a). It is true that there are a few positive characterisations of the Absolute in this passage; but the general description of it is, as may be easily remarked, couched only in negative terms. It is impossible for any absolutist philosophy to say anything, and to say at the same time that it is not outside itself.

However much a rigorously monistic philosophy may describe the Absolute in negative terms, the very negation becomes affirmation, and it cannot rid itself entirely of some positive characterisation at least of the Absolute. It was this that happened in the case of the Upanishadic Absolute. The Bṛihadāraṇyaka describes the Absolute as "the not-gross and the not-subtle, the not-short and the not-long, the not-glowing and the not-shadowy, the not-dark, the not-attached, the flavour-less, the smell-less, the eye-less, the ear-less, the speech-less, the mind-less, the Prāṇa-less, the mouth-less, the un-internal, the un-external, consuming nothing, and consumed by none" (S. 27. b). This is a purely negative characterisation of the Absolute in the Bṛihadāraṇyaka. The Kaṭha mixes up negative and positive characteristics of it, as does the Muṇḍakopanishad. The Kaṭha tells us that the Brahman is "sound-less, touch-less, form-less, taste-less, imperishable, smell-less, beginning-less, end-less, greater than the great and eternal, garnering which one is able to escape the clutches of death" (S. 27. c). The Muṇḍaka tells us that the Brahman is "unpointable, ungraspable, without family and without caste, without eye and without ear, without hands and without feet, eternal, all-pervading, omnipresent, extremely subtle, imperishable, and the source of all beings" (S. 27. d). The typical formulation of the negative characterisation of the Absolute is in the famous formula "Neti Neti," which, as we shall presently point out, is itself interpreted in a negative as well as a positive signification. In most of the passages from the Bṛihadāraṇyaka in which this famous expression occurs, the intended meaning is that the Absolute is characterless and indefinable; that whatever may be predicated of it falls outside it and thus fails to define it. "The Ātman is ungraspable for he cannot be grasped;

he is indestructible for he cannot be destroyed; he is unattached because he clings to nothing; he is unbound, he does not wriggle, he is not injured...... Know this to be the secret of immortality, said Yājñavalkya to Maitreyi, and forthwith he entered the order of Saṁnyāsa" (S. 27. e). There is, however, one passage from the Bṛihadāraṇyaka where an attempt is made to give a positive connotation to the expression Neti Neti: "It is for this reason that they describe the Absolute as Neti Neti: there is *nothing* which exists *outside* it, the Brahman being all-inclusive" (S. 27. f). The inclusive character of the Absolute leads to a transcendental view about it in a later passage of the Bṛihadāraṇyaka where the Absolute is described as full both "of light and not-light, of desire and not-desire, of anger and not-anger, of law and not-law, having verily filled all, both the near and the far-off, the this and the that, the subject and the object" (S. 27. g). We thus see how the Upanishadic characterisation of the Absolute passes from the negative stage of neither-nor, through the affirmative stage of inclusiveness, to the transcendental state of either-or.

Sankara's Doctrines of Identity, Creation and Immortality.

22. What is Śaṅkara's answer to the question of the relation between the Self and the Absolute? It is true that the Absolute *sub specie æternitatis* is the only reality; but what can we say about the reality of what we empirically call the Self? Śaṅkara answers that the Self is empirically real, but transcendentally ideal. From the phenomenal point of view, we say that it exists as a separate entity; but transcendentally, it is identical with the Absolute. There are many passages in the Upanishads which support this view of Śaṅkara. The Chhāndogya tells us that "the Self which inhabits the body is verily the Brahman, and that as soon as the mortal coil is thrown over, it will finally merge in Brahman" (S. 28. a). In the Śvetāśvatara we are told that "the individual Self flutters like a swan in the wheel of Brahman considering itself and its Mover as separate entities; but it is only when it becomes one with it that it becomes immortal" (S. 28. b). The Bṛihadāraṇyaka tells us that "he who worships the deity as separate from himself is merely the beast of the gods" (S. 28. c). In the Taittirīya an identity is asserted between the person in the Man and the person in the Sun (S. 28. d). The Muṇḍakopanishad teaches the identity of the Soul pent up in the recesses of the human heart with the Supreme Person, and identifies both with the Universe (S. 28. e). Finally, in that oft-repeated instruction which Āruṇi imparts to Śvetaketu, he teaches the absolute identity of the Self and Brahman (S. 28. f). These passages are verily a crux to the non-Advaitic interpreters of the Upanishads. What does Śaṅkara say, again, to the question of Creation? What, according to him, is the relation that subsists between the world and the souls on the one hand and Brahman on the other so far as creation is concerned? To explain creation empirically, Śaṅkara draws upon the Muṇḍakopanishad which tells us that "just as a spider creates and retracts its thread, as the herbs and trees grow upon the surface of the earth, just as from a living person the hairs of the head and the body grow, similarly, from this immutable Brahman does all this universe spring" (S. 29. a); and yet again "just as from a fire well-lit thousands of scintillations arise, and into it are resolved, similarly, from this immutable Brahman manifold beings come into existence and into it are merged" (S. 29. b). As regards the doctrine of Immortality, Śaṅkara asserts the impersonal immortality of the liberated Souls in their final mergence in the Absolute. "Just as rivers, which flow into the ocean, disappear in it after having thrown away their name and form, similarly, the Sage after having thrown off his name and form enters the highest heavenly Person (S. 30. a). "His breath does not expire; being Brahman himself, he goes to Brahman; as a serpent may throw off his slough, even so does the Sage cast off his mortal body" (S. 30. b). This last passage implies also the state of "Jīvanmukti," inasmuch as it asserts that having realised his identification with Brahman even while life lasts, he merges in Brahman when he has thrown off his mortal coil.

Three theories about the origin of the Doctrine of Maya.

23. We now come to discuss a problem, upon which there has been a great deal of difference of opinion among interpreters of Vedāntic philosophy, namely, problem of the sources of the doctrine of Māyā. There are, on the whole, three different theories which try to account for the doctrine of Māyā, as found in Śaṅkara and later writers, in three different ways: according to the first, the doctrine of Māyā is a mere fabrication of the fertile genuis of Śaṅkara; according to the second, the doctrine of Māyā as found in Śaṅkara is to be traced entirely to the influence of the Śūnyavāda of the Buddhists; according to the third, Śaṅkara's doctrine of Māyā is to be found already full-fledged in the Upanishads, of which he is merely an exponent. To say that the doctrine of Māyā is a fabrication of Śaṅkara is to deny outright the presence of its sources in the Upanishads. To say that it is the outcome of the nihilism of the Buddhists is to give, in addition, merely a negativistic, nihilistic interpretation to the philosophy of Śaṅkara. To say, again, that the doctrine of Māyā is to be found full-fledged in the Upanishads is to deny the process of the development of thought, especially in such a well-equipped mind as that of Śaṅkara. All these theories could be disproved if we find sufficient justification for the sources of the doctrine of Māyā in the Upanishads, and if Śaṅkara's philosophy be shown to have developed these, and brought them to maturity. One of the chief ways in which an attempt is generally made to trace the source of the doctrine of Māyā in the Upanishads is to find in a Concordance references to a word like Māyā, and to argue therefrom as to the presence or otherwise of that doctrine in the Upanishads. Such a procedure is an entirely ridiculous one, inasmuch as it finds the existence of a doctrine like that of Māyā in words rather than in ideas. To find out whether the doctrine of Māyā is present in the Upanishads or not, we must examine the ideology of the Upanishads, and see whether this affords us sufficient justification for saying that the doctrine is to be met with there. We shall see in the sequel of this chapter that there are definite traces of that doctrine to be met with in Upanishadic literature, and that so far from Śaṅkara having fabricated a new conception altogether, or having owed it to the influence of the nihilistic school of thought, he may definitely be said to have gone back to the Upanishads to find his inspiration there, and as may befit a true thinker and philosopher, to have elaborated it out of the inchoate mass supplied to him by the Upanishads. Our conclusion, therefore, is that Śaṅkarāchārya only elaborated the ideas that he found in the Upanishads, and wove them into the contexture of his Advaitic philosophy.

24. As we have said, we shall examine the ideas instead of the words in the Upanishads, and see whether the traces of the Māyā doctrine cannot be found in them. The Īśopanishad tells us that truth is veiled in this universe by a vessel of gold, and it invokes the grace of God to lift up the golden vessel and allow the truth to be seen (S. 31. a). The veil that covers the truth is here described as golden, as being so rich, gaudy, and dazzling that it takes away the mind of the observer from the inner contents, and rivets it upon itself. Let us not be dazzled by the appearance of gold, says the Upanishad, everything that glitters is not gold. Let us penetrate deeper and see the reality that lies ensconced in it. We have thus, first, the conception of a veil which prevents truth from being seen at first glance. Then, again, we have another image in the Kaṭhopanishad of how people living in ignorance, and thinking themselves wise, move about wandering, like blind men following the blind, in search of reality, which they would have easily seen had they lodged themselves in knowledge instead of ignorance (S. 31. b). We have here the conception of blindfoldness, and we are told that we deliberately shut our eyes to the truth before us. Then, thirdly, ignorance is compared in the Muṇḍakopanishad to a knot which a man has to untie before he gets possession of the Self in the recess of his own heart (S. 31. c). Fourthly, the Chhāndogyopanishad tells us how knowledge is power, and ignorance impotence (S. 31. d). We, who are moving in this world without having attained to the knowledge of Ātman, are exhibiting at every stage the power of the impotence that lies in us. Not unless we have attained to the knowledge of Ātman can we be said to have attained power. Then, fifthly, the famous prayer in the Bṛihadāraṇyaka, in which a devotee is praying to God to carry him from Not-Being to Being, from

The Doctrine of Maya in the Upanishads.

Darkness to Light, from Death to Immortality, merely voices the sentiment of the spiritual aspirant who wishes to rid himself of the power of Evil over him. Unreality is here compared to Not-Being, to Darkness, or to Death (S. 31. e). The Kaṭhopanishad declares that the Sages never find reality and certainty in the unrealities and uncertainties of this world (S. 31. f). Māyā is here described as an "adhruva"—an Unreality, or an Uncertainty. The Chhāndogya again tells us that a cover of Untruth hides the ultimate Truth from us, just as the surface of the earth hides from us the golden treasure that is hidden inside it. We, who unconsciously move to the region of Truth day after day, do yet labour under the power of Untruth, for we do not know the Ātman. This Ātman is verily inside our own hearts. It is only he, who reaches Him every day, that is able to transcend the phenomenal world (S. 31. g). Māyā is here compared to an Untruth, an "anṛita." Then again, the Praśnopanishad tells us that we cannot reach the world of Brahman unless we have shaken off the crookedness in us, the falsehood in us, the illusion (Māyā) in us (S. 31. h). It is important to remember that the word Māyā is directly used in this passage, and almost in the sense of an illusion. In the same sense is the word Māyā used in the Śvetāśvatara where we are told that it is only by meditation upon God, by union with Him, and by entering into His Being, that at the end there is the cessation of the great world-illusion (S. 31. i). Here again, as before, the word Māyā can mean nothing but illusion. It must be remembered, however, that the word Māyā was used so far back as at the time of the Ṛigveda in a passage, which is quoted by the Bṛihadāraṇyaka, where Indra is declared to have assumed many shapes by his "Māyā" (S. 31. j). There, apparently, the word Māyā meant "power" instead of "illusion"—a sense in which the Śvetāśvatara later uses it, when it describes its God as a Māyin, a magician, a powerful Being who creates this world by his powers, while the other, namely, the individual soul is bound down again by "Māyā") (S. 31. k). Here it must be remembered that there is yet no distinction drawn, as in later Vedāntic philosophy, between the Māyā that envelops Īśvara and the Avidyā that envelops Jīva: for both the generic word Māyā is used, and in the passage under consideration it means only "power"—almost the same sense which Küno Fişcher gives to the "Attributes" of Spinoza. Then again, in the Śvetāśvatara, Māyā is once more identified with Prakṛiti (S. 31. l), a usage which prevailed very much later, as may be seen from the way in which even the author of the Kusumāñjali had no objection in identifying the two even for his theistic purpose. The Śvetāśvatara also contains passages which describe the Godhead as spreading his meshes and making them so manifold that he catches all the beings of the universe in them, and rules over them (S. 31. m). Here we have the conception of a net or meshes, inside which all beings are entangled. Then again, a famous passage from the Bṛihadāraṇyaka, which we have already considered, which speaks of "as if there was a duality," implying thereby that there is really no duality, signifies the identification of Māyā with a semblance, an as-it-were, an appearance (S. 31. n). Finally, in that celebrated conversation between Śvetaketu and Āruṇi which we have also had the occasion to consider, we are told that everything besides the Ātman is merely a word, a mode, and a name (S. 31. o). We thus see from an examination of the various passages in the Upanishads that even though the word Māyā may not have been used for many times in the Upanishads, still the conception that underlies Māyā is already present there, and even though we do not find there the full-fledged doctrine of illusion in its philosophical aspects as in Gauḍapāda and later writers, still we do find in the Upanishads all the material that may have easily led Śaṅkara to elaborate a theory of Māyā out of it. When we consider that we have the conceptions of a veil, of blind-foldness, of a knot, of ignorance, of not-being, of darkness, of death, of unreality and uncertainty, of untruth, of crookedness and falsehood and illusion, of the power of God, of this power as identical with nature, of meshes, of semblance, an as-it-were and an appearance, and finally, of a word, a mode and a name, let no man stand up and say that we do not find the traces of the doctrine of Māyā in the Upanishads!

Vicissitudes in the historical development of the doctrine of Maya.

25. Having traced the source of the doctrine of Māyā in the Upanishads, it is but proper that we should give a very brief account of the vicissitudes of that doctrine in its historical development in the post-Upanishadic period, and especially of the transformation of it which was effected by Gauḍapāda and Śaṅkara, inasmuch as this particularly concerns the question as to how far Śaṅkara may be said to have elaborated his full-fledged doctrine from the teachings of the Upanishads and from those of his spiritual ancestor, Gauḍapāda. In the post-Upanishadic period, as early as even in the days of the Bhagavadgītā, we do not find the doctrine stated in the terms in which the philosophers Gauḍapāda and Śaṅkara state it. In the Bhagavadgītā, the word Māyā is used in the sense almost of magical power, and God, the great magician, is declared to cause the spirit-host to revolve as by the power of His divine magic (XVIII. 61), and yet again the beings in the world are declared to be resorting to the demoniacal sort of life when God robs them of their wisdom by his power (VII. 15). Moreover, it must be remembered, that here again we have to investigate the doctrine of Māyā in ideas rather than in words. Also, the Bhagavadgītā is a short treatise compared with the Upanishads, nor does the theistic-mystic trend of the argument leave much room for a philosophical development of the conception of Māyā. When we come to Gauḍapāda, however, we find that a great stride forward is taken in the development of that doctrine. Gauḍapāda uses Buddhistic terminology, but sets forth an original doctrine. He tries to write a systematic treatise on philosophy instead of only giving a lift to the spiritual impulse of man in the manner of the Bhagavadgītā. Hence he states his opinion deliberately and fully, and we find him in his Kārikās maintaining the doctrine, not simply that the world is an appearance or an illusion, but that the world was never created at all! His was what has been known in the history of Indian Thought as the doctrine of "Ajātavāda," the doctrine of Non-creation. "If there were a universe, the question might arise whether it would hide from our view; but the universe is not; duality is only Māyā; non-duality is the only reality" (I. 17). The sage Gauḍapāda, however, is not decided as to whether he should regard the world as a dream or an illusion, or not. In one place, he praises those who have called the world an illusion: he calls such people the "well-versed in the Vedāntic science" (II. 31). On the other hand, when he is enumerating the various views about the creation of the universe, he is stating the view that the world is a dream or an illusion as a view which is held by others besides himself, "Some people regard the universe as the greatness of God, others as his creation, others as a dream, others as an illusion, others regard it as merely the will of God,......still others the object of His enjoyment, some people call it the play-thing of God, and yet others regard it as God's nature" (I. 7–9). As contrasted with these views, he states his position that he is at one with those who maintain the doctrine that the universe was not created at all (IV. 4-5). But it must be remembered that for the purposes of spiritual perfection and ethical conduct, Gauḍapāda has to take account of the world as a verity. "That is the state of the highest Samādhi, in which all talk is at an end, all anxiety is at an end, which is full of the highest tranquillity and eternal illumination" (III. 37); and, again, "creation has been recommended by the sages for the benefit of those who cannot but find the world to be real (Upālambhāt) and who must needs be led on the path of good conduct (Samāchārāt)" (IV. 42). We thus see how even the sage Gauḍapāda has to take some cognisance at least of the world as real, though it may be for the perfection of mystical endeavour or ethical conduct, even though, philosophically, he may regard it as not having been created at all. Śaṅkara profits by all the conceptions that have preceded him, and weaves his full-fledged doctrine out of the strands left at his disposal by the Upanishads and Gauḍapāda. If we examine carefully the expressions which Śaṅkara uses about Māyā in his great Commentary on the Brahmasūtras and elsewhere, namely those of inexplicability (sadasadanirvachanīyasvarūpatva), super-imposition (atasmin tadbuddhiḥ), and illicit transformation (rajusarpa and śuktikārajata) on the one hand, and those of subjective modification (ākāśe talamalinatvādi), and postulation of negation (khapushpa, mṛigatṛishṇikā, aindrajālika, śaśavishāṇa and vandhyāputra) on the other, all to designate the phenomenal appearance of the world, we shall see that Śaṅkara is placing himself between the doctrines of lesser reality and illusion; but his meaning is entirely unmistakable, that the world is merely an appearance on the background of Brahman. We cannot enter here into greater details about the doctrine of Māyā as Śaṅkara develops it. But we cannot leave unmentioned even in the short space at our disposal here the objections which Rāmānuja raises against Śaṅkara's doctrine of Māyā, in order that we may be able to understand the real meaning of Śaṅkara's doctrine better. Rāmānuja asks—What is the seat of Māyā, the Soul or Brahman?—How does the ever-luminous Brahman come to be hidden?—Is Māyā real or unreal? If real, it cannot be an illusion; if unreal, it cannot be an "upādhi" of Brahman—Is not the description of Brahman that it is incapable of definition a definition itself?—What is the criterion of the proof of Māyā?—Is it not a contradiction in terms to say that Māyā ceases by the knowledge of the attributeless Brahman?—Is not the removal of ignorance, once established, for ever impossible?—all these objections would seem to be merely an *ignoratio elenchi*, if we only consider for a while Śaṅkarāchārya's criticism of the Vijñānavādins and the Śūnyavādins in his exposition of the Brahmasūtra "Nābhāva upalabdheḥ" (II. 2. 28), where by a severe criticism of theories which hold that the world is merely an idea, or that the world is merely a naught, Śaṅkarāchārya proves himself to be neither an epistemological idealist, nor an epistemological nihilist. To Śaṅkara, the world is real, but only phenomenally real. Noumenally, *sub specie æternitatis*, it is unreal. We shall entirely mistake Śaṅkara's point of view if we do not consider the great distinction that he draws between the "pāramārthika" and the "vyāvahārika" views of reality. Like his later successor in Germany, he was the first in India to bring into vogue the distinction between empirical reality and transcendental ideality. Kant was himself charged with having been an Idealist in spite of his celebrated Refutation of Idealism. In like manner has Śaṅkara been charged with having been an idealist-nihilist in spite of his celebrated criticism of these doctrines. The recognition of the distinction between the Vyāvahārika and the Pāramārthika views of reality, added to the recognition of the Prātibhāsika and the Svāpnika views, which may also be gathered from his philosophy elsewhere, yields us a doctrine of the Degrees of Reality, which is all the while implicit in Śaṅkara, though it is never explicitly stated. Greater reality than the reality of the world of illusion belongs to the world of dream; greater reality than the reality of the world of dream belongs to the world of life; greater reality than the reality of the world of life belongs to the world of the Self, or God, or the Absolute, which are all ultimately identical with one another. Every system of philosophy must needs take account of some sort of appearance. From the days of Parmenides, Plato, and Plotinus to the days of Berkeley, Hegel, and Bradley, there has been the same cry. There is an extraordinary "moral" meaning in the doctrine of Appearance which critics of that doctrine systematically ignore. To quote the words of Carlyle: "Where is the cunning eye and ear to whom that God-written Apocalypse will yield articulate meaning? We sit as in a boundless Phantasmagoria and Dream-grotto; boundless, for the faintest star, the remotest century, lies not even nearer the verge thereof: sounds and many-coloured visions flit round our sense; but Him, the Unslumbering, whose work both Dream and Dreamer are, we see not; except in rare half-waking moments, suspect not. Creation, says one, lies before us, like a glorious Rainbow; but the Sun that made it lies behind us, hidden from us. Then, in that strange Dream, how we clutch at shadows as if they were substances; and sleep deepest while fancying ourselves most awake! ......Where now is Alexander of Macedon?...... Napoleon too, and his Moscow Retreats and Austerlitz campaigns! Was it all other than the veriest Spectre-hunt?......That warrior on his strong war-horse, fire flashes through his eyes; force dwells in his arm and heart: but warrior and war-horse are a vision; a revealed Force, nothing more. Stately they tread the Earth, as if it were a firm substance: fool! the Earth is but a film; it cracks in twain, and warrior and war-horse sink beyond plummet's sounding, Plummet's? Fantasy herself will not follow them. A little while ago, they were not; a little while, and they are not, their very ashes are not......Thus, like a God-created, fire-breathing Spirit-host, we emerge from the Inane; haste stormfully across the astonished Earth; then plunge again into the Inane......... But whence?—O Heaven, whither? Sense knows not; Faith knows not; only that it is through Mystery to Mystery, from God and to God."

SOURCES IV

1 (*a*) तद्ध एक आहुरसदेवेदमग्र आसीत् । एकमेवाद्वितीयम् ।
तस्मादसतः सज्जायत । छां. VI. 2. 1.

(*b*) येयं प्रेते विचिकित्सा मनुष्ये अस्तीत्येके नायमस्तीति चैके ।
क. I. 1. 20.

(*c*) श्वोभावा मर्त्यस्य यदन्तक एतत्सर्वेन्द्रियाणां जरयन्ति तेजः ।

अपि सर्वं जीवितमल्पमेव ॥ अभिध्यायन् वर्णरतिप्रमोदान्
अतिदीर्घे जीविते को रमेत ॥ क. I. 1. 26, 28.

(d) ते ह स्म पुत्रैषणायाश्च वित्तैषणायाश्च लोकैषणायाश्च व्युत्थाय अथ भिक्षाचर्यं चरन्ति। बृ. IV. 4. 22.

(e) इमानि पञ्चमहाभूतानि .... अण्डजानि च जारुजानि च स्वेदजानि च उद्भिज्जानि च अश्वा गावः पुरुषाः.... यत्किंचेदं प्राणि जंगमं च पतत्रि च यच्च स्थावरं सर्वं तत्प्रज्ञानेत्रं प्रज्ञाने प्रतिष्ठितम्।

ऐ. III. 3.

(f) आहर सोम्य हस्तम्। आर्तभागौ आवामेव एतस्य वेदिष्यावः। न नावेतत्सजन इति। तौ ह उत्क्रम्य मन्त्रयांचक्राते। तौ ह यदूचतुः कर्म हैव तदूचतुः अथ यत्प्रशशंसतुः कर्म हैव तत्प्रशशंसतुः। पुण्यो वै पुण्येन कर्मणा भवति पापः पापेनेति। बृ. III. 2. 13.

(g) योनिमन्ये प्रपद्यन्ते शरीरत्वाय देहिनः। स्थाणुमन्येऽनुसंयन्ति यथाकर्म यथाश्रुतम्। क. II. 5. 7.

2 (a) तत्कारणं सांख्ययोगाधिगम्यं ज्ञात्वा देवं मुच्यते सर्वपाशैः।

श्वे. VI. 13.

(b) यदग्ने रोहितं रूपं तेजसस्तद्रूपं, यच्छुक्लं तदपां, यत्कृष्णं तदन्नस्य, अपागादग्नेरग्नित्वं, वाचारंभणं विकारो नामधेयं त्रीणि रूपाणि इत्येव सत्यम्। छां. VI. 4. 1.

अजामेकां लोहितशुक्लकृष्णां बह्वीः प्रजाः सृजमानां सरूपाः। श्वे. IV. 5.

3 (a) इन्द्रियेभ्यः परा ह्यर्था अर्थेभ्यश्च परं मनः। मनसस्तु परा बुद्धिर्बुद्धेरात्मा महान्परः। महतः परमव्यक्तं अव्यक्तात्पुरुषः परः। पुरुषान्न परं किंचित् सा काष्ठा सा परा गतिः॥

क. I. 3. 10, 11.

(b) यच्छेद्वाङ्मनसि प्राज्ञः तद्यच्छेज्ज्ञान आत्मनि। ज्ञानमात्मनि महति नियच्छेत् तद्यच्छेच्छांतआत्मनि॥

क. I. 3. 13.

4 (a) इहैवान्तःशरीरे सोम्य स पुरुषो यस्मिन्नेताः षोडशकलाः प्रभवन्तीति। प्र. VI. 2.

(b) स प्राणमसृजत, प्राणाच्छ्रद्धां, खं, वायुः, ज्योतिः, आपः

पृथिवी, इन्द्रियं, मनः, । अन्नं, अन्नाद्वीर्यं, तपो, मन्त्राः, कर्म, लोकाः, लोकेषु च नाम च ॥ प्र. VI. 4.

(c) स यथेमा नद्यः स्यन्दमानाः समुद्रं प्राप्य अस्तं गच्छन्ति । भिद्येते तासां नामरूपे समुद्र इत्येवं प्रोच्यते । एवमेवास्य परिद्रष्टुरिमाः षोडशकलाः पुरुषं प्राप्य अस्तं गच्छन्ति । भिद्येते तासां नामरूपे, पुरुष इत्येवं प्रोच्यते । स एषोऽकलोऽमृतो भवति । प्र. VI. 5.

(d) अरा इव रथनाभौ कला यस्मिन्प्रतिष्ठिताः । तं वेद्यं पुरुषं वेद, यथा मा वो मृत्युः परिव्यथा इति ॥

प्र. VI. 6.

5 (a) यच्च स्वभावं पचति विश्वयोनिः, पाच्यांश्च सर्वान् परिणामयेद्यः । सर्वमेतद्विश्वमधितिष्ठत्येको, गुणांश्च सर्वान् विनियोजयेद्यः ॥ श्वे. VI. 5.

(b) प्रधानक्षेत्रज्ञपतिर्गुणेशः । श्वे. VI. 16.

(c) यस्तूर्णनाभ इव तन्तुभिः प्रधानजैः स्वभावतो देव एकः समावृणोत् । श्वे. VI. 10.

6 (a) मायां तु प्रकृतिं विद्यान्मायिनं तु महेश्वरम् । श्वे. VI. 10.

(b) अस्मान्मायी सृजते विश्वमेतत्तस्मिंश्चान्यो मायया संनिरुद्धः श्वे. VI. 9.

7 (a) अजो ह्येको जुषमाणोऽनुशेते जहात्येनां भुक्तभोगामजोऽन्यः । श्वे. IV. 5.

(b) कर्माध्यक्षः सर्वभूताधिवासः साक्षी चेता केवलो निर्गुणश्च । श्वे. VI. 1.

8 (a) ऋषिं प्रसूतं कपिलं यस्तमग्रे ज्ञानैर्बिभर्ति जायमानं च पश्येत् । श्वे. V. 2.

(b) हिरण्यगर्भं जनयामास पूर्वम् । श्वे. III. 4.

हिरण्यगर्भं पश्यत जायमानं स नो बुद्ध्या शुभया संयुनक्तु । श्वे. IV. 12.

(c) यो ब्रह्माणं विदधाति पूर्वं यो वै वेदांश्च प्रहिणोति तस्मै । श्वे. VI. 18.

9 (a) त्रिरुन्नतं स्थाप्य समं शरीरं हृदीन्द्रियाणि मनसा संनिवेश्य । ब्रह्मोडुपेन प्रतरेत विद्वान्स्रोतांसि सर्वाणि भयावहानि ॥

प्राणान्प्रपीड्येह स युक्तचेष्टः क्षीणे प्राणे नासिकयोच्छ्वसीत । दुष्टाश्वयुक्तमिव वाहमेनं विद्वान्मनो धारयेताप्रमत्तः ॥ समे शुचौ शर्कराविह्निवालुकाविवर्जिते शब्दजलाश्रयादिभिः। मनोऽनुकूले न तु चक्षुपीडने गुहानिवाताश्रयणे प्रयोजयेत् ॥ नीहारधूमार्कानलानिलानां खद्योतविद्युत्स्फटिकशशिनाम् । एतानि रूपाणि पुरःसरणि ब्रह्मण्यभिव्यक्तिकराणि योगे ॥ पृथ्व्यप्तेजोऽनिलखे समुत्थिते पञ्चात्मके योगगुणे प्रवृत्ते । न तस्य रोगो न जरा न मृत्युः प्राप्तस्य योगाग्निमयं शरीरम् ॥ लघुत्वमारोग्यमलोलुपत्वं वर्णप्रसादः स्वरसौष्ठवं च । गन्धः शुभो मूत्रपुरीषमल्पं योगप्रवृत्तिं प्रथमां वदन्ति ॥ यथैव बिम्बं मृदयोपलिप्तं तेजोमयं भ्राजते तत्सुधातम् । तद्वात्मतत्त्वं प्रसमीक्ष्य देही एकः कृतार्थो भवते वीतशोकः ॥ यदात्मतत्त्वेन तु ब्रह्मतत्त्वं दीपोपमेनेह युक्तः प्रपश्येत् । अजं ध्रुवं सर्वतत्त्वैर्विशुद्धं ज्ञात्वा देवं मुच्यते सर्वपाशैः ॥

श्वे. II. 8–15.

(*b*) यदा पञ्चावतिष्ठन्ते ज्ञानानि मनसा सह । बुद्धिश्च न विचेष्टति तामाहुः परमां गतिम् ॥ तां योगमिति मन्यन्ते स्थिरामिन्द्रियधारणाम् । अप्रमत्तस्तदा भवति योगो हि प्रभवाप्ययौ ।

क. II. 6. 10–11.

(*c*) ध्याननिर्मथनाभ्यासाद्देवं पश्येन्निगूढवत् ।

श्वे. I. 14.

(*d*) तयोरन्यः पिप्पलं स्वाद्वत्ति अनश्नन्न्यो अभिचाकशीति ।

मुं. III. 1. 1.

सूर्यो यथा सर्वलोकस्य चक्षुः न लिप्यते चाक्षुषैर्बाह्यदोषैः । एकस्तथा सर्वभूतान्तरात्मा न लिप्यते लोकदुःखेन बाह्यः ॥

क. II. 5. 11.

(*e*) भगवन्नस्थिचर्मस्नायुमज्जामांसशुक्रशोणितश्लेष्माश्रुदूषिते विण्मूत्रवातपित्तकफसंघाते दुर्गन्धे निःसारेऽस्मिञ् शरीरे किं कामोपभोगैः । मै. I. 2.

(*f*) हिता नाम पुरुषस्य नाड्यो हृदयात्पुरीततमभिप्रतन्वन्ति । तद्यथा सहस्रधा केशो विपाटितस्तावदण्व्यः पिङ्गलस्याणिम्ना तिष्ठन्ते, शुक्लस्य, कृष्णस्य, पीतस्य, लोहितस्य च। तासु तदा भवति यदा सुप्तः स्वप्नं न कंचन पश्यति ॥

कौ. IV. 19.

(*g*) अथ या एता हृदयस्य नाड्यस्ताः पिङ्गलस्याणिम्नस्तिष्ठन्ति शुक्लस्य नीलस्य पीतस्य लोहितस्येत्यसौ वा आदित्यः पिङ्गल एष शुक्ल एष नील एष पीत एष लोहितः।

छां. VIII. 6. 1.

(*h*) ता वा अस्यैता हिता नाम नाड्यो यथा केशः सहस्रधा भिन्नस्तावताणिम्ना तिष्ठन्ति शुक्लस्य नीलस्य पिङ्गलस्य हरितस्य लोहितस्य पूर्णाः।

बृ. IV. 3. 20.

10 (*a*) अथ यदा सुषुप्तो भवति यदा न कस्यचन वेद, हिता नाम नाड्यो द्वासप्ततिसहस्राणि हृदयात् पुरीततमभिप्रतिष्ठन्ते, ताभिः प्रत्यवसृप्य पुरीतति शेते स यथा कुमारो वा महाराजो वा महाब्राह्मणो वा अतिघ्नीमानन्दस्य गत्वा शयीत एवमेवैष एतच्छेते। बृ. II. 1. 19.

(*b*) येनावृतं नित्यमिदं हि सर्वं ज्ञः कालकालो गुणी सर्वविद्यः। तेनेशितं कर्म विवर्तते ह पृथिव्यप्तेजोऽनिलखानि चिन्त्यम्॥

श्वे. VI. 2.

(*c*) आकाशेनाह्वयति, आकाशेन शृणोति, आकाशेन प्रतिशृणोति। आकाशमुपास्स्वेति।

छा. VII. 12. 1.

11 अन्धं तमः प्रविशन्ति ये अविद्यामुपासते। ततो भूय इव ते ो य उ विद्यायां रताः। अन्यदेवाहुर्विद्यया अन्यदाहुरविद्यया। इति शुश्रुम धीराणां येनस्तद्विचचक्षिरे। विद्यां चाविद्यांच यस्तद्वेदोभयं सह। अविद्यया मृत्युं तीर्त्वा विद्ययामृतमश्नुते। ई. 9, 11.

12 (*a*) संयुक्तमेतत्क्षरमक्षरं च व्यक्ताव्यक्तं भरते विश्वमीशः। अनीशश्चात्मा बध्यते भोक्तृभावात् ज्ञात्वा देवं मुच्यते सर्वपाशैः॥ श्वे. I. 8.

(*b*) एको हि रुद्रो न द्वितीयाय तस्थुः य इमान् लोकान् ईशत ईशनीभिः। प्रत्यङ्जनास्तिष्ठति संचुकोपान्तकाले संसृज्य विश्वा भुवनानि गोपाः॥

श्वे. III. 2.

(*c*) घृतात्परं मण्डमिवातिसूक्ष्मं ज्ञात्वा शिवं सर्वभूतेषु गूढम्। विश्वस्यैकं परिवेष्टितारं ज्ञात्वा देवं मुच्यते सर्वपाशैः॥

श्वे. IV. 16.

(d) एकैकं जालं बहुधा विकुर्वन् अस्मिन्क्षेत्रे संचरत्येष देवः। भूयःसृष्ट्वा यतयस्तथेषः सर्वाधिपत्यं कुरुते महात्मा॥

श्वे. V. 3.

13 (a) न जायते म्रियते वा विपश्चिन्नायं कुतश्चिन्न बभूव कश्चित्। अजो नित्यः शाश्वतोऽयं पुराणो न हन्यते हन्यमाने शरीरे॥

क. I. 2. 18.

(b) हन्ता चेन्मन्यते हन्तुं हतश्चेन्मन्यते हतम्। उभौ तौ न विजानीतो नायं हन्ति न हन्यते॥

क. I. 2. 19.

(c) श्रवणायापि बहुभिर्यो न लभ्यः शृण्वन्तोऽपि बहवो यन्न विद्युः। आश्चर्यो वक्ता कुशलोऽस्य लब्धाश्चर्यो ज्ञाता कुशलानुशिष्टः॥ क. I. 2. 7.

(d) सर्वे वेदा यत्पदमामनन्ति तपांसि सर्वाणि च यद्वदन्ति। यदिच्छंतो ब्रह्मचर्यं चरन्ति तत्ते पदं संग्रहेण ब्रवीम्योमित्येतत्॥ क. I. 1. 15.

(e) तद्य इत्थं विदुर्ये चेमेऽरण्ये श्रद्धा तप इत्युपासते तेऽर्चिषमभिसंभवन्त्यर्चिषोऽहरह्न आपूर्यमाणपक्षमापूर्यमाणपक्षाद्यान्षडुदङ्ङेति मासांस्तान्॥ मासेभ्यः संवत्सरं संवत्सरादादित्यमादित्याच्चन्द्रमसं चन्द्रमसो विद्युतं तत्पुरुषोऽमानवः स एनान्ब्रह्म गमयत्येष देवयानः पन्था इति॥ अथ य इमे ग्राम इष्टापूर्ते दत्तमित्युपासते ते धूममभिसंभवन्ति धूमाद्रात्रिं रात्रेरपरपक्षं अपरपक्षाद्यान्षड्दक्षिणैति मासांस्तान्नैते संवत्सरं अभिप्राप्नुवन्ति ॥..॥ तस्मिन्यावत्संपातमुषित्वा अथ एतमेवाध्वानं पुनर्निवर्तन्ते।

छां. V. 10. 1–5.

14 (a) कुर्वन्नेवेह कर्माणि जिजीविषेच्छतं समाः। एवं त्वयि नान्यथेतोऽस्ति न कर्म लिप्यते नरे॥

ई. 2.

(b) अग्निर्मूर्धा, चक्षुषी चन्द्रसूर्यौ, दिशः श्रोत्रे, वाग् विवृताश्च वेदाः। वायुः प्राणो, हृदयं विश्वमस्य पद्भ्यां पृथिवी ह्येष सर्वभूतान्तरात्मा॥

मुं. II. 1. 4.

(c) इन्द्रियेभ्यः पराह्यर्था अर्थेभ्यश्च परं मनः। मनसस्तु परा बुद्धि बुद्धेरात्मा महान्परः॥ महतः परमव्यक्तं अव्यक्त-

त्पुरुषः परः। पुरुषान्न परं किंचित् सा काष्ठा सा परा गतिः॥
क. I. 3. 10–11.

15 (a) सोऽहं भगवो मन्त्रविदेवास्मि, नात्मवित्, श्रुतं ह्येव मे भगवद्दृशेभ्यस्तरति शोकमात्मविदिति सोऽहं भगवः शोचामि, तं मा भगवान् शोकस्य पारं तारयत्विति ॥
छां. VII. 1.

(b) उद्धर्तुमर्हसीत्यन्धोदपानस्थो भेक इवाहमस्मिन्संसारे भगवंस्त्वं नो गतिस्त्वं नो गतिः।
मै. I. 7.

(c) तं विश्वरूपं भवभूतमीड्यं देवं स्वचित्तस्थमुपास्य पूर्वम्।
श्वे. VI. 2.

(d) यस्य देवे परा भक्तिर्यथा देवे तथा गुरौ। श्वे. VI. 53.

16 ऊर्ध्वमूलोऽवाक्शाख एषोऽश्वत्थः सनातनः। तदेव शुक्रं तद्ब्रह्म तदेवामृतमुच्यते। तस्मिँल्लोकाः श्रिताः सर्वे तदु नात्येति कश्चन। एतद्वै तत्।
क. II. 6. 1.

17 स यदशिशिषति यत्पिपासति यन्न रमते ता अस्य दीक्षाः। अथ यदश्नाति यत्पिबति यद्रमते तदुपसदैरेति॥ अथ यद्धसति यज्जक्षति यन्मैथुनं चरति स्तुतशस्त्रैरेव तदेति। अथ यत्तपो दानमार्जवमहिंसा सत्यवचनमिति ता अस्य दक्षिणाः। तस्मादाहुः सोष्यत्यसोष्टेति। पुनरुत्पादनमेवास्य तन्मरणमेवावभृथः। तद्धैतद् घोर आङ्गिरसः कृष्णाय देवकीपुत्रायोक्त्वोवाचापिपास एव स बभूव सोऽन्तवेलायामेतत्त्रयं प्रतिपद्येताक्षितमस्यच्युतमसि प्राणसंशितमसीति। छां. III. 17. 1–6.

18 (a) ऋतं पिबन्तौ सुकृतस्य लोके गुहां प्रविष्टौ परमे परार्धे। छायातपौ ब्रह्मविदो वदन्ति॥
क. I. 3. 1.

(b) द्वा सुपर्णा सयुजा सखाया समानं वृक्षं परिषस्वजाते। तयोरन्यः पिप्पलं स्वाद्वत्त्यनश्नन्नन्यो अभिचाकशीति॥
मुं. III. 1. 1.

19 (a) एको देवः सर्वभूतेषु गूढः सर्वव्यापी सर्वभूतान्तरात्मा।
श्वे. VI. 1. 1.

(*b*) यस्मात्परं नापरमस्ति किंचित् यस्मान्नाणीयो न ज्यायोऽस्ति कश्चित् । वृक्ष इव स्तब्धो दिवि तिष्ठत्येकस्तेनेदं पूर्णं पुरुषेण सर्वम् ॥ श्वे. III. 9.

(*c*) विश्वतश्चक्षुरुत विश्वतोमुखो विश्वतोबाहुरुत विश्वतस्पात् । संबाहुभ्यां धमति सं पतत्रैर्द्यावाभूमी जनयन् देव एकः ॥
श्वे. III. 3.

20 (*a*) यतो वा इमानि भूतानि जायन्ते येन जातानि जीवन्ति यत्प्रयन्त्यभिसंविशन्ति तद्विजिज्ञासस्व तद्ब्रह्मेति ।
तै. III. 1.

(*b*) तस्माद्वा एतस्मादात्मन आकाश संभूतः आकाशाद्वायुः वायोरग्निः अग्नेरापः अद्भ्यः पृथिवी पृथिव्या ओषधयः ओषधिभ्योऽन्नम् ।
तै. II. 1.

21 स य एवमेतद्राजनं देवतासु प्रोतं वेद एतासामेव देवतानां सलोकतां सार्ष्टितां सायुज्यं गच्छति ।
छां. II. 20. 2.

22 (*a*) ज्ञाज्ञौ द्वावजावीशानीशावजा ह्येका भोक्तृभोगार्थयुक्ता । अनन्तश्चात्मा विश्वरूपो ह्यकर्ता त्रयं यदा विन्दते ब्रह्ममेतत् ॥
श्वे. I. 9.

(*b*) एतज्ज्ञेयं नित्यमेवात्मसंस्थं नातःपरं वेदितव्यं हि किंचित् । भोक्ता भोग्यं प्रेरितारं च मत्वा सर्वं प्रोक्तं त्रिविधं ब्रह्ममेतत् ॥ श्वे. I. 12.

23 (*a*) वेत्थ नु त्वं काप्य तत्सूत्रं येनायं च लोकः परश्च लोकः सर्वाणि च भूतानि संदृब्धानि भवन्तीति... वेत्थ नु त्वं काप्य तमंतर्यामिणं य इमं च लोकं परं च लोकं सर्वाणि च भूतानि योऽन्तरो यमयतीति..यस्तत्काप्य सूत्रं विद्यात् तं च अन्तर्यामिणमिति स ब्रह्मवित् स लोकवित् स वेदवित् स भूतवित् स आत्मवित् स सर्वविदिति । ... वायुर्वै गौतम तत्सूत्रम् । याज्ञवल्क्य अन्तर्यामिणं ब्रूहीति । यः पृथिव्यां तिष्ठन् पृथिव्या अन्तरो, यं पृथिवी न वेद, यस्य पृथिवी शरीरं, यः पृथिवीमन्तरो यमयत्येष त आत्माऽन्तर्याम्यमृतः । °अप्सु, अग्नौ, अन्तरिक्षे, वायौ, दिवि, आदित्ये, दिक्षु, चन्द्रतारके, आकाशे, तमसि, तेजसि,

सर्वेषु भूतेषु, प्राणे, वाचि, चक्षुषि, श्रोत्रे, मनसि, त्वचि, विज्ञाने, रेतसि।..।एष त आत्मान्तर्याम्यमृतोऽतोऽन्यदार्तम्।

बृ. III. 7

(b) तत्सृष्ट्वा तदेवानुप्राविशत् । तदनुप्रविश्य सच्च त्यच्चाभवत् । निरुक्तं चानिरुक्तं च । निलयनं चानिलयनं च । विज्ञानं चाविज्ञानं च । सत्यं चानृतं च । सत्यमभवत् यदिदं किंच तत्सत्यमित्याचक्षते ।

तै. II. 6.

24 (a) स वा अयमात्मा सर्वेषां भूतानां राजा, तद्यथा रथनाभौ च रथनेमौ चाराः सर्वे समर्पिताः एवमेवास्मिन्नात्मनि सर्वाणि भूतानि सर्वे देवाः सर्वे लोकाः सर्वे एत आत्मानः समर्पिताः ।

बृ. II. 5. 15.

(b) यथाग्नेः क्षुद्राः विस्फुलिङ्गा व्युच्चरन्त्येवमेव अस्मादात्मनः सर्वे प्राणाः सर्वे लोकाः सर्वे देवाः, सर्वाणि भूतानि व्युच्चरन्ति । तस्य उपनिषत् सत्यस्य सत्यमिति । प्राणाः वै सत्यं, तेषामेष सत्यम् ।

बृ. II. 1. 20.

(c) द्वे वाव ब्रह्मणो रूपे मूर्तं चैवामूर्तंच, मर्त्यं चामृतं, च स्थितं च यच्च, सच्च त्यच्च ॥ .. ॥ अथ नामधेयं सत्यस्य सत्यमिति, प्राणा वै सत्यं तेषामेष सत्यम् ।

बृ. II. 3. 1–6.

25 (a) यदा पश्यः पश्यते रुक्मवर्णं कर्तारमीशं पुरुषं ब्रह्मयोनिम् । तदा विद्वान् पुण्यपापे विधूय निरञ्जनः परमं साम्यमुपैति ॥

मुं. III. 1. 3.

(b) वेदान्तविज्ञानसुनिश्चितार्थाः संन्यासयोगाद्यतयः शुद्धसत्त्वाः। ते ब्रह्मलोकेषु परान्तकाले परामृताःपरिमुच्यन्ति सर्वे ॥

मुं. III. 2. 6.

26 (a) मनसैवेदमाप्तव्यं नेह नानास्ति किंचन । मृत्योः स मृत्युं गच्छति य इह नानेव पश्यति ॥

क. II. 4. 11.

(b) तं ह पितोवाच श्वेतकेतो यन्नु सोम्य इदं महामना अनूचानमानी स्तब्धोऽस्युत तमादेशमप्राक्ष्यः ॥ येनाश्रुतं श्रुतं भवति अमतं मतमविज्ञातं विज्ञातमिति कथं नु भगवः स आदेशो भवतीति ॥ यथा सोम्यैकेन मृत्पिण्डेन सर्वं मृन्मयं विज्ञातं स्याद्वाचारंभणं विकारो नामधेयं मृत्तिकेत्येव

सत्यम् ॥ यथा सोम्य लोहमणिना सर्वं लोहमयं विज्ञातं स्याद्वाचारंभणं विकारो नामधेयं लोहमित्येव सत्यम् ॥ यथा सोम्यैकेन नखनिकृंतनेन सर्वं कार्ष्णायसं विज्ञातं स्याद्वाचारंभणं विकारो नामधेयं कृष्णायसमित्येव सत्यमेवं सोम्य स आदेशो भवतीति ॥ न वै नूनं भगवन्तस्त एतदवेदिषुर्यद्ध्येतदवेदिष्यन् कथं मे नावक्ष्यन्निति भगवांस्त्वेव तद्ब्रवीत्विति तथा सोम्येति होवाच ॥

छां. VI. I. 2–7.

(*c*) इदं ब्रह्म इदं क्षत्रं इमे लोकाः इमे देवाः इमानि भूतानि इदं सर्वं यदयमात्मा । स यथा दुंदुभेर्हन्यमानस्य न बाह्यान् शब्दान् शक्नुयाद्ग्रहणाय दुंदुभेस्तु ग्रहणेन दुंदुभ्याघातस्य वा शब्दो गृहीतः ॥ स यथा शंखस्य ध्मायमानस्य न बाह्यान् शब्दान् शक्नुयाद्ग्रहणाय शंखस्य तु ग्रहणेन शंखध्मस्य वा शब्दो गृहीतः ॥ स यथा वीणायै वाद्यमानायै न बाह्यान् शब्दान् शक्नुयाद्ग्रहणाय वीणायै तु ग्रहणेन वीणावादस्य वा शब्दो गृहीतः ॥

बृ. II. 4. 6–9.

(*d*) सा होवाच मैत्रेयी अत्रैव मा भगवान् अमूमुहत् न प्रेत्य संज्ञास्तीति स होवाच याज्ञवल्क्यो न वा अरेऽहं मोहं ब्रवीमि ॥ यत्र हि द्वैतमिव भवति तदितर इतरं जिघ्रति तदितर इतरं पश्यति तदितरं इतरं शृणोति तदितर इतरं अभिवदति तदितर इतरं मनुते तदितर इतरं विजानाति यत्र वा अस्य सर्वमात्मैवाभूत् तत्केन कं जिघ्रेत् तत्केन कं पश्येत् तत्केन कं शृणुयात् तत्केन कं अभिवदेत् तत्केन कं मन्वीत तत्केन कं विजानीयात् येनेदं सर्वं विजानाति तं केन विजानीयात् । विज्ञातारमरे केन विजानीयादिति ॥

बृ. II. 4. 13, 14.

(*e*) यद्वै तन्न पश्यति, पश्यन्वै तन्न पश्यति, नहि द्रष्टुर्दृष्टेर्विपरिलोपो विद्यतेऽविनाशित्वात् । न तु तद्द्वितीयमस्ति ततोऽन्यद्विभक्तं, यत्पश्येत् । °जिघ्रति °रसयते °वदति °शृणोति °मनुते °स्पृशति °विजानाति । यत्र वा अन्यदिव स्यात् तत्र अन्यो अन्यत्पश्येत् जिघ्रेत् रसयेत् वदेत् शृणुयात् मन्वीत स्पृशेत् विजानीयात् ।

बृ. IV. 3. 23–31.

27 (*a*) एष सर्वेश्वरः एष सर्वज्ञः एषोऽन्तर्याम्येष योनिः सर्वस्य प्रभवाप्ययौ हि भूतानाम्॥ नान्तःप्रज्ञं न बहिष्प्रज्ञं नोभयतः-प्रज्ञं न प्रज्ञानघनं न प्रज्ञं नाप्रज्ञम्। अदृष्टमव्यवहार्यमग्राह्य-मलक्षणमचिन्त्यमव्यपदेश्यमेकात्मप्रत्ययसारं प्रपंचोपशमं शान्तं शिवं अद्वैतं चतुर्थं मन्यन्ते स आत्मा स विज्ञेयः॥

मां. 6, 7.

(*b*) स होवाचैतद्वै तदक्षरं गार्गि ब्राह्मणाः अभिवदन्ति। अस्थूलं, अनणु, अन्हस्वं, अदीर्घं, अलोहितं, अच्छायं, अतमो, असंगं, अरसं, अगंधं, अचक्षुष्कं, अश्रोत्रं, अवाक्, अमनो, अप्राणं, अमुखं, अनन्तरं, अबाह्यं, न तदश्नाति किंचन, न तदश्नाति कश्चन। बृ. II. 8. 8.

(*c*) अशब्दमस्पर्शमरूपमव्ययं, तथाऽरसं नित्यमगंधवच्च यत्। अनाद्यनंतं महतः परं ध्रुवं निचाय्य तन्मृत्युमुखात्प्रमुच्यते॥

क. I. 3. 15.

(*d*) यत्तद्द्रेश्यमग्राह्यमगोत्रमवर्णमचक्षुःश्रोत्रं तदपाणिपादम्। नित्यं विभुं सर्वगतं सुसूक्ष्मं तदव्ययं यद्भूतयोनिं परि-पश्यन्ति धीराः॥ मुं. I. 1. 6.

(*e*) स एष नेति नेतीत्यात्माऽगृह्यो न हि गृह्यते, अशीर्यो न हि शीर्यते, असंगो न हि सज्यते, असितो न व्यथते न रिष्यति अलमृतत्वमिति होक्त्वा याज्ञवल्क्यो विजहार।

बृ. IV. 5. 15; cf. also बृ. III. 9. 26; IV. 2. 4; IV. 4 22.

(*f*) अथात आदेशः नेति नेति। "न" हि एतस्मादिति "न" इति अन्यत्परमस्ति। बृ. II. 3. 6.

(*g*) तेजोमयोऽतेजोमयः, काममयोऽकाममयः, क्रोधमयोऽक्रो-धमयः, धर्ममयोऽधर्ममयः, सर्वमय तद्यदेतत् इदंमयोऽदो-मयः॥ बृ. IV. 4. 5.

28 (*a*) एष म आत्माऽन्तर्हृदय एतद्ब्रह्म एतमितः प्रेत्याभिसंभ-वितास्मीति। छा. III. 14. 4.

(*b*) अस्मिन् हंसो भ्राम्यते ब्रह्मचक्रे। पृथगात्मानं प्रेरितारं च मत्वा जुष्टस्ततः तेनामृतत्वमेति॥ श्वे. I. 6.

(*c*) ब्रह्म वा इदमग्र आसीत् तदात्मानमवेत् अहं ब्रह्मास्मीति। तस्मात् तत्सर्वं अभवत् तद्यो यो देवानां प्रत्यबुध्यत स एव तदभवत् तथा ऋषीणां तथा मनुष्याणाम्...य एवं

वेद अहं ब्रह्मास्मीति स इदं सर्वं भवति । अथ योऽन्यां देवतां उपास्ते अन्योऽसौ अन्योऽहमस्मीति, न स वेद यथा पशुरेवं स देवानाम् । बृ. I. 4. 10.

(*d*) स यश्चायं पुरुषे यश्चासावादित्ये स एकः ॥ तै. II. 8.

(*e*) पुरुष एवेदं विश्वं...एतद्यो वेद निहितं गुहायां सोऽविद्याग्रंथिं विकिरतीह सोम्य ॥ मुं. II. 1. 10.

(*f*) स य एषोऽणिमा ऐतदात्म्यमिदं सर्वं तत्सत्यं स आत्मा, तत्त्वमसि श्वेतकेतो । छां. VI. 8. 7.

29 (*a*) यथोर्णनाभिः सृजते गृह्णते च यथा पृथिव्यामोषधयः संभवन्ति । यथा सतः पुरुषात्केशलोमानि तथाक्षरात्संभवतीह विश्वम् ॥ मुं. I. 1. 7.

(*b*) तदेतत्सत्यं यथा सुदीप्तात्पावकाद्विस्फुलिंगाः सहस्रशः प्रभवन्ते सरूपाः । तथाक्षराद्विविधाः सोम्य भावाः प्रजायन्ते तत्र चैवापियन्ति ॥ मुं. II. 1. 1.

30 (*a*) यथा नद्यः स्यंदमानाः समुद्रे अस्तं गच्छन्ति नामरूपे विहाय । तथा विद्वान् नामरूपाद्विमुक्तः परात्परं पुरुषमुपैति दिव्यम् ॥ मुं. III. 2. 8.

(*b*) न तस्य प्राणा उत्क्रामन्ति ब्रह्मैव सन् ब्रह्माप्येति...तद्यथाऽहिनिर्ल्वयनी वल्मीके मृता प्रत्यस्ता शयीत एवमेव इदं शरीरं शेते । बृ. IV. 4. 6–7.

31 (*a*) हिरण्मयेन पात्रेण सत्यस्यापिहितं मुखम् । तत्त्वं पूषन्नपावृणु सत्यधर्माय दृष्टये ॥ ई. 15.

(*b*) दूरमेते विपरीते विषूची अविद्या या च विद्येति ज्ञाता । अविद्यायामन्तरे वर्तमानाः स्वयंः धीराः पंडितं मन्यमानाः दंद्रम्यमाणाः परियन्ति मूढा अन्धेनैव नीयमाना यथांधाः ॥ क. I. 2. 4, 5.

(*c*) पुरुष एवेदं विश्वम्..एतद्यो वेद निहितं गुहायाम् । सोऽविद्याग्रंथिं विकिरतीह सोम्य ॥ मुं. II. 1. 10.

(*d*) नाना तु विद्या च अविद्या च । यदेव विद्यया करोति श्रद्धयोपनिषदा तदेव वीर्यवत्तरं भवतीति ॥ छा. I. 1. 10

(*e*) असतो मा सद्गमय । तमसो मा ज्योतिर्गमय । मृत्योर्मा अमृतं गमय । बृ. I. 3. 28

(*f*) अथ धीरा अमृतत्वं विदित्वा ध्रुवं अध्रुवेष्विह न प्रार्थयन्ते । क. II. 4. 2.

(*g*) त इमे सत्याः कामाः अनृतापिधानाः तेषां सत्यानां सतां अनृतमपिधानम् । यो यो हि अस्य इतः प्रैति न तमिह दर्शनाय लभते ।..तद्यथा हि हिरण्यनिधिं निहितं अक्षेत्रज्ञा उपर्युपरि संचरन्तो न विन्देयुः एवमेव इमाः सर्वाः प्रजाः अहरहर्गच्छंत्यः एतं ब्रह्मलोकं न विन्दन्ति अनृतेन हि प्रत्यूढाः । स वा एष आत्मा हृदि..अहरहर्वा एवंवित्स्वर्गं लोकमेति । छां. VIII. 3. 1–3.

(*h*) तेषां असौ विरजो ब्रह्मलोको न येषु जिह्मं अनृतं न माया चेति । प्र. I. 16.

(*i*) तस्याभिध्यानात् योजनात् तत्त्वभावात् भूयश्चान्ते विश्वमायानिवृत्तिः । श्वे. I. 10.

(*j*) रूपं रूपं प्रतिरूपो बभूव तदस्य रूपं प्रतिचक्षणाय । इंद्रो मायाभिः पुरुरूप ईयते युक्ता ह्यस्य हरयः शतादश ॥
बृ. II. 5. 19; cf.also ऋ. VI. 47. 18.

(*k*) अस्मान्मायी सृजते विश्वमेतत् । तस्मिंश्चान्यो मायया संनिरुद्धः । श्वे. IV. 9.

(*l*) मायां तु प्रकृतिं विद्यान्मायिनं तु महेश्वरम् ।

श्वे. IV. 10.

(*m*) य एको जालवानीशत ईशनीभिः सर्वान् लोकान् ईशत ईशनीभिः । श्वे. III. 1.

एकैकं जालं बहुधा विकुर्वन् अस्मिन्क्षेत्रे संचरत्येष देवः ।
भूयः सृष्ट्वा यतयस्तथेशः सर्वाधिपत्यं कुरुते महात्मा ॥

श्वे. V. 3.

(*n*) यत्र हि द्वैतमिव भवति तदितर इतरं पश्यति ।

बृ. II. 4. 14.

(*o*) यथा सोम्य एकेन मृत्पिण्डेन सर्वं मृण्मयं विज्ञातं स्यात् वाचारंभणं विकारो नामधेयं मृत्तिका इत्येव सत्यम् ।
छां. VI. 1. 4.

CHAPTER V

THE PROBLEM OF ULTIMATE REALITY IN THE UPANISHADS

The Supreme Philosophical Problem.

1. In the midst of all the metaphysical conflicts that we have witnessed in the last chapter, there arises one supreme question—what, if any, is the core of Upanishadic teaching? Shall our minds be only tossed on the waves of philosophical conflicts, or can we have a ballast which will give the necessary poise to our philosophical speculations? Shall our minds be only sunk in the mire of the metaphysical conflicts of Pluralism, Qualified Monism, and Monism as we find them in the Upanishads? Is there not, at the basis of these various attempts at the solution of the central metaphysical problem, one fundamental conception, which will enable us to string together the variegated philosophical speculations of the Upanishads? This raises a very important problem—the problem of Ultimate Reality as understood by the Upanishadic seers. As we shall notice in this chapter, the Upanishadic philosophers solved the problem by taking recourse to the conception of Ātman, a word which originally signified the breathing principle in man, but which came in the end to denote the essence of the Universe. Readers of Greek philosophy need hardly be reminded of the close parallel that exists between this Upanishadic conception of Ātman and the Platonic conception of the αὐτὸ καθ' αὑτό. The Ātman, as we shall see in the course of this chapter, is the ultimate category of existence to the Upanishadic seers.) How they arrived at this conception, and what use they made of it in the solution of the fundamental philosophical problem will form the theme of the present discourse.

The three approaches to the Problem in the history of thought: cosmological, theological, psychological.

2. If we look at the history of philosophic thought, we shall see that there are various ways in which the problem of Ultimate Reality has been approached. The three chief types of approach are the Cosmological, the Theological, and the Psychological. Dr. Caird has said, that, by the very constitution of man's mind, there have been only three ways of thinking open to man: "He can look outward upon the world around him; he can look inward upon the Self within him; and he can look upward to the God above him, to the Being who unites the outward and inward worlds, and who manifests himself in both."[1] According to him, the consciousness of objects is prior in time to self-consciousness, and the consciousness of both subject and object is prior to the consciousness of God. As he also elsewhere expresses it: "Man looks outward before he looks inward, and he looks inward before he looks upward."[2] The question arises: Is this account of the development of the consciousness of Reality ultimately valid? Is it necessary that man must look at the outside world before he looks within, and must he always look within before he can look up to God? The solutions which the history of philosophy gives to this problem are not exactly as Caird would have them. The Cartesian solution does not start by saying that the

1 Evolution of Religion, I. 77.

2 Evolution of Religion, II. 2.

outside world is real. For Descartes, the Self is the primary reality, self-consciousness the primary fact of existence, and introspection the start of the real philosophical process. From the Self, says Descartes, we arrive at the conception of God, who is the cause of the Self, and whom we must therefore regard as more perfect than the Self. Finally, it is from God that we arrive at the world which we started by negating, by regarding as the creation of a deceptive evil spirit. On the other hand, to the God-intoxicated philosopher, Spinoza, neither the Self nor the world is the primary reality. To him, God is the be-all and the end-all of all things, the alpha and the omega of existence. From God philosophy starts, and in God philosophy ends. The manner of approach of the Upanishadic philosophers to the problem of ultimate reality was neither the Cartesian nor the Spinozistic one. The Upanishadic philosophers regarded the Self as the ultimate existence and subordinated the World and God to the Self. The Self, to them, is more real than either the World or God. It is only ultimately that they identify the Self with God, and thus bridge over the gulf that exists between the theological and psychological approaches to Reality. They start, no doubt, by looking out into the world, but they find that the solution of the ultimate problem cannot come from the world without : it is necessary for us, they say, to go back to the psychololgical category. Then they try another experiment : they go by the theological approach to the problem of reality, but they find that also to be wanting. Finally, they try the psychological approach, and arrive at the solution of the problem of ultimate existence. We thus see that the problem of ultimate Reality to the Upanishadic philosophers is a cosmo-theo-psychological problem : finding both the cosmological and theological approaches deficient, they take recourse to the psychological approach and arrive at the conception of the Self, which they call the Ātman. We shall proceed to show at length in this chapter how the Upanishadic philosophers regarded the cosmological and theological approaches as only ancillary, and the psychological approach as the only true approach to the ultimate solution.

I—THE COSMOLOGICAL APPROACH

Regress from the cosmological to the physiological categories.

3. We shall first discuss the cosmological approach, and see how it was found deficient. The naive mind of the natural man is likely to consider the forces of nature as ultimate realities; but a deeper speculation and a greater insight into events show that the phenomenal forces cannot be taken to be ultimate realities. This fact is illustrated by a story in the Chhāndogya Upanishad, where we are told how one student, Upakosala, lived for instruction with his preceptor, Satyakāma Jābāla, and served him assiduously for twelve years; how even though the ordinary period of tutelage was over, his teacher would not leave him; how the wife of the teacher asked her husband why it was that he would not leave this one disciple while he had left the others; how, when Upakosala had once gone to the forest, the three sacrificial Fires, whom he had assiduously served in his master's house, rose in bodily form before him; how the first, namely Gāhrapatya, told him that the ultimate reality was to be found in the sun; how the second, namely Anvāhāryapachana, told him that it was to be found in the moon; how, the last, namely Āhavanīya, told him that it was to be found in the lightning; how, in fact, Upakosala seemed to be temporarily satisfied with the

instruction imparted to him by the three Fires; how, when he returned home, his teacher asked him why it was that his face shone as if with spiritual illumination; how the student told him that the spiritual illumination, if at all, was due to the instruction imparted to him by the three Fires; how the teacher replied that the teaching imparted to him by the Fires was deficient and inferior to the teaching which he himself knew; how he ultimately imparted that teaching to his disciple, which consisted in saying that the ultimate reality was to be found neither in the sun, nor in the moon, nor in the lightning, but in the image of the person reflected in the human eye. "It is this image," said Satyakāma Jābāla, "which is the Ātman. It is this image which is fearless, and the ultimate reality. It is this image which brings all blessings. It is this image which is the most resplendent thing in all the worlds. He who knows it to be so will himself be resplendent in the worlds" (S. 1). This passage evidently indicates a regress from the cosmological to the physiological category. Not satisfied with objective existences being regarded as ultimate reality, Satyakāma declares that ultimate reality is to be found in a physiological category, namely, the eye. This, in itself, as we shall see later on, is only an inferior truth, though evidently it has the merit of taking us from the outside world to the physiological sphere. In a similar spirit, in another passage of the Chhāndogya Upanishad, we are told how the light "which shines in the high heavens in transcendent space is the same light which is within man, and of this we have tactual proof, namely, when we feel the warmth in the body, and audible proof when after closing our ears we hear what may be regarded as the thunder of heaven, or the bellowing of an ox, or the sound of a burning fire. He who meditates on ultimate reality as thus dwelling in the human body becomes himself conspicuous and celebrated" (S. 2. a). This same idea is expressed in the Maitri Upanishad when the author of that Upanishad speaks of the ultimate reality in man as being verily the sound which a man hears after shutting his ears (S. 2. b). We thus see that in these passages we have a regress from the cosmological to the physiological categories, namely, the eye, or bodily warmth, or the sound that man hears after closing his ears. The cosmological approach has been tried and found wanting. It seems necessary for the Upanishadic philosophers to halt at the caravansary of the physiological categories[1] before they can proceed to the psychological destination.

Regress from the cosmological and physiological to the psychological categories.

4. In a passage which occurs both in the Kaushītaki and the Bṛihadāraṇyaka Upanishads, we are told how both the cosmological and physiological categories must be regarded as deficient, and how they must, therefore, necessarily pave the way for the psychological category. There is here a discussion as to how the proud Bālāki once went to Ajātaśatru, the king of Kāśī, and how he tried to impose upon him by saying that he would impart superior wisdom to him; how Ajātaśatru welcomed this great man who told him that he would impart superior knowledge; how the proud Bālāki began by saying that true wisdom consisted in regarding the sun as ultimate reality; how he went on to say that the ultimate reality was to be found, one after another, in such objects as the moon, the lightning, the thunder, the wind, the sky, the fire, the water, the mirror, the image, the echo, the

1 There is the same distinction between physiology and psychology as Matthew Arnold would say between the poetries of Byron and Wordsworth.

sound, the body, the right eye and the left eye; how ultimately Bālāki's mouth was gagged when he could proceed no further in his peculiar way of philosophising; how Ajātaśatru took Bālāki by the hand, went to a man who had fallen in deep sleep, and called upon him saying 'Thou great one, clad in white raiment, O king Soma'; how the man, who had fallen in deep sleep, still remained lying; how he rose at once when Ajātaśatru pushed him with his stick; and how, finally, Ajātaśatru told Bālāki that in the person who had gone to sleep, the sleeping consciousness may be regarded as ultimate reality (S. 3). In this passage we have evidently the deficiency of both the cosmological and physiological categories brought out in favour of the psychological category, namely, the deep-sleep consciousness. We shall see later how even this is an inferior answer to the problem that has been raised; and, therefore, we shall not stop at this place to discuss the final psychological answer of the Upanishadic philosophers on this head.

The cosmological argument for the existence of God: God is all-powerful.

5. The cosmological approach has been tried and found wanting in favour either of physiological or psychological categories. But it does not by any means follow that the cosmological speculations of the Upanishadic philosophers did not lead them independently to the positing of Absolute Existence. If we look deeper, we shall find in them the same kind of cosmological proof for the existence of the Absolute, as we find, for example, in the history of Greek Philosophy. A passage of the Taittirīya Upanishad declares that behind the cosmos there must be an existence which must be regarded as responsible for its origin, sustenance, and absorption: "that from which all these beings come

into existence, that by which they live, that into which they are finally absorbed, know that to be the eternal verity, the Absolute" (S. 4. a). And, again, a cryptic formula of the Chhāndogya Upanishad declares that a man must compose himself in the belief that the world has come out of, lives in, and is finally absorbed in the Absolute. The philosopher of this Upanishad expresses this whole conception by means of a single word *tajjalān*, which means that it is from the Absolute that the world has sprung, it is into it that it is dissolved, and it is by means of it that it lives (S. 4. b). This "cosmological" proof for the existence of an eternal verity behind the cosmos by reference to the origin, existence, and destruction of the world is known to all students of philosophy, and we find the same thing in the Upanishads also. It is true that the same kind of objections that were advanced by Kant against the traditional cosmological argument may likewise be advanced against this way of argumentation in the Upanishads ; but the fact cannot be gainsaid that the argument is there. When once an eternal verity behind the cosmos has been postulated, the Upanishadic philosophers have no hesitation in making it the fount and source of all power whatsoever. They consider it to be the source of Infinite Power which is only partially exhibited in the various phenomena of Nature. Thus the forces of Nature that we are aware of are ultimately only partial manifestations of the power that is in the Absolute. There is a very interesting parable in the Kenopanishad which tells us how this is so. Parables and myths in philosophical works are to be understood as merely allegorical representations of philosophical truths, and it is thus that the story in that Upanishad of Brahman, the eternal Verity, showing its prowess against the arrogant godlings of Nature, must be understood. The story runs, that there was, once upon a time, a great fight between the gods and the demons, and the gods were successful. The gods thought that the success was due entirely to their own power, and forgetting that this power was only a manifestation of the power of Brahman in them, they became proud. The Brahman, knowing this, suddenly made its appearance before them, and the gods were greatly wonderstruck, not knowing what it was. Then they sent forth one of them, namely, the god of fire, as an emissary to Brahman, and charged him with the task of learning the real nature of that Great Being. The god of fire ran in pride to Brahman. Brahman asked him who he was, and the god of fire proudly answered that he was Jātavedas, in whom lay the power of burning the whole of the earth if he pleased. Then Brahman threw before him a small blade of grass, and asked him to burn it if he could. The god of fire was unable to burn it with all his might. He became disappointed and returned to the gods. Then the gods sent another godling of nature, the god of wind, and charged him with the same mission. The god of wind ran in pride to Brahman, and, being asked who he was, said that he was Mātariśvan, in whom lay the power of blowing away anything from off the surface of the earth. Brahman again threw a blade of grass before him. Not with all his might was the god of wind able to move it to an infinitesimal distance. Then the god of wind returned in shame, not being able to know the nature of that Great Being. Then the gods sent Indra and charged him with the same mission. Indra was a more modest god than either the god of fire or the god of wind. He ran to Brahman to know its nature, and Brahman disappeared from his sight, for the simple reason, it seems, that Indra was more humble than either of the gods previously sent.

Then suddenly sprang before Indra one very beautiful celestial damsel, from whom Indra inquired what that Great Being was, which had made its sudden disappearance from before him. Then that damsel told him that it was Brahman, and said further, that it was due to the power of the Brahman that the gods had gained victory over the demons, and not to their own personal power. God Indra was shrewd enough and understood that the power of the gods was only a manifestation of the power of the Absolute. It was on account of this humility, which made it possible for him to go to Brahman and touch him nearest, that he became the foremost of the gods. " It is verily the power of Brahman which flashes forth in the lightning and vanishes again. It is the power of Brahman which manifests itself as the motion of the soul in us and bethinks itself " (S. 5. a). This parable tells us that all physical as well as mental power is to be regarded merely as a manifestation of the power of Brahman. We thus see how the philosopher of the Kenopanishad arrives cosmologically at the conception of an unmanifested Power which lies at the back of the so-called manifest powers of nature and mind, and which must therefore be understood as the primary reality.

God is supreme resplendence.

6. It is not merely that all the power in the world is ultimately due to Brahman : the very resplendence and illumination that we meet with in the world are also to be regarded as manifestations of the great unmanifest luminosity of the Absolute. " Does the sun shine by his own power ?" asks the Kaṭhopanishad ; " Do the moon and the stars shine by their own native light ? Does the lightning flash forth in its native resplendence ?—Not to speak of the paltry

earthly fire, which obviously owes its resplendence to something else ?" Shall we say that all these so-called resplendent things are resplendent in their own native light, or must we assert that they derive their power of illumination from a primal eternal verity which lies at the back of them all, and whose illumination makes possible the illumination of the so-called luminous objects of nature ? "Before Him the Sun does not shine, before Him the moon and the stars do not shine, before Him the lightning does not shine; far less this earthly fire. It is only when the Absolute shines first, that all these objects shine afterwards. It is by His luminosity that they become luminous" (S. 5. b).

God is the subtle essence underlying phenomenal existence.

7. The Brahman, therefore, which must be posited as the fount and source of all existence, and which must be regarded as the origin of all power and resplendence, must also be taken, say the Upanishadic thinkers, as the subtle essence underlying all the gross manifestations that we meet with in the world. Another parable, this time from the Chhāndogya Upanishad, tells us how in the conversation that took place between a teacher and his pupil, the teacher, in order to convince his pupil of the subtlety of the underlying essence, directed him to bring to him a small fruit of the Nyagrodha tree; how, when the disciple had brought one, the teacher directed him to break it open; how, when it was broken open, he asked him to see what was inside the fruit of the tree; how, when the disciple looked into it, he saw that there were seeds infinite in number, and infinitesimal in size; how when the teacher again directed him to break open one of those seeds, the disciple did so, and, being asked to see further what was there, said "Nothing,

Sir ", upon which the teacher told him, " My dear boy, it is of the very subtle essence that you do *not* perceive there—it is of this very essence that the great Nyagrodha tree is made. Believe it, my dear boy " (S. 6). This parable tells us how the underlying essence of things is to be regarded as subtle and unmanifest, and how the gross and manifested objects are to be understood as merely phenomenal appearances. There is, however, a further point in the parable which we must duly notice. When the teacher told his disciple that behind the Nyagrodha tree there lay a subtle essence which was unmanifest, he also told him that it was to be identified with the Self, and further, that the disciple must identify himself with it (S. 6). We see here the limitation of the mere cosmological conception of an underlying essence of things, and it seems as if cosmology must invoke the aid of psychological categories once more before the essence underlying the cosmos could be identified with the essence that lies at the back of the human mind. Thus the whole Universe becomes one, only when we suppose that there is the same subtle essence underlying both the world of nature and the world of mind.

The physico-theological argument.

8. The cosmological argument, as it happens in the history of thought, seems also to take the help of the physico-theological proof and the two together seem to offer a formidable front to the thinking mind. Likewise does it happen in the case of Upanishadic philosophy. The argument from design and the argument from order are merely the personal and impersonal aspects of the physico-theological argument. Those who believe in God believe in design. Those who believe in an impersonal Absolute believ

only in order. Very often, as in the case of the Upanishadic thinkers, the personal and impersonal aspects are fused together, and we are told how the Self as personal existence is yet "an impersonal bund which holds the river of existence from flowing by. Neither night nor day, neither age nor death, neither grief nor good nor evil, are able to transgress this eternal bund of existence" (S. 7. a). "It is at the command of this imperishable existence," says the Bṛihadāraṇyaka Upanishad, "that the sun and the moon stand bound in their places. It is due to the command of this Absolute that the heaven and the earth stand each in its own place. It is due to the command of this imperishable Brahman that the very moments, the hours, the days, the nights, the months, the seasons, and the years have their appointed function in the scheme of things. It is at the command of this Brahman that some rivers flow to the east from the snow-clad mountains, while others flow to the west" (S. 7. b). We shall not try to disentangle here the personal and impersonal aspects of the physico-theological proof, the aspect of design and the aspect of order. Suffice it to say that the physico-theological proof is present in the Upanishads, pointing out that the Absolute must be regarded as the ballast of the cosmos, preventing it from rocking to and fro at the slightest gust of chance.

II—THE THEOLOGICAL APPROACH

Regress from polytheism to monotheism.

9. We shall now see how the Upanishadic philosophers went by the theological approach to the conception of reality. They began by inquiring how many gods must be supposed to exist in the universe. They could not rest content until they arrived at the idea of one God, who was the ruler of the whole universe. Ultimately, they identified this God with the

inner Self in man. In this way did theological categories become subservient to the psychological category of the Self. We shall see how this happens. In the controversy which took place between Vidagdha Śākalya and the sage Yājñavalkya as reported in the Bṛihadāraṇyaka, we are told that the former asked Yājñavalkya how many gods must be regarded as existing in the world, to which the first answer of Yājñavalkya was "three and three hundred," Yājñavalkya closely following upon this by saying that there were "three and three thousand." Not satisfied with the answers, Śākalya asked again how many gods there were. Yājñavalkya replied there were thirty-three gods. Śākalya was again dissatisfied and asked again. Yājñavalkya replied there were six gods. In answer to further inquiries from Śākalya, Yājñavalkya went on to say that there were three gods, and then two gods, and even one-and-a-half (!) god, and finally that there was only one God without a second. Yājñavalkya was merely testing the insight of Śākalya as to whether he would rest satisfied with the different answers that he first gave, and when Śākalya did not seem satisfied, he finally said that there was only one God. By mutual consent, Śākalya and Yājñavalkya came to the conclusion that He alone is the God of the Universe, "whose body the earth is, whose sight is fire, whose mind is light, and who is the final resort of all human souls" (S. 8. a).

The theistic conception of God and His identification with the Self.

10. The Śvetāśvatara Upanishad develops this conception of a personal God. In a theistic vein it declares how the one God, whom it calls Rudra, beside whom there is no second, and who rules the worlds with his powers, stands behind all persons, creates all the worlds, and, in the end of time, rolls them up again. He has his eyes everywhere, and his face everywhere; his hands and feet are also omnipresent. He creates the men of earth and endows them with hands. He creates the fowl of air and endows them with wings. He is the only God who has created the heaven and the earth (S. 8. b). In a later passage of the same Upanishad, the author inquires further into the nature and attributes of this God. He calls him the only Lord of the universe, the creator, the preserver, and the destroyer of all. He ends by declaring that it is only to those who regard this God as identical with the Self within,—to those belongs eternal happiness, to none else: "Some so-called wise men, being under a great philosophic delusion, regard Nature, and others Time, as the source of being. They forget that it is the greatness of the Lord, which causes the wheel of Brahman to turn round. It is by Him that all this has been covered. He is the only knower, he is death to the god of death, the possessor of all qualities and wisdom. It is at His command that creation unfolds itself, namely, what people call earth, water, fire, air and ether. He is the permanent as well as the accidental cause of unions. He is beyond the past, the present, and the future, and is truly regarded as without parts. That universal God, who is immanent in all these beings, should be meditated upon as dwelling in our minds also—that God who is the Lord of all gods, who is the Deity of all deities, who is the supreme Master of all masters, and who is the adorable Ruler of the universe. There is no cause of Him, nor any effect. There is none equal to Him, nor any superior. The great power inherent in Him manifests itself alike in the form of knowledge and action. There is no master of Him in this world, nor any ruler, nor is there anything which we might regard as His sign. He is the only Cause, the Lord of all those who possess sense-organs. There is no generator of Him, nor any protector. He is the self-subsistent mover of the unmoving manifold, who causes the one seed to sprout in infinite ways. It is only to those who regard this Universal Being as immanent in their own Selves, to them belongs eternal happiness, to none else " (S. 8. c). In this theistic description of the Śvetāśvatara Upanishad we are told how God is the only cause of the world, and how ultimately he is to be regarded as identical with the Self within. Here again the purely theological category becomes subservient to the psychological category of the Self ; and it seems as if the ultimate category of existence to the Upanishadic philosophers is God-Ātman.

The immanence-transcendence of God.

11. The Upanishads are not without reference to the immanence and transcendence of God. There are some passages which declare merely his immanence, others merely his transcendence ; others again bring together the two aspects of the immanence and transcendence of God. Thus, for example, we are told in the Śvetāśvatara Upanishad that " God is to be regarded as being present in fire and in water, in all the universe, in the herbs and plants." In the Bṛihadāraṇyaka Upanishad we are told how God-Ātman is immanent in us from top to toe, as a razor is entirely closed up within the razor-box, or again, as a bird is pent up within its nest. A story from the Chhāndogya Upanishad also brings into relief this aspect of the immanence of God. We are told there how the disciple was asked by his teacher to place a small piece of salt in water at night, and come to him in the morning ; how the disciple did as he was commanded ; how, when the teacher asked

him what had become of the salt, the disciple could not find it out because it had already melted in the water; how when the teacher asked him to taste the water from the surface, then from the middle, and then from the bottom, the disciple replied that it was salt in all places; then how the teacher told him that the salt, even though it seemed to have disappeared in the water, was thoroughly present in every part of it. Thus, verily, says the clever teacher, is that subtle Ātman immanent in the universe, whom we may not be able to see, but whom we must regard as existing as the supreme object of faith (S. 9. a). All these passages speak of the thorough immanence of God. A passage from the Kaṭhopanishad, which reminds us of a similar one from the Republic of Plato, which speaks of the Sun of the world of Ideas, tells us how the universal Self is to be regarded as beyond all the happiness and the misery of the world—"like the celestial Sun who is the eye of all the universe and is untouched by the defects of our vision" (S. 9. b). Here the transcendence of God is clearly brought into relief. In other passages, we are also told how God is to be regarded as having "filled the whole world and yet remained beyond its confines." "Like the fire and the wind which enter the world and assume various forms, the universal Ātman is immanent in every part of the universe and protrudes beyond its confines." "Verily motionless like a lone tree does this God stand in the heaven and yet by Him is this whole world filled." This is how the Śvetāśvatara Upanishad declares the transcendence and immanence of God (S. 9. c). We see from all these passages how God-Ātman is to be regarded as having filled every nook and cranny of the Universe, and yet having overflowed it to a limitless extent. In any case, the God in the universe is to be regarded as identical with the Self within us : it is only when this identification takes place that we arrive, according to the Upanishadic philosophers, at the ultimate conception of Reality.

III—THE PSYCHOLOGICAL APPROACH

The conception of the Self reached by an analysis of the various physiological and psychological categories.

12. Let us now proceed to see how the Upanishadic philosophers reached the idea of ultimate reality by the psychological method. In a conversation which took place between King Janaka and Yājñavalkya as reported in the Bṛihadāraṇyaka Upanishad, we find that Yājñavalkya asked Janaka as to what psychological doctrines he had heard about the nature of ultimate reality. Janaka was a very inquisitive and philosophically inclined king, and he had therefore known all the opinions on that head which had been imparted to him by different sages. He proceeded to tell Yājñavalkya the opinions of these various philosophers. "Jitvan Śailini told me," said king Janaka, "that speech was the ultimate reality." Yājñavalkya answered that this was merely a partial truth. Then king Janaka told him that Udaṅka Śaulbāyana had said to him that breath was the ultimate reality. This also, said Yājñavalkya, was only a partial truth. Varku Vārshṇi had told him, said Janaka, that the eye was the final reality. This again, said Yājñavalkya, was only a partial truth. Then the king went on to say how Gardabhī-vipīta Bhāradvāja had told him that the ear was the final reality; how Satyakāma Jābāla had said that the mind was the final reality; how Vidagdha Śākalya had told him that the heart was the final reality;—all of which opinions, said Yājñavalkya, were only partial truths (S. 10. a). In this enumeration of the opinions of different Upanishadic philosophers as re-

gards the various physiological or psychological categories as constituting the ultimate reality, and in Yājñavalkya's rejection of each one of them in turn, there lies implicitly the conception that ultimate reality can be found only in the Self, and not in the accidental adjuncts with which the Self may come to be clothed. This same idea has been developed in the Kena Upanishad where we are told that "the Self must be regarded as the ear of ear, as the mind of mind, as the speech of speech, as the breath of breath, as the eye of eye. Those who know the Self thus are released from this world and become immortal." "That which speech is unable to give out, but that which itself gives out speech, know that to be the ultimate reality, not that which people worship in vain. That which the mind is unable to think, but which thinks the mind, know that to be the ultimate reality; that which the eye is unable to see, but that which enables us to see the eye, know that to be the ultimate reality; that which the ear does not hear, but that which enables us to perceive the ear, that which breath is not able to breathe, but that by which breath itself is breathed, know that to be the final reality" (S. 10. b.). In this passage we are told that the Self must be regarded as the innermost existence, while all the physiological and psychological elements are only external vestures, which clothe reality but which do not constitute it.

The states of consciousness: waking-consciousness, dream-consciousness, sleep-consciousness, Self-consciousness.

13. We now come to a very famous parable in the Chhāndogya Upanishad which unmistakably tells us how we must arrive at the conception of the Self-conscious Being within us as constituting the ultimate reality. In a very clever analysis of the psychological states

through which a man's soul passes, the author of that Upanishad brings out how the ultimate reality must not be mistaken with bodily consciousness; how it must not be confused with the dream-consciousness; how it transcends even the deep-sleep-consciousness; how, finally, it is the pure Self-consciousness, which is beyond all bodily or mental limitations. We are told in the Chhāndogya Upanishad that the gods and demons were, once upon a time, both anxious to learn the nature of final reality, and they therefore went in pursuit of it to Prajāpati. Prajāpati had maintained that "that entity, which is free from sin, free from old age, free from death and grief, free from hunger and thirst, which desires nothing, and imagines nothing, must be regarded as the ultimate self." The gods and demons were anxious to know what this Self was. So the gods sent Indra and the demons Virochana as their emissaries to learn the final truth from Prajāpati. They dwelt there as pupils at first for a period of thirty-two years, which condition was necessary before a master could impart spiritual wisdom to his disciples. Then Prajāpati asked them what it was that had brought them there. Indra and Virochana told him that they had come to him in order that they might know the nature of the Self. Now Prajāpati would not immediately tell them the final truth. He tried to delude them by saying first that the Self was nothing more than the image that we see in the eye, in water, or in a mirror. It was this, he said, which must be regarded as the immortal and fearless Brahman. Indra and Virochana became complacent in the belief that they had understood the nature of the Self. They bedecked themselves by putting on excellent clothes and ornaments, cleaned themselves, looked into a water-pan, and imagined they had visualised the ultimate Self, and went altogether composed in mind. Virochana told the demons that he had been in possession of the ultimate secret, namely, that the so-called Self was no other than the image that one sees in the eye, in a mirror, or in a pan of water, thus identifying the Self with the mere image of the body. The Upanishad tells us how there are a certain set of people who take this as final gospel, which it calls the gospel of the Asuras. There must be a slight reference here to those, who, like the later Chārvākas, maintained that the Self was nothing more than the mere consciousness of body. Indra, however, unlike Virochana, bethought himself that Prajāpati must not have given him the final answer in the matter of the knowledge of ultimate reality. There was this difficulty that pressed itself before him. "It is true," he said, "that, when the body is well adorned, the Self is well adorned; when the body is well dressed, the Self is well dressed; when the body is well cleaned, the Self is well cleaned; but what if the body were blind, or lame, or crippled? Shall not the Soul itself be thus regarded as blind, or lame, or crippled"? He thought that there was this great difficulty in the teaching that had been imparted to him by Prajāpati, and so he went back again to Prajāpati to request him once more to tell him what ultimate reality was. Prajāpati advised him to practise penance once more for thirty-two years, and, when Indra had performed that penance, Prajāpati supplied him with another piece of knowledge. "The true Self is he," said Prajāpati, "who moves about happy in dreams. He is the immortal, the fearless Brahman." In fact, Prajāpati told him that dream-consciousness must be regarded as identical with the Self. This seemed to please Indra and he went back; but before he reached the gods, he saw again that there was another difficulty in the information that had been imparted to him by Prajāpati. "Do we not feel," he asked himself, "as if we are struck, or chased in our dreams? Do we not experience pain, and do we not shed tears in our dreams? How can we account for this difficulty if the Self were to be identified with dream-consciousness"? So he went back to Prajāpati again, and told him that the knowledge which he had imparted to him could not be final, inasmuch as the dream-consciousness seemed to him to be affected with feelings of pain and fear. The true Self could experience neither pain nor fear. Prajāpati saw that Indra was a pupil worthy to know better things, and so he asked him once more to practise penance for another thirty-two years, at the end of which time he imparted to him another piece of knowledge which was yet not the highest knowledge, namely, when he said, that the true Self must be regarded as identical with the deep-sleep consciousness in which there is perfect repose and perfect rest. Indra was satisfied with the answer which Prajāpati had given and returned. But before he reached the gods, he again saw that the real Self could not be identified even with deep-sleep consciousness for the simple reason that in deep-sleep we are conscious neither of our own selves nor of objects. In fact, in deep-sleep we are as if we were only logs of wood. There is neither consciousness of self nor consciousness of the objective world. Feeling this great difficulty in the teaching that had been imparted to him by Prajāpati, he went back again and told him that he could not be satisfied with the knowledge which had been imparted to him, namely that the ultimate Self was to be found in the consciousness of deep-sleep. For, he said, in that state there was neither self-consciousness, nor any consciousness of the objective world; and it seemed as if the soul was entirely annihilated in that state. This could not be regarded, said Indra, as the final wisdom. Prajāpati now saw that Indra by his shrewd insight had made himself worthy of receiving the highest knowledge. So he asked Indra once more, and this time finally, to practise penance for five years again. Indra practised penance for five years, thus completing the round of penance for a hundred and one years. At the end of that period, he went in all humility to Prajāpati and implored him to give him an insight into the final knowledge. Prajāpati said, " Verily, O Indra, this body is subject to death, but it is at the same time the vesture of an immortal Soul. It is only when the Soul is encased in the body, that it is cognisant of pleasure and pain. There is neither pleasure nor pain for the Soul once relieved of its body. Just as the wind and the cloud, the lightning and the thunder, are without body, and arise from heavenly space and appear in their own form, so does this serene being, namely, the Self, arise from this mortal body, reach the highest light, and then appear in his own form. This Serene Being, who appears in his own form is the highest Person." There is here an indication of the true nature of ultimate reality as being of the nature of self-consciousness. That which sees itself by itself, that which recognises itself as identical with itself in the light of supreme knowledge—that must be regarded as the final reality. The final reality, therefore, according to the Chhāndogya Upanishad, is reached in that theoretic, ecstatic, self-spectacular state in which the Self is conscious of nothing but itself. (S. 11). There is a great meaning which runs through this parable. By an analysis of the different states of consciousness, the philosopher of the Chhāndogya Upanishad points out that the bodily consciousness must not be mistaken for final reality, nor the consciousness in dreams, nor that in deep sleep.

The Soul is of the nature of pure self-consciousness, the Kantian "I am I." Those who mistake the ultimate Self as identical with bodily consciousness are the materialists. Those who identify it with the consciousness in the dream-state rise a little higher no doubt, but they mistake the Self for what the modern Theosophists call the "etheric double." Those, on the other hand, who regard the Self as identical with deep-sleep consciousness also misunderstand its nature, because there is in that state no consciousness either of the object world or of the Self. The true Self could only be the self-conscious Being, shining in his own native light, thinking of nothing but his own thought, the νόησις νοήσεως of Aristotle, the supreme theoretic Being, the eternal Self-spectator.

The ontological argument for the existence of the Self.

14. We have hitherto seen how the philosopher of the Chhāndogya Upanishad arrives at the conception of Self-consciousness as constituting the ultimate reality. We have seen also how the Upanishadic philosophers generally regard God as identical with this pure self-consciousness. The philosopher of the Taittirīya Upanishad gives us certain characteristics of this final reality which enable us to regard his argument as almost an ontological characterisation of reality. "The Absolute," he says, "is Existence, Consciousness, and Infinity" (S. 12. a). In this identification of the Absolute with Consciousness, we have again the real nature of the Ātman brought out in bold relief. Existence to that philosopher means Consciousness. The same idea is repeated elsewhere in the Aitareya Upanishad, where the author of that Upanishad speaks "of the gods of the heaven and the beings of the earth, whether produced from eggs, or embryo, or sweat, or from the earth, everything

that moves, or flies, or is stationary—Self-consciousness is the eye of all these. They are rooted in Self-consciousness. Self-consciousness is the eye of the world; it is Self-consciousness which is the Absolute" (S. 12. b). Here we have unmistakably the ontological argument, namely, that ultimate Existence must be identified with Self-consciousness. Thus by a survey of the different approaches to the problem of Reality, namely, the cosmological, the theological, and the psychological, we see that the Upanishadic philosophers try to establish Reality on the firm footing of Self-consciousness. Self-consciousness to them is the eternal verity. God to them is not God, unless he is identical with Self-consciousness. Existence is not Existence if it does not mean Self-consciousness. Reality is not reality, if it does not express throughout its structure the marks of pure Self-consciousness. Self-consciousness thus constitutes the ultimate category of existence to the Upanishadic philosophers.

IV—THE SIGNIFICANCE OF SELF-CONSCIOUSNESS

Self-consciousness: its epistemological and metaphysical significance contrasted with the mystical.

15. The great question that now confronts the Upanishadic seeker after truth is: if Self-consciousness is the final reality, how would it be possible for us to realise it? Can bare intellect suffice to give us a vision of this final reality, or is there any other process beyond the reach of intelligence which has the power of taking us within the portals of pure Self-consciousness? The Upanishadic answer is that mere intellect would be lame to enable us to realise pure Self-consciousness. Pure Self-consciousness could only be reached in a state of mystic realisation. Whether the mystical faculty, which may be called intuition, is higher than, analogous to, or included in the faculty of intellect, whose product all philosophy is, we shall not stop here to consider. It raises a large problem which does not lie within the scope of this work. We shall, however, try to describe it partly in our last Chapter on "The Intimations of Self-Realisation," where we shall see how it would be possible mystically to realise Self-consciousness. Our answer there would evidently be the super-sensuous and the super-intellectual answer. Intuition, as we shall see, is a superior faculty to either mere sensuous perception, or intellective apprehension. At present, however, we are concerned merely with the "philosophic" aspect of pure Self-consciousness, which may be looked at from two different points of view, the epistemological and the metaphysical. We shall see first what the epistemological aspect of Self-consciousness is according to the Upanishads, and then shall end this chapter by bringing out its full metaphysical significance, reserving the mystical aspect of it for our last chapter.

The Epistemology of Self-consciousness.

16. Epistemologically, we are told in various passages of the Upanishads, it would not be possible for us to know the Self in the technical meaning of the word "knowledge." Our readers might bring to mind the fact that Kant equally well regarded Reality, as consisting of God and the Self, as technically unknowable. These were, he said, merely matters of faith. The Upanishadic answer is that it is true that God and the Self are unknowable, but they are not merely objects of faith, they are objects of mystical realisation. Then, again, the Upanishads do not regard the Self as unknowable in the agnostic sense of the word, for example, in the sense in which Spencer understands it. Rather, it is "unknowable" from the standpoint of philosophic humility.

(i) The Ātman, say the Upanishadic philosophers, is unknowable in his essential nature. "That, from which our speech turns back along with mind, being unable to comprehend its fulness, is the ultimate reality," says the Taittirīya Upanishad. "That where the eye is unable to go, where neither speech nor mind is able to reach—what conception can we have of it, except that it is beyond all that is known, and beyond all that is unknown!" says the Kenopanishad. The philosopher of that Upanishad says in an Augustinian mood that he who thinks he knows does not know, while he who thinks he doesnotknow does really know. *Cognoscendo ignorari, et ignorando cognosci.* The Kaṭhopanishad in a similar vein says that "the Self is not in the first instance open to the hearing of men, but that even having heard him, many are unable to know him. Wonderful is the man, if found, who is able to speak about him; wonderful, indeed, is he who is able to comprehend him in accordance with the instruction of a teacher" (S. 13. a). We see in all these passages how the Ātman is to be regarded as unknowable in his essential nature.

(ii) There is, however, another side to the subject of the unknowability of Ātman. The Ātman is unknowable because He is the Eternal Subject who knows. How could the Eternal Knower, ask the Upanishads in various places, be an object of knowledge? "The Ātman is the Great Being," says the Śvetāśvatara Upanishad "who knows all that is knowable; who can know him who himself knows?" In the Bṛihadāraṇyaka Upanishad, in various passages, we are put in possession of the bold speculations of the philosopher Yājñavalkya. "That by whom everything is known, how could he himself be known ? It is impossible to know the knower." "It would not be possible for us to see the seer, to hear the hearer, to think the thinker, and to apprehend him by whom everything is apprehended." "He is the eternal seer without himself being seen ; he is the eternal hearer without himself being heard ; he is the only thinker without himself being thought ; he is the only comprehender without any one to comprehend him ; beyond him there is no seer, beyond him there is no hearer, beyond him there is no thinker, beyond him there is no being who comprehends"(S. 13. b.) We thus see that the question of the unknowability of Ātman has another aspect also, namely, that He is unknowable because He is the Eternal Subject of knowledge, and cannot be an object of knowledge to another beside Him.)

(iii) But this raises another fundamental question. Granted that the Self is the eternal knower of objects, granted also there is no other knower of him, would it be possible for the knower to know himself ? This very subtle question was asked of Yājñavalkya in another passage of the Bṛihadāraṇyakopanishad, and here again we see the brilliant light which the sage Yājñavalkya throws on the problem. It *is* possible, he says, for the knower to know himself. In fact, Self-knowledge or Self-consciousness is the ultimate category of existence. The Self can become an object of knowledge to himself. According to the philosophy of Yājñavalkya, nothing is possible, if self-consciousness is not possible. Self-consciousness is the ultimate fact of existence. We see here how boldly Yājñavalkya regards both introspection and self-consciousness as the verities of experience. We also see the nudity of the doctrines of Kant and Comte when they try to deny the fact of introspection. Introspection is a psychological process corresponding to Self-consciousness as a metaphysical reality. Self-consciousness is possible only through the process of introspection. The Self is endowed with the supreme power of dichotomising himself. The empirical conditions of knowledge are inapplicable to the Self. The Self can divide himself into the knower and the known. It is wonderful how Kant should have posited the " I am I " as the supreme metaphysical category, which he called the transcendental, original, and synthetic unity of apperception, and yet should have denied the reality of the corresponding psychological process of introspection. The answer of Yājñavalkya is that Self-consciousness *is* possible, and is not only possible, but alone real. King Janaka asked Yājñavalkya what was the light of man. Yājñavalkya first said that the light of man was the sun. It is on account of the sun that man is able to sit and to move about, to go forth for work, and to return. " When the sun has set, O Yājñavalkya, " asked king Janaka " what is the light of man ?" Yājñavalkya said that then the moon was the light of man. For, having the moon for light, man could sit, and move about, and do his work, and return. " When both the sun and the moon have set, " asked king Janaka, " what is the light of man ?" " Fire indeed, " said Yājñavalkya, " is man's light. For having fire for his light, man can sit and move about, do his work, and return." " When the sun has set, when the moon has set, and when the fire is extinguished, what is the light of man ?" asked Janaka. " Now, verily, " says Yājñavalkya, " you are pressing me to the deepest question. When the sun has set, when the moon has set, and when the fire is extinguished, the Self alone is his light" (S. 13. c.). Yājñavalkya is here clearly positing what Aristotle called "theoria," the act of pure self-contemplation in which the Self is most mysteriously both the subject and object of knowledge.

The Metaphysics of Self-consciousness.

17. We have seen, hitherto, the epistemological significance of the conception of pure Self-consciousness in the Upanishads. We have seen that the Self is regarded as unknowable in his essential nature, as well as because he cannot be an object of knowledge. We have seen also that he can dichotomise himself and make himself at once the knower and the known. It remains for us now to discourse on what may be called the metaphysical significance of the conception of Self-consciousneess. In the preceding Chapter we have seen how the whole field of philosophic thought was torn by the conflicts of the metaphysicians, some regarding the Self as entirely distinct from the Absolute, others regarding it as a part of the Absolute, and yet others regarding the Self and the Absolute as entirely identical. These constitute respectively the fundamental positions of the three great metaphysical schools—the dualistic, the quasi-monistic, and the monistic. Never has any land possibly experienced such bitter and prolonged argumentative battles as were witnessed in India throughout the history of its thought. The question arises: Is there any way out of the difficulty? How is it that each of these different metaphysical schools comes to interpret the same Upanishadic passages as confirming its own special metaphysical doctrines? Shall we not say that the Upanishads are higher than the Commentators? Is there not a common body of metaphysical doctrine in the Upanishads which each of the metaphysical schools has only partially envisaged? Is the utterance of that greatest of Indian philosophers to be regarded as vain, when he said that the Schools may battle among themselves, but yet that Philosophy is above the Schools? May we not find a supreme clue to the reconciliation of these different battling doctrines? We must go back to the Upanishads themselves, with our mind entirely purged of all scholastic interpretation. Let us make our mind a *tabula rasa*, an unwritten slate upon which there is no hurtful imprint of scholastic superstition, and we shall see that there is a clue through the labyrinth and mazes of the philosophic conflicts. It is true that the reconciliation of the different schools must come, if at all, only through mystical experince. It is only in mystic experience that each school and each doctrine can have its own appointed place and level. But it may also be granted to us to look even philosophically at the problem, to go back to the texts of the Upanishads themselves, to arrange them in a serial order of developing philosophical propositions, and finally to see a vista of supreme reconciliation spreading out before us among the battling forces.

The Ladder of Spiritual Experience.

18. We may arrange the different stages of spiritual experience, as developed in the Upanishads, philosophically interpreted, in a series of five developing propositions. We may regard them as constituting the ladder of spiritual experience with a series of five ascending steps. The first stage of spiritual experience would consist, according to Bṛihadāraṇyaka Upanishad, in realising the Self, in mystically apprehending the glory of the Self within us, as though we were distinct from him (S. 14. a). Now comes the second stage. Another passage from the Bṛihadāraṇyaka Upanishad tells us that the Being, which calls itself the "I" within us, must be identified with the Self that is hithertofore realised. We must experience that we are really the very Self, and that we are neither the bodily, or the sensuous, or the intellectual, or the emotional vestures; that we are in our essential nature entirely identical with the pure Self. This is the second stage (S.14. b). In the third stage of spiritual experience, we must come to realise, according to Bṛihadāraṇyaka Upanishad, that the Self that we have realised is identical with the Absolute. This same identification of the Ātman and the Brahman, of the Individual Spirit and the Universal Spirit, of the Self and the Absolute, is also proclaimed by the epistolary stanza of the Īśa and its cognate Upanishads, where we are told that the Ātman must be regarded as verily the Brahman, that the Ātman is infinite in its nature as also the Brahman, that the Ātman derives its being from Brahman, that subtracting the infinity of the Ātman from the infinity of the Brahman, the residuum is even infinite. Thus does that epistolary stanza pile infinities over infinities, and, taking the mathematical lead, speak as if when the infinity of the Ātman is deducted from the infinity of the Brahman, the remainder itself is infinite. The inner meaning of this assertion is that we should see that there is no difference between the Self and the Absolute. This constitutes the third stage (S.14.c). Now comes the fourth. If the Being that calls itself the "I" within us is the Ātman according to our second proposition, and if it is to be entirely identified with the Brahman according to our third proposition; that is, in other words, if I am the Self, and the Self is the Absolute; then, it follows syllogistically that I am the Absolute. This is unmistakably inculcated by a passage of Bṛihadāraṇyaka Upanishad, where we are told that we must identify the " I " with the Absolute. Another aspect of the same doctrine is proclaimed in the Chhāndogya Upanishad, where the " Thou " comes also to be " projectively " identified with the Absolute. This constitutes the fourth stage (S. 14. d.). If now the " I " is the Absolute, and if also the " Thou " is equally the Absolute, if, in other words, both the subject and object are the Absolute, then it follows that everything that we see in this world, Mind and Nature, the Self and the not-Self, equally constitute the Absolute. Whatever falls within the ken of apprehension, equally with whatever we are, goes to make up the fulness of the Absolute. The Brahman according to the Chhāndogya Upanishad is verily the " ALL " (S. 14. e). To such a giddy height does the philosophic ladder take us on the rising steps of philosophic thought. This is verily the position of Absolute Monism. Whether this state of Absolute Monism is to be merely intellectually apprehended, or mystically realised, depends upon whether we are by nature destined to be merely torch-bearers or mystics in the spiritual pilgrimage. That we should prefer the second alternative will be evident in our last Chapter on the " Intimations of Self-Realisation."

SOURCES V

1 उपकोसलो ह वै सत्यकामे जाबाले ब्रह्मचर्यमुवास । तस्य ह द्वादशवर्षाण्यग्नीन्परिचचार । स ह स्मान्यानन्तेवासिनः समावर्तयंस्तं ह स्मैव न समावर्तयति । तं जायोवाच

तप्तो ब्रह्मचारी कुशलमग्नीन् परिचचारीन् मा त्वाग्नयः परि-
प्रवोचन् प्रब्रूह्यस्मा इति तस्मै हाप्रोच्यैव प्रवासांचक्रे ।...।
अथ हाग्नयः समूदिरे तप्तो ब्रह्मचारी कुशलं नः पर्यचारी-
द्धन्तास्मै प्रब्रवामेति तस्मै होचुः ।...। अथ हैनं गार्हपत्यो-
नुशशास पृथिव्यग्निरन्नमादित्य इति । य एष आदित्ये
पुरुषो दृश्यते सोहमस्मि स एवाहमस्मीति ।...। अथ हैनं
अन्वाहार्यपचनोऽनुशशास आपो दिशो नक्षत्राणि चंद्रमा
इति । य एष चंद्रमसि पुरुषो दृश्यते सोहमस्मि स एवा-
हमस्मीति ।...। अथ हैनं आहवनीयोऽनुशशास प्राण
आकाशो द्यौर्विद्युदिति । य एष विद्युति पुरुषो दृश्यते
सोऽहमस्मि स एवाहमस्मीति ।...। ते होचुरुपकोसल
एषा सोम्य तेऽस्मद्विद्या आत्मविद्या च आचार्यस्तुते गतिं
वक्तेत्याजगाम हास्याचार्यः । तमाचार्योऽभ्युवाद उपको-
सल ३ इति । भगव इति ह प्रतिशुश्राव । ब्रह्मविद इव
सोम्य ते मुखं भाति कोनु त्वानुशशासेति ।...। य एषोऽ-
क्षिणि पुरुषो दृश्यत एष आत्मेति होवाच एतदमृतमभय-
मेतद् ब्रह्मेति ।...। एतं संयद्वाम इत्याचक्षत...एष उ एव
वामनीः...एष उ एव भामनीः सर्वेषु लोकेषु भाति य
एवं वेद ।

छां. IV. 10. 15.

2 (a) अथ यदतः परो दिवो ज्योतिर्दीप्यते विश्वतः पृष्ठेषु सर्वतः
पृष्ठेषु अनुत्तमेषु उत्तमेषु लोकेषु इदं वाव तद्यदिदमस्मि-
न्नन्तःपुरुषे ज्योतिस्तस्यैषा दृष्टिः यत्र एतद् अस्मिन्
शरीरे संस्पर्शेनोष्णिमानं विजानाति । तस्यैषा श्रुतिर्यत्रैत-
त्कर्णावपिगृह्य निनदमिव नदथुरिव अग्नेरिव ज्वलत उप-
शृणोति । तदेतद्दृष्टं च श्रुतं चेत्युपासीत चक्षुष्यः श्रुतो
भवति य एवं वेद ।

छां. III. 13.

(b) अन्यत्राप्युक्तम् । अयमग्निर्वैश्वानरो योऽयमंतःपुरुषे । येनेद-
मन्नं पच्यते । यदिदमद्यते तस्यैष घोषो भवति । यमेतत्कर्णा-
वपिधाय शृणोति ।

मै. II. 6.

3 अथ ह वै गार्ग्यो बालाकिरनूचानः संस्पष्ट आस...स
हाजातशत्रुं काश्यमेत्योवाच ब्रह्म ते ब्रवाणीति । तं होवाचा-

जातशत्रुः सहस्रं दद्मस्त एतस्यां वाचि । स होवाच
बालाकिर्य एवैष आदित्ये पुरुषस्तमेवाहमुपास इति ।
°चंद्रमसि °विद्युति °स्तनयित्नौ °वायौ °आकाशे °अग्नौ
°अप्सु °आदर्शे °छायायां °प्रतिशुत्कायां °शब्दे °शरीरे
°दक्षिणेऽक्षिणि °सव्येऽक्षिणि । तत उ ह बालाकिस्तूष्णी-
मास ।...। तं होवाचाजातशत्रुः...एहि व्येव त्वा ज्ञपयि-
ष्यामिति । तं ह पाणावभिपद्य प्रवव्राज तौ ह सुप्तं पुरुष-
मीयतुस्तं हाजातशत्रुरामंत्रयांचक्रे बृहत्पांडरवासः सोम
राजन्निति ।

कौ. IV. 1–18; also बृ. II. 1. 1–15.

4 (*a*) यतो वा इमानि भूतानि जायंते । येन जातानि जीवंति ।
यत्प्रयंति अभिसंविशंति । तद्विजिज्ञासस्व । तद्ब्रह्मेति ।

तै. III. 1.

(*b*) तज्जलानिति शान्त उपासीत ।

छां. III. 14. 1.

5 (*a*) ब्रह्म ह देवेभ्यो विजिग्ये तस्य ह ब्रह्मणो विजये देवा
अमहीयन्त । त ऐक्षन्त । अस्माकमेवायं विजयोऽस्माक-
मेवायं महिमेति । तद्धैषां विजज्ञौ । तेभ्यो ह प्रादुर्बभूव
तन्न व्यजानन्त किमिदं यक्षमिति । तेऽग्निमब्रुवन् जातवेद
एतद्विजानीहि किमेतद्यक्षमिति । तथेति । तदभ्यद्रवत्
तमभ्यवदत्कोऽसीत्यग्निर्वा अहमस्मीत्यब्रवीज्जातवेदा वा
अहमस्मीति । तस्मिंस्त्वयि किं वीर्यमित्यपीदं सर्वं दहेयं यदिदं
पृथिव्यामिति । तस्मै तृणं निदधावेतद्दहेति तदुपप्रेयाय
सर्वजवेन तन्न शशाक दग्धुम् । स तत एव निववृते नैतद-
शकं विज्ञातुं यदेतद्यक्षमिति । अथ वायुमब्रुवन् वायवेतद्वि-
जानीहि किमेतद्यक्षमिति । तथेति । तदभ्यद्रवत् तमभ्य-
वदत् कोऽसीति वायुर्वा अहमस्मीत्यब्रवीन्मातरिश्वा वा
अहमस्मीति । तस्मिंस्त्वयि किं वीर्यमित्यपीदं सर्वमाददीयं
यदिदं पृथिव्यामिति । तस्मै तृणं निदधावेतदादत्स्वेति
तदुपप्रेयाय सर्वजवेन तन्न शशाकादातुम् । स तत एव
निववृते । नैतदशकं विज्ञातुं यदेतद्यक्षमिति । अथेन्द्रम-
ब्रुवन् मघवन् एतद्विजानीहि किमेतद्यक्षमिति । तथेति
तदभ्यद्रवत् । तस्मात्तिरोदधे । स तस्मिन्नेवाकाशे स्त्रिय-
माजगाम बहुशोभमानां उमां हैमवतीं तां होवाच किमेत-

यक्षमिति । सा ब्रह्मेति होवाच ब्रह्मणो वा एतद्विजये महीय-
ध्वमिति ततो हैव विदांचकार ब्रह्मेति ।...। तस्माद्वा इंद्रो-
ऽतितरामिवान्यान्देवान् स ह्येनन्नेदिष्ठं पस्पर्श स ह्येनत्
प्रथमो विदांचकार ब्रह्मेति । तस्यैष आदेशो यदेतद्विद्युतो
व्यद्युतदा ३ इतीति न्यमीमिषदा ३ इति...यदेतद्गच्छतीव
च मनोऽनेन चैतदुपस्मरत्यभीक्ष्णं संकल्पः ।

के. III. IV.

(*b*) न तत्र सूर्यो भाति न चंद्रतारकं नेमा विद्युतो भाति कुतो-
ऽयमग्निः । तमेव भांतमनुभाति सर्वं तस्य भासा सर्वमिदं
विभाति ॥ क. II. 5. 15.

6 न्यग्रोधफलमत आहरेति । इदं भगव इति । भिन्द्धीति ।
भिन्नं भगव इति । किमत्र पश्यसीति । अण्व्य इवेमा धाना
भगव इति । आसामङ्ग एकां भिन्द्धीति । भिन्ना भगव इति
किमत्र पश्यसीति न किंचन भगव इति । तं होवाच यं
वै सोम्य एतमणिमानं न निभालयस एतस्य वै सोम्य
एषोऽणिम्न एवं महान्न्यग्रोधस्तिष्ठति । श्रद्धत्स्व सोम्येति ।
स य एषोऽणिमैतदात्म्यमिदं सर्वं तत्सत्यं स आत्मा तत्त्व-
मसि श्वेतकेतो इति ।

छां. VI. 12.

7 (*a*) अथ य आत्मा स सेतुर्विधृतिरेषां लोकानामसंभेदाय नैतं
सेतुमहोरात्रे तरतः न जरा न मृत्युर्न शोको न सुकृतं न
दुष्कृतम् ।

छां. VIII. 4. 1.

(*b*) एतस्य वा अक्षरस्य प्रशासने गार्गि सूर्याचंद्रमसौ विधृतौ
तिष्ठतः, एतस्य वा अक्षरस्य प्रशासने गार्गि द्यावापृथिव्यौ
विधृते तिष्ठतः, एतस्य वा अक्षरस्य प्रशासने गार्गि निमेषा
मुहूर्ता अहोरात्राण्यर्धमासा मासा ऋतवः संवत्सरा इति
विधृतास्तिष्ठन्ति, एतस्य अक्षरस्य प्रशासने गार्गि प्राच्यो-
ऽन्या नद्यः स्यंदन्ते श्वेतेभ्यः पर्वतेभ्यः प्रतीच्योऽन्याः ।

बृ. III. 8. 9.

8 (*a*) अथ हैनं विदग्धः शाकल्यः पप्रच्छ कति देवा याज्ञवल्क्येति
त्रयश्च त्री शता, त्रयश्च त्री च सहस्रेत्योमिति होवाच ।
कत्येव देवा याज्ञवल्क्येति त्रयस्त्रिंशदित्योमिति होवाच ।

कत्येव देवा याज्ञवल्क्येति षडित्योमिति होवाच । कत्येव
देवा याज्ञवल्क्येति त्रय इत्योमिति होवाच । कत्येव देवा
याज्ञवल्क्येति द्वावित्योमिति होवाच । कत्येव देवा याज्ञ-
वल्क्येत्यध्यर्ध इत्योमिति होवाच । कत्येव देवा याज्ञवल्क्ये-
त्येक इत्योमिति होवाच ।...। कतम एको देव इति...
पृथिव्येव यस्यायतनमग्निर्लोको मनो ज्योतिः यो वै तं
पुरुषं विद्यात्सर्वस्यात्मनः परायणं स वै वेदिता स्याद्याज्ञ-
वल्क्य वेद वा अहं तं पुरुषं सर्वस्यात्मनः परायणम् ।

बृ. III. 9. 1–10.

(*b*) एको हि रुद्रो न द्वितीयाय तस्थुर्य इमांल्लोकानीशत ईश-
नीभिः । प्रत्यङ्जनास्तिष्ठति संचुकोपान्तकाले संसृज्य
विश्वा भुवनानि गोपाः ॥ विश्वतश्चक्षुरुत विश्वतोमुखो
विश्वतोबाहुरुत विश्वतस्पात् । सं बाहुभ्यां धमति सं
पतत्रैर्द्यावाभूमी जनयन्देव एकः ॥

श्वे. III. 2. 3.

(*c*) स्वभावमेके कवयो वदंति कालं तथान्ये परिमुह्यमानाः ।
देवस्यैष महिमा तु लोके येनेदं भ्राम्यते ब्रह्मचक्रम् ॥ येना-
वृतं नित्यमिदं हि सर्वं ज्ञः कालकालो गुणी सर्वविद्यः । तेने-
शितं कर्म विवर्तते ह पृथ्व्यप्तेजोऽनिलखानि चिन्त्यम् ॥..।
आदिः स संयोगनिमित्तहेतुः परस्त्रिकालादकलोऽपि दृष्टः । तं
विश्वरूपं भवभूतमीड्यं देवं स्वचित्तस्थमुपास्य पूर्वम् ॥...
तमीश्वराणां परमं महेश्वरं तं देवतानां परमं च दैवतम् ।
पति पतीनां परमं परस्ताद्विदाम देवं भुवनेशमीड्यम् ॥
न तस्य कार्यं करणं च विद्यते न तत्समश्चाभ्यधिकश्च
दृश्यते । परास्य शक्तिर्विविधैव श्रूयते स्वाभाविकी ज्ञान-
बलक्रिया च ॥ न तस्य कश्चित्पतिरस्ति लोके न चेशिता
नैव च तस्य लिंगम् । स कारणं करणाधिपाधिपो न चास्य
कश्चिज्जनिता न चाधिपः ॥..॥ एको वशी निष्क्रियाणां
बहूनामेकं बीजं बहुधा यः करोति । तमात्मस्थं येऽनुप-
श्यंति धीरास्तेषां सुखं शाश्वतं नेतरेषाम् ॥

श्वे. VI. 1–12.

9 (*a*) यो देवोऽग्नौ योऽप्सु यो विश्वं भुवनमाविवेश । य ओष-
धिषु यो वनस्पतिषु तस्मै देवाय नमो नमः ॥

श्वे. II. 17.

स एष इह प्रविष्ट आनखाग्रेभ्यो यथा क्षुरः क्षुरधानेऽवहितः स्याद्विश्वंभरो वा विश्वंभरकुलाये तं न पश्यन्ति ।

बृ. I. 4. 7.

लवणमेतदुदकेऽवधायाथ मा प्रातरुपसीदथा इति । स ह तथा चकार । तं होवाच यद्दोषा लवणमुदकेऽवाधा अंग तदाहरेति तद्धावमृश्य न विवेद यथा विलीनमेव । अंग अस्य अंतादाचामेति कथमिति लवणमिति । मध्यादाचामेति कथमिति लवणमिति । अंतादाचामेति कथमिति । लवणमिति । अभिप्रास्यैनदथ मोपसीदथा इति । तद्ध तथा चकार । तच्छश्वत्संवर्तते । तं होवाचात्र वाव किल सत्सोम्य न निभालयसेऽत्रैव किलेति । स य एषोऽणिमा..तत्सत्यं स आत्मा तत्त्वमसि श्वेतकेतो ।

छां. VI. 13. 1–3.

(*b*) सूर्यो यथा सर्वलोकस्य चक्षुर्न लिप्यते चाक्षुषैर्बाह्यदोषैः । एकस्तथा सर्वभूतांतरात्मा न लिप्यते लोकदुःखेन बाह्यः ॥

क. II. 5–11.

(*c*) स भूमिं विश्वतो वृत्वाऽत्यतिष्ठद्दशांगुलम् ॥

श्वे. III. 14 (also RV. X. 901).

अग्निर्यथैको भुवनं प्रविष्टो रूपं रूपं प्रतिरूपो बभूव । एकस्तथा सर्वभूतांतरात्मा रूपं रूपं प्रतिरूपो बहिश्च ॥ वायुर्यथैको भुवनं प्रविष्टो रूपं रूपं प्रतिरूपो बभूव । एकस्तथा सर्वभूतांतरात्मा रूपं रूपं प्रतिरूपो बहिश्च ॥

क. II. 5. 9, 10.

वृक्ष इव स्तब्धो दिवि तिष्ठत्येकस्तेनेदं पूर्णं पुरुषेण सर्वम् ।

श्वे. III. 9.

10 (*a*) यत्ते कश्चिदब्रवीत्तच्छृणवामेत्यब्रवीन्मे जित्वा शैलिनिर्वाग्वै ब्रह्मेति..एकपाद्वा एतत्सम्राडिति । ... । अब्रवीन्म उदङ्कः शौल्बायनः प्राणो वै ब्रह्मेति...एकपाद्वा एतत्सम्राडिति ।...। अब्रवीन्मे वर्कुर्वार्ष्णः चक्षुर्वै ब्रह्मेति...एकपाद्वा एतत्सम्राडिति ।...। अब्रवीन्मे गर्दभीविपीतो भारद्वाजः श्रोत्रं वै ब्रह्मेति...एकपाद्वा एतत्सम्राडिति । ... । अब्रवीन्मे सत्यकामो जाबालो मनो वै ब्रह्मेति...एकपाद्वा एतत्सम्राडिति । ...। अब्रवीन्मे विदग्धः शाकल्यो हृदयं ब्रह्मेति...एकपाद्वा एतत्सम्राडिति ।

बृ. IV. 1. 2–7.

(*b*) श्रोत्रस्य श्रोत्रं मनसो मनो यद्वाचो ह वाचं स उ प्राणस्य प्राणः। चक्षुषश्चक्षुरतिमुच्य धीराः प्रेत्यास्माल्लोकादमृता भवंति ॥ ... ॥ यद्वाचानभ्युदितं येन वागभ्युद्यते। तदेव ब्रह्म त्वं विद्धि नेदं यदिदमुपासते ॥ यन्मनसा न मनुते येनाहुर्मनो मतम्। तदेव ब्रह्म त्वं विद्धि नेदं यदिदमुपासते। यच्चक्षुषा न पश्यति येन चक्षूंषि पश्यति। तदेव ब्रह्म त्वं विद्धि नेदं यदिदमुपासते ॥ यच्छ्रोत्रेण न शृणोति येन श्रोत्रमिदं श्रुतम्। तदेव ब्रह्म त्वं विद्धि नेदं यदिदमुपासते। यत्प्राणेन न प्राणिति येन प्राणः प्राणीयते। तदेव ब्रह्म त्वं विद्धि नेदं यदिदमुपासते ॥

के. I. 2. 8.

11 तद्धोभये देवासुरा अनुबुबुधिरे...इन्द्रो हैव देवानामभिप्रवव्राज, विरोचनोऽसुराणां, तौ...समित्पाणी प्रजापतिसकाशमाजग्मतुः...तौ ह प्रजापतिरुवाच य एषोऽक्षिणि पुरुषो दृश्यते एष आत्मेति होवाच...योयं भगवोऽप्सु परिख्यायते यश्चायमादर्शे। ... । तौ ह साध्वलंकृतौ सुवसनौ परिष्कृतौ भूत्वोदशरावेऽवेक्षांचक्राते...एष आत्मेति होवाच एतदमृतमभयमेतद्ब्रह्मेति । तौ ह शान्तहृदयौ प्रवव्रजतुः ।...। शान्तहृदय एव विरोचनोऽसुरानाजगाम ।... अथ हेन्द्रोऽप्राप्यैव देवानेतद्भयं ददर्श यथैव खल्वयमस्मिञ्शरीरे साध्वलंकृते साध्वलंकृतो भवति सुवसने सुवसनः परिष्कृते परिष्कृतः एवमेवायमस्मिन्नन्धेऽन्धो भवति स्रामे स्रामः परिवृक्णे परिवृक्णः...नाहमत्र भोग्यं पश्यामीति स समित्पाणिः पुनरेयाय ।...। तस्मै (इन्द्राय) होवाच य एष स्वप्ने महीयमानश्चरत्येष आत्मेति होवाच एतदमृतमभयमेतद्ब्रह्मेति । स ह शान्तहृदयः प्रवव्राज स ह अप्राप्यैव देवानेतद्भयं ददर्श...अप्रियवेत्तेव भवति, अपि रोदितीव नाहमत्रभोग्यं पश्यामीति समित्पाणिः पुनरेयाय।...। तस्मै (इन्द्राय) होवाच तद्यत्रैतत् सुप्तः संप्रसन्नः स्वप्नं न विजानात्येष आत्मेति होवाच...स ह शान्तहृदयः प्रवव्राज स ह अप्राप्यैव देवानेतद्भयं ददर्श न खलु अयमेवं संप्रत्यात्मानं जानात्ययमहमस्मीति नो एव इमानि भूतानि विनाशमेवापीतो भवति नाहमत्र भोग्यं पश्यामीति स समित्पाणिः पुनरेयाय ।...। तस्मै (इन्द्राय) होवाच। मघवन् मर्त्यं वा इदं शरीरमात्तं मृत्युना। तदस्य अमृतस्य अशरी-

रस्य आत्मनोऽधिष्ठानम्। आत्तो वै सशरीरः प्रियाप्रियाभ्यां न वै सशरीरस्य सतः प्रियाप्रिययोरपहतिरस्ति। अशरीरं वाव सन्तं न प्रियाप्रिये स्पृशतः। अशरीरो वायुरभ्रं विद्युत्स्तनयित्नुः अशरीराण्येतानि तद्यथैतान्यमुष्मादाकाशात्समुत्थाय परं ज्योतिरुपसंपद्य स्वेन स्वेन रूपेणाभिनिष्पद्यन्ते एवमेवैष संप्रसादोऽस्माच्छरीरात्समुत्थाय परं ज्योतिरुपसंपद्य स्वेन रूपेणाभिनिष्पद्यते स उत्तमः पुरुषः।

छां. VIII. 7. 12.

12 (*a*) सत्यं ज्ञानमनन्तं ब्रह्म यो वेद निहितं गुहायां परमे व्योमन्।

तै. II. 1.

(*b*) एष ब्रह्मा एष इन्द्रः...एते सर्वे देवा इमानि च पंचमहाभूतानि...अंडजानि च जारुजानि च स्वेदजानि च उद्भिज्जानि।...। यत्किंचेदं प्राणि जंगमं च पतत्रि च यच्च स्थावरम्। सर्वं तत्प्रज्ञानेत्रं प्रज्ञाने प्रतिष्ठितं प्रज्ञानेत्रो लोकः प्रज्ञा प्रतिष्ठा प्रज्ञानं ब्रह्म।

ऐ. III. 3.

13 (*a*) यतो वाचो निवर्तन्ते अप्राप्य मनसा सह।

तै. II. 4.

न तत्र चक्षुर्गच्छति न वाग्गच्छति नो मनो न विद्मो न विजानीमो यथैतदनुशिष्यादन्यदेव तद्विदितादथो अविदितादधि। के. I. 3.

यस्यामतं तस्य मतं मतं यस्य न वेद सः। अविज्ञातं विजानतां विज्ञातमविजानताम्॥

केन. II. 3.

श्रवणायापि बहुभिर्यो न लभ्यः शृण्वंतोऽपि बहवो यं न विद्युः। आश्चर्यो वक्ता कुशलोऽस्य लब्धाऽऽश्चर्यो ज्ञाता कुशलानुशिष्टः॥ क. I. 27.

(*b*) स वेत्ति वेद्यं न च तस्यास्ति वेत्ता। तमाहुरग्र्यं पुरुषं महान्तम्।

श्वे. III. 19.

येनेदं सर्वं विजानाति तं केन विजानीयात्। विज्ञातारमरे केन विजानीयादिति।

बृ. II. 4. 14.

न दृष्टेर्द्रष्टारं पश्येर्न श्रुतेः श्रोतारं शृणुयार्न मतेर्मंतारं मन्वीथा न विज्ञातेर्विज्ञातारं विजानीयाः।

बृ. III. 4. 2.

अदृष्टो द्रष्टाऽश्रुतः श्रोताऽमतो मन्ताऽविज्ञातो विज्ञाता, नान्योऽतोस्ति द्रष्टा, नान्योऽतोस्ति श्रोता, नान्योऽतोस्ति मंता, नान्योऽतोऽस्ति विज्ञाता।

बृ. III. 7. 23.

(*c*) याज्ञवल्क्य, किंज्योतिरयं पुरुष इति। आदित्यज्योतिः सम्राडिति होवाच आदित्येनैवायं ज्योतिषास्ते पल्ययते कर्म कुरुते विपल्येतीत्येवमेवैतद्याज्ञवल्क्य। अस्तमित आदित्ये याज्ञवल्क्य किंज्योतिरेवायं पुरुष इति चंद्रमा एवास्य ज्योतिर्भवतीति...। अस्तमित आदित्ये याज्ञवल्क्य चंद्रमस्यस्तमिते किंज्योतिरेवायं पुरुष इति अग्निरेवास्य ज्योतिर्भवतीति..। अस्तमित आदित्ये याज्ञवल्क्य चंद्रमस्यस्तमिते शान्तेऽग्नौ किंज्योतिरेवायं पुरुष इति आत्मैवास्य ज्योतिर्भवतीति।

बृ. IV. 3. 2–6.

14 (*a*) आत्मा वा अरे द्रष्टव्यः। बृ. II. 4. 5.

(*b*) आत्मानं विजानीयादयमस्मीति पूरुषः।

बृ. IV. 4. 12.

(*c*) अयमात्मा ब्रह्म। बृ. II. 5. 19.

पूर्णमदः पूर्णमिदं पूर्णात्पूर्णमुदच्यते। पूर्णस्य पूर्णमादाय पूर्णमेवावशिष्यते॥ शांतिः॥

(*d*) अहं ब्रह्मास्मि। बृ. I. 4. 10.

तत्त्वमसि। छां. VI. 8. 7.

(*e*) सर्वं खल्विदं ब्रह्म। छां. III. 14. 1.

CHAPTER VI

THE ETHICS OF THE UPANISHADS

Metaphysics, Morality, and Mysticism.

1. After a discussion in the last chapter of the central metaphysical position reached in the Upanishads, and after a suggestion that that position is to be attained more by the way of mysticism than by the way of thought, it would behove us for a while to bestow our attention on the moral problem in the Upanishads, which might easily be seen to be connected with their metaphysics on the one hand, and mysticism on the other. The problem of the relation of metaphysics and morality has been a much-debated problem from very ancient times; nor is the problem of the relation of morality and mysticism in any way a less important problem. For, just as it is hard to decide as to which of the two—metaphysics and morality—should receive the primacy in the discussion of the development of man's consciousness as a whole, similarly, it is equally hard to decide which of the two—morality and mysticism—plays a more important part in that development. If we take into account, however, the integrity of man's consciousness as a whole, it would seem absolutely impossible, in the interest of the highest development of which man's consciousness is capable, to sunder the intellectual from the moral, as the moral from the mystical element. Intelligence without the moral backbone might only degenerate into the cleverest forms of chicanery, and a mystic without morality, if such a one were possible,

might only be a hideous creature who is a blot on the spiritual evolution of man. And, again, just as morality, to be ratiocinative, must be firmly linked to the intellect, similarly for its consummation, it must end in the mystical attitude, which alone is the goal and end of the life of man. In short, Metaphysics, Morality and Mysticism are as inseparable from each other in the interest of the highest spiritual development of man, as intellect, will, and emotion are inseparable for his highest psychological development. It would thus seem necessary for a while to linger on the discussion of the moral problem in the Upanishads, as the connecting link between the metaphysical position reached therein and the final mystical realisation taught in the Upanishads.

Progress of the Chapter.

2. At a time when moral reflection in other lands had hardly reached even the gnomic stage, it is interesting to note that, in the Upanishads, we have a fairly good discussion of all the more important ethical problems ; while, in certain cases at least, the solution reached might be contemplated upon with great profit even by present-day moralists, because the solution which the Upanishads attempt is a solution which is based upon the eternal truths of Ātmanic experience. It is true that in the Upanishads we have not a very full discussion of the theories of the moral standard as apart from the theories of the moral ideal, inasmuch as thought is required to be necessarily more abstract in the discussion of the former, while in that of the latter it has to deal with the concrete problem of the end of human life. In the course of the present chapter, we shall first discuss the rudiments of the theories of the moral standard as we find them in the Upanishads,

and after a consideration of the limitations of the theories so advanced, we shall proceed to a discussion of the theories of the moral ideal. Of these latter, two at least are specially noteworthy—the Doctrine of Beatificism, and the Doctrine of Self-realisation. After having considered these theories, we shall next go on to the discussion of practical ethics in the Upanishads, and thus survey the lists of virtues enumerated in the various Upanishads, considering more especially the virtue of Truth. It is undoubtedly true that in the discussion of the practical side of ethics, the Upanishadic period is surpassed by the Neo-Upanishadic period, for there the metaphysical interest having waned, interest in practical conduct got the upper hand. Then, after a short discussion of the problem of the freedom of the will as considered in the Upanishads, we shall conclude the chapter by a short portrayal of the ideal of the Upanishadic Sage, bringing out the contrast between the Upanishadic Sage on the one hand and the Stoic and Christian Sages on the other.

I—THEORIES OF THE MORAL STANDARD

Heteronomy.

3. Coming to the consideration of the theories of the moral standard as advanced in the Upanishads, we have to note at the outset, that, as in the childhood of man, so in the childhood of the race, heteronomy is the first principle which serves to dictate rules for moral conduct. Reference is always made in such cases to the conduct of others, of those who are better situated morally than ourselves as dictating to us the principle of conduct for our own behoof. Not without reason did Aristotle think that the opinion of men of trained character should count as the principle of moral authority in cases when one is not able, on ac-

count of one's ignorance, to choose the way of moral action for oneself. [1]The Taittirīyopanishad contains a celebrated passage, where the disciple is told that "he should follow only the good actions of the spiritual teacher; that he might even more profitably follow the good actions of those who are still better situated than the spiritual teacher; that if ever he should seek to find out the intimate nature of duty or conduct, then he should always be guided by this one principle only, namely, how the Brahmins, who are cautious, gentle, and intent upon the law, conduct themselves in that particular case" (S. 1). This quotation evidently implies the maxim that we should always mould our conduct on the pattern of the conduct of those who are better than ourselves and are in a position to give us rules of conduct by their example. The opinion of Society in general, or the opinion of the State, are rather vague terms for defining the nature of heteronomic duty. It may not be possible for either the Society or the State to always impart to us one uniform principle of moral conduct. On the other hand, if we penetrate deeper, we shall find that the opinions of the Society or the State are themselves based upon the maxims of conduct which are supplied to them by Wise Men. There is an oligarchy in Morality, as there is an oligarchy in the Society or the State, and it is the voice of the Moral Oligarchy which, according to the Taittirīyopanishad, ought to prevail in supplying us with the pattern of conduct.

Theonomy.

4. Theonomy is also a sort of heteronomy, inasmuch as the "theos" is also a "heteros" from the properly moral point of view. But it is convenient to consider Theonomy as separate from Heteronomy, inasmuch as

1. Nicomachean Ethics I. 4.

the Law of God stands in a somewhat different category from the Law of Man. Unless it were possible to know the wishes of God in every particular case affecting moral conduct, unless it were possible even so much as to note what principles in general might be regarded as constituting the wishes of God—if we were not to understand these as identical with the dictates of Conscience which is the candle of the Lord within us—it might not seem very possible to set down in detail the Laws of God as enjoining the performance of certain duties upon us, in preference to, or in cancelment of, other duties. But in communities which entertain a vague fear about God as a Being who is separate from ourselves, the laws which are after all "attributed" to God by man ever hang like the sword of Damocles on the moral agent, and theophobia instead of theopathy supplies the rules for moral life. It was thus that the sage of the Kaṭhopanishad said that "God is that great fearful Thunderbolt which is raised over our head, by knowing which alone can man become immortal. For is it not through His fear, that the fire burns, the sun shines, the god of gods, the wind, and death as the fifth, run about doing their work?" Of the same import is the passage from the Taittirīyopanishad which only reiterates the passage from the Kaṭha with slight alterations (S. 2). But when all has been said in favour of the Law of God, on a careful consideration of the intimate nature of moral action, it may become evident that the law issuing from anybody except one's own Self can never be regarded as a sufficient guarantee for the moral tone of actions.

Autonomy.

5. It is thus that moralists have arrived at the conception of autonomy which alone supplies the true principle of moral conduct. It is neither the Society, nor the

State, nor God, who can give us the essential rule for moral conduct. This must spring entirely from within ourselves. We cannot say that the Upanishadic seers envisaged this principle of moral action unless of course we see it in that quotation from the Chhāndogya Upanishad where we are told that the mind should be meditated upon as the Ultimate Reality (S. 3. a), or even again in that other quotation from the same Upanishad where we are asked to regard the mind as verily the Ātman in us, as also the Ultimate Reality (S. 3. b). These passages have been understood by a recent writer on Hindu Ethics as involving the theory of Intuitionism. But it may be easily seen that inasmuch as it is the Mind which is here equated with the Highest Reality and not the Self which is mentioned as apart from it, we can only understand the passage as involving a lower intuitionism instead of the higher intuitionism of autonomy. Instances are not wanting even in the history of European Morals where aesthetic or sympathetic intuitionism prepares the way for the higher intuitionism of autonomy. It was not till the days of the Bhagavadgītā in the history of Hindu Ethics that the real nature of autonomy was clearly appreciated, and the categorical imperative of duty with all its Kantian purism severely inculcated. We have thus to regard the Upanishadic Ethics as on the whole deficient in the principle of autonomy as supplying the rules for moral conduct.

II—THEORIES OF THE MORAL IDEAL

Anti-Hedonism.

6. It is however when we come to the formulation of the theories of the Moral Ideal that the Upanishadic seers are at their best. We have said above that the

formulation of such theories is a more concrete problem than the formulation of the theories of the Moral Standard, which is by the very nature of the case bound to be abstract. As there is a variety of Metaphysical theories in the Upadishadic literature as we saw in a previous chapter, similarly there is a variety of theories about the nature of the Moral Ideal. To begin with, we have an entirely anti-hedonistic theory advocated by the author of the Kaṭhopanishad. We are told there that "there are two different paths, the path of the good and the path of the pleasant, and that these two diverse paths try to seduce a man each to itself. Of these, he who follows the path of the good is ultimately rewarded by the fulfilment of his aim, while he who follows the path of the pleasant loses the goal which he is pursuing. When the good and the pleasant present themselves before a man, he looks about him if he be wise, and decides which of them to choose. The wise man chooses the good before the pleasant, while the fool chooses the pleasant before the good" (S. 4. a). In these two verses from the Kaṭhopanishad we have a classical expression of the conflict between the good and the pleasant as experienced even in the Upanishadic days. Who will not say that the story of the conflict between the Good and the Pleasant in the Kaṭhopanishad trying to attract a man to themselves reminds one of a similar story of the choice of Hercules in Xenophon, where the two maidens, Pleasure and Virtue, present themselves before Hercules with their several seductions, and Hercules chooses Virtue? As with Hercules, so with Nachiketas. Even though the God of Death tries to seduce Nachiketas by the offer of a life of pleasure and glory, Nachiketas refuses to be imprisoned in the chains which Yama has forged for him (S. 4. b), and therein proves that he is not like the ordinary run of mankind which hugs to its heart the path of plesaure and glory to be only ultimately disillusioned in its choice. Nachiketas, true anti-hedonist as he is, refuses to be seduced by the life of pleasure.

Pessimism.

7. It is likely, however, that anti-hedonism may degenerate into an utter pessimism, and so likewise does it happen in the case of certain Upanishads. The Kaṭhopanishad asks in a pessimistic vein : " what decaying mortal here below would delight in a life of the contemplation of the pleasures of beauty and love, when once he has come to taste of the kind of life enjoyed by the unageing immortals ?" (S. 5. a). This is almost in the spirit of Schopenhauer who said that the best thing for man here below is not to have been born at all, and the second best to have died young. In a similar spirit, the Kaṭhopanishad condemns the desire for a long life of sensual enjoyment in preference to even a momentary contemplation of the life immortal. This pessimistic mood is most expressively brought forth in the Maitri Upanishad, where, our attention having been called to the contemplation of the universal evil that exists in the world and the impermanence of things having been most poetically expressed, life is described as the source of eternal misery. " What is the use of the satisfaction of desires," asks Bṛihadratha, " in this foul-smelling and unsubstantial body, which is merely a coglomeration of ordure, urine, wind, bile and phlegm, and which is spoilt by the content of bones, skin, sinews, marrow, flesh, semen, blood, mucus and tears ? What is the use of the satisfaction of desires in this body which is afflicted by lust, anger, covetousness, fear, dejection, envy, separation from the desired, union with the undesirable, hunger, thirst, old age, death,

disease and grief? Verily all this world merely decays. Look at the flies and the gnats, the grass and the trees, that are born merely to perish. But what of these? The great oceans dry up, the mountains crumble, the pole-star deviates from its place, the wind-cords are broken, the earth is submerged, and the very gods are dislocated from their positions" (S. 5. b.). Contemplating such a situation, Bṛhadratha entreats Śākāyanya to save him "as one might save a frog from a waterless well." This pessimistic attitude of Bṛihadratha is the logical outcome, only carried to an excess, of the anti-hedonistic attitude put into the mouth of Nachiketas.

Asceticism, Satyagraha, and Quietism.

8. Closely connected with pessimism is the theory of asceticism and its monastic practices. Unless a man begins to feel the interest in life waning for him, he does not see the necessity of harbouring the ascetic virtues. It is only when his heart begins to be set on the Eternal that he wishes to adopt the life of renunciation. It was in this way, we are told by the Bṛihadāraṇyakopanishad, that the wise men of old began to feel that there was no use for them of any wealth or fame or progeny. "What shall we do with progeny," they asked, "if it does not bring to us nearer the Eternal?" In this manner did they leave all ambition for progeny and wealth and fame and adopt the life of an ascetic (S. 6. a). The Kaushītaki Upanishad goes even further, and by a curious analogical explanation advocates the attitude of Satyāgraha. "Just as Prāṇa which is identical with Brahman is served by the mind as its messenger, the eye as its guard, the ear as its informant, the speech as its tire-woman, and just as all the senses bring offerings to Prāṇa even though it does

not solicit them, similarly all these beings will bring offerings to a man who knows this secret even though he does not solicit them. For him the rule of life is 'Beg not'. When he has gone to alms in a village and does not find any, he may sit down with the resolve that he shall not partake of anything that may be offered to him, and those who had formerly refused him shall come near him and speak to him good words—for this is verily what happens to a man who does not solicit alms—and bring offerings to him and say they shall give" (S. 6. b). This passage from the Kaushītaki enjoins upon an ascetic the attitude of non-begging in the firm belief that when he does not beg, things will come to him of their own accord. The Bṛihadāraṇyakopanishad gives further characteristics of the ascetic life, inasmuch as it tells us that "a Brahmin ought to grow disgusted with all wisdom, and lead a life of child-like simplicity" (S. 7. a); believing in the quietistic life, "he should never give himself up to too many words, for that is verily a weariness of the flesh" (S. 7. b).

Spiritual Activism.

9. There is, however, a positive side to the quietistic life taught in certain Upanishads. The Muṇḍakopanishad tells us that "we should verily leave away all words, but should devote ourselves to the knowledge of the Ātman, for the Ātman is the bund of immortality. Meditate upon the Ātman with the help of the symbol Om; for thus alone may it be possible for you to go beyond the ocean of darkness. Sages see Him by the help of the light of knowledge, for he manifests himself, the Immortal One, in the form of bliss" (S. 8. a). We must therefore remember that even though we are told that we should lead a quietistic life, that is only as a sort of recoil from the unreal and empty world of

sense; within itself, however, it may contain the marrow of self-realisation. "It was thus," says the Bṛihadāraṇyakopanishad, "that one who lived a peaceful life, of self-control, of cessation from activity, and of patient suffering, having collected himself, saw the Ātman within himself, saw in fact everything as verily the Ātman. Evils cease to have any power over him, for he has overcome all evil. Sin has ceased to torment him, for he has burnt all sin. Free from evil, free from impurity, free from doubt, he has become properly entitled to the dignity of a Brāhmaṇa" (S. 8. b). The Muṇḍakopanishad makes a more positive assertion by telling us that "a man who has left off all argument in the superiority of his spiritual illumination begins to play with the Ātman, and to enjoy the Ātman, for that verily constitutes his action. Thus does he become foremost among those who have known Brahman" (S. 8. c). Here we are told that though, to all appearances, such a person may be leading a life of freedom from the bustle of society, alone to himself in the privacy of spiritual solitude, he still has an object to play with, an object to enjoy, namely the Ātman. In fact, his life in Ātman is a life of intense spiritual activity, and not, as it may seem to others, a life of retirement and quietude.

Phenomenal Activism.

10. Contrasted with this kind of Activism, however, stands that other kind of Activism, with which alone people are ordinarily familiar, namely, what we may call Phenomenal Activism. The Īśopanishad tells us that "a man should try to spend his life-span of a hundred years only in the constant performance of actions. It is thus only that he can hope not to be contaminated by actions" (S. 9. a). It is important to note that even though this passage

from the Īśopanishad tells us that we should spend our life-time in doing actions, the actions that are here implied have no further range than possibly the small circumference of "sacrifice"; and further, the way in which, even in the midst of a life of action, freedom from contagion with the fruit of action may be secured is not here brought out with sufficient clearness. It is only later, when we come to the days of the Bhagavadgītā, that we see how even in the midst of the life of action actionlessness may be secured, only if attachment to action is annihilated once for all and no calculating desire is entertained for the fruit of action. The Īśopanishad does not supply these two links between the life of action and the goal of actionlessness and point out that actionlessness may be secured in the midst of action only through freedom from attachment to action, and the annihilation of any desire for the end of action. But, at any rate, it is evident that the Īśopanishad goes very much beyond the other Upanishads when it tries to reconcile the life of action with the life of knowledge. "To pitchy darkness do they go," it tells us, "who pursue the path of ignorance, namely the path of action. To greater darkness still do they go who devote themselves to the life of knowledge for its own sake. Sages have told us from very ancient times that knowledge leads to the one result, while action leads to the other. But he alone who can synthesise the claims of knowledge and action is able by means of action to cross the ocean of death and by means of knowledge to attain to immortality" (S. 9. b). In this way does the Īśopanishad try to reconcile the claims of knowledge and action, telling us that the life of bare contemplation and the life of bare activity are alike fraught with evil; but that he alone may be said to attain the goal of life who knows how to harmonise the two different paths. Thus we may see how the later claims of Aristotle for the contemplative life, and of Bacon for the active life, are prophetically reconciled by the philosopher of the Īśopanishad.

Eudaemonism.

11. When the phenomenal side of Activism is thus recognised, it is not very difficult to deduce from it a theory of the moral ideal which must needs take account of phenomenal good. The moral good may not be regarded as the Summum Bonum, and the worldly good may come to be recognised as at least on a par with it in the formation of the conception of the Summum Bonum. On the other hand, the verse from the Śvetāśvataropanishad which comes at the end of its fourth chapter is an echo of the spirit of Vedic prayer, where worldly good is craved for as being even a superior moment in the conception of the highest good. " Make us not suffer in our babies or in our sons," says the Upanishad ; " make us not suffer in lives, or in cows, or in horses ; kill not our powerful warriors, O Rudra, so may we offer to thee our oblations for ever and ever !" (S. 10. a). When the eye of the moral agent is not turned inwards, the good he seeks is evidently the external good only. On the other hand, when as in the case of the Taittirīya Upanishad, the internal good comes also to be recognised as of no meaner value, we are asked to choose both Truth and Law which have moral, along with Happiness and Prosperity which have material value (S. 10. b). It was thus that even that great idealistic philosopher Yājñavalkya, when he went to the court of King Janaka and was asked as to whether he desired wealth and cattle, or victory and controversy, said he wanted both : he wanted the cows along with their golden coin, as well as victory in the argumentative battle with the

other philosophers in Janaka's court. The apology which Yājñavalkya apparently offered for his conduct was that "he was enjoined by his father not to take away any wealth without having imparted spiritual instruction" (S. 10. c). It is evident that Yājña-valkya desired both material as well as spiritual good; and in spite of his otherwise supremely idealistic teaching, he possibly wanted to set an example by showing that the consideration of external good cannot be entirely ignored even by idealists as constituting a moment in the conception of the highest good.

Beatificism.

12. The author of the Taittirīyopnishad goes even a step further, and tells us that probably there is no distinction of kind between physical good and spiritual good, and that we may thus regard the two as commensurable in terms of each other. In a famous passage he makes for us an analysis of the conception of bliss. Physical good to him is itself an aspect of "bliss," as spiritual good constitutes the acme of "bliss"; and according to that author, there is a scale of values connecting the so-called physical bliss on the one hand with the highest spiritual bliss on the other. What, according to him, is the unit of measurement? We are told that the unit of measurement may be taken to be "the happiness of a young man of noble birth and of good learning, who is very swift and firm and strong, and to whom is granted the possession of the whole earth full of wealth. Of a hundred such blisses is made the bliss of the human genii; of a hundred blisses of these genii is made the bliss of the divine genii; of a hundred of these latter blisses is made the bliss of the fathers; of a hundred blisses of the fathers is made the bliss of the gods who are born gods; of a hundred of these is made the bliss of the gods who have become gods by their actions; of a hundred such blisses is made the bliss of the highest gods; of a hundred blisses of these gods is made the bliss of Indra; a hundred blisses of Indra constitute the bliss of Bṛihaspati; of a hundred such blisses is made the bliss of Prajāpati; and a hundred blisses of Prajāpati make the bliss of Brahman: and each time we are told that all the blisses, severally and progressively, belong to the Sage who is free from all desires" (S. 11). It is important to note that there is here no distinction of kind brought out between physical good on the one hand and spiritual bliss on the other, unless of course it were intended by the author that the physical good may be taken to be as good as naught before the highest bliss. That, however, does not seem to be the trend of argument by which the beatific calculus is arrived at after such labour by the author of the Taittirīyopanishad with the help of a physico-mythological scale of measurement. It is also equally important to remember that all these various blisses are said at all times to belong to the Sage who is free from all desires. If, in short, desirelessness is to constitute the highest bliss, there is no meaning in saying that the highest good could be measured in terms of the unit of physical good. In any case, it does not seem possible that spiritual good can be of the same kind as physical good: the two are probably entirely incommensurate, differing not in degree but in kind. The bliss of the Sage, who has realised Brahman, cannot be measured in terms of the physical happiness of any beings whatsoever, however highly placed or however divine they may be.

13. Indeed, there cannot be any physical scale for the measurement of spiritual values. The bliss of Self-realisation is entirely of its own kind, absolutely *sui generis*. But

Self-realisation.

to cavil at the theory of Self-realisation by saying that the Self "is realised" already, and that therefore there is no necessity of "realising" the Self seems to us to be merely a listless evasion of the true significance of Self-realisation. When Canon Rashdall says that the Self is realised already, he is speaking about a metaphysical fact. On the other hand, when it is said that the Self is to be realised, we are asked to take into account the whole ethical and mystical process by which the allurements of the not-Self naturally ingrained in the human being are to be gradually weaned out, and the Self to be made to stand in its native purity and grandeur. It is in the doctrine of Self-realisation that the ethical and mystical processes meet, a fact to which we shall have to allude presently. It need hardly be said that by Self-realisation, as the Upanishadic seers understand that expression, is meant the unfoldment and the visualisation of the Ātman within us, instead of the incipid and soul-less realisation of the various "faculties" of man, namely, the intellectual, the emotional and the moral, in which sense Bradley and other European moralists have understood that expression. The Bṛihadāraṇyakopanishad tells us that the Ātman, who constitutes the Reality within us as without us, is and ought to be the highest object of our desire, higher than any phenomenal object of love, such as progeny, or wealth, or the like, because, the Upanishad tells us, the Ātman, being the very kernel of our existence, is nearmost to us. "If a man may say there is another object of love dearer to him than the Ātman, and if another replies that if there be God overhead he shall destroy his object of love, verily it shall so happen as this man says. Hence it is that we ought to meditate on the Ātman as the only object of desire. For him who worships the Ātman in this way, nothing dear shall ever perish" (S. 12. a). There is a further reason why, according to the same Upanishad, the Self should be regarded as the highest object of desire ; because, when one has attained the Self, there are for him no desires left to be fulfilled, and he becomes entirely desireless (S. 12. b). But the Upanishadic doctrine of Self-realisation implies more than that the Ātman is the sole object of desire. In a very celebrated conversation between Yājñavalkya and Maitreyī in the Bṛihadāraṇyakopānishad, we are told that when Yājñavalkya wanted to make a partition of his estate between his two wives, Kātyāyanī and Maitreyī, Maitreyī chose rather the spiritual portion of her husband's estate, saying "Supposing I obtain the possession of the whole earth full of wealth, by that I shall never attain to immortality." "Verily not," replied Yājñavalkya, "thy life will be only like the life of those who have all kinds of convenience for them ; but there is no hope of immortality by the mere possession of wealth." Maitreyī thereupon replied: "What shall I then do with that by which I may not grow immortal?" "Verily most dear to me art thou, my wife, who art talking thus," said Yājñavalkya, "Come, I shall instruct thee in spiritual wisdom. It is not for the sake of the husband, that the husband is dear, but for the sake of the Ātman ; it is not for the sake of the wife that the wife is dear, but for the sake of the Ātman ; it is not for the sake of the children that the children are dear, but for the sake of the Ātman ; it is not for the sake of wealth that wealth is dear, but for the sake of the Ātman....It is not for the sake of everything that everything is dear, but for the sake of the Ātman. This Ātman, O Maitreyi, ought to be seen, ought to be heard, ought to be thought about, ought to be meditated upon ; for it is only when the Ātman is seen and heard and thought about and meditated upon does all this become verily known " (S. 13). It is important to remember that this passage is not to be interpreted in the interest of an egoistic theory of morals, as some have done, but only in the interest of the theory of Self-realisation. We have not to understand that the wife or the husband or the sons are dear for one's own sake, interpreting the word Ātman in an egoistic sense. The word Ātman which comes at the end of the passage in the expression *Ātmā vā are drashṭavyo* forbids an egoistic interpretation of that word in the previous sentences. We are thus obliged to interpret the word Ātman throughout the passage in the sense of the Self proper, the Ultimate Reality, and, therefore, to understand that the love that we bear to the wife or the husband or the sons is only an aspect of, or a reflection of, the love that we bear to the Self. It is, in fact, for the sake of the Self that all these things become dear to us. This Self the Bṛihadāraṇyaka enjoins upon us to realise by means of contemplation.

The ethical and mystical sides of Self-realisation.

14. The ethical and mystical sides of Self-realisation are fused together nowhere better than in that celebrated passage from the Chhāndogya Upanishad, where having started an inquiry as to what it is that induces a man to perform actions, and having answered that it is the consideration of happiness which impels him to do so,—for, we are told, had he experienced unhappiness in his pursuit, he would not have gone in for the actions at all,—the author of the Chhāndogya Upanishad comes to tell us that real happiness is the happiness that one enjoys in the vision of the Infinite, and that every other kind of happiness is only so-called, and of really no value whatsoever as contrasted with it. It thus comes about that, according to the author of that Upanishad, there are two radically different kinds of happiness, namely what he calls the Great and the Small. Great happiness consists in seeing, hearing, and meditating upon the Ātman. Little happiness consists in seeing, hearing and meditating upon other things besides the Ātman. Great happiness is immortal; Little happiness is perishable. If the question be asked, in what this Great happiness consists, the answer may be given, in Herakleitean fashion, that it consists in its own greatness, and possibly not in its own greatness! People say that cows and horses, elephants and gold, servants and wives, lands and houses—these constitute greatness. No, says the author, these rest in something else, but the Infinite rests in itself. Great happiness is experienced when the Infinite is seen above and below, before and behind, to the right and to the left, and is regarded as identical with everything that exists; when the Being, that calls itself the I within us, is realised above and below, before and behind, to the right and to the left, and is regarded as identical with everything that exists; when the Ātman is seen above and below, before and behind, to the right and to the left and is regarded as identical with everything that exists. He who thus realises the triune unity of the Infinite, the I, and the Ātman, and experiences the truth of the sentence *So Aham Ātmā*, is alone entitled to enjoy the highest happiness. One who comes to see this, and think about this, and meditate on this, really attains Swārājya: he loves his Self, plays with his Self, enjoys the company of his Self, and revels in his Self (S. 14). In this way, according to the Chhāndogya Upanishad, the ethical Summum Bonum consists in the mystical realisation of the triune unity as the goal of the aspirant's one-pointed endeavour.

Supermoralism.

15. We must not fail to take account, however, of a phase of the theory of the moral ideal as propounded in the Upanishads. This is the theory of what we may call Supermoralism, the state of being beyond good and bad, the ethical counterpart of the metaphysical theory of Absolutism. There is, however, a distinction between the supermoralism of Bradley and Nietzsche on the one hand, and the supermoralism of the Upanishads on the other. Neitzsche's supermoralism affects only the superman, who, in the possession of absolute strength, defies, and therefore rises above, all conceptions of good and bad. The Bradleyan supermoralism affects only the Absolute, which in its absoluteness is to be regarded as being beyond both good and bad. On the other hand, the Upanishadic supermoralism affects the Individual as well as the Absolute, and the Individual only so far as he may be regarded as having realised the Absolute in himself. The passage from the Kaṭhopanishad which tells us that " the Absolute is beyond duty and beyond non-duty, beyond action and beyond non-action, beyond the past and beyond the future," supported likewise by the passage from the Chhāndogya Upanishad which tells us that " the bodiless Ātman is beyond the reach of the desirable and the undesirable" (S. 15. a), has its counterpart in the passage from the Muṇḍakopanishad which tells us that " the Moral Agent shakes off all conceptions of merit and demerit, that is, in other words, goes beyond the reach of virtue and vice, and good and bad, when he has attained to divine assimilation after realising the golden-coloured Being who is the lord and governor of all" (S. 15. b). Similarly, we are told in the Bṛihadāraṇyakopanishad that the Ātman who lives in the citadel of our heart, and who is the lord and protector of all, grows neither great by good actions nor small by evil actions (S. 16. a), while he who contemplates upon this Ātman himself attains a like virtue, when his greatness ceases to grow by good actions, or diminish by bad actions (S. 16. b). These passages tell us that the Moral Agent goes beyond the reach of good and bad, when and only so far as he has attained to likeness with, or becomes merged in, the Ātman, who is himself, metaphysically speaking, beyond the reach of good and bad.

III—Practical Ethics

Virtues in the Bṛiadaranyaka.

16. We have discussed hitherto the theories of the Moral Standard and the Moral Ideal which have been advanced in the Upanishads. We shall now go on to a consideration of the practical side of Ethics, namely the enumeration and inculcation of certain virtues in the various Upanishads. And first, about the three cardinal virtues which are enumerated in the Bṛihadāraṇyakopanishad. There we are told how "once upon a time the gods, men, and demons all went to their common father, Prajāpati, and asked him to communicate to them the knowledge which he possessed. To the gods, Prajāpati communicated the syllable Da, and having asked them whether they had understood what he had said to them, received the answer that they had understood that they were asked to practice self-control (*Dāmyata*), upon which Prajāpati expressed satisfaction. To the men he also communicated the syllable Da, and after having asked them whether they had understood what he had said to them, received the answer that they had understood that they should practise charity (*Datta*), upon which Prajāpati said he was satisfied. To the demons likewise, Prajāpati communicated the syllable Da, and having asked them whether they had understood what he had said to them, received the answer that they had understood that they should practise compassion (*Dayadhvam*), upon which Prajāpati expressed satisfaction again "(S. 17. a). Even though thus Prajāpati gave the same instruction to the different inquirers, they understood the import of the instruction according to their different capacities, and learnt what was for them the right thing to do. We are told by the author of the Upanishad that " when the celestial voice, the Thunderbolt, repeats Da, Da, Da, it intends to communicate the three different sets of virtues, namely, Self-control, Charity, and Compassion." These, then, are the three cardinal virtues for people who are born with the Sāttvika, the Rājasa and the Tāmasa elements predominating in them. To those who, like the gods, occupy an elevated position, the divine voice says : " Be self-controlled, for otherwise, out of your elation, you might do acts of unkindness." To those who are in the position of men, equals among equals, the divine voice says : " Be charitable, and love your fellows." To those, again, who, like the demons, have in them the capacity of doing infinite harm, the divine voice says: " Be compassionate. Be kind to those with whom you would otherwise be cruel." Thus we are told in the above passage that Self-control, Charity, and Compassion constitute the three different cardinal virtues for the three different sets of people, each one of them having a certain predominating psychological temperament.

Virtues and Vices in the Chhandogya.

17. So far about the Bṛihadāraṇyakopanishad. In the Chhāndogya Upanishad we meet with a different list of virtues in the conversation between Ghora Āṅgirasa and Kṛishṇa, the son of Devaki.

Who this Krishna was, and what the purport of the instruction which Ghora Āṅgirasa imparted to Kṛishṇa might be taken to be, we have had occasion to consider in a previous chapter. At present we are concerned merely with the list of virtues that are enumerated there, and their ethical significance. We are told that the chief virtues of man are austerity, charity, straightforwardness, harmlessness, and truthfulness : these according to Ghora Āṅgirasa constitute the chief virtues of man (S. 17. b). We have already seen the analogy which the enumeration of these virtues bears to the enumeration of a similar list of virtues in the Bhagavadgītā (XVI. 1. 2). Then, in the Chhāndogya Upanishad again, a little later on, we find the mention of the five chief different sins of which man is capable. We are told there that "he who steals gold, he who drinks wine, he who pollutes the bed of his teacher, he who kills a Brahmin, all these go down to perdition ; likewise also he, who even associates with them" (S. 17. c). In this passage we are told what were regarded, by the Upanishadic seers, the five chief different kinds of sin. The thief, the drunkard, the adulterer, the Brahmocide, and the man who associates with them, are all regarded as worthy of capital punishment : this is very much like the later injunctions in Manu and Yājña-valkya (III. 5. 227), where the same crimes are described as the greatest of all sins.

The hortatory precepts in the Taittirīya.

18. The Taittirīya Upanishad is evidently the most hortatory of all the Upanishads. It adopts a deliberately didactic tone, and impresses a number of virtues to be observed, the study and teaching of the Sacred Scriptures forming the burthen of the discourse. We are asked to respect the Law, to tell the Truth, to practise Penance, Self-control, and Tranquillity, to offer ceremonial as well as daily Oblations to the Fire, to receive guests with Hospitality, to practise Humanity, and to Increase and Multiply. We are also told the opinions of three different moralists, each of whom insisted upon a special virtue. The sage Satyavachas Rāthītara taught the virtue of Truth. The sage Taponitya Pauruśishṭi insisted upon the virtue of Penance. Finally, the sage Nāka Maudgalya said that there was no virtue higher than the Study and Teaching of the Sacred Books, for that, he said, constituted penance—that verily constituted penance (S. 18.). On the other hand, a little further on, we have in the same Upanishad a direct moral advice imparted by the teacher to the out-going pupil. When the pupil has finished the course of his studies at his master's house, the master by way of a parting advice, tells him to speak the Truth, to respect the Law, and not to swerve from the Study of the Vedas; after having offered to the preceptor the kind of wealth he would choose, he should go out into the world to marry and to produce children, so that the family lineage may not be broken. The pupil is further advised not to swerve from the duties that are due to the Gods and the Fathers; to regard the Mother as his god; to regard the Father as his god; to regard the Preceptor as his god; to regard the Guest as his god. In general, the pupil is advised only to perform those actions which might be regarded as faultless by the society. Those, says the Spiritual Teacher, who are higher than ourselves in Brahminhood, should be respected "by giving a seat"—an expression which is otherwise interpreted as implying also that "in the presence of such, not a word should be breathed by the disciple." Finally, the Teacher imparts to his disciple the various conditions of Charity: Charity should be practised with

Faith, and not with Un-Faith, with Magnanimity, with Modesty, with Awe, and with Sympathy (S. 19). We thus see how the author of the Taittirīya Upanishad enumerates the different virtues that are necessary for practical life.

Truth, the Supreme Virtue.

19. More, however, than any of the other virtues, Truth seems to find particular favour with the Upanishdic seers. Illustrations of this virtue are scattered in the various Upanishads. When audacious potentates speak from the viceregal chair that in Indian Scriptures there does not seem to be any consideration made of the supreme virtue of Truth, it were much to be wished that they had studied the Upanishads, where Truth is inculcated as the supreme virtue, before they made their daring statements. In a famous passage of the Chhāndogya Upanishad we are told how Satyakāma, the son of one Jabālā, who had led a wanton life in her youth, asked his mother when he came of age, as to who it was from whom he was born, how the mother answered that she could only tell him that he was born of her though she was not quite sure from what father he was born, how when Satyakāma went to his spiritual teacher in order to get himself initiated, he was asked by the teacher as to what family it was from which he had come, how the youth Satyakāma gave a straightforward reply saying that he did not really know from what family he had come, but that he only knew his mother's name, and that she had told him that she did not know from what father he was born, herself having led a very wanton life in her youth. "Heigh !" exclaimed the spiritual teacher to Satyakāma, "these words could not come from a man who was not born of a Brahmin.

Come, I shall initiate you, because you have not swerved from the Truth" (S. 20). This story tells us how even the son of a wanton girl could be elevated to the position of a Brahmin merely for having told the pure and unadulterated Truth. Then, again, in that same Upanishad, we are told how Truth has the power of saving a man even from death, for Truth, we are told, is merely the counterpart of Reality. "When a man who has committed theft is brought handcuffed to the place of trial, they heat an axe for him, and if he has really committed the theft, then he covers himself with untruth, catches hold of the axe and is burnt to death. On the other hand, if he has not committed the theft, he covers himself with truth, catches hold of the axe, and is not burnt at all, but acquitted" (S. 21). This is how they used to distinguish the culprit from the true man in ancient times. Whatever may be said in modern times of the efficacy of such a trial, the fact remains that underlying the idea of this trial, there lies an unshakable belief in the power of Truth. Be true and fear not. Your strength would be as the strength of ten, if only your heart is pure. On the other hand, if you hide the canker of Untruth in your bosom, in mortal fear you shall walk even in the midday sun. Of like import is the utterance of Bhāradvāja in the Praśnopanishad where we are told that if a man may tell the Untruth he shall be dried up from the very roots; hence it is, he says, he dare not tell the Untruth (S. 22. a). On the other hand, the Muṇḍakopanishad tells us, that Truth alone becomes victorious in the world, and not a lie; by Truth is paved the path of the gods, by which travel the sages, who have all their desires fulfilled, to where lies the highest Repository of Truth (S. 22. b). This is how the practice of Truth as a moral virtue enables one to reach the Absolute. Finally, in the conversation between Nārada and Sanatkumāra, when Nārada had gone to his teacher to receive instruction from him in regard to the nature of Truth, the teacher answered it was only when a man had realised the Ultimate that he might be said to tell the Truth, while other truths were truths only by sufferance (S. 22. c). This is verily in the spirit of the jesting Pilate who asked what truth was, and would not stay for an answer. While, however, Pilate expressed a doubt as to the nature of truth, Sanatkumāra gives a more positive interpretation of it when he says that ultimate Truth is to be found only in the attainment of Reality. What people call truth is really no Truth at all. It is Truth only by sufferance. Thus we see how Truth is regarded by the Chhāndogya Upanishad as the ultimate moral correlate of the realisation of the Absolute.

Freedom of the Will.

20. We next come to the treatment of the problem of the Freedom of the Will. It may be easily admitted that a proper discussion of this problem requires a very high stage in the development of moral philosophy; hence there is not much wonder if the treatment of the problem of the Freedom of the Will in the Upanishads is but scanty. There are, however, a few remarks showing a rather acute insight in regard to the problem, and we must not fail to give the credit for them to the Upanishadic philosophers. The Bṛihadāraṇyakopanishad tells us that man is merely a conglomeration of desire, will, and action: "as his desire is, so is his will; as is his will, so is the action that he performs; as his action is, so is the fruit that he procures for himself" (S. 23). There is here a very clever discussion of the relation between desire, will, action, and the effect of action—a contribution indeed of the Upanishadic

sages to the Psychology of the Moral Self. In the Kaushītaki Upanishad, again, we have the enunciation of a theological determinism, inasmuch as we are told there that man is but a puppet in the hands of God, who makes him do good actions if he wishes him to rise, and bad actions if he wishes him to fall (S. 24. a). This is a regular denial of the freedom of man, and we are told that man does not possess true freedom at all as moral philosophy understands that expression. On the other hand, in the Chhāndogya Upanishad, we are told that even though true freedom cannot be said to belong to man before the realisation of Ātman, still we can say that it does belong to him after that realisation. Man in the foolishness of the contemplation of his small success regards himself to be the lord of all he surveys; he believes that he may be the master of any situation in which he may be placed, and that he may compel nature any time to bend to his sovereign will; but events in life prove that these are after all false expectations, and that even though a little freedom may be granted to man in small matters, he is yet not free in the highest sense of the term. Pent up within the gaol, he thinks like a prisoner that he is free; but he is free only to drink and eat and not to move about. Like a falcon to whose foot a string is tied, he can only fly in the limited sphere described by the length of the tether, but he is bound beyond that region. Similarly, man may vainly imagine that he is free to do any actions he pleases, but his freedom is the freedom of the tethered falcon. The Chhāndogya Upanishad tells us that it is only when we have known the Ātman that there is freedom for us in all the worlds; but if we have not known the Ātman, there is no freedom for us at all (S. 24. b). The same Upanishad tells us again a little later, that when we have known the Ātman we can obtain any object we please, thus testifying to the sovereignty of man's will over nature, which proceeds from the realisation of the Ātman (S. 24. c). Finally, even though there is no discussion in the early Upanishads of the conflict of motives which leads to the moral choice, still in the Muktikopanishad we have a passage where we are told that the river of desire runs between the banks of good and bad, but that, by the effort of our will, we should compel it to move in the direction of the good (S. 25)—a contribution, though a belated one, to the psychological aspect of the problem of freedom.

The Ideal of the Sage.

21. What is now the Ideal of the Upanishadic Sage? It may be seen by reference to the progress of the argument in the Chapter that moral values are by the Upanishadic seers almost invariably linked with mystical values and that just as there can be no true mysticism unless it is based upon the sure foundation of morality, so morality to be perfect must end in the mystical attitude. In the Upanishads, there is no mere moral agent whose morality does not consummate in mystical realisation. Thus, the Upanishadic Sage differs on the one hand from the Stoic Sage, who represents in himself the acme of moral perfection connected with an intellectual contemplation instead of a mystical realisation of the Absolute. On the other hand, he differs from the Christian Sage, who no doubt sticks rightly to the triadic norm of conduct, faith, hope, and charity, but who centres his hopes for mystical perfection in a *heteros*—Jesus Christ—and not in himself. The Upanishadic Sage believes in the possibility of greater or less mystical realisation for every being according to the greater or less worth of his character, belief, and endeavour: he sees the Ātman in all, and sees the Ātman alone. The Īśopanishad tells us that "for a man to whom all these beings have become the Ātman, what grief, what infatuation, can there possibly be, when he has seen the unity in all things ?" (S. 26. a). He has gone to the end of sorrow, and has torn asunder the ether-like skin of desire that had so long enveloped him in darkness and despair (S. 26.b). All his desires have been at an end, because he has attained to the fulfilment of the highest desire, namely the realisation of the Ātman (S. 26. c). As drops of water may not adhere to the leaf of a lotus, even so may sin never contaminate him (S. 26. d). There is no feeling of repentance for him : he never bethinks himself as to why it was that he did not do good actions, or why he did only evil ones (S. 26.e). He has come to learn of the nature of Reality, and has thus gone beyond the reach of these duals (S. 26. f). If ever anybody may intend evil to him, or try to persecute him, his hopes will be shattered, as anything dashing itself against an impenetrable rock may shatter itself to pieces, for, verily, the Sage is an impenetrable rock (S. 27). He has attained to eternal tranquillity, because as the Upanishad puts it, he has "collected" the Godhead (S. 28. a). All his senses along with the mind and intellect have become motionless on account of the contemplation of the Absolute in the process of Yoga (S. 28. b), and having realised the Ātman, he has found eternal happiness everywhere (S. 28. c). How this mystical perfection can be attained, and how morality may thus culminate in mysticism, will form the theme of our next Chapter.

SOURCES VI

1 यान्यस्माकं सुचरितानि तानि त्वयोपास्यानि नो इतराणि ।...। ये के चास्मच्छ्रेयांसो ब्राह्मणाः... । अथ यदि ते कर्मविचिकित्सा वा वृत्तविचिकित्सा वा स्यात्, ये तत्र ब्राह्मणाः... संमर्शिनः अलूक्षाः धर्मकामाः स्युः यथा ते तत्र वर्तेरन् तथा तत्र वर्तेथाः । एष आदेशः । एष उपदेशः । एषा वेदोपनिषत् ।

तै. I. 11.

2 महद्भयं वज्रमुद्यतं य एतद्विदुरमृतास्ते भवंति । भयादस्याग्निस्तपति भयात्तपति सूर्यः । भयादिंद्रश्च वायुश्च मृत्युर्धावति पंचमः ॥

क. II. 6. 2–3.

भीषाऽस्माद्वातः पवते भीषोदेति सूर्यः । भीषाऽस्मादग्निश्च इंद्रश्च मृत्युर्धावति पंचम इति ॥ तै. II. 8.

3 (*a*) मनो ब्रह्मेत्युपासीत । छां. III. 18. 1.

(*b*) मनो ह्यात्मा...मनो हि ब्रह्म मन उपास्स्वेति ।

छां. VII. 3. 1.

4 (*a*) अन्यच्छ्रेयोऽन्यदुतैव प्रेयस्ते उभे नानार्थे पुरुषं सिनीतः । तयोः श्रेय आददानस्य साधुर्भवति हीयतेऽर्थाद्य उ प्रेयो वृणीते ॥ श्रेयश्च प्रेयश्च मनुष्यमेतस्तौ संपरीत्य विविनक्ति धीरः । श्रेयो हि धीरोऽभिप्रेयसो वृणीते प्रेयो मंदो योगक्षेमाद् वृणीते ॥

क. I. 2. 1–2.

(*b*) स त्वं प्रियान्प्रियरूपांश्च कामानभिध्यायन्नचिकेतोऽत्यस्राक्षीः । नैतां सृंकां वित्तमयीमवाप्तो यस्यां मज्जन्ति बहवो मनुष्याः ॥

क. I. 2. 3.

5 (*a*) अजीर्यताममृतानामुपेत्य जीर्यन्मर्त्यः कधस्थः प्रजानन् । अभिध्यायन्वर्णरतिप्रमोदानतिदीर्घे जीविते को रमेत ॥

क. I. 1. 28.

(*b*) भगवन्नस्थिचर्मस्नायुमज्जामांसशुक्रशोणितश्लेष्माश्रुदूषिते विण्मूत्रवातपित्तकफसंघाते दुर्गन्धे निःसारेऽस्मिञ्छरीरे

किं कामोपभोगैः । कामक्रोधलोभभयविषादेर्ष्येष्टवियोगानिष्टसंप्रयोगक्षुत्पिपासाजरामृत्युरोगशोकाद्यैरभिहतेऽस्मिञ्छरीरे किं कामोपभोगैः । सर्वं चेदं क्षयिष्णु पश्यामो यथेमे दंशमशकादयस्तृणवनस्पतय उद्भूतप्रध्वंसिनः ... । अथ किमेतैर्वान्यानां शोषणं महार्णवानां शिखरिणां प्रपतनं ध्रुवस्य प्रचलनं व्रश्चनं वातरज्जूनां निमज्जनं पृथिव्याः स्थानादपसरणं सुराणां इत्येतद्विधेऽस्मिन्संसारे किं कामोपभोगैः ।

मै. I. 2–7.

6 (*a*) एतमेव प्रव्राजिनो लोकमिच्छंतः प्रव्रजन्ति । एतद्ध स्म वै तत् पूर्वे विद्वांसः प्रजां न कामयन्ते किं प्रजया करिष्यामो येषां नोऽयमात्माऽयं लोक इति । ते ह स्म पुत्रैषणायाश्च वित्तैषणायाश्च लोकैषणायाश्च व्युत्थायाथ भिक्षाचर्यं चरन्ति ।

बृ. IV. 4. 22.

(*b*) प्राणो ब्रह्मेति ह स्माह कौषीतकिः । तस्य ह वा एतस्य प्राणस्य ब्रह्मणो मनो दूतं, चक्षुर्गोप्तृ, श्रोत्रं संश्रावयितृ, वाक्परिवेष्ट्री । तस्मै वा एतस्मै प्राणाय ब्रह्मण एताः सर्वा देवता अयाचमानाय बलिं हरन्ति । एवं हैवास्मै सर्वाणि भूतान्ययाचमानायैव बलिं हरन्ति य एवं वेद । तस्योपनिषन्न याचेदिति । तद्यथा ग्रामं भिक्षित्वाऽलब्ध्वोपविशेन्नाहमतो दत्तमश्नीयामिति त एवैनमुपमंत्रयंते ये पुरस्तात्प्रत्याचक्षीरन् । एष धर्मोऽयाचतो भवति । अन्नदास्त्वेवैनमुपमंत्रयन्ते ददाम त इति ।

कौ. II. 1.

7 (*a*) एवं वै तमात्मानं विदित्वा ब्राह्मणाः पुत्रैषणायाश्च वित्तैषणायाश्च लोकैषणायाश्च व्युत्थायाथ भिक्षाचर्यं चरन्ति ... । तस्माद् ब्राह्मणः निर्विद्य बाल्येन तिष्ठासेत् ।

बृ. III. 5. 1.

(*b*) तमेव धीरो विज्ञाय प्रज्ञां कुर्वीत ब्राह्मणः । नानुध्यायाद् बहून् शब्दान् वाचो विग्लापनं हि तत् ।

बृ. IV. 4. 21.

8 (*a*) तमेवैकं जानथात्मानं अन्या वाचो विमुंचथ अमृतस्यैष सेतुः । ओमित्येवं ध्यायथ आत्मानं स्वस्ति वः पराय तमसः

परस्तात् । तद्विज्ञानेन परिपश्यंति धीराः आनंदरूपममृतं यद्विभाति ।

मुं. II. 2. 5–7.

(b) तस्मादेवंविच्छांतो दान्त उपरतस्तितिक्षुः समाहितो भूत्वा आत्मन्यात्मानं पश्यति । सर्वमात्मानं पश्यति । नैनं पाप्मा तरति, सर्वं पाप्मानं तरति, नैनं पाप्मा तपति, सर्वं पाप्मानं तपति, विपापो विरजोऽविचिकित्सो ब्राह्मणो भवति ।   बृ. IV. 4. 23.

(c) प्राणो ह्येष यः सर्वभूतैर्विभाति विजानन्विद्वान्भवते नातिवादी । आत्मक्रीड आत्मरतिः क्रियावानेष ब्रह्मविदां वरिष्ठः ॥   मुं. III. 1. 4.

9 (a) कुर्वन्नेवेह कर्माणि जिजीविषेच्छतं समाः । एवं त्वयि नान्यथेतोऽस्ति न कर्म लिप्यते नरे ॥

ई. 2.

(b) अंधं तमः प्रविशंति येऽविद्यामुपासते । ततो भूय इव ते तमो य उ विद्यायां रताः ॥ अन्यदेवाहुर्विद्ययाऽन्यदाहुरविद्यया । इति शुश्रुम धीराणां ये नस्तद्विचचक्षिरे ॥ विद्यां चाविद्यां च यस्तद्वेदोभयं सह । अविद्यया मृत्युं तीर्त्वा विद्ययामृतमश्नुते ॥   ई. 9–11.

10 (a) मा नस्तोके तनये मा न आयुषि मा नो गोषु मा नो अश्वेषु रीरिषः । वीरान्मा नो रुद्र भामिनोऽवधीर्हविष्मंतः सदमित्वा हवामहे ।

श्वे. IV. 22.

(b) सत्यान्न प्रमदितव्यम् । धर्मान्न प्रमदितव्यम् । कुशलान्न प्रमदितव्यम् । भूत्यै न प्रमदितव्यम् ।

तै. I. 11. 1.

(c) तं होवाच “ याज्ञवल्क्य, किमर्थमचारीः, पशूनिच्छन् अण्वन्तानिति ” । उभयमेव सम्राडिति होवाच ।

बृ. IV. 1. 1.

स होवाच याज्ञवल्क्यः । पिता मेऽमन्यत नाननुशिष्य हरेतेति ।

बृ. IV. 1. 7.

11 सैषाऽऽनंदस्य मीमांसा भवति । युवा स्यात्साधुयुवा-

व्यायकः । आशिष्ठो द्रढिष्ठो बलिष्ठः । तस्येयं पृथिवी सर्वा वित्तस्य पूर्णा स्यात् । स एको मानुष आनंदः । ते ये शतं मानुषा आनंदाः । स एको मनुष्यगंधर्वाणामानंदः । श्रोत्रियस्य चाकामहतस्य । इत्यादि ।

तै. II. 8.

12 (*a*) तदेतत्प्रेयः पुत्रात्प्रेयो वित्तात्प्रेयोऽन्यस्मात्सर्वस्मादंतरतरं यदयमात्मा । स योऽन्यमात्मनः प्रियं ब्रुवाणं ब्रूयात् प्रियं रोत्स्यतीतीश्वरो ह तथैव स्यादात्मानमेव प्रियमुपासीत स य आत्मानमेव प्रियमुपास्ते न हास्य प्रियं प्रमायुकं भवति ।

बृ. I. 4. 8.

(*b*) तद्वा अस्यैतदाप्तकामं आत्मकामं अकामं रूपं शोकान्तरम् ।

बृ. IV. 3. 2.

योऽकामो निष्काम आप्तकाम आत्मकामः ।

बृ. IV. 4. 6.

13 सा होवाच मैत्रेयी "यन्नु म इयं भगोः सर्वा पृथिवी वित्तेन पूर्णा स्यात् कथं तेनामृता स्यामिति "। " नेति " होवाच याज्ञवल्क्यः " यथैवोपकरणवतां जीवितं तथैव ते जीवितं स्यात् अमृतत्वस्य तु नाशास्ति वित्तेनेति " । सा होवाच मैत्रेयी " येनाहं नामृता स्यां किमहं तेन कुर्याम् ।...। " स होवाच याज्ञवल्क्यः प्रिया बतारे नः सती प्रियं भाषस एह्यास्स्व व्याख्यास्यामि ते ।..। स होवाच न वा अरे पत्युः कामाय पतिः प्रियो भवति, आत्मनस्तु कामाय पतिः प्रियो भवति । ज्यायायै° पुत्राणां°, वित्तस्य°, ब्रह्मणः°, क्षत्रस्य°, लोकानां°, देवानां°, भूतानां°, सर्वस्य° । आत्मा वा अरे द्रष्टव्यः श्रोतव्यो मन्तव्यो निदिध्यासितव्यः । आत्मनो वा अरे दर्शनेन श्रवणेन मत्या विज्ञानेनेदं सर्वं विदितम् ।

बृ. II. 4. 2-5.

14 यदा वै सुखं लभतेऽथ करोति, नासुखं लब्ध्वा करोति सुखमेव लब्ध्वा करोति, सुखं त्वेव विजिज्ञासितव्यम्... । यो वै भूमा तत्सुखं, नाल्पे सुखमस्ति । भूमा त्वेव विजिज्ञासितव्यः । यत्र नान्यत्पश्यति नान्यच्छृणोति, नान्यद्विजानाति स भूमा । अथ यत्रान्यत्पश्यति, अन्यच्छृणोति, अन्यद्विजानाति तदल्पम् । यो वै भूमा तदमृतं अथ यदल्पं तन्मर्त्यम् । स (भूमा) भगवः कस्मिन्प्रतिष्ठित इति स्वे

महिम्नि यदि वा न महिम्नि इति । गोअश्वमिह महिमेत्याचक्षते हस्तिहिरण्यं दासभार्यं क्षेत्राण्यायतनानीति । नाहमेवं ब्रवीमि । स एवाधस्तात्, स उपरिष्टात्, स पश्चात्, स पुरस्तात्, स दक्षिणतः, स उत्तरतः, स एवेदं सर्वं इत्यथातो अहंकारादेशः अहमेवाधस्तात्, अहमुपरिष्टात्, अहं पश्चात्, अहं पुरस्तात्, अहं दक्षिणतो, अहमुत्तरतो, अहमेवेदं सर्वमित्यथात आत्मादेशः आत्मैवाधस्तात्, आत्मोपरिष्टात्, आत्मा पश्चात्, आत्मा पुरस्तात्, आत्मा दक्षिणतः, आत्मोत्तरतः, आत्मैवेदं सर्वमिति । स वा एष एवं पश्यन्नेवं मन्वान एवं विजानन्नात्मरतिरात्मक्रीड आत्ममिथुन आत्मानंदः स स्वराड् भवति तस्य सर्वेषु लोकेषु कामचारो भवति ।

छां. VII. 22–25.

15 (*a*) अन्यत्र धर्मादन्यत्राधर्मादन्यत्रास्मात्कृताकृतात् । अन्यत्र भूताच्च भव्याच्च यत्तत्पश्यसि तद्वद ॥

क. I. 2. 14.

अशरीरं वाव सन्तं न प्रियाप्रिये स्पृशतः ।

छां. VIII. 12. 1.

(*b*) यदा पश्यः पश्यते रुक्मवर्णं कर्तारमीशं पुरुषं ब्रह्मयोनिम् । तदा विद्वान्पुण्यपापे विधूय निरंजनः परमं साम्यमुपैति ॥

मुं. III. 1. 3.

16 (*a*) य एषोऽन्तर्हृदय आकाशस्तस्मिन्शेते सर्वस्य वशी सर्वस्येशानः सर्वस्याधिपतिः स न साधुना कर्मणा भूयान्नो एव असाधुना कनीयान् ।

बृ. IV. 4. 22.

(*b*) एष नित्यो महिमा ब्राह्मणस्य न वर्धते कर्मणा नो कनीयान् ।

बृ. IV. 4. 23.

17 (*a*) त्रयाः प्राजापत्याः प्रजापतौ पितरि ब्रह्मचर्यमूषुर्देवा मनुष्या असुरा उषित्वा ब्रह्मचर्यं देवा ऊचुर्ब्रवीतु नो भवानिति तेभ्यो हैतदक्षरमुवाच द इति व्यज्ञासिष्टा३ इति व्यज्ञासिष्मेति होचुर्दाम्यतेति न आत्थेत्योमिति होवाच व्यज्ञासिष्टेति । अथ हैनं मनुष्या ऊचुर्ब्रवीतु नो भवानिति तेभ्यो हैतदेवाक्षरमुवाच द इति व्यज्ञासिष्टा३ इति व्यज्ञासिष्मेति होचुर्दत्तेति न आत्थेत्योमिति होवाच व्यज्ञासिष्टेति । अथ

ह्येनमसुरा ऊचुर्ब्रवीतु नो भवानिति तेभ्यो हैतदेवाक्षरमुवाच द इति व्यज्ञासिष्टा ३ इति व्यज्ञासिष्मेति होचुर्दयध्वमिति न आत्थेत्योमिति होवाच व्यज्ञासिष्टेति तदेतदेवैषा दैवी वागनुवदति स्तनयित्नुर्द द द इति दाम्यत दत्त दयध्वमिति तदेतत् त्रयं शिक्षेद्दमं दानं दयामिति॥

बृ. V. 2. 1–3.

(*b*) अथ यत्तपो दानमार्जवमहिंसा सत्यवचनमिति ता अस्य दक्षिणाः। छां. III. 17. 4.

(*c*) स्तेनो हिरण्यस्य, सुरां पिबंश्च, गुरोस्तल्पमावसन्, ब्रह्महा चैते पतन्ति चत्वारः पंचमश्चाचरंस्तैरिति।

छां. V. 10. 9.

18 ऋतं च स्वाध्यायप्रवचने च। सत्यं च°। तपश्च°। दमश्च°। शमश्च°। अग्नयश्च°। अग्निहोत्रं च°। अतिथयश्च°। मानुषं च°। प्रजा च°। प्रजनश्च°। प्रजातिश्च°। सत्यमिति सत्यवचा राथीतरः। तप इति तपोनित्यः पौरुशिष्टिः। स्वाध्यायप्रवचने एवेति नाको मौद्गल्यः। तद्धि तपस्तद्धि तपः।

तै. I. 9.

19 वेदमनूच्याचार्योऽन्तेवासिनमनुशास्ति। सत्यं वद धर्मं चर स्वाध्यायान्मा प्रमदः। आचार्याय प्रियं धनमाहृत्य प्रजातंतुं मा व्यवच्छेत्सीः।... देवपितृकार्याभ्यां न प्रमदितव्यम्। मातृदेवो भव, पितृदेवो भव, आचार्यदेवो भव, अतिथिदेवो भव। यान्यनवद्यानि कर्माणि तानि सेवितव्यानि नो इतराणि।...। ये के चास्मच्छ्रेयांसो ब्राह्मणाः तेषां त्वयाऽऽसनेन प्रश्वसितव्यम्। श्रद्धया देयं, अश्रद्धयाऽदेयम्। श्रिया देयं, ह्रिया देयं, भिया देयं, संविदा देयम्।

तै. I. 11. 1-3.

20 सत्यकामो ह जाबालो जबालां मातरमामन्त्रयांचक्रे ब्रह्मचर्यं भवति विवत्स्यामि किं गोत्रोऽहमस्मीति। सा हैनमुवाच नाहमेतद्वेद तात यद्गोत्रस्त्वमसि बह्वहं चरन्ती परिचारिणी यौवने त्वामलभे साहमेतन्न वेद यद्गोत्रस्त्वमसि जबाला तु नामाहमस्मि सत्यकामो नाम त्वमसि स सत्यकाम एव जाबालो ब्रुवीथा इति। स ह हारिद्रुमतं गौतममेत्योवाच ब्रह्मचर्यं भगवति वत्स्याम्युपेयां भगवन्तमिति तं होवाच किंगोत्रो नु सोम्यासीति स होवाच नाहमेत-

वेद भो यद्गोत्रोऽहमस्म्यपृच्छं मातरं सा मा प्रत्यब्रवीत् बह्वहं चरन्ती परिचारिणी यौवने त्वामलभे साहमेतन्न वेद यद्गोत्रस्त्वमसि जबाला तु नामाहमस्मि सत्यकामो नाम त्वमसीति सोऽहं सत्यकामो जाबालोऽस्मि भो इति । तं होवाच नैतदब्राह्मणो विवक्तुमर्हति समिधं सोम्याहरोप त्वा नेष्ये न सत्यादगा इति ।

छां. IV. 4. 1–5.

21 पुरुषं सोम्योत हस्तगृहीतमानयन्त्यपहार्षीत्तत् परशुमस्मै तपतेति स यदि तस्य कर्ता भवति तत एवानृतमात्मानं कुरुते सोऽनृताभिसंधोऽनृतेनात्मानमन्तर्धाय परशुं तप्तं प्रतिगृह्णाति स दह्यतेऽथ हन्यते । अथ यदि तस्याकर्ता भवति तत एव सत्यमात्मानं कुरुते स सत्याभिसंधः सत्येनात्मानमन्तर्धाय परशुं तप्तं प्रतिगृह्णाति स न दह्यतेऽथ मुच्यते ।

छां. VI. 16. 1–2.

22 (a) समूलो वा एष परिशुष्यति योऽनृतमभिवदति । तस्मान्नार्हाम्यनृतं वक्तुम् ।

प्र. VI. 1.

(b) सत्यमेव जयते नानृतं सत्येन पन्था विततो देवयानः । येनाक्रमन्त्यृषयो ह्याप्तकामा यत्र तत्सत्यस्य परं निधानम् ॥

मुं. III. 1. 6.

(c) सत्यं भगवो विजिज्ञास इति ।...। यदा वै विजानात्यथ सत्यं वदति नाविजानन् सत्यं वदति विजानन्नेव सत्यं वदति ।

छां. VII. 16, 17.

23 अथो खल्वाहुः काममय एवायं पुरुष इति । स यथाकामो भवति तत्क्रतुर्भवति, यत्क्रतुर्भवति तत्कर्म कुरुते, यत्कर्म कुरुते तदभिसंपद्यते ।

बृ. IV. 4. 5.

24 (a) एष ह्येव साधु कर्म कारयति तं यमेभ्यो लोकेभ्य उन्निनीषत एष उ एवासाधु कर्म कारयति तं, यमधो निनीषत, एष लोकपालः एष लोकाधिपतिरेष लोकेशः स म आत्मेति विद्यात् स म आत्मेति विद्यात् ।

कौ. III. 9.

(b) य इहात्मानमननुविद्य व्रजन्ति तेषां सर्वेषु लोकेष्वकामचारो भवति । य इहात्मानं अनुविद्य व्रजन्ति तेषां सर्वेषु लोकेषु कामचारो भवति ।

छां. VIII. 1. 6.

(c) यं यं अन्तं अभिकामो भवति यं यं कामयते सोऽस्य संकल्पादेव समुत्तिष्ठति तेन संपन्नो महीयते ।

छां. VIII. 2, 10.

25 शुभाशुभाभ्यां मार्गाभ्यां वहंती वासनासरित् । पौरुषेण प्रयत्नेन योजनीया शुभे पथि । अशुभेषु समाविष्टं शुभेष्वेवावतारयेत् । मुक्तिक II. 5, 6.

26 (a) यस्मिन् सर्वाणि भूतानि आत्मैवाभूद्विजानतः । तत्र को मोहः कः शोकः एकत्वमनुपश्यतः । ई. 7.

(b) यदा चर्मवदाकाशं वेष्टयिष्यन्ति मानवाः । तदा देवमविज्ञाय दुःखस्यांतो भविष्यति ॥

श्वे. VI. 20.

(c) पर्याप्तकामस्य कृतात्मनस्तु इहैव सर्वे प्रविलीयंति कामाः ।

मुं. III. 2. 2.

(d) यथा पुष्करपलाश आपो न श्लिष्यंत एवमेवंविदि पापं कर्म न लिप्यते । छां. IV. 14. 3.

(e) एतं ह वाव न तपति किमहं साधु नाकरवम् । किमहं पापमकरवमिति ।

तै. II. 9.

(f) स य एवं विद्वान् एते आत्मानं स्पृणुते, उभे ह्येवैष एते आत्मानं स्पृणुते । तै. II. 9.

27 एवं यथाश्मानमाखणं ऋत्वा विध्वंसत, एवं हैव स विध्वंसते य एवंविदि पापं कामयते यश्चैनं अभिदासति स एषोऽश्माखणः । छां. I. 2. 8.

28 (a) तमीशानं वरदं देवमीड्यं निचाय्येमां शान्तिमत्यंतमेति ।

श्वे. IV. 11.

(b) यदा पंचावतिष्ठंते ज्ञानानि मनसा सह । बुद्धिश्च न विचेष्टति तामाहुः परमां गतिम् । तां योगमिति मन्यन्ते स्थिरामिंद्रियधारणाम् । क. II. 6. 10–11.

(c) तमात्मस्थं येऽनुपश्यन्ति धीरास्तेषां सुखं शाश्वतं नेतरेषाम् । श्वे. VI. 12.

CHAPTER VII

INTIMATIONS OF SELF-REALISATION

Philosophy is to Mysticism as Knowledge is to Being.

1. In a previous Chapter we have seen how the Upanishadic seers arrived at the conception of a unitary Ātman who fills the whole world of nature as of mind, from whom the world comes into being, in whom the world lives, and into whom the world is finally absorbed. It is this conception of Ātman which we saw to be the quintessence of the philosophical teachings of the Upanishads ; it is this conception which enables us to bridge over the disputes between the various contending theological schools ; and finally, it is this conception which gives a proper place to the various constructions of reality in the ultimate explanation of things. We also suggested in that Chapter that the Upanishads afforded a practical lesson for the realisation of Ātman. They are not content with merely constructing an intellectual explanation of Reality, but suggest means for the practical attainment of it. It is true that, in the very nature of things, the problem of Self-realisation could not be expected to be expounded in a deliberate fashion by the Upanishadic Seers. They only throw hints and suggest the way for realising the Self, only too cognizant of the fact that any description of the great mystic experience by word of mouth would fall short of reality, as much as any mediate, intellectual, or expressible knowledge would fall short of immediate, intuitive, first-hand experience. There is the same gulf between the expression of an experience

and the enjoyment of it, as there is between knowledge and being. Nevertheless, mystic experience has itself to be suggested and communicated in a concealed fashion so as to enable the seekers after mystic life in their otherwise dark journey to know the lamp-posts on the mystic way. It is thus that we find in the various Upanishads mystical intimations of the realisation of the Self, which are hidden like jewels beneath an intellectual exterior, and which he alone who has the eye for them can discern to be of immeasurable value.

The Lower Knowledge and the Higher Knowledge.

2. The Upanishadic seers fully realise the fact that no amount of mere intellectual equipment would enable us to intuitively apprehend Reality. They draw the same distinction between Aparā Vidyā and Parā Vidyā, between lower and higher knowledge, as the Greek philosophers did between Doxa and Epistemē, between opinion and truth. The Muṇḍakopanishad tells us that there are two different kinds of knowledge to be known, one the higher, the other, the lower knowledge. Of these the lower knowledge is the knowledge of the Vedas, of grammar, of etymology, of metre, of the science of the heavens; while the higher knowledge is that by which alone the imperishable Being is reached (S. 1. a). The same typical distinction between the way of knowledge and the way of realisation is brought out in a conversation between Nārada and Sanatkumāra, where Nārada, the spiritual disciple, goes to his Teacher to learn the science of realisation. Asked to say what branches of knowledge he has hitherto studied, Nārada tells Sanatkumāra that he has studied all the Vedas, as well as all history and mythology; he has studied the science of the manes, mathe-

matics, the science of portents, the science of time, logic, ethics, the science of the gods, the science of Brahman, the science of the demons, the science of weapons, astronomy, as well as the science of charms, and fine arts. But he tells his master that grief fills him that so much knowledge is not competent to land him beyond the ocean of sorrow. He has studied only the different Mantras ; but he has not known the Self. He has known erewhile from persons revered like his Spiritual Teacher that he alone is able to go beyond the ocean of sorrow who can cross it by the saving bund of Ātman. Would his Spiritual Teacher enable him to cross over the ocean of ignorance and grief ? (S. 1. b). This passage brings into relief the distinction between the lower knowledge and the higher knowledge, and sets the knowledge of Self on such a high pedestal indeed that all intellectual knowledge seems to be merely verbal jugglery, or an utter weariness of the flesh, as contrasted with it. Finally, the extremely practical character of the Upanishadic Seers towards the problem of Self-realisation is exhibited in the Kenopanishad, where we are told that the end of life may be attained only if the Self were to be realised even while the body lasts ; for if Self-knowledge does not come while the body lasts, one cannot even so much as imagine what ills may be in store for him after death (S. 2. a). The same idea is urged with a slightly different emphasis in the Kaṭhopanishad, where we are told that unless a man is able to realise the Self while the body lasts, he must needs have to go from life to life through a series of incarnations (S. 2. b).

3. The question now arises—if the Ātman is capable of being realised even while the body lasts, why is it that all people do not realise him in their life-time, or yet

again, if he can be realised by some, what can we regard to be their qualifications for that realisation? The Upanishads abound in references to the qualifications necessary for the spiritual life.

Qualifications for Self-realisation.

The first quality requisite for a spiritual aspirant is, the Kaṭhopanishad tells us, introversion: "Our senses have been created by God with a tendency to move outwards. It is for this reason that man looks outside himself rather than inside himself. Rarely a wise man, who is desirous of immortal life, looks to his inner Self with his eye turned inwards" (S. 3. a). The same out-moving tendency of the senses is emphasised in the Śvetāśvataropanishad, where we are told that the individual self lives pent up in its citadel of nine doors with a tendency to flutter every time outside its prison-house (S. 3. b). In order to bend the wand to the other extreme, it thus seems necessary for the spiritual aspirant at the outset to entirely shut himself up to the outside world so as to be able to look entirely within himself. This is the stage of introversion. After "introversion" comes "catharsis." The Kaṭhopanishad tells us that unless a man has stopped from doing wrong, unless he has entirely composed himself, it may not be possible for him, however highly-strung his intellect may be, to reach the Self by force of mere intellect (S. 4. a). The Muṇḍakopanishad insists upon truth and the life of penance, right insight and the life of celibacy, as essential conditions for the unfoldment of the Self within us (S.4.b). The Kaṭhopanishad brings into relief the non-intellectual, in the sense of the super-intellectual, character of Self-realisation, when it declares that the Self can be reached neither by much discourse, nor by keen intellect, nor by polymathy (S. 4. c). The Īśāvāsyopanishad in a very famous passage inculcates the same logophobia as in the Kaṭhopanishad, when it tells us that knowledge is even more dangerous than ignorance, inasmuch as those who pursue the path of ignorance go after death to a region of pitchy darkness, while those who pride themselves upon their possession of knowledge go to greater darkness still) (S. 4. d). The Muṇḍakopanishad points out that the Ātman can not be realised by a man who has not sufficient grip and tenacity to lead the severe life of spirituality, nor can he be reached by a man whose life is a bundle of errors (S. 4. e). The same Upanishad gives further characteristics of the life of Self-realisation. "Unless a man feels disgusted with the worlds to which his actions may bring him, and unless he believes firmly that the world which is beyond the reach of actions can never be obtained by any actions howsoever good," unless, in other words, he regards the life of Self-realisation as uniquely superior to the life of action, "he has no right to enter into the spiritual world, to seek which he must forthwith go in a humble spirit, fuel in hand, to a Spiritual Teacher who has realised the Self" (S. 4. f). We thus see that, for the realisation of the Self, the Upanishads inculcate a life of introversion, with an utter disgust for the world and catharsis from sins, a spirit of humbleness, and a life of tranquillity, truth, penance, insight, strength, and right pursuit. Unless these conditions are fulfilled, the aspirant after spiritual life may never hope to realise the Self.

Necessity of Initiation by a Spiritual Teacher.

4. When the equipment in moral virtues is thus being perfected, the next step in the path of Self-realisation is initiation by a worthy Spiritual Teacher. Time and oft have the Upanishads inisted upon the necessity of initiation

by a Guru. Satyakāma in the Chhāndogya Upanishad is merely voicing the opinions of many when he tells his teacher that he has heard erewhile from people as revered as his own spiritual teacher that unless one be initiated by a Guru in the path of Self-realisation, one cannot attain the goal of mystic life (S. 5. a). The Kaṭhopanishad believing in the natural descent of spiritual knowledge from a higher to a lower level tells us that "unless the spiritual teacher be really of a superior calibre, spiritual knowledge would be hard of attainment, and again, that unless the initiation comes from a Spiritual Teacher who has realised his identity with the Self, There can be no knowledge of the subtle path which transcends all power of logic and argumentation. Let us not divert our intellect into wrong ways by mere logic-chopping; for, how can we hope to attain to the knowledge of Ātman unless we are initiated by another"? (S. 5. b). "Arise," says the same Upanishad in another passage, "Awake, and learn from those who are better than ye; for the path of realisation is as hard to tread as the edge of a razor. Very wisely have sages called it an inaccessible path" (S. 5. c). These and other passages make it clear that the knowledge of Self could not be attained by an individual striving for himself on his own behalf; for, we are told, the knowledge is so subtle and mystic that nobody could by his own individual effort ever hope to attain it. Secondly, it is necessary that the Teacher to whom we go to seek wisdom must have realised his identity with the ultimate Self. For, unless the Teacher has realised such an identity, unless, in other words, he stands on the lofty pedestal of unitive experience, the knowledge which he can impart can never be expected to be fructified in any individual who receives it.) Doubt has oftentimes been expressed as to the necessity of having a spiritual teacher from whom to learn spiritual wisdom. Why, it is contended, may we not hope to attain it by reference to books ? Persons who put forth this objection must remember what Plato said about the comparative value of the knowledge to be obtained from books, and the knowledge to be obtained from a teacher by word of mouth. The first is entirely lifeless ; the second is the outcome of the full-fledged life of the master. This makes all the difference in the world ; for, books can never be expected to solve the actual difficulties in the path of Self-realisation, while a Teacher who has walked on the path may take his aspiring disciple from step to step on the ladder of spiritual perfection.

The parable of the blindfolded man.

5. There is a very interesting parable in the Chhāndogya Upanishad to illustrate how the disciple is carried by his Spiritual Teacher from step to step on the path of Self-realisation. There we are told how a man was once led away from his country, namely the Gāndhāras, by some robbers who took him, with his eyes covered, to a very lonely and uninhabited place, and there left him to roam as best he might in any direction he pleased ; how, as he was piteously crying for help and instruction to be able to reach his original home, he was told by a person who suddenly happened to come there, "Go in that direction : in that direction are the Gāndhāras"; and how, thereupon, exercising his intelligence as best as he could, he asked his way from village to village on his return journey, and finally came back after much travail to his original home (S. 6). This parable of the blindfolded man is as full of spiritual wisdom as the parable of the cave in the Republic of Plato. It exhibits in a very typical fashion the whole process of the original

benightment of the Soul and its later illumination. Our real country is the country of Brahman, from which we are led away by the thieves, namely, the passions, into the forest of utter ignorance, with our eyes blindfolded by lust for unreal things. Then we cry aloud and piteously that some help may come, which may give us more light and lead us back to Brahman. Suddenly, we meet with a Spiritual Teacher, probably as the consequence of our having previously performed meritorious actions. The Teacher imparts to us knowledge of the way to our original home, and then, exercising our faculties as best we may, we go from stage to stage in the spiritual path until we reach back the country of Brahman which was our original home.

Precautions to be observed in imparting spiritual wisdom.

6. There are, however, certain necessary precautions which must be observed by the Spiritual Teacher before he imparts the mystic knowledge to his aspiring disciple. The Muṇḍakopnishad tells us that unless a disciple has perfomed such a difficult task as that of carrying fire over his head, his Spiritual Teacher should not impart the knowledge of the mystic way to him (S. 7. a). The passage which gives this admonition is also otherwise interpreted as embodying the principle that no man has the right of entrance into the mystic path unless he is a "shaveling." This implies that only a Samnyāsin can be a worthy student of the spiritual science. We have no intention to discredit the order of Samnyāsa, but we may say that other passages from the Upanishads do not always describe Samnyāsa as being the only fit mode of life for receiving mystic wisdom. The Chhāndogya Upanishad tells us that "mystic knowledge may be imparted to either the eldest son,

or to a worthy disciple who has lived with his master for a long time, but to none else. Not even a treasure which fills the whole sea-girt earth would be a sufficient recompense for communicating mystic knowledge" (S. 7. b). The passage from the Śvetāśvataropanishad which is a comparatively later passage, and which introduces the word "Bhakti" for the first time in Upanishadic literature, tells us that unless the disciple has absolute Faith (Bhakti) in God as in the Master, the spiritual secret should not be imparted to him (S. 7. c). We thus see how a Spiritual Teacher must be very jealous of imparting the knowledge of the mystic path. The Bhagavadgītā (XVIII. 67), taking up the same word Bhakti, later tells us that the mystic knowledge should not be imparted to one who does not make himself worthy of it by long penance, who has no faith either in God or the Master, who has no desire to listen to the spiritual wisdom, or else who harbours within himself an antagonism to spiritual knowledge.

Meditation by means of Om, the way to Realisation.

7. The actual means of meditation which a Spiritual Teacher imparts to his disciple is described unanimously in the Upanishads as being the symbol Om. It is also to be noticed that Om is described as not merely the supreme means of meditation, but the goal to be reached by the meditation itself. The Om occupies in Indian philosophy the same position which the Logos occupies in Christology. The Upanishads repeat from time to time the efficacy of meditation by means of the supreme symbol. "The word which the Vedas declare and which is the subject of all austerities, desiring which men lead the life of religious studentship, that word, I tell thee, is briefly Om; that

word is the Supreme Brahman; that word is the Supreme Symbol; that word is the Supreme Support" (S. 8. a). In these terms does the Kaṭhopanishad identify the means of meditation with the goal to be reached by it; the symbol, in short, stands for both the means and the end of spiritual life. The Chhāndogya Upanishad declares that all speech is interwoven on this symbol Om, in the same manner as the leaves of a tree are woven together on a stalk (S. 8. b). The Muṇḍakopanishad tells us by the help of a very happy simile that "we should take into our hand the bow of the Upanishads, and put upon it the arrow of the Soul, sharpened by devotion. We should next stretch it with concentrated attention, and penetrate the mark which is the Supreme Brahman. The mystic symbol Om is the bow; the arrow is the Soul; and Brahman is the mark to be pierced. We should penetrate it with undistracted attention, so that the arrow may become one with the mark" (S. 9). We are told here how devotion is necessary for the whetting of the point of the arrow, how concentrated attention and undistracted effort are necessary for making the arrow of the Soul pierce the target of Brahman, how, finally, the arrow is to become so absorbed in the target that it ceases to exist as a separate entity. If unitive life is to be expressed by any metaphor,—and all verbal expressions, it must be remembered, fall short of the experience of reality, —the metaphor of the arrow and the target invented by the Muṇḍakopanishad must be considered a very happy one, as most fittingly characterising the communion of the lower and the higher selves so as to involve the utter destruction of the separate individuality of the lower self. Further, the Om has not merely an individual, but a cosmic efficacy as well. It not merely serves to help the meditation of the individual person, but the Sun himself, we are told, travels the universe, singing the symbol Om (S. 10). Finally, the moral efficacy of meditation by means of Om is brought out in the Praśnopanishad where Satyakāma inquires of his teacher as to what happens to a man by his continuing to meditate by means of that symbol till the hour of his death, and the answer is given that "just as a snake is relieved of its slough, similarly is the man who meditates on Om relieved of his sins, and, by the power of his chants, is lifted to the highest world where he beholds the Person who informs the body, and who stands supreme above any living complex whatsoever" (S. 11).

The Mandukyan exaltation of Om.

8. The Māṇḍukya Upanishad supplies us with a unique exaltation of Om and its spiritual significance. We are told there that Om consists not merely of the three moræ A U M, which it might easily be seen to contain, but that it contains also a fourth mora-less part. The reason for this four-fold division of Om lies manifestly in the author's intention of bringing into correspondence with the parts of Om the states of consciousness on the one hand, and the kinds of soul on the other. The Om is supposed to represent in miniature the various states of consciousness, as well as the various kinds of soul. Thus, on the one hand, it stands for the state of wakefulness, the state of dream, and the state of deep-sleep, as well as the supreme self-conscious state which is called the Turyā. On the other hand, it stands for the different kinds of soul, namely the Vaiśvānara, the Taijasa, the Prājña, as well as the fourth, namely the Ātman. The mora-less part of Om has correspondence with the fourth dimension of psychology, namely the Turyā,

as well as with the fourth dimension of metaphysics, namely the Ātman. The Vaiśvānara is the enjoyer of gross things, as the Taijasa is the enjoyer of the subtle. The Prājña is described as the equivalent of what philosophy calls God, " the Lord of all, the all-knowing, the inner controller of all, the origin and end of all beings." Contrasted with these stands the Ātman, which is the Māṇḍukyan equivalent of what philosophy calls the Absolute. It is described as " neither inwardly nor outwardly cognitive, nor yet on both sides together. It is not a cognition-mass, and is neither knower nor not-knower. It is invisible, impractiable, incomprehensible, indescribable, unthinkable, and unpointable. Its essence is the knowledge of its own self. It negates the whole expanse of the universe, and is tranquil and blissful and without a second" (S. 12). The spiritual significance of the psycho-metaphysical correspondence of the parts of Om lies in the great help that is supposed to be given by meditation on it in intuiting the Ātman in the Turyā state of consciousness after a negation of the other kinds of Soul in the other states of consciousness. Nowhere else as in the Māṇḍukya Upanishad do we find such an exaltation of Om, and the great value for spiritual life of meditation by means of that symbol.

Practice of Yoga.

9. The aim of the Upanishads is a practical one, and we find scattered throughout the Upanishads certain hints for the practical realisation of the Godhead by means of Yoga. In the Śvetāśvataropanishad we are told that our body should be regarded as the lower stick and meditation on Praṇava as the upper one, and that by rubbing together these two sticks, we have to churn out the fire of God that is hidden

in us (S. 13. a). The reference to the body and the Praṇava as the lower and the upper sticks in the process of spiritual churning which we meet with in this passage of the Śvetāśvataropanishad is a remarkable one, as it enables us to interpret correctly another passage from the Kaṭhopanishad, where a reference to the sticks is to be met with again, and where we are told that just as the earthly fire is ensconced within the two churning sticks like a fœtus in the womb of a pregnant woman, and just as this fire is to be worshipped with offerings day after day by people who keep awake for that purpose, similarly in between the two sticks in the practice of Yoga,—namely, as we can *now* interpret the expression by reference to the Śvetāśvatara, the body and the Praṇava,—between these sticks is ensconced the spiritual fire, which we have to worship day after day by keeping ourselves awake, and giving it the offerings of the psychical tendencies in us (S. 13. b). This passage in the Kaṭhopanishad can also be interpreted in another way, as we find a little later on in the same Upanishad that the two sticks in the process of Yoga may also be regarded as the upper breath and the lower breath, the Prāṇa and the Apāna, and that between the two is seated the beautiful God whom all our senses worship (S. 14. a). Instead of regarding the two Araṇis as the body and the Praṇava as in the Śvetāśvataropanishad, we might as well take them to mean the upper and the lower breaths, in between which is seated the beautiful Ātman; and a reference from the Muṇḍakopanishad is also not wanting, where we are told that the mind for its purification is dependent upon the Prāṇas, and that it is only when the mind is purified after an initial control of the Prāṇas that the Ātman reveals himself (S. 14. b).

Yoga doctrine in Svetasvatara.

10. The Yoga doctrine in the Śvetāśvataropanishad is a more developed one than in the other Upanishads, and we have in the second chapter of that Upanishad a classic and almost systematic description of the practices and effects ot Yoga, which may be said to carry the Upanishad quite near to the time when the Yoga doctrine came to be systematised in a new school of philosophy.) We are told that "we should hold our body with its three erect parts quite even, and that we should pen our mind, along with our senses, in the heart. We should concentrate upon Brahman, and, with the help of that boat cross all the fearful streams that bar our spiritual progress. Controlling our breath and with our actions quite measured, we should throw out by the nose our Prāṇa when it becomes quite exhausted in the process of inspiration, and we should regulate our mind which is like a chariot to which are yoked very evil horses. We should sit for the practice of Yoga on an even and pure piece of ground which is free from pebbles, fire, and sand, and which is also free from sounds and watery resorts. The place where we sit for practice should be delightful to the mind, and not jarring to the eye; and we should choose for practice a place in the still recesses of a cave" (S. 15. a). The Śvetāśvataropanishad also lets us into the mystery of the physiological effects achieved by this practice of Yoga. "When the five-fold result of Yoga arising from the different elements, namely, earth, water, fire, air, and ether comes well to operate, the practiser of Yoga knows neither disease, nor old age, nor death, for verily his body has become full of the fire of Yoga. His body now becomes very light, the pulse of health beats within him, he becomes free from desires, his complexion becomes clear, and his pronunciation very pleasing. He emits a smell which is holy, and his excretions become very slight; it is by these marks that one should know that the novice in Yoga is being well established in his practice" (S. 15. b). The spiritual effects of the practice of Yoga which are given in the Śvetāśvataropanishad will be discussed somewhat later in this chapter, our present concern being only the details of the manner of Yoga-practice, and its physiological effects.

The Faculty of God-realisation.

11. The end of the practice of Yoga is evidently the realisation of God. But before we discuss the nature of God-realisation, we must answer a previous question—By what Faculty is it that a mystic is able to realise God? Is it Sense, or is it Thought, or is it any super-sensuous and super-intellectual faculty of Intuition, by means of which one is able to realise God? The Kaṭhopanishad tells us that the form of God does not fall within the ken of our vision. "Never has any man been able to visualise God by means of sight, nor is it possible for one to realise Him either by the heart, or by the imagination, or by the mind. It is only those who know this sublime truth that become immortal" (S. 16. a). Later writers have translated the above passage in a different way. They tell us that even though it may not be possible for us to "visualise" the form of God, still it "may be possible for us to realise Him by means of the heart, or by the imagination, or by the mind." It is true that the grammatical construction of the above passage does not come in the way of this interpretation also. But it must be remembered that the verse from the Kaṭhopanishad which comes almost immediately after it makes it quite clear that it is "not possible to realise God either by word of mouth, or by the mind, or by the eye. It is only those who know that God is, to them alone, and to none else, is God revealed" (S. 16. b). We are here told that it is not possible at all to realise God by means of the mind, which makes it quite clear that we have to "understand" in the earlier verse from the Kaṭhopanishad the negative adverb in the second part, which would then imply that it is never by means of the mind that one can realise God. It is also noteworthy from the later verse from the Kaṭhopanishad that the nature of God-realisation is like that of a "fact." You can never question it. You can never argue about it. You can never think about it. If you only know that God is, then alone is God realised by you. The value of a fact can never be disturbed by any probings into its *pros* and *cons*, by logical manipulation about its nature, or by any imaginative or highly-strung intellectual solutions. It thus becomes clear that neither Sense nor Thought enables us to realise God. But a further question arises—if God can be realised at all, has man got any Faculty by means of which he can so realise Him? To that question, another verse from the Kaṭhopanishad supplies an answer. "This Ātman who is hidden in all beings is not patent to the eyes of all. It is only the subtle seers who can look with the one-pointed and piercing faculty of Intuition (Buddhi) that are able to realise God" (S. 16. c). Opinions differ as to whether even this Buddhi can lead us to the vision of God. In one passage of the Bhagavadgītā (VI. 21) we are told that the happiness of God-realisation can be apprehended by means of Buddhi; on the other hand, we are told in another passage of that same work (III. 42), that just as God is beyond all senses and mind, similarly He is beyond even this faculty of Buddhi or Intuition. But when words fail to exactly describe the nature of the Faculty of God-realisation, it may become serviceable psychologically to "invent" a term, to call it either Buddhi or Intuition, and then to make it responsible for the vision of God. The Upanishads, however, take yet another turn, and look at the question of God-realisation not from the psychological but from the moral point of view. The Muṇḍakopanishad tells us that "it is only when a perfect katharsis of the whole moral being takes place by the clearness of illumination, that one is able to realise the immaculate God after meditation; for He can be attained neither by sight, nor by word of mouth, nor by any other sense, nor by penance, nor by any actions whatsoever" (S. 17. a). Of like import is that other passage from the Kaṭhopanishad which tells us that "it is only when the whole moral being is purged of evil that one is able to realise the greatness of God" (S. 17. b). We prefer to understand the reading "Dhātuprasāda" instead of "Dhātuḥprasāda" in the above passage, for to our mind the idea of Dhātṛi or Creator is absolutely irrelevant to the passage and can only be illegitimately smuggled into it, the purification of the moral being yielding quite a necessary and legitimate sense.

The thorough immanence of God.

12. Time and oft we are told in the Upanishads, as in the passage above quoted from the Kaṭhopanishad, that the mystic is able to "see" God. Another passage from the same Upanishad tells us that "we ought to extract the Ātman courageously from our body, as one extracts a blade of grass from its sheath. When the Ātman is thus drawn out, let a man know that he is the lustrous Immortal Being—yea, the lustrous Immortal Being" (S. 18. a). The process of the extraction of the Ātman from this frail body implies a thorough immanence of the Ātman in the body. The Ātman is to the body what the wheat is to the chaff. The wheat must be separated from the chaff, even though the chaff may temporarily cover it. Even so must the Ātman be extracted from the body, even though, for a while, the body may serve as a covering for it. "Just as a razor is laid in a razor-case or a bird is pent up in its nest, even so is this Conscious Being placed in the body up to the very nails, up to the very hair of the body" (S. 18. b). In this wise does the Kaushītaki Upanishad declare the immanence of Ātman. The Śvetāśvataropanishad tells us that just as oil is hidden in sesamum, or ghee in curds, just as water is hidden in springs, or fire in the churning sticks, even so is the Ātman immanent in the body" (S. 18. c). Another passage from the Śvetāśvataropanishad tells us that "just as there is an extremely subtle film on the surface of ghee, even so does the Godhead who is immanent in all beings envelop the whole universe, by knowing Whom alone is a man released from all bonds" (S. 18. d). The essence of all this teaching about the immanence of God is that if man may but try in the proper way, he may be able to realise God even within himself.

Types of mystical experience.

13. It is just the possibility of God-realisation within himself that vindicates the mystic's search after God by a long process of purification and contemplation. References are not wanting in the Upanishads, though we cannot say they are to be met with there to the fullest extent, to the visions and auditions which the mystic experiences on his spiritual journey. Four types of experience on the whole are to be found scattered in the Upanishads, which bear respectively on the forms, the colours, the sounds, and the lights which are experienced by the mystic in the process of contemplation. These we shall indicate from the various Upanishads, without trying to sever the different experiences from one another. In the second chapter of the Śvetāśvataropanishad, there is a classic reference to the different forms and lights that are experienced by the mystic on the threshold of his spiritual pilgrimage. We are told that he experiences forms such as those of "mist and smoke, the sun, the fire and the wind, the fire-fly and the lightning, the crystal and the moon" (S. 19. a). An early passage from the Bṛihadāraṇyakopanishad tells us almost in the same strain that to the vision of the advancing mystic appear such forms as those of the saffron-coloured raiment, of the red-coloured beetle, of a flame of fire, of a lotus-flower, and of a sudden flash of lightning: these constitute the glory of the advancing mystic" (S. 19. b). It seems, however, on the whole, that the Upanishadic mystics are either morphists, or photists, rather than audiles. There are only few references to the experience of audition in the Upanishads, and these also are not well accounted for. In the Bṛihadāraṇyaka, as in the Maitri Upanishad, we are told that the mystic hears certain sounds within himself which are attributed by the authors of those Upanishads to the process of digestion that is going on within the system. We are told that "the sound is a result of the processes of digestion and assimilation, that a man is able to hear it merely by shutting his ears, and finally that when a man is dying he is not able to hear the sound" (S. 20. a). The Chhāndogya Upanishad in a similar strain tells us that the indication of the presence of Reality within us can be obtained merely by shutting our ears, and by being able to hear sounds like those of the roaring of an ox, or the peal of a thunder, or the crackling of fire (S. 20.b). Mystic expereince has shown that it is not merely by shutting our ears that we are able to hear the mystic sound, that we can hear it even with our ears quite open, and that finally even a deaf man who cannot hear anything else is yet able to hear this sound. Then, again, we cannot call the mystic sound a result of the processes of digestion and assimilation within us. It is true that the mystic sound is to a certain extent dependent upon physiological circumstances. But to call the sound a result of those circumstances is like putting the cart before the horse. We thus see that even though a reference is unmistakebly made to the auditions experienced by a mystic, the Upanishadic seers are not correct in giving their *raison dêtre*, nor even in defining their exact nature. On the other hand, when they come to deal with the photic experiences, the Upanishadic mystics are evidently at their best. "On a supreme disc set with gold," says the Muṇḍakopanishad, "is the spotless and immaculate Brahman, which is the light of all lights which the seekers after Ātman experience" (S. 21. a). The Chhāndogya Upanishad tells us that "after having crossed the bund of phenomenal existence, even though a man may be blind, he ceases to be blind; even though he may be pierced, he is as good as unpierced; after having crossed this bund, the very night becomes like day, for before the vision of the aspiring mystic the spiritual world is suddenly and once for all illumined" (S. 21. b). Another passage from the Chhāndogya Upanishad tells us that before such a mystic, there is neither ever any sunset nor any sun-rise. "Only if this be true," says the author of the Upanishad, "may I not break my peace with God! When there is neither any sun-rise nor any sun-set, there is eternal day before the aspiring soul" (S. 21. c). Finally, this same idea is reiterated once more in the Śvetāśvataropanishad, where we are told that "when there is neither day nor night before the mystic, when there is neither being nor not-being, God alone is", thus testifying to the transcendence of God beyond both night and day, beyond both being and not-being, as the result of an utter cancelment of these in divine omnipresence (S. 21. d).

The acme of mystic realisation.

14. The photic or auditive experiences which we have referred to above, though they may be called the harbingers of a full-fledged realisation to come, do not yet constitute the acme of Self-realisation. One very celebrated passage of the Muṇḍakopanishad tells us that the Ātman cannot be realised except by one whom the Ātman himself chooses : before such a one does the Ātman reveal his proper form (S. 22. a). This is verily the doctrine of Grace. It implies that man's endeavours after a full-fledged realisation of God may always fall short of the ideal, unless Grace comes from above. It is only when the Ātman chooses the saint for the manifestation of his supreme glory that the mystic will be able to perceive Him. It is only then that the golden-coloured Being of the Chhāndogya Upanishad who can be seen on the Sun, "with golden mustaches, and golden hair, and who shines like gold up to his very toes," can come to be identified, as by the sage of the Īśopanishad, with the Being within oneself (S. 22. b). It is only then that the Individual Spirit can become one with the Universal Spirit. The Śvetāśvataropanishad tells us that "just as a mirror which is cleaned of its impurities becomes lustrous and capable of reflecting a lustrous image, even thus does the mystic see Himself at the height of his spiritual experience and reach the goal of his endeavour. Just, again, as with the help of a lamp one is able to see an object, similarly by the help of the Individual Self he sees the lustrous Universal Self, who is unborn, who is the highest reality, and who is beyond all existences" (S. 22. c). The mystic imagery implied in the above quotations from the Śvetāśvatara is made absolutely clear in the teaching of the great sage Maitri who imparted to his disciple "the highest secret of the Upanishads" when he said that at the acme of spiritual expreience the mystic sees his own form in a flood of supreme light arising from within himself, which indeed constitutes the realisation of the immortal and fearless Ātman (S. 22. d).

Reconciliation of contradictions in the Ātman.

15. The Upanishads abound in passages which try to reconcile opposite qualities in the Ātman as realised. The Śvetāśvataropanishad tells us that "the Ātman is neither male nor female, nor is the Ātman of an intermediate sex: what body He takes, in that body does He lie ensconced" (S. 23. a). The Īśopanishad tells us that "the Ātman may be said to move and yet not to move. He is far as well as near. He is inside all things as well as outside all things." A daring mystic of the Kaṭhopanishad asks—Who except himself has been able to realise the Ātman who rejoices and rejoices not, who can walk in a sitting posture and move about everywhere in a lying one? In the Muṇḍakopanishad an attempt is made to reconcile the infinite greatness of the Ātman with his infinite subtlety: "Great and lustrous is that incontemplatable Being, and yet he is subtler than the subtle. He is farther than any far-off end, and yet quite near to us, being shut up in the cave of our heart." In like manner does the Kaṭhopanishad tell us in an oft-quoted passage that the Ātman is subtler than the subtle and greater than the great, and is pent up within the recesses of our heart. On the other hand, passages are not wanting, as in the Śvetāśvataropanishad and the Kaṭhopanishad, where the Ātman is described as being of the size of a thumb and glorious like the sun; or even again as being as small as the tip of a needle, or a hundredth part of the end of a hair divided into a hundred infinitesimal portions (S. 23. b). What is meant exactly by saying that the Ātman is neither male nor female, that He moves and yet does not move, that He is both far and near, that He is greater than the great and smaller than the small, or that He is of the size of a thumb, only the mystics can know. We, who judge from the outside, can have no idea of how the seeming contradictions may be reconciled in the infinite variety and greatness of the Ātman.

Effects of realisation on the Mystic.

16. The Upanishads discuss in many places the psychological and other effects which the realisation of God produces upon the perfected Mystic. "One who knows his identity with the Self and comes to realise that he is the Ātman—for what reason should such a man enter into any feverish bodily activity, for his desires are fulfilled and his end is gained?" (S. 24. a). This is as much as to say that when the identification with Ātman comes to take the place of the identification with body in a perfected Mystic, all his desires for bodily accommodation vanish immediately. Then, secondly, " the knots of his heart are broken, all his doubts are solved, and the effects of his actions are annihilated, when once he has seen God who is higher than the highest " (S. 24. b). The doubts which had so long harassed his mind, and the actions from whose result he used to suffer, break away immediately; while one may know the perfected Mystic by this one principal mark, that he has left no doubts to solve. If he is once for all in sure possession of reality—what doubts can he any further have? Then, thirdly, in the Muṇḍakopanishad, we have the great contrast between the want of power in the Mystic before Self-realisation, and the obtainment of power after it. "Though the individual Soul was lying so long with the universal Soul on the same tree, he was yet infatuated and was grieving on account of his complete impotence, but when he has once become atoned with the Highest, who is the source of all power, his grief vanishes immediately, and he begins to participate in the other's infinite power" (S. 24. c). Fourthly, we have in the Taittirīya Upanishad a classic description of the illimitable bliss that a perfected Mystic experiences after his communion with the Highest—a description which we have had occasion to notice in our account of the beatific calculus in a previous chapter. But the Bṛihadāraṇyakopanishad, in the vein of an almost erotic mysticism, tells us further that the only earthly analogue which we can have for the bliss of God-realisation,—indeed a very imperfect and partial analogue after all,—is the bliss arising from union with a dear wife. "Just as when a man is embraced by his dear wife, he knows nothing outside nor anything inside; similarly when the individual Self is embraced by the universal Self, he knows nothing outside nor anything inside; for he has attained an end which involves the fulfilment of all other ends, being verily the attainment of Ātman which leaves no other ends to be fulfilled" (S. 24. d). We do not know how far to justify this analogy. But it seems after all that there might be a difference of kind between the two blisses which the Bṛihādaraṇyakopanishad is comparing, instead of merely a difference of degree ; or, at least, that the one kind of bliss is so insignificant as contrasted with the other that there is as much analogy between them as there is between the light of a candle and the light of the sun. Further, all such erotic analogues have this defect in them, that those who betake themselves to sexual enjoyment may be thereby vainly made to imagine that they are after all experiencing an iota at least of the great divine bliss. In our opinion, it is foolish to regard the relation between the Self and God as in any way analogous to the relation between the bride and the bridegroom, and still more foolish to regard it as analogous to the inverted relation between the bridegroom and the bride as in certain pseudo-mystic teachings. In fact, there ought to be and can be no analogue for the unique relation between the Self and God in the state of ecstasy. To return to our argument, however, fifthly, we are told in the Taittirirīya Upanishad that the direct result of the enjoyment of divine bliss is that the Mystic is divested once for all of all feeling of fear. The one kind of emotion kills the other, and the feeling of bliss kills once for all the emotion of fear. Whom and what may such a perfected Mystic fear, when he finds infinite joy in all directions and at all times ? " He becomes fearless, " says the Taittirīya Upanishad, " because he has obtained a lodgment in that invisible, incorporate, indefinable, fearless, supportless support of all " (S. 24. e). Finally, we are told in the Chhāndogya Upanishad that " if such a Mystic should ever want to have any end fulfilled at all, he should wait upon the Ātman, and pray to him, without the slightest touch of egoism, for the fulfilment of his desire : immediately is the end fulfilled for him for which he had prayed to God" (S. 25. a). "The Ātman," says the Chhāndogya Upanishad, "is sinless, without age, without death, without fear, without any hunger or thirst, and has all his desires or ends fulfilled. This Ātman should be sought after; this Ātman should be known. He who realises the Ātman in this way after having sought after him, for him all the worlds are gained, and all desires fulfilled" (S. 25. b). The Muṇḍakopanishad tells us also that "a man can have all his desires fulfilled, and obtain any world he may seek, even if he only waits upon and worships a Mystic who has realised the Self" (S. 25. c). We thus see, on the whole, that the immediate effects of God-realisation upon the Mystic are the entire abatement of bodily excitement, the resolution of all doubts, the obtainment of infinite power, the enjoyment of illimitable joy, the destruction of all fear, and the fulfilment of any end that may be contemplated by the Mystic.

Raptures of mystic ecstasy.

17. The Upanishads have preserved for us a few mystic monologues which contain the essence of the raptures of spiritual experience. The Sage of the Muṇḍakopanishad, when he came to realise the immortal Brahman, fell into mystic raptures when he saw that "the Brahman was before him and behind him, to his right and to his left, above and below," and broke forth into the Leibnitzian exclamation that "this was the best of all possible worlds" (S. 26). He considered himself fortunate that he was ever born into this world at all, for, was it not his appearance on the terrestrial globe that led him, by proper means and through adequate stages, to the vision of the Godhead wherever his eye was cast? The Sage Vāmadeva of the Bṛihadāraṇyakopanishad came to know that "just as, at the origin of things, Brahman came to self-consciousness and then understood that it was verily the All, similarly, whoever among the gods, or the mortals, or the sages comes to self-consciousness becomes verily the All"; and thus the Sage, to whom the infinite past was like an eternal now, broke forth into the exclamation that "he it was who had lived in Manu, and that he it was who had given light to the Sun" (S. 27),—even like the Maratha saint Tukaram, who, at a later date, exclaimed that, in bygone ages, when Śuka had gone to the mountains to reach Self-realisation, he was himself present to watch that Great Act in spirit, if not in body. The Mystic of the Chhāndogya Upanishad declares that even as a horse might shake its mane, similarly had he himself shaken off all his sin, that even as the Moon might come out entire after having suffered an eclipse from Rāhu, even so, having been freed from the mortal coil, had he obtained the eternal life in the Ātman (S. 28). Then, again, the utterances of Triśaṅku in the Taittirīya Upanishad are remarkable for the grandeur of the ideas involved in them. After Triśaṅku had reached Self-realisation, he tells us he felt as if he was the "Mover of the Tree." What is the Tree to which Triśaṅku is referring? It may be the Tree of the Body, or it may even be the Tree of the World. It is not uncustomary for Upanishadic and post-Upanishadic writers to speak of the Body or the World as verily a Tree. In fact, Triśaṅku tells us that, like the true Soul that he was, he could move the Tree of the bodily or worldly coil. He tells us, furthermore, that his glory was "like the top of a mountain," which is as much as to say that when he had come to realise the Self, he felt that everything else looked so mean and insignificant to him from the high pedestal of Ātmanic experience that he felt as if he was on the top of all things whatsoever. Triśaṅku tells us furthermore that "the source from which he had come was Purity itself." May this not refer to the Purity of the Divine Life from which all existence springs? Then, again, Triśaṅku tells us that he was as it were "the Immortal Being in the Sun,"—an identification Īśāvāsya-wise of the Individual and Universal Spirit. Furthermore, Triśaṅku says that he regarded himself as "a treasure of unsurpassable value," referring probably to the infinite wealth of Ātmanic experience that he had obtained. Finally, he tells us that he was verily "the intelligent, the immortal and the imperishable One," thus identifying himself with Absolute Spirit (S. 29). Finally, that greatest of the Mystics whose post-ecstatic monologue is preserved for us in the Taittirīya Upanishad, tells us in a passage of unsurpassed grandeur throughout both Upanishadic as well as post-Upanishadic literature that when he had transcended the limitations of his earthly, etheric, mental, intellective, and beatific sheaths, he sat in the utter silence of solipsistic solitude, singing the song of universal unity: "How wonderful, how wonderful, how wonderful; I am the food, I am the food, I am the food; I am the food-eater, I am the food-eater, I am the food-eater; I am the maker of their unity, I am the maker of their unity, I am the maker of their unity," which utterances only mean, metaphysically, that he was himself all matter and all spirit as well as the connecting link between them both, and epistemologically, that he was himself the subject-world and the object-world as well as the entire subject-object relation—a stage of spiritual experience which has been well characterised by a modern idealistic thinker as a stage where the difference between the field, the fighter, and the strife vanishes altogether—the culmination of the unitive song being couched in terms which are only too reminiscent of like mystic utterances from other lands, "I am the first-born of the Law; I am older than the gods; I am the navel of Immortality; he that gives me, keeps me; him, who eats all food, I eat as food; I envelop the whole universe with splendour as of the Sun" (S. 30.)

SOURCES VII

1 (*a*) द्वे विद्ये वेदितव्ये इति ह स्म यद् ब्रह्मविदो वदंति परा चैवापरा च। तत्र अपरा ऋग्वेदो यजुर्वेदः सामवेदोऽथर्ववेदः शिक्षा कल्पो व्याकरणं निरुक्तं छंदो ज्योतिषमिति। अथ परा यया तदक्षरमधिगम्यते॥

मुं. I. 1. 4–5.

(*b*) स होवाच ऋग्वेदं भगवोऽध्येमि यजुर्वेदं राशिं दैवं निधिं वाकोवाक्यमेकायनं देवविद्यां ब्रह्मविद्यां भूतविद्यां क्षत्रविद्यां नक्षत्रविद्यां* सर्पदेवजनविद्यामेतद्भगवोऽध्येमि सोऽहं भगवो मंत्रविदेवास्मि नात्मविच्छ्रुतं ह्येव मे भगवद्दृशेभ्यस्तरति शोकमात्मविदिति सोऽहं भगवः शोचामि तं मा भगवान् शोकस्य पारं तारयत्विति।

छां. VII. 1. 2–3.

2 (*a*) इह चेदवेदीदथ सत्यमस्ति न चेदिहावेदीन्महती विनष्टिः।

के. II. 13.

(*b*) इह चेदशकद्बोद्धुं प्राक् शरीरस्य विस्रसः। ततः सर्गेषु लोकेषु शरीरत्वाय कल्पते॥

क. II. 6. 4.

3 (*a*) पराञ्चि खानि व्यतृणत्स्वयंभूस्तस्मात्पराङ्पश्यति नान्तरात्मन्। कश्चिद्धीरः प्रत्यगात्मानमैक्षदावृत्तचक्षुरमृतत्वमिच्छन्॥

क. II. 4. 1.

(*b*) नवद्वारे पुरे देही हंसो लेलायते बहिः।

श्वे. III. 18.

4 (a) नाविरतो दुश्चरितान्नाशांतो नासमाहितः । नाशान्तमानसो वापि प्रज्ञानेनैनमाप्नुयात् ॥

क. I. 2. 24.

(b) सत्येन लभ्यस्तपसा ह्येष आत्मा सम्यग्ज्ञानेन ब्रह्मचर्येण नित्यम् । अंतःशरीरे ज्योतिर्मयो हि शुभ्रो यं पश्यंति यतयः क्षीणदोषाः ॥

मुं. III. 1. 5.

(c) नायमात्मा प्रवचनेन लभ्यो न मेधया न बहुना श्रुतेन ।

क. I. 2. 22.

(d) अंधं तमः प्रविशन्ति येऽविद्यामुपासते । ततो भूय इव ते तमो य उ विद्यायां रताः ॥

ई. 9.

(e) नायमात्मा बलहीनेन लभ्यो न च प्रमादात्तपसो वाप्यलिंगात् ।

मुं. III. 2. 4

(f) परीक्ष्य लोकान् कर्मचितान् ब्राह्मणो निर्वेदमायान्नास्त्यकृतः कृतेन । तद्विज्ञानार्थं स गुरुमेवाभिगच्छेत्समित्पाणिः श्रोत्रियं ब्रह्मनिष्ठम् ॥

मुं. I. 2. 12.

5 (a) श्रुतं ह्येव मे भगवद्दृशेभ्यः आचार्याद्धयेव विद्या विदिता साधिष्ठं प्रापयतीति ।

छां. IV. 9. 3.

(b) न नरेणावरेण प्रोक्त एष सुविज्ञेयो बहुधा चिन्त्यमानः । अनन्यप्रोक्ते गतिरत्र नास्ति अणीयान् ह्यतर्क्यमणुप्रमाणात् ॥ नैषा तर्केण मतिरापनेया प्रोक्तान्येनैव सुज्ञानाय प्रेष्ठ ।

क. I. 2. 8–9.

(c) उत्तिष्ठत जाग्रत प्राप्य वरान्निबोधत । क्षुरस्य धारा निशिता दुरत्यया दुर्गं पथस्तत्कवयो वदन्ति ॥

क. I. 3. 14.

6 यथा सोम्य पुरुषं गंधारेभ्योऽभिनद्धाक्षमानीय तं ततोऽतिजने विसृजेत्स यथा तत्र प्राङ्वोदङ्वाऽधराङ्वा प्रत्यङ्वा प्रध्मायीताभिनद्धाक्ष आनीतोऽभिनद्धाक्षो विसृष्टः ॥ १ ॥ तस्य यथाभिनहनं प्रमुच्य प्रब्रूयादेतां दिशं गंधारा एतां दिशं व्रजेति स ग्रामाद् ग्रामं पृच्छन् पण्डितो मेधावी गंधारानेवोपसंपद्येत एवमेवेहाचार्यवान् पुरुषो वेद तस्य तावदेव चिरं यावन्न विमोक्ष्येऽथ संपत्स्य इति ॥ २ ॥

छां. VI. 14. 1–2.

7 (a) क्रियावन्तः श्रोत्रिया ब्रह्मनिष्ठाः स्वयं जुह्वत एकर्षिं श्रद्ध-
यंतः । तेषामेवैतां ब्रह्मविद्यां वदेत शिरोव्रतं विधिवद्यैस्तु
चीर्णम् ॥ मुं. III. 2. 10.

(b) इदं वाव तज्ज्येष्ठाय पुत्राय पिता ब्रह्म प्रब्रूयात्प्रणाय्याय
वान्तेवासिने । नान्यस्मै कस्मैचन यद्यप्यस्मा इमामद्भिः
परिगृहीतां धनस्य पूर्णां दद्यादेतदेव ततो भूय इत्येतदेव
ततो भूय इति ॥

छां. III. 11. 5-6.

(c) वेदान्ते परमं गुह्यं पुराकल्पे प्रचोदितम् । नाप्रशान्ताय
दातव्यं नापुत्रायाशिष्याय वा पुनः ॥ यस्य देवे परा भक्तिः
यथा देवे तथा गुरौ । तस्यैते कथिता ह्यर्थाः प्रकाशन्ते
महात्मनः प्रकाशन्ते महात्मनः ॥

श्वे. VI. 22-23.

8 (a) सर्वे वेदा यत्पदमामनन्ति तपांसि सर्वाणि च यद्वदन्ति ।
यदिच्छंतो ब्रह्मचर्यं चरन्ति तत्ते पदं संग्रहेण ब्रवीम्यो-
मित्येतत् ॥ एतद्ध्येवाक्षरं ब्रह्म एतद्ध्येवाक्षरं परं एतद्ध्ये-
वाक्षरं ज्ञात्वा यो यदिच्छति तस्य तत् ॥
क. I. 2. 15-17.

(b) तद्यथा शंकुना सर्वाणि पर्णानि संतृण्णानि एवमोंकारेण
सर्वा वाक् संतृण्णा ॐकार एवेदं सर्वम् ।

छां. II. 23. 3.

9 धनुर्गृहीत्वौपनिषदं महास्त्रं शरं ह्युपासानिशितं संधयीत ।
आयम्य तद्भावगतेन चेतसा लक्ष्यं तदेवाक्षरं सोम्य
विद्धि ॥ ३ ॥ प्रणवो धनुः शरो ह्यात्मा ब्रह्म तल्लक्ष्यमुच्यते ।
अप्रमत्तेन वेद्धव्यं शरवत्तन्मयो भवेत् ॥ ४ ॥

मुं. II. 2. 3-4.

10 ॐ इति ह्येष स्वरन्नेति । छां. I. 5. 1, 3.

11 अथ हैनं शैब्यः सत्यकामः पप्रच्छ । स यो ह वैतद् भगव-
न्मनुष्येषु प्रायणान्तमोंकारमभिध्यायीत । कतमं वाव स
तेन लोकं जयतीति । तस्मै स होवाच " एतद्वै सत्यकाम
परं चापरं च ब्रह्म यदोंकारः । तस्माद्विद्वानेतेनैवायतने-
नैकतरमन्वेति ।.....यथा पादोदरस्त्वचा विनिर्मुच्यत
एवं ह वै स पाप्मना विनिर्मुक्तः स सामभिरुन्नीयते ब्रह्म-

लोकं स एतस्माज्जीवघनात्परं पुरिशयं पुरुषमीक्षते ”।

प्र. V. 1–5.

12 भूतं भवद्भविष्यदिति सर्वमोंकार एव । यच्चान्यत्त्रिका-
लातीतं तदप्योंकार एव ॥१॥ सर्वं ह्येतद् ब्रह्मायमात्मा ब्रह्म ।
सोऽयमात्मा चतुष्पात् ॥ २ ॥ जागरितस्थानो बहिःप्रज्ञः
सप्तांग एकोनविंशतिमुखः स्थूलभुग्वैश्वानरः प्रथमः
पादः ॥ ३ ॥ स्वप्नस्थानोऽन्तःप्रज्ञः सप्तांग एकोनविंशति-
मुखः प्रविविक्तभुक् तैजसो द्वितीयः पादः ॥ ४ ॥ यत्र
सुप्तो न कंचन कामं कामयते न कंचन स्वप्नं पश्यति
तत्सुषुप्तम् । सुषुप्तस्थान एकीभूतः प्रज्ञानघन एवानंदमयो
ह्यानंदभुक् चेतोमुखः प्राज्ञस्तृतीयः पादः ॥ ५ ॥ एष सर्वे-
श्वर एष सर्वज्ञ एषोऽन्तर्याम्येष योनिः सर्वस्य प्रभवाप्ययौ
हि भूतानाम् ॥ ६ ॥ नान्तःप्रज्ञं न बहिःप्रज्ञं नोभयतःप्रज्ञं
न प्रज्ञानघनं न प्रज्ञं नाप्रज्ञम् । अदृष्टमव्यवहार्यमग्राह्यमल-
क्षणमचिन्त्यमव्यपदेश्यमेकात्मप्रत्ययसारं प्रपञ्चोपशमं शान्तं
शिवमद्वैतं चतुर्थं मन्यन्ते स आत्मा स विज्ञेयः ॥ ७ ॥
सोऽयमात्माऽध्यक्षरमोंकारोऽधिमात्रं पादा मात्रा मात्राश्च
पादा अकार उकार मकार इति ॥ ८ ॥ ....॥ अमात्रश्चतुर्थो-
ऽव्यवहार्यः प्रपंचोपशमः शिवोऽद्वैतं एवमोंकार आत्मैव
संविशत्यात्मनात्मानं य एवं वेद य एवं वेद ॥ १२ ॥

मां. 1–12.

13 (*a*) स्वदेहमरणिं कृत्वा प्रणवं चोत्तरारणिम् । ध्याननिर्मथना-
भ्यासाद्देवं पश्येन्निगूढवत् ॥

श्वे. I. 14.

(*b*) अरण्योर्निहितो जातवेदा गर्भ इव सुभृतो गर्भिणीभिः ।
दिवे दिव ईड्यो जागृवद्भिर्हविष्मद्भिः मनुष्येभिरग्निः ॥

क. II. 4. 8.

14 (*a*) ऊर्ध्वं प्राणमुन्नयत्यपानं प्रत्यगस्यति । मध्ये वामनमासीनं
विश्वे देवा उपासते ॥

क. II. 5. 3.

(*b*) प्राणैश्चित्तं सर्वमोतं प्रजानां यस्मिन्विशुद्धे विभवत्येष
आत्मा । मुं. III. 1. 9.

15 (*a*) त्रिरुन्नतं स्थाप्य समं शरीरं हृदींद्रियाणि मनसा संनि-
वेश्य । ब्रह्मोडुपेन प्रतरेत विद्वान् स्रोतांसि सर्वाणि भया-

वहानि ॥ ८ ॥ प्राणान्प्रपीड्येह स युक्तचेष्टः क्षीणे प्राणे
नासिकयोच्छ्वसीत । दुष्टाश्वयुक्तमिव वाहमेनं विद्वान्मनो
धारयेताप्रमत्तः ॥ ९ ॥ समे शुचौ शर्कराबह्निवालुका-
विवर्जिते शब्दजलाश्रयादिभिः । मनोनुकूले न तु चक्षु-
पीडने गुहानिवाताश्रयणे प्रयोजयेत् ॥ १० ॥

श्वे. II. 8–10.

(*b*) पृथिव्यप्तेजोऽनिलखे समुत्थिते पंचात्मके योगगुणे प्रवृत्ते ।
न तस्य रोगो न जरा न मृत्युः प्राप्तस्य योगाग्निमयं
शरीरम् ॥ १२ ॥ लघुत्वमारोग्यमलोलुपत्वं वर्णप्रसादः
स्वरसौष्ठवं च । गंधः शुभो मूत्रपुरीषमल्पं योगप्रवृत्तिं
प्रथमां वदन्ति ॥ १३ ॥ श्वे. II. 12–13.

16 (*a*) न संदृशे तिष्ठति रूपमस्य न चक्षुषा पश्यति कश्चनैनम् ।
हृदा मनीषा मनसाभिक्लृप्तो य एतद्विदुरमृतास्ते भवन्ति ॥

क. II. 6. 9.

(*b*) नैव वाचा न मनसा प्राप्तुं शक्यो न चक्षुषा । अस्तीति
ब्रुवतोऽन्यत्र कथं तदुपलभ्यते ॥

क. II. 6. 12.

(*c*) एष सर्वेषु भूतेषु गूढोत्मा न प्रकाशते । दृश्यते त्वग्र्यया बुद्ध्या
सूक्ष्मया सूक्ष्मदर्शिभिः ॥

क. I. 3. 12.

17 (*a*) न चक्षुषा गृह्यते नापि वाचा नान्यैर्देवैस्तपसा कर्मणा
वा । ज्ञानप्रसादेन विशुद्धसत्वः ततस्तु तं पश्यते निष्कलं
ध्यायमानः ॥

मुं. III. 1. 8.

(*b*) तमक्रतुः पश्यति वीतशोको धातुप्रसादान्माहिमानमात्मनः ।

क. I. 2. 20.

18 (*a*) तं स्वाच्छरीरात्प्रवृहेन्मुञ्जादिवेषीकां धैर्येण । तं विद्याच्छु-
क्रममृतं तं विद्याच्छुक्रममृतमिति ॥

क. II. 6. 17.

(*b*) तद्यथा क्षुरः क्षुरधाने हितः विश्वंभरो वा विश्वंभरकुलाये
एवमेव एष प्रज्ञात्मा इदं शरीरं अनुप्रविष्टः आलोमभ्यः
आनखेभ्यः ।

कौ. IV. 20.

(*c*) तिलेषु तैलं दधिनीव सर्पिरापः स्रोतःस्वरणीषु चाग्निः ।

एवमात्मात्मनि गृह्यतेऽसौ सत्येनैनं तपसा योऽनुपश्यति ॥
श्वे. I. 15.

(d) घृतात्परं मंडमिवातिसूक्ष्मं ज्ञात्वा शिवं सर्वभूतेषु गूढम् ।
विश्वस्यैकं परिवेष्टितारं ज्ञात्वा देवं मुच्यते सर्वपापैः ॥
श्वे. IV. 16.

19 (a) नीहारधूमार्कानलानिलानां खद्योतविद्युत्स्फटिकशशिनाम् ।
एतानि रूपाणि पुरःसराणि ब्रह्मण्यभिव्यक्तिकराणि योगे ॥
श्वे. II. 11.

(b) तस्य ह एतस्य पुरुषस्य रूपं यथा महारजनं वासो, यथा पाण्ड्वादिकं, यथेंद्रगोपो, यथा अग्न्यार्चिः, यथा पुण्डरीकं, यथा सकृद्विद्युत् । ते ह वा अस्य श्रीर्भवति य एवं वेद ।
बृ. II. 3. 6.

20 (a) अयमग्निर्वैश्वानरो योयमंतःपुरुषे येनेदमन्नं पच्यते यदिदमद्यते तस्यैष घोषो भवति यमेतत्कर्णावपिधाय शृणोति स यदोत्क्रमिष्यन् भवति नैनं घोषं शृणोति ॥
बृ. V. 9. 1; मै. II. 6.

(b) तदस्मिञ् शरीरे संस्पर्शेनोष्णिमानं विजानाति । तस्यैषा श्रुतिः । यत्र कर्णावपिगृह्य निनदमिव, नदथुरिव, अग्नेरिव ज्वलत उपशृणोति । छां. III. 13. 8.

21 (a) हिरण्मये परे कोशे विरजं ब्रह्म निष्कलं । तच्छुभ्रं ज्योतिषां ज्योतिस्तद्यदात्मविदो विदुः ॥९॥
मुं. II. 2. 9.

(b) एतं सेतुं तीर्त्वा अंधः सन्ननंधो भवति, विद्धः सन्नविद्धो भवति, तस्माद्वा एतं सेतुं तीर्त्वापि नक्तमहरेवाभिनिष्पद्यते । सकृद्विभातो ह्येवैष ब्रह्मलोकः ॥
छां. VIII. 4. 2.

(c) न वै तत्र न निम्लोच नोदियाय कदाचन । देवास्तेनाहं सत्येन मा विराधिषि ब्रह्मणा ॥ २ ॥ न ह वा अस्मा उदेति न निम्लोचति सकृद्दिवा हैवास्मि भवति य एतां ब्रह्मोपनिषदं वेद ॥ ३ ॥
छां. III. 11. 2–3.

(d) यदाऽतमः तन्न दिवा न रात्रिर्न सन्न चासन् शिव एव केवलः । श्वे. IV. 18.

22 (*a*) यमेवैष वृणुते तेनैव लभ्यः तस्यैष आत्मा विवृणुते तनूं स्वाम् ।

मुं. III. 2. 3.

(*b*) य एषोऽन्तरादित्ये हिरण्मयः पुरुषो दृश्यते हिरण्यश्मश्रुर्हिरण्यकेश आप्रणखात् सर्व एव सुवर्णः ।

छां. I. 6. 6.

योऽसावसौ पुरुषः सोऽहमस्मि । ई. 16.

(*c*) यथैव बिंबं मृदयोपलिप्तं तेजोमयं भ्राजते तत्सुधातम् । तद्वात्मतत्वं प्रसमीक्ष्य देही एकः कृतार्थो भवते वीतशोकः ॥ १४ ॥ यदात्मतत्त्वेन तु ब्रह्मतत्त्वं दीपोपमेनेह युक्तः प्रपश्येत् । अजं ध्रुवं सर्वतत्त्वैर्विशुद्धं ज्ञात्वा देवं मुच्यते सर्वपाशैः ॥ १५ ॥

श्वे. II. 14–15.

(*d*) अयं वाव खल्वात्मा ते । यः कतमो भगव इति । तं होवाच । अथ य एष संप्रसादोऽस्माच्छरीरात्समुत्थाय परं ज्योतिरुपसंपद्य स्वेन रूपेणाभिनिष्पद्यत इत्येष आत्मेति होवाच एतदमृतमभयमेतद् ब्रह्मेति । अथ खल्वियं ब्रह्मविद्या सर्वोपनिषद्विद्या वा राजन्नस्माकं भगवता मैत्रिणाऽख्याता ।

मै. II. 1–3.

23 (*a*) नैष स्त्री न पुमानेष न चैवायं नपुंसकः । यद्यच्छरीरमादत्ते तेन तेन स रक्ष्यते ॥

श्वे. V. 10.

(*b*) अनेजदेकं मनसो जवीयो नैनद्देवा आप्नुवन् पूर्वमर्शत् ।... तदेजति तन्नैजति तद्दूरे तद्वन्तिके । तदन्तरस्य सर्वस्य तदु सर्वस्यास्य बाह्यतः ॥

ई. 4, 5.

आसीनो दूरं व्रजति शयानो याति सर्वतः । कस्तं मदामदं देवं मदन्यो ज्ञातुमर्हति ॥

क. I. 2. 21.

बृहच्च तद्दिव्यमचिन्त्यरूपं सूक्ष्माच्च तत्सूक्ष्मतरं विभाति । दूरात्सुदूरे तदिहान्तिके च पश्यत्स्विहैव निहितं गुहायाम् ॥

मुं III. 1. 7.

अणोरणीयान्महतो महीयानात्मास्य जंतोर्निहितो गुहायाम् । क. I. 2. 20.

अंगुष्ठमात्रो रवितुल्यरूपः संकल्पाहंकारसमन्वितो यः ।
बुद्धेर्गुणेनात्मगुणेन चैव आराग्रमात्रो ह्यवरोऽपि दृष्टः ॥ ८ ॥
बालाग्रशतभागस्य शतधा कल्पितस्य च । भागो जीवः स
विज्ञेयः स चाऽऽनंत्याय कल्पते ॥ ९ ॥

श्वे. V. 8—9.

अंगुष्ठमात्रः पुरुषोन्तरात्मा सदा जनानां हृदये संनिविष्टः ।

क. II. 6. 17.

24 (*a*) आत्मानं चेद्विजानीयादयमस्मीति पूरुषः । किमिच्छन् कस्य कामाय शरीरमनुसंज्वरेत् ॥

बृ. IV. 4. 12.

(*b*) भिद्यते हृदयग्रंथिश्छिद्यंते सर्वसंशयाः । क्षीयंते चास्य कर्माणि तस्मिन् दृष्टे परावरे ॥

मुं. II. 2. 8.

(*c*) समाने वृक्षे पुरुषो निमग्नोऽनीशया शोचति मुह्यमानः ।
जुष्टं यदा पश्यति अन्यमीशमस्य महिमानमिति वीतशोकः॥

मुं. III. 1. 2.

(*d*) तद्यथा प्रियया स्त्रिया संपरिष्वक्तो न बाह्यं किंचन वेद, नांतरं, एवमेवायं पुरुषः प्राज्ञेनात्मना संपरिष्वक्तो न बाह्यं किंचन वेद, नान्तरम्, तद्वा अस्य एतदाप्तकामं आत्मकामं अकामं रूपम् ॥

बृ. IV. 3. 21.

(*e*) आनंदं ब्रह्मणो विद्वान् न बिभेति कदाचन ।

तै. II. 4.

यदा ह्येवैष एतस्मिन्नदृश्ये अनात्म्येऽनिरुक्तेऽनिलयनेऽभयं प्रतिष्ठां विन्दते । अथ सोऽभयं गतो भवति ।

तै. II. 7.

25 (*a*) आत्मानमंते उपसृत्य स्तुवीत कामं ध्यायन् अप्रमत्तो, अभ्याशो ह यत् , अस्मै स कामः समृध्येत यत्कामः स्तुवीतेति ॥ छां. I. 3. 12.

(*b*) य आत्मा ऽपहतपाप्मा विजरो, विमृत्युः, विशोकोऽविजिघत्सोऽपिपासः, सत्यसंकल्पः, सोन्वेष्टव्यः, स विजिज्ञासितव्यः । स सर्वांश्च लोकानाप्नोति सर्वांश्च कामान् यस्तमात्मानमनुविद्य विजानातीति ।

छां. VIII. 7. 1.

(c) यं यं लोकं मनसा संविभाति विशुद्धसत्त्वः कामयते यांश्च कामान् । तं तं लोकं जयते तांश्च कामांस्तस्मादात्मज्ञं ह्यर्चयेद् भूतिकामः ॥

मुं. III. 1. 10.

26 ब्रह्मैवेदममृतं पुरस्ताद् ब्रह्म पश्चाद् ब्रह्म दक्षिणतश्चोत्तरेण । अधश्चोर्ध्वं प्रसृतं ब्रह्मैवेदं विश्वमिदं वरिष्ठम् ॥

मुं. II. 2. 11.

27 ब्रह्म ह वा इदमग्र आसीत्तदात्मानमवेत् । अहं ब्रह्मास्मीति । तस्मात् तत्सर्वमभवत् । तद्यो यो देवानां प्रत्यबुध्यत स एव तदभवत् तथा ऋषीणां, तथा मनुष्याणाम् । तद्धैतत्पश्यन् ऋषिर्वामदेवः प्रतिपेदेऽहं मनुरभवं सूर्यश्चेति ।

बृ. I. 4. 10.

28 अश्व इव रोमाणि विधूय पापं, चंद्र इव राहोर्मुखात्प्रमुच्य, धूत्वा शरीरं, अकृतं कृतात्मा ब्रह्मलोकमभिसंभवामीति ।

छां. VIII. 13. 1.

29 अहं वृक्षस्य रेरिवा । कीर्तिः पृष्ठं गिरेरिव । ऊर्ध्वपवित्रो वाजिनीव स्वमृतमस्मि । द्रविणं सवर्चसम् । सुमेधा अमृतोऽक्षितः । इति त्रिशंकोर्वेदानुवचनम् ।

तै. I. 10.

30 स य एवंवित् । अस्माल्लोकात्प्रेत्य । एतमन्नमयमात्मानमुपसंक्रम्य । एतं प्राणमयमात्मानमुपसंक्रम्य । एतं मनोमयमात्मानमुपसंक्रम्य । एतं विज्ञानमयमात्मानमुपसंक्रम्य । एतमानंदमयमात्मानमुपसंक्रम्य । इमाँल्लोकान्कामान्नीकामरूप्यनुसंचरन् । एतत्साम गायन्नास्ते । हा ३ वु हा ३ वु हा ३ वु । अहमन्नमहमन्नमहमन्नम् । अहमन्नादो ३ ऽहमन्नादो ३ ऽहमन्नादः । अह ३ श्लोककृदह ३ श्लोककृदह ३ श्लोककृत् । अहमस्मि प्रथमजा ऋता ३ स्य । पूर्वं देवेभ्योऽमृतस्य ना ३ भायि । यो मा ददाति स इदेव मा ३ वाः । अहमन्नमन्नमदन्तमा ३ द्मि । अहं विश्वं भुवनमभ्यभवा ३ म् । सुवर्न ज्योतीः ॥

तै. III. 10. 5–6.

GENERAL INDEX.

A.

D.

G.

H.

I.

N.

O.

S.

T.

U.

V.

UPANISHAD INDEX

BṚIHADĀRAṆYAKA UPANISHAD.

CHHĀNDOGYA UPANISHAD.

ĪŚĀVĀSYA UPANISHAD.

KENA UPANISHAD.

AITAREYA UPANISHAD.

TAITTIRĪYA UPANISHAD.

KAUSHĪTAKI UPANISHAD.

KAṬHA UPANISHAD.

MUṆḌAKA UPANISHAD.

ŚVETĀŚVATARA UPANISHAD

PRAŚNA UPANISHAD

MAITRI UPANISHAD.

MĀṆḌŪKYA UPANISHAD.

BIBLIOGRAPHICAL NOTE

1. TEXTS.

A handy edition of the texts of the Upanishads can be had at the Nirnayasagar Press, Bombay, entitled *Twenty-eight Upanishads*, which contains almost all of the more prominent Upanishads, excluding the Maitri. Another edition of the Twenty-eight Upanishads is published also at the Venkateshwar Press, Bombay. The Anandashram Press, Poona, has published an edition of *Thirty-two Upanishads*, which excludes the famous ten Upanishads, with an inclusion, however, of Kaushītaki and Maitri along with other Minor Upanishads. This edition of Minor Upanishads is printed with the commentaries of Nārāyaṇa and Śaṅkarānanda. Jacob has brought out an edition of the *Eleven Ātharvaṇa Upanishads* in the Bombay Sanskrit Series, which also contains Upanishads beyond the ordinary ten. An excellent edition of the Miscellaneous Upanishads can be had at the Adyar Library, Madras, edited by the Director of the Manuscripts Library. Dr. Schrader, who was the Director of that Library in 1912, brought out an edition of the *Saṁnyāsa Upanishads* during that year, but when he was required to go to Europe during the war, his place was taken up by his successor A. Mahadev Shastri, who has recently brought out editions of the *Yoga Upanishads* in 1920, *Vedānta Upanishads* in 1921, and *Vaishṇava Upanishads* in 1923. It seems only one volume on Śaiva Upanishads from out of the original plan yet remains to be edited. All the Upanishads have been edited with the commentary of Upanishad-Brahmayogin. The get-up of the volumes leaves nothing to be desired, and we cannot recommend to our readers a more beautiful or more handy edition of the Minor Upanishads than the edition of the four volumes brought out from Adyar.

As regards the Hundred and Eight Upanishads, there was an edition brought out by Subrahmanya Shastri at Madras in 1883. Later on, the Tattvavivechak Press, Bombay, brought out an edition of the same Hundred and Eight Upanishads, while a handy edition of the *Hundred and Eight Upanishads* can now be had even at the Nirnayasagar Press, Bombay. In the absence of a more reliable edition, we can recommend this to all students of Upanishadic literature, who care for the canon of the Upanishadic literature "in extenso." There are a number of other Upanishads which exist beyond the so-called Hundred and Eight, which have been catalogued in the volume on the bibliography of the Upanishads published at Adyar, as well as with greater fulness and precision in the "Creative Period of Indian Philosophy" by S. K. Belvalkar and R. D. Ranade.

It is strange that there should not have been even a single exceedingly reliable edition of the Texts of the Upanishads. We recommend the production of such a one to all those who are interested in the literary side of the Upanishads. Lanman's dictum ("Beginings of Hindu Pantheism") remains only too true that "a critical text of all the old Upanishads conveniently assembled in one volume with a philologically accurate translation and various useful appendices is still one of the pressing needs of Indology."

Colonel Jacob has laid all students of Upanishadic literature under immense obligations by editing a *Concordance to the Principal* (56) *Upanishads*, along with the Bhagavadgītā. This piece of literary work is exceedingly creditable to one who was serving in the Indian Army. One wishes that there were more happy surprises of that kind from the Indian Army!

II. COMMENTARIES.

All the great Schools of Vedānta Philosophy have had their own commentaries on the Upanishads, as on the Brahma-Sūtras, and the Bhagavadgītā. The *Commentaries of Śaṅkara* on the various Upanishads have been printed in the Anandasram Press, Poona, as also in the collected edition of his works printed at Vanivilas Press. They are also edited in one volume by H. R. Bhagavat, Poona. Śaṅkara's commentary on the Kārikās of Gauḍapāda, which are themselves a commentary on the Māṇḍūkyopanishad, is most famous, as well as his commentary on the Bṛihadāraṇyaka. This last has been again commented on by Sureśvarāchārya in his Vārtika. Doubt has sometimes been thrown upon Śaṅkara's commentary on the Śvetāśvatara Upanishad ; but his commentaries on the other Upanishads have been regarded as authentic. There has been a very good one-volume edition of the principal Eleven Upanishads commented on by Swami Achintya Bhagawan and printed at the Nirnayasagar Press, 1910, which follows in substance the commentary of Śaṅkara on the Upanishads. If one wishes to have an epitome of Śaṅkara's commentaries on the Upanishads, one can have it in this edition of Swami Achintya Bhagawan. The edition is also beautifully printed and is handy. Another running commentary on the substance of the various Upanishads, following the Advaita school of Philosophy, is entitled " Anubhūtiprakāśa, " and has been written by the famous Mādhavāchārya.

The *Commentaries of Rāmānuja* on the Upanishads are not so well-known as his commentary on the Brahma-Sūtras. There is a mention of the existence of his commentaries on the Upanishads in an edition printed at Madras, which is however, in any case, not very accessible. On the other hand, the commentaries of Raṅga Rāmānuja on the various Upanishads following the Viśishṭādvaita school of thought are better known. The Anandashram Press has printed Raṅga Rāmānuja 's commentaries on the Bṛihadāraṅyaka, the Chhāndogya, the Kaṭha and the Kena Upanishads. The last two Upanishads with Raṅga Rāmānuja 's commentary have been also edited by Shridharashastri Pathak, of the Deccan College, Poona.

The *Commentaries of Madhva* on the Upanishads can be had in the Sarvamūla Series edited at the Madhavavilas Book Depot,

Kumbhakonam. Extracts from Madhva's commentaries along with the original Upanishads and translations have been published at the Panini Office, Allahabad.

The *Brahma-sūtras* themselves are an aphoristic summary of the Upanishads, borrowing words and ideas from them, and linking them together in a theologico-philosophical context. It is the commentaries of the great Teachers on the Brahma-sūtras, which are, however, more famous than the commentaries on the Upanishads themselves. These commentaries constitute the later Vedānta proper, and use the scholastico-logical method, as has been pointed out in the Preface, instead of the mystico-intuitional one.

III. TRANSLATIONS.

The most important work that has been hitherto done on the Upanishads is the work of Translation. Through a long period of years the Upanishads have afforded a temptation for the aspiring Translator to try his hand at in various languages. The first known translation of the Upanishads was done into Persian during the years 1656-1657 by the Pandits in the court of Dara, the son of Shah Jahan. The first notice of the Upanishads to the Western world was through Anquetil du Perron's translation entitled the "Oupnek'hat," two volumes, Strassburg, 1801-1802, which was a rendering into Latin of the Persian translation above referred to. The substance of the Latin translation appeared in French in the year 1832 in J. D. Lanjuinais's "Recherches sur les Langues, la Littérature, la Religion et la Philosophie des Indiens," 1832. Ram Mohan Roy published his translation of the Īśa, Kena, Kaṭha, and Muṇḍaka Upanishads during the same year, namely, 1832. Exactly fifty years later, the Oupnek'hat was translated into German at Dresden, 1882. It may thus be seen how the Sanskrit Upanishads were rendered into Persian at the time of Dara, how the Persian translation in its turn was rendered into Latin by Anquetil du Perron in 1801-1802, and how the Latin translation was itself rendered both into the French and German languages during the course of the last century.

One of the earliest translators of the Upanishads into English was Röer, who published his translations of nine Upanishads, Īśa, Kena, Kaṭha, Praśna, Muṇḍaka, Māṇḍūkya, Aitareya, Taittirīya, and Śvetāśvatara at Calcutta in 1853. His translation of the Bṛihadāraṇyaka came also later on. Max Müller was the first systematic translator of all the chief Upanishads at the Clarendon Press in two volumes, 1879-1884. Whitney published a review of this translation in the American Journal of Philology in 1886, in an essay entitled "The Upanishads and their latest Translation". Paul Deussen's monumental "Sechzig Upanishad's des Veda," pp. 946, was published at Leipzig, 1897, and contains a translation of all the fifty Upanishads included in the Oupnek'hat, as well as ten other Ātharvaṇa Upanishads. It is unfortunate that Deussen's translation has not yet been rendered into English. It contains very useful introductions to all the Upanishads, as well as to each section of them. This work was reviewed by Böhtlingk in an essay entitled "Bemerkungen zu einigen Upanishaden" in 1897, where he pointed out a number of points in which he differed from Deussen.

G. R. S. Mead's translation of the Upanishads in collaboration with J. C. Chhattopadhyaya in 1896, in two volumes, was published by the London Theosophical Society. Volume I. contains translations of the Īśa, Kena, Kaṭha, Praśna, Muṇḍaka, and Māṇḍūkya Upanishads, and Volume II, of the Taittirīya, Aitareya and Śvetāśvatara Upanishads. Mead's translation excited such an interest in the European world that it was translated both into the French and Dutch languages in 1905 and 1908. S. Sitaram Shastri and Ganganath Jha's Translation of the Upanishads in five volumes with Śaṅkara's commentary (Natesan, Madras, 1898-1901) contains texts of the Īśa, Kena, Muṇḍaka, Kaṭha, Praśna, Chhāndogya, Aitareya and Taittirīya Upanishads, and is so neatly done and so finely printed that it perforce invites the study of the beginner in Upanishadic literature. One wishes very much that Natesan might add the translation of the five remaining Upanishads, Māṇḍūkya, Bṛihadāraṇyaka, Śvetāśvatara, Kaushītaki, and Maitri to the already translated eight, so as to make a fine set of volumes of the Translations of the chief Upanishads along with Texts. Sitanatha Tattvabhushan's Translation of the Upanishads in three volumes, Calcutta, 1900, contains all the thirteen principal Upanishads except Maitrāyaṇī. S. C. Vasu has edited the Īśa, Kena, Kaṭha, Praśna, Muṇḍaka, and Māṇḍūkya Upanishads with extracts from Madhva 's commentary, Panini Office, Allahabad, 1911. He has translated the Chhāndogya and the Bṛihadāraṇyaka Upanishads likewise with extracts from the commentary of Madhva. Tukaram Tatya has brought out an eclectic edition of the Translations of the Twelve principal Upanishads which includes the translation of the Īśa, Kena, Kaṭha, Praśna, Muṇḍaka, Māṇḍūkya, Aitareya, Taittirīya, Śvetāśvatara and Bṛihadāraṇyaka Upanishads by Röer, of the Chhāndogya by Rajendralal Maitra, and of the Kaushītaki by Cowell. The Maitri is unrepresented in this volume. R. E. Hume 's translation of the Thirteen Principal Upanishads, Oxford, 1921, is the latest, most handy, and most serviceable of all. Mr. Hume has profited by the translations of all his predecessors, while his Bibliography is remarkably clear and useful. Our own Bibliographical Note owes not a little to him.

Of the translations of the Upanishads in the Vernaculars, there are many. We might mention C. G. Bhanu's translation of the various Upanishads in Marathi along with the commentary of Śaṅkara in a series of volumes, and H. R. Bhagavat's text and translation in Marathi of various Upanishads in two volumes, the first containing the more important and classical Upanishads, and the other a few of the minor Upanishads. Vishnu Shastri Bapat's translation of the Upanishads in Marathi as well as his translation of the Bhāshya of Śaṅkara on the Upanishads are the most painstaking of Marathi translations. There are translations of the Upanishads in every language of India, and particularly the Bengali. The Bibliography would be inordinately swollen if we were to mention all the translations in the various languages.

As regards the translations of single Upanishads in serial order, we might mention first Aurobindo Ghose's translations of the Īśa, Kaṭha, and other Upanishads, which are interspersed with the philosophical reflections of the author. Prof. M. Hiriyanna's translations of the Kena, Kaṭha, and other Upanishads with the commentary of Śaṅkara have appeared recently, while the Kenopanishad has been transliterated and translated by Oertel, Professor at Yale, 1894. The Kaṭhopanishad seems to find particular favour with translators, and there are numerous translations of it in various languages. Thus Paul Regnaud published a translation of the Kaṭhopanishad in French, Paris, 1898, while the same Upanishad was also translated into Swedish by Butenschön, Stockholm, 1902, and into Italian by Belloni-Filippi, Pisa, 1905. Whitney's translation of the Kaṭhopanishad, Boston, 1890, is a remarkable piece of work, in which he proposes a number of textual emendations, and adds a critical introduction.

Johannes Hertel has recently published a critical edition of the Muṇḍakopanishad, Leipzig, 1924. Hertel's is an ambitious method of editing. He goes into questions of Metre and Language, differentiates the Traditional from the Original text, then gives a Restored text, and then discusses the contents, the origin, and the age of the Muṇḍakopanishad, along with its references to Jainism. After this prelude, Hertel prints the text of the Muṇḍakopanishad by the anastatic method, borrowing it from the Bibliotheca Indica. Hertel may have been inspired to adopt his method of the discussion of the Muṇḍakopanishad from attempts like that of Father Zimmermann on the Mahānārāyaṇa Upanishad, which was his Ph. D. Thesis, in which he discusses the Sources and the Relation between the different recensions of that Upanishad. Prof. Zimmermann goes into the text-parallels of the Upanishad, and the relation of them, and then proceeds to point out the contents and the sources of the Upanishad, and then ends with an arrangement of matter. In fact, such a method of procedure should be made applicable to every Upanishad.

M. N. Dvivedi's translation of the Māṇḍūkya Upanishad with the Kārikās of Gauḍapāda and the Bhāshya of Śaṅkara, 1894, is remarkable in many respects. It was the first notice of that great Heracleitian philosopher Gauḍapāda in English. Recently an amount of literature is coming out on Gauḍapāda and on his relation to the Mādhyamika Sūtras. Prof. Vidushekhara Bhattacharya, Shantiniketan, is making a special study of Gauḍapāda, and one feels no doubt that when Gauḍapāda is rendered well into English, his relation to the Mādhyamika Sūtras is pointed out, and a survey is taken of his contribution to Philosophy, he is bound to startle the world of thought. As regards the Taittirīya Upanishad, A. Mahadeva Shastri has brought out a classical edition of that Upanishad with an English translation and the Commentaries of Śaṅkarāchārya, Sureśvarāchārya, and Vidyāraṇya, pp. 791, Mysore, 1903, which would be most serviceable to all the students of that Upanishad.

Otto Böhtlingk has done very classic work in turning out the editions of two of the biggest Upanishads, namely the Bṛihadāraṇyaka and the Chhāndogya, the one printed at St. Petersburg, and the other at Leipzig. It is remarkable that the two editions were printed simultaneously, and appeared in the same year, namely 1889. While both the editions have been carefully edited, the Chhāndogya has particularly a very beautiful appearance. The principle of paragraphing is retained in both the Upanishads, and Böhtlingk has emended the text in various places, though not always successfully. For example, for the reading Vijitāya (Chhāndogya IV. I. 4) Böhtlingk substitutes Vijitvarāya, and for Tajjalāniti, he reads Tajjānānīti (Chhāndogya III.14.1), of which the first is unnecessary, and the second awkward. Nevertheless, the editions of the Bṛihadāraṇyaka and the Chhāndogya edited with text and translation by Böhtlingk have remained quite classical, though they are somewhat inaccessible in India. Böhtlingk soon followed this achievement by his editions of the Kaṭha, Aitareya and Praśna Upanishads, with their texts in Devanāgari, and translation and notes in German, Leipzig, 1891. Whitney published a review of Böhtlingk's translations of the various Upanishads in the American Journal of Philology, subjecting them to a very detailed examination, and Böhtlingk replied to these criticisms in 1891. All this is a matter of literary give and take, which would certainly be enjoyed by those who take a philological interest in the Upanishads.

E. B. Cowell's translations of the Kaushītaki and the Maitri Upanishads with the commentary of Rāmatīrtha (1861,1870), have also remained classical works on those two Upanishads. A. Mahadeva Shastri's edition of the Amṛitabindu and Kaivalya Upanishads, text and translation, is a handy little volume. Narayanaswami Iyer has translated Thirty Minor Upanishads at Madras, 1914. Finally, S. K. Belvalkar's "Four Unpublished Upanishads," containing texts and translations of the Bāshkala, the Chhāgaleya, the Ārsheya, and the Śaunaka Upanishads (1925), of which the first was printed by Dr. Schrader but the rest were only in MS. form in the Adyar Library, has been published by the Academy of Philosophy and Religion, and can be had at its Poona Branch, Poona, India.

IV. SELECTIONS.

One of the earliest of books of Selections from the Upanishads was by Paul Regnaud entitled *Matériaux pour servir à l'histoire de la philosophie de l'Inde*, Paris, 1876. It contains numerous passages from the original Upanishads in transliterated form together with French translation and topical arrangement. Regnaud had intended this book for a short account of the ancient philosophy of India. Another book on *Selections from the Upanishads* in English by John Murdoch, Madras 1895, is intended not so much to illustrate the philosophy of the Upanishads, as to prove the superiority of Christianity to the philosophy of Hinduism. L. D. Barnett's *Some Sayings from the Upanishads* London, 1905, as well as his *Brahma-Knowledge*, London 1906, are sprightly little volumes which take us to the heart of Upanishadic teaching. Deussen 's *Die Geheimlehre des Veda*, Leipzig, 1907, is intended as a summary of the "Sechzig Upanishad's" and contains selections from fourteen Upanishads. Hillebrandt, the famous Vedic scholar, has produced a work of selections entitled *Aus Brāhmaṇas und Upanishaden*, Jena, which contains typical passages from the Brāhmaṇas as well as the Upanishads to illustrate the early philosophy of India. Hillebrandt does not make a sufficient differentiation between the Brāhmaṇas on the one hand and the Upanishads on the other, and hence finds "ritual and superstition freely mixed with pure ideas of philosophy" in his little volume. He says that he is satisfied that he has many agreements with Oldenberg, particularly when the latter says that the philosophy of the Upanishads cannot, in any way, be compared to the philosophies of Kant and Schopenhauer, and is therefore open to the same criticism which we have made against Oldenberg in the Preface. As a sprightly little volume, Johannes Hertel's *Die Weisheit der Upanishaden*, Munchen, 1921, is more stimulating than Hillebrandt's selections, though occasionally one-sided. Hertel brings together selections from the Īśa, Kena, Kaṭha, Chhāndogya, Bṛihadāraṇyaka, Aitareya, and Kaushītaki Upanishads, and says that he wants to present the Upanishads in readable German, not that his book is intended specifically for Indologists. Hertel's work whets thought, even though his conclusions are not always satisfactory. We have noticed in the Preface how in two little points we disagree with the meaning which Hertel finds in the Kenopanishad. Hertel gives introductions to all his selections, which makes the book more valuable than Hillebrandt's, which does not contain such introductions. Paul Eberhardt 's *Der Weisheit letzter Schluss*, Jena, 1920, is also a book of selections from the Upanishads, and contains thirty-seven passages topically arranged. The author of the present work has also an intention of bringing out an edition of *Selections from the Upanishads* from the specifically spiritual point of view. It was Ram Mohan Roy's deliberate opinion that Selections from the Upanishads published and largely circulated would contribute more than anything else to the moral and religious elevation of his countrymen, and it may seem as if the spiritual Selections from the Upanishads which the author of the present work intends to bring out will satisfy this urgent need.

V. REFERENCES.

The references to Upanishadic literature are vast and various. We can tabulate here only the principal among them under three different heads, references in the Histories of Literature, references in the Histories of Religion, and references in the Histories of Philosophy. Weber 's *Indische Studien* Vols. I. and II. contain series of articles on almost all of the Upanishads in this volume, with the exception of the Aitareya and the Bṛihadāraṇyaka. We have also a treatment of the Upanishads in his *History of Indian Literature,* as well as in Monier Williams's *Indian Wisdom.* Other references to the philosophy of the Upanishads are to be found in Leopold von Schroeder 's *Indiens Literatur und Cultur,* 1887, in Prof. Macdonell 's *History of Sanskrit Literature,* pp. 218-243, as well as in Winternitz's *Geschichte der indischen Litteratur* Vol. I., pp. 210-229. All these try to sum up concisely the teachings of the Upanishads, and indicate their general place in the history of Sanskrit Literature.

So far as the Histories of Religion are concerned, we may mention Hopkins's *Religions of India,* and [illegible] den 's *Studies in Eastern Religions*, as well as his later *Studies in the Religions of the East.* These indicate the religious place of the Upanishads in Indian thought.

Among Histories of Indian Philosophy we might make special mention of Prof. Radhakrishnan's *Indian Philosophy* Volume I., and Das Gupta's *History of Indian Philosophy* Vol. I., which contain recent pronouncements on the philosophy of the Upanishads. Strauss 's *Indische Philosophie* contains a treatment of the philosophy of the Old Upanishads at pp. 42-61, and of the New Upanishads at pp. 62-85, which would amply repay perusal.

Among other references to Upanishadic literature, we might make mention of Prof. Keith 's chapter on the Upanishadic Period in the *Cambridge History of India* Vol. I, chapter 5, wherein he points out that the theory of Transmigration was a new theory in the Upanishadic days, having been entirely absent in the Brāhmaṇa period. He also suggests that it would not be correct to suppose that the Brahman Doctrine was the reaction of the noble class against the devotion of the priests to the ritual. On the other hand, he points out that it must have been through policy that the Brahmins ascribed the Brahman doctrine to the noble class (pp. 142-144). We have pointed out in the third chapter of this book how the idea of Transmigration could be traced even to the Vedic days ; hence it was not entirely new to the Upnishads. Also, we have suggested at the end of the first chapter that the doctrine of Brahman could be regarded neither as Brahmanic nor as Kshatriyan, and that anybody, who came to "know', to whatever class he might have belonged, was regarded as a Sage. To attribute policy to the Brahmins would not be a satisfactory solution.

A last reference to Upanishadic literature we should make mention of is an Article on the Upanishads in the *Encycyclopaedia of Religion and Ethics* by the Rev. A. S. Geden, the Translator of Deussen 's Philosophy of the Upanishads. The editor of the Encyclopaedia could not have pitched upon a more suitable person to write the article on the "Upanishads." The article also contains a useful little Bibliography at the end of it.

VI. ESSAYS AND WORKS.

There are a number of important essays and systematic treatises connected with either a part or the whole of Upanishadic Philosophy. We must begin by noting a somewhat brilliant idea in Otto Wecker's *Der Gebrauch der Kasus in der älteren Upanishad-literatur*, Tübingen, 1905, wherein by a consideration of the various cases in ten of the principal Upanishads he comes at a chronological order of the Upanishads relative to the age of

Pāṇini. This is rather an important idea; for, Pāṇini seems to have flourished before the Upanishadic era had faded away, and therefore, some Upanishads wherein the Pāṇinian uses do not occur may safely be taken to be pre-Pāṇini, while others where they do occur may be taken to be post-Pāṇini. With this important hint, Wecker arranges the Upanishads in four groups; Group one consists of the Bṛihadāraṇyaka, the Chhāndogya, and the Kaushītaki; Group two, of the Aitareya, the Taittirīya, and the Kaṭha; Group three, of the Kena, and the Īśa; Group four, of the Svetāśvatara and the Maitri. The first two are evidently pre-Pāṇini, the third possibly pre-Pāṇini, while the last is post-Pāṇini. In fact, this procedure of Wecker, in which he tries to arrive at a date of the Upanishads from a grammatical point of view is far more valid than that which avails itself of the presence or absence of the idea of Transmigration which we have noted in the first chapter of this work. One wonders why the idea of Incarnation has not been similarly requisitioned for such purposes. In an essay on *The Dramatic Element in the Upanishads* in the Monist, 1910, Charles Johnston discusses certain dialogues from the Bṛihadāraṇyaka, the Chhāndogya, and other Upanishads. A. H. Ewing writes a study in Upanishadic psycho-physics by considering the *Hindu conception of the function of Breath.* Dr. Betty Heimann offers a review of the Upanishadic speculations on deep-sleep in his *Die Tiefschlaf-Spekulation der alten Upanishaden*, 1922, while Rumball has written an essay on *The Conception of Sin in the Upanishads*, Open Court, 1909. We thus see how a searching analysis of the Upanishads has been made in the interest of the different studies pursued by Scholars.

Similar is the case with certain other essays on Upanishadic subjects. We have already pointed out in our Preface how in his *Die Sāṁkhya-Philosophie*, Leipzig, 1894, Richard Garbe goes into a detailed survey of the relation of the Upanishads to the Sāṁkhya system, and comes to the conclusion that the Sāṁkhya system originated in the mid-Upanishadic period. Dr. Macnicol's chapter on the Theism of the Upanishads in his work on *Indian Theism* is a very clever analysis of the theistic teaching of the Upanishads. Macnicol 's thesis is that we may suppose that the Upanishads maintain the theistic theory, because, as he says, the doctrine of Māyā is unknown to the Upanishads. Macnicol comes to the conclusion that the Upanishadic theory of God is theistic-mystic, instead of pantheistic: "Dr. Caird in his luminous exposition of the closely parallel speculation of Plotinus has distinguished the body of ideas to which it appears to me the reflection of the Upanishads belongs as Mysticism from what is properly to be denominated Pantheism" (p. 59). We cannot go with Dr. Macnicol when he says that the Doctrine of Māyā is unknown to the Upanishads; but we do agree with him when he speaks about the mystic trend of Upanishadic doctrine, though a mysticism need not always be a mere theism. Professor John McKenzie's *Hindu Ethics*, Oxford, contains an excellent essay on the Ethics of the Upanishads (pp. 67-99). We entirely agree with Mr. McKenzie that the Upanishadic ethical thinking is conducted in full view of the wider implications of human existence, namely, in other words, that the Upanishadic Ethics reposes on a solid Metaphysical basis: but we do not agree that the Upanishadic morality is ultimately unreal, or only Antinomian. A survey of the various views on Upanishadic Ethics in our Chapter VI would surely disprove all such partial views.

Of the strictly philosophical essays on Upanishadic subjects, we have, in the first place, Josiah Royce 's essay on the Mystical Conception of Being, as illustrated primarily from the Upanishads, in his *World and the Individual.* Royce tells us that he dwells so long on the Upanishads, because, as he says, "they contain already the entire story of the mystic faith so far as it had a philosophical basis" (p. 175). Royce characterises the mystical method as immediacy, and though he is not himself in sympathy with mysticism, nobody could have explained the mystic position better than Royce has done. Prof. Radhakrishnan's *Reign of Religion in Contemporary Philosophy*, McMillan, 1920, ends with a chapter on "Some suggestions for an approach to Reality based on the

Upanishads ". We might see from this how Prof. Radhakrishnan himself regards the Upanishads as capable of giving us a point of view in contemporary thought. Prof. G. H. Langley, of Dacca University, writes an essay on the *Conception of the Universal Spirit in the Upanishads, and its identity with the Individual Spirit* in the Indian Philosophical Review, edited by A. G. Widgery and R. D. Ranade, April, 1920. Herein also he points out how the Upanishads differ from Kant. Not that Kant himself, according to Prof. Langley, is ultimately right, "for Kant regards that the Self in synthesising the given intuitions distorts the representations of the real object which give rise to them. On the other hand, Croce must be regarded as nearer the truth than Kant, when he says that the Self in synthesising is not distorting that which is given in experience, but is exercising only the essential function of spirit in revealing its true nature " (pp. 126-127). Finally, Dr. Barua in his *Pre-Buddhistic Philosophy*, Calcutta, 1921, goes into a very detailed analysis of all the Thinkers of India before the days of Buddha, and naturally has to consider *in extenso* the teachings of Upanishadic philsophers like Uddālaka, Yājñavalkya, Pippalāda, and others. The great difficulty in the case of these Upanishadic Philosophers is, however, to clinch their personalities and doctrines, and if this could be successfully done,a volume on the " Philosophers of the Upanishads " could well be written on the lines followed by Dr. Burnet in his Early Greek Philosophy. Rudiments of such a possible work have been already indicated in the first chapter of the present volume.

It is to the great credit of the Christian Missions in India that they should have instituted research in various departments of Indian thought, and the Upanishads have not escaped their close attention. Even though the views that they take are bound to be in the interest of Christianity, nobody could question the labour they bestow upon the subjects they deal with. Slater's book on *Studies in the Upanishads*, Madras, 1897, is a very good and clever production ; only Slater does not suppose that the Upanishads are capable of supplying the idea of a universal religion :

"If the dream of a universal religion be true—and we have but one science of the universe; and if the Fatherhood of God and the Brotherhood of man be true, there can be but one bond of spiritual union for such a family—that religion cannot possibly be based on the Upanishads. If you make them your religion, then you must be content to see it confined to a small corner of the globe, and to a select coterie even in that corner. For if, as it has often been urged, this ancient system can be properly understood only in the original Sanskrit, then true religion at its highest, depends, not only on superior intellect, but also on special linguistic talent, and talent to study a dead language! The thing, at lowest, is impracticable" (pp. 72). We fail to see what connection the idea of a universal religion has with language; it has to do only with spirit, and not with the expression of it in any language. H. D. Griswold's treatise on *Brahman: a study in the History of Indian Philosophy* discusses at length the doctrine of Brahman in the Upanishads, and considers its religious, ethical, and philosophical consequences. Urquhart's *Upanishads and Life*, Calcutta, 1916, the argument of which work he also pursues further in his larger book on *Pantheism and the Value of Life*, discusses the theism and the pessimism of the Upanishads, their metaphysical inadequacy, their religious and ethical effects, and ends with the message of Christianity for India.

Of the more systematic works on Upanishadic Philosophy as a whole, we have to mention first A. E. Gough's *Philosophy of the Upanishads*, London 1882, which is probably the earliest of the kind, and which is a brilliantly written work, though it has a somewhat unsympathetic tone. Gough's view about the relation of Śaṅkara to the Upanishads is that his philosophy may be supposed to be a legitimate outcome of the teachings of the Upanishads—an opinion which has been challenged by critics who point out that Śaṅkara's philosophy is not the legitimate outcome of the teachings of the Upanishads. Deussen's *Philosophy of the Upanishads*, which has been translated by the Rev. A. S. Geden, 1906, is the next most systematic work on the Upanishads.

Having spent a number of years on his "Sechzig Upanishad's", Deusen could speak with a master's voice on the central teachings of the Upanishads. Deussen 's work is entirely indispensable to students of Upanishadic thought. Prof. Radhakrishnan 's *Philosophy of the Upanishads*, a separate print from his Indian Philosophy Vol. I., which has lately appeared, is a masterly and running survey of the teachings of the Upanishads, and comes from the hand of one who is deeply read in Western thought. Dr. S. K. Belvalkar and R. D. Ranade 's *Creative Period of Indian Philosophy* which will be published under the patronage of the University of Bombay, has been in the Press for some time past, and gives a detailed analysis of the contents of the various Upanishads arranged in their chronological and stratificatory order. There is also a very exhaustive survey in that book of a Century of Minor Upanishads, most of which have never been hitherto translated, and some of which have never been even printed.

There remain, however, two masterly treatises on the Philosophy of the Upanishads, one by Oltramare and the other by Oldenberg. Oltramare 's *L 'Histoire des Idées théosophiqes dans l 'Inde*, Paris, 1907, contains a full account of Upanishadic philosophy in French, pp. 63-131. Oltramare first discusses such topics as Brahman, the Individual Soul, and the Identity of the Brahman with the Individual Soul. Then he proceeds to tell us how to know the Individual Soul is to know Brahman. He proceeds next to the question of the individualisation of Brahman, as well as the relation of the World to Brahman and Soul. Further, Oltramare proceeds to discuss the doctrines of Saṁsāra and Moksha. Under these headings, he discusses such problems as the Mechanism of Metempsychosis, Works and Salvation, Knowledge and Salvation, and finally, the Meaning of Salvation. Lastly, he winds up by discussing the new tendency of religious thought in the Upanishads, as well as by an examination of the intellectual and moral influence of the Upanishads. Oldenberg 's *Die Lehre der Upanishaden und die Anfänge des Buddhismus*, Göttingen, 1915, pp. 374, is entirely worthy of the veteran scholar. In part one of this work, Oldenberg discusses the old Upanishads ; in part two, the new Upanishads and the beginnings of Sāṁkhya and Yoga ; while in part three, he discusses the beginnings of Buddhism. After a preliminary chapter discussing such topics as the Land and Folk, the pre-historic back-ground, the Vedic gods, Death and the other world, and so forth, Oldenberg goes to the central conceptions of the Upanishads, namely those of Brahman and Ātman, and their identification. He then discusses the problem of the relation of the Absolute to the World, and the meaning of the One and the Many. He proceeds next to discuss the question of the Absolute in itself, and the problem of the Personal and the Impersonal. He then applies himself to the question of "Seelenwanderung", as well as to that of the Worth of Existence. He proceeds to discuss the question of Emancipation, the relation of Knowledge and Works, and the problem of the knowability of the Absolute. He ends his first part by a review of the literary form of the Upanishads, namely the prose and poetry of the Upanishads, their dialogues, and such other similar matters. In part two, he considers the beginnings of Sāṁkhya and Yoga, wherein he discusses such problems as the Guṇas, the Purusha and the Prakṛiti, the discipline of Prāṇa, the Āsanas, and Miracles. In part three, he discusses the origin of Buddhism in a survey spreading over about sixty pages. We might easily see from these contents of Oltramare 's and Oldenberg's works that, like their great predecessor in the field, Deussen 's Philosophy of the Upanishads, they are fully philosophical in tone, and grapple with the central problems of Upanishadic thought. But they aim less at construction than at mere exposition, and they have been written from the standpoint of the philosophy of the past. It might be easily seen, therefore, how a constructive presentation of Upanishadic Philosophy from the standpoint of contemporary thought was the necessity of the hour.

ERRATA

Page

22. (10th line from the bottom) heliolatory, *read* heliolatry

63. (3rd line from the bottom) roof of philosophy in Greec *read* root of philosophy in Greece

75 ff. For Cosmogony, insert Heading Chapter II : Cosmogony

81. *τό ὄν* *read* *τό μὴ ὄν*

95. (3rd line from the top) whatoever *read* whatsoever

153. ἀνάμνησις *read* ἀνάμνησις

223 (18th line from the top) problem *read* the problem

228 (7th line from the top) śaṅkara *read* Śaṅkara

277 (5th line from the bottom) it is *read* the Ātman is

295 (10th line from the bottom) to us nearer *read* us nearer to

304 (10th line from the top) *drashṭavyo* read *drashṭavyaḥ*

306 (10th line from the top) Neitzsche *read* Nietzsche

330 (14th line from the top) There *read* there

344 (15th line from the top) unmistakebly *read* unmistakably

106 कठ II. 5	कठ II. 5. 9
112 (*e*) श्वे. VI. 1	(*e*) श्वे. VI. 5
170 बृ. II. 15-17	बृ. II. 1. 15-17
172 कठ II. 2.12	कठ II. 4.12
कठ I. 2.21	कठ I. 2.22
175 बृ. IV. 4. 9-7	बृ. IV. 4. 6-7
177 छां. VI. 6.10	छां. VI. 9-10
235 श्वे. VI. 5.	श्वे. V.5
श्वे. VI. 10	श्वे. IV. 10
श्वे. VI. 9.	श्वे. IV. 9
श्वे. VI. 1.	श्वे. VI. 11
237 ई. 9, 11.	ई. 9-11.
238 कठ I. 1.15	कठ I. 2. 15
239 श्वे. VI. 2.	श्वे. VI. 5.
श्वे. VI. 53	श्वे.VI. 23
श्वे. VI. 1. 1	श्वे. VI. 11
243 बृ. II. 8.8	बृ. III. 8.8
279 मै. II. 6	मै. II. 8.
282 श्वे. III. 2.3	श्वे. III. 2,3.
283 कठ II. 5-11	कठ II. 5.11
ऋ. X. 901	ऋ. X. 90.1
284 केन I. 2. 8	केन I. 2-8
285 छां. VIII. 7.12	छां. VIII. 7-12
कठ I. 27	कठ I. 2.7
320 बृ. IV. 3. 2	बृ. IV. 3.21.

AN ENCYCLOPAEDIC HISTORY OF INDIAN PHILOSOPHY.

The Academy of Philosophy and Religion has undertaken the preparation and publication of an Encyclopædic History of Indian Philosophy in sixteen volumes, much like the Cambridge Modern History, or the Cambridge History of English Literature, making use of the specialised labours of the many great *savants* of Philosophy in India, and bringing their researches to a focus in the Encyclopædic History, the volumes of which may be set down as follows :—

Vol. I. The Philosophy and Religion of the Vedas.

Vol. II. A Constructive Survey of Upanishadic Philosophy (Now out.)

Vol. III. Philosophy and Religion of the Mahābhārata, and the Bhagavadgīta.

Vol. IV. The Philosophy of Buddhism.

Vol. V. The Philosophy of Jainism.

Vol VI. Philosophy of the Darśanas: Sāmkhya, Yoga, and Pūrva-mīmānsā.

Vol. VII. Philosophy of the Darśanas: Nyāya and Vaiśeshika.

Vol. VIII. The Philosophy of Advaitism.

Vol. IX. Non-Advaitic Vedānta.

Vol. X. Indian Mysticism: Mysticism in Mahārāshṭra (In the press).

Vol. XI. Indian Mysticism: Mysticism outside Mahārāshṭra.

Vol. XII. Tendencies of Contemporary Thought.

Vol. XIII. Sources.

Vol. XIV. Sources.

Vol. XV. Sources.

Vol. XVI. Index.

The following persons, whose names have been alphabetically arranged, constitute, among others, the Contributors to the series, the asterisk signifying Member of the Editorial Board:—

* 1. Dr. S. K. Belvalkar, M. A. Ph. D., Professor of Sanskrit, Deccan College, Poona.

2. Principal Vidhushekhara Bhattacharya, Vishva-Bharati University, Shantiniketan.

3. Prof. A. Chakravarti M. A., Professor of Philosophy, Presidency College, Madras.

* 4. Prof. S. N. Das Gupta, M. A. Ph. D., Presidency College, Calcutta.

* 5. Principal A. B. Dhruva, M. A., Professor of Sanskrit, Hindu University, Benares.

6. Prof. M. Hiriyanna, M. A., Professor of Sanskrit, Maharaja's College, Mysore.

7. Prof. Krishnaswami Iyengar, M. A., Professor of History, University of Madras, Madras.

8. V. Subramanya Iyer Esqr., B. A., Registrar, University of Mysore, Mysore.

* 9. Dr. Ganganath Jha, M. A. D.Litt., Vice-Chancellor, University of Allahabad, Allahabad.

10. Prof. K. Subramanyam Pillay, M. A. M. L., Law College, Madras.

*11. Prof. S. Radhakrishnan, M. A., Professor of Philosophy, University of Calcutta, Calcutta.

*12. Prof. R. D. Ranade, M. A., Director of the Academy of Philosophy and Religion, Poona Branch, Poona.

*13. Dr. Brajedranath Seal, M. A. Ph. D. D. Sc., Vice-Chancellor University of Mysore, Mysore, Chairman.

14. Prof. Kuppuswami Shastri, M. A., Professor of Sanskrit, Presidency College, Madras.

15. Prof. E. A. Wodehouse, M. A., Professor of English, Deccan College, Poona.

16. Prof. R. Zimmermann, S. J., Ph. D., Professor of Sanskrit, St. Xavier's College, Bombay.

It has been decided to bring out the Series at as early a date as possible ; but, a period, say, of about ten years, may safely be predicted for the publication of the entire series. More information about the Encyclopaedic History of Indian Philosophy, or about the Academy of Philosophy and Religion, can be had from the Director of the Academy of Philosophy and Religion, Poona Branch, Poona.